Piracy and the Origins of Universal Jurisdiction

Queen Mary Studies in International Law

Edited by

Malgosia Fitzmaurice
Sarah Singer

VOLUME 34

The titles published in this series are listed at *brill.com/qmil*

Piracy and the Origins of Universal Jurisdiction

On Stranger Tides?

By

Mark Chadwick

BRILL
NIJHOFF

LEIDEN | BOSTON

Library of Congress Cataloging-in-Publication Data

Names: Chadwick, Mark, (Law teacher), author.
Title: Piracy and the origins of universal jurisdiction : on stranger tides?
/ By Mark Chadwick.
Description: Leiden : Brill Nijhoff, 2018. | Series: Queen Mary studies in International Law ; VOLUME 34 | Includes bibliographical references and index.
Identifiers: LCCN 2018053434 | ISBN 9789004331198 (hardback : alk. paper)
Subjects: LCSH: Piracy. | Universal jurisdiction . | International law.
Classification: LCC KZ7212 .C425 2018 | DDC 345/.0264--dc23
LC record available at https://lccn.loc.gov/2018053434

Typeface for the Latin, Greek, and Cyrillic scripts: "Brill". See and download: brill.com/brill-typeface.

ISSN 1877-4822
ISBN 978-90-04-33119-8 (hardback)
ISBN 978-90-04-39046-1 (e-book)

This book is printed on acid-free paper and produced in a sustainable manner.

Printed by Printforce, the Netherlands

For my parents

Contents

Acknowledgements

> The buccaneers were true to each other and as time went on their organisation became astonishingly sound. Those afloat could rely upon the integrity of those ashore and *vice versa*. Indeed, they formed a community of singularly united villains.*

Piracy is never a solo enterprise. It would have been impossible to "hoist the black flag" without the support of a rich network of supporters, be they fellow crew, financial sponsors, buyers of stolen goods, sympathetic locals or crooked local nobles. Similarly, it would have been impossible to survive the book-writing process (originally a thesis-writing process) without the assistance of my own villainous crew.

First and foremost, I must extend my deepest thanks to my PhD supervisors, Professors Dino Kritsiotis and Olympia Bekou, for their incisive observations, an apparently endless supply of patience, and warm encouragement through uncertain times. This work also could not have come to pass without the kind and constructive advice of my examiners, Professors Malgosia Fitzmaurice and Sarah Dromgoole, to whom my thanks are also due.

Thanks are also due to the Arts and Humanities Research Council for funding the PhD thesis upon which this book is based, as well as the School of Law at the University of Nottingham and the Graduate School for their constant support. I wish to thank everyone who helped me throughout my time at Nottingham, both academically and personally, either by taking an interest in my work or offering your support; you are too many to mention, but I am eternally grateful for all your help.

I am also lucky to have supportive colleagues at Nottingham Trent University, particularly all those who have lent an ear to my ideas. Special mentions are due to Tom Lewis, Elizabeth Kirk, Elizabeth Chadwick, David Ong, Olivier Yambo, Luigi Daniele, Jonathan Doak, Lydia Davies-Bright, Simon Boyes, Alex Kastrinou, Helen O'Nions, Danny Gough, Dawn Sedman, Marc Wesley and Janine Griffiths-Baker.

I would also like to thank Carl Dundas for his help with translation work, my friend Nigel Phillips, whose passion for all things pirate kept me going when all seemed lost, my partner Gillian, whose support and patience appears

* Basil Fuller and Ronald Leslie-Melville, *Pirate Harbours and Their Secrets* (London: Stanley Paul & Co., 1935), 76–77.

boundless, and of course my parents whose encouragement and understanding make anything possible. Finally, I would like to thank to all at BRILL, especially Ingeborg van der Laan, for her help and perseverance.

It's been a long journey, but an adventure too – one that the pirates of old might just have been proud of.

CHAPTER 1

Of Pirates and Nazis: Introducing the "Piracy Analogy"

> [T]he substantive basis underlying the exercise of universal jurisdiction in respect of the crime of piracy also justifies its exercise in regard to the crimes with which we are dealing in this case.[1]

∵

These words, proclaimed by the Supreme Court of Israel in the 1961 *Eichmann* case, mark a watershed moment in the history of international criminal justice.[2] Seeking to justify the controversial arrest and prosecution of Nazi logistician Adolf Eichmann to a global audience, the Court redefined their suspect as a "pirate", an "enemy of all mankind"[3] against whose punishment none could object.

It is a comparison that might not immediately seem appropriate. Adolf Eichmann – a lieutenant colonel in the *Schutzstaffel* (more commonly known by the abbreviation "SS") and "an expert on the Jewish question"[4] – had facilitated The Holocaust by overseeing the transfer of six million Jews to Nazi concentration camps during the 1940s.[5] Standing before a court room in

1 Supreme Court of Israel, *Eichmann v. A-G Israel*, 36 *International Law Reports* (1968) 227, para. 12.

2 This term is intended, broadly, to refer to the law and procedure and relating to the "core" international crimes within the jurisdiction of the International Criminal Court (ICC) (*i.e.* genocide, crimes against humanity, war crimes and aggression), which are enforceable in international courts (such as the ICC) or in State courts; definition taken from Antonio Cassese and Paola Gaeta, *Cassese's International Criminal Law* (Oxford: OUP, 2013), 3.

3 *Supra* n01, para 11, citing from Permanent Court of International Justice, *The Case of the S.S. "Lotus" (France v Turkey)*, 7 September 1927, dissenting opinion of Judge Moore, 70.

4 Hannah Arendt, *Eichmann in Jerusalem: A Report on the Banality of Evil* (1963) (New York: Penguin, 2006), 36.

5 The first instance District Court judgement held that Eichmann had "caused the deaths of millions of Jews" (*A-G Israel v. Eichmann* (1961), 36 *International Law Reports* (1968) 5, para.

 | DOI:10.1163/9789004390461_002

Jerusalem after several years in hiding,[6] Eichmann faced a fifteen-charge indictment "of unsurpassed gravity"[7] derived from the 1950 Nazis and Nazi Collaborators (Punishment) Law.[8] The charge sheet encompassed four counts of "crimes against the Jewish people" (the formulation of which resembled the definition of genocide as set out in the 1948 Convention on the Prevention and Punishment of the Crime of Genocide),[9] seven counts of "crimes against humanity" (charges which covered the extermination of non-Jews, including ethnic Poles, Slovenes and Gypsies), one count of a "war crime" and three counts of "membership of a hostile organisation".[10] Eichmann was found guilty on all counts.[11]

Even the most infamous of pirates (with whom Eichmann was seemingly being compared) could not compare to this level of depravity. Blackbeard, for instance, was a violent and fearful individual who held colonial Charleston to ransom,[12] maimed crewmembers on a whim (lest they would "forget who he was"),[13] and terrorised the shipping lanes of the Caribbean in the 1710s.[14] They are actions that are certainly despicable (despite literary and celluloid celebration) but that do not measure up to the atrocities of the Nazi regime. Nevertheless, pirates have been bestowed the dubious title of "*hostes humani generis*, the enemies to all mankind"[15] and described as "worse than ravenous beasts".[16] Piracy is an offence that, since ancient times, has attracted categorical hostility, inviting all States to unite in its eradication and exercise a collective right

---

244). The figure of six million was conceded by Eichmann himself: para. 161. See also Lucy Dawidowicz, *The War Against the Jews* (New York: Bantam, 1986).

6 As documented in, e.g., Bettina Stangneth, *Eichmann Before Jerusalem: The Unexamined Life of a Mass Murderer* (Melbourme: Scribe, 2014).

7 *Eichmann* (District Court) *supra* no5, para. 1.

8 William Schabas, "The Contribution of the *Eichmann* Trial to International Law", 26 *Leiden Journal of International Law* (2013) 667, 670.

9 *Eichmann* (Supreme Court), *supra* no1, para. 10.

10 Transcript of 11 April 1961.

11 *Eichmann* (District Court) *supra* no5, para. 243. Eichmann was acquitted of suspected offences where the conduct in question took place prior to 1941.

12 Captain Charles Johnson, *A General History of the Robberies and Murders of the Most Notorious Pirates* (1724) (with an introduction and commentary by David Cordingly) (London: Conway Maritime Press, 1998), 49.

13 *Ibid.*, 59.

14 David Cordingly, *Spanish Gold: Captain Woodes Rogers and the Pirates of the Caribbean* (London: Bloomsbury, 2011), 167–178.

15 *Kidd's Trial*, 14 Howell's State Trials (1701) 123.

16 *Tryal of Captain Thomas Green and his crew*, 14 Howell's State Trials (1705), 1199.

(a "universal jurisdiction") to punish it.[17] This universality of approach uniquely abrogates typical State claims to jurisdiction, where some direct interest in the offence is required.[18]

The history of piracy provided an existing source of universal enmity on which the Israeli District and Supreme Courts could base their moral and legal right to prosecute Adolf Eichmann. By reference to the "piracy analogy"[19] Eichmann could be considered, like the pirates of old, an "outlaw, an enemy of all mankind"[20] whose crimes "[shook] the stability of the international community to its very foundations",[21] violating the "universal moral values and humanitarian principles [...] adopted by civilized nations".[22] Recourse to the "piracy analogy" in this way was in fact unnecessary for the purpose of ensuring Eichmann's conviction (the District Court had already held that it was required "to give effect to the law of the Knesset, and we cannot entertain the contention that this law conflicts with the principles of international law").[23] The introduction of this line of argument nevertheless served an additional purpose: it allowed the Court to play on international feeling about the seriousness of Eichmann's offences, appealing not only to those directly affected by The Holocaust but also Jewish diaspora and non-Jews.[24] In so doing, Israel did what it claimed *any* State could have done; it became an enforcer not simply of Israeli law, but of international law.[25]

---

17 See e.g.: Judge Moore, *supra* no3, 70–71; International Court of Justice, *Arrest Warrant of 11 April 2000* (*Democratic Republic of the Congo v. Belgium*) (2002), Joint Separate Opinion of Judges Higgins, Kooijmans and Buergenthal, 81, and Separate Opinion of Judge Guillame, 42; *In re Piracy Jure Gentium,* [1934] A.C., 589; *United States v Smith*, 18 US 5 Wheat 153 (1820), 162; Michael Akehurst, "Jurisdiction in International Law", 46 *British Yearbook of International Law*, (1972–1973) 145, 160; and Georges Abi-Saab, "The Proper Role of Universal Jurisdiction", 1 *Journal of International Criminal Justice*, (2003) 596, 599–600.

18 State jurisdiction is predominantly asserted based on some *nexus* to the suspect, discussed in greater detail *infra*, 1.1.1.

19 As this phenomenon has been termed by Eugene Kontorovich, in "The Piracy Analogy: Modern Universal Jurisdiction's Hollow Foundation" 45 *Harvard International Law Journal* (2004) 183.

20 Judge Moore in *Lotus, supra* no3, 70, cited in *Eichmann* (Supreme Court), *supra* no1, para. 11.

21 *Eichmann, ibid.*, para. 12.

22 *Ibid.*, para. 11.

23 *Eichmann* (District Court), *supra* no5, para. 10.

24 Deborah E. Lipstadt, *The Eichmann Trial* (New York: Schocken, 2011), 33–34.

25 Petros A. Papadatos, *The Eichmann Trial* (London: F.A. Praeger, 1964), 46.

Today, genocide,[26] crimes against humanity,[27] grave breaches of the Geneva Conventions (or, more broadly, "war crimes"),[28] aggression[29] and torture[30] are all arguably subject to universal jurisdiction, theoretically exercisable by any State regardless of where and by whom the offence was committed. Based on a

---

26 *Restatement (Third) of the Foreign Relations Law of the United States* (1988) s404; Principle 2 of *The Princeton Principles on Universal Jurisdiction* (Princeton University, 2001), 29; *Demjanjuk v. Petrovsky*, 776 F.2d 571, (US, 6th Circuit, 1985; extradition hearing), 580–583; International Court of Justice, *Case Concerning Application of the Convention on the Prevention and Punishment of the Crime of Genocide* (*Bosnia and Herzegovina v. Serbia and Montenegro*) 26 February 2007, 227; European Court of Human Rights, *Jorgić v. Germany* (Application no. 74613/01), 12 July 2007, paras 68–70; *Draft Code of Crimes Against the Peace and Security of Mankind*, articles 8, 9 and 17, adopted by the International Law Commission at its Forty-Eighth Session (1996 U.N. Doc. A/51/10); Kenneth C. Randall, "Universal Jurisdiction under International Law", 66 *Texas Law Review* (1987–1988) 785, 834–836. This is notwithstanding the absence of universal jurisdiction in the 1948 *Convention on the Prevention and Punishment of the Crime of Genocide*; see discussion in Luc Reydams, *Universal Jurisdiction: International and Municipal Legal Perspectives* (Oxford: OUP, 2003), 47–53.

27 *Eichmann* (Supreme Court), *supra* no1, para. 11; *Princeton* Principle 2, *ibid.*; *Draft Code, ibid*, articles 8, 9 and 18; M. Cherif Bassiouni, "The History of Universal Jurisdiction and Its Place in International Law" in Stephen Macedo (ed.), *Universal Jurisdiction: National Courts and the Prosecution of Serious Crimes under International Law* (Philadelphia: University of Pennsylvania Press, 2004) 39, 52–53; Randall, *ibid.*, 799–814.

28 The 1949 Geneva Conventions oblige States to prosecute a suspect "regardless of nationality" (or, alternatively, to extradite them) if suspected of having committed a "grave breach" of the conventions: Articles 49/50/129/146 of Conventions I-IV respectively. "Grave breaches" are defined in Articles 50/51/130/147 of Conventions I-IV respectively, in addition to Articles 85(3) and (4) of Additional Protocol I (1977). See also Jean-Marie Henckaerts and Louise Doswald-Beck, ICRC *Customary International Humanitarian Law, Volume I: Rules* (Cambridge: CUP), 604 (Rule 157, "Jurisdiction over War Crimes"), noting a right under customary international law for States "to vest universal jurisdiction in their national courts over war crimes" in addition to the obligations imposed by the Geneva Conventions.

29 *Princeton* Principle 2, *ibid.*; *Draft Code, supra* no26, articles 8, 9 and 16. See also Michael P. Scharf, "Universal Jurisdiction and the Crime of Aggression" 53 *Harvard International Law Journal* (2012) 358, suggesting, at 379, that "it is reasonable for states to conclude that Nuremberg and its progeny provide a customary international law basis for prosecuting the crime of aggression under universal jurisdiction".

30 *Convention Against Torture and Other Cruel, Inhuman or Degrading Treatment or Punishment* (adopted by General Assembly resolution 39/46 of 10 December 1984, entered into force 26 June 1987), Articles 5 and 7; *Princeton* Principle 2, *supra* no26; *Prosecutor v Anto Furundžija*, Judgement (Trial Chamber, International Criminal Tribunal for the former Yugoslavia), 10 December 1998, para. 156; European Court of Human Rights, *Ely Ould Dah v France*, Application No. 13113/03, ECHR (Fifth Section), 17 March 2009, para. 60; International Court of Justice, "Questions Relating to the Obligation to Prosecute or Extradite" (*Belgium v. Senegal*), Judgment Of 20 July 2012, 455; International Law Commission, Report of the Work of Its Sixty-Sixth Session, U.N. Doc. A/69/10 (2014), 149–150.

reading of *Eichmann*, it might be reasonable to assume that the pre-existence of universal jurisdiction over piracy ensures "enduring value [...] by supporting the extension of universal jurisdiction to certain modern offences".[31] Yet the propriety of analogising such crimes to piracy has been criticised.[32] The argument *against* the analogy to piracy is based on the premise that piracy was never actually considered to be a particularly heinous crime, making comparisons to offences such as genocide seem disingenuous.[33] This argument, in turn, removes the purported historical basis for modern day exercises of universal jurisdiction, which must instead find substantiation from some alternative theory.[34] The problem is more than merely academic, as the very idea of universal jurisdiction remains controversial for many scholars and, indeed, for many States.[35]

The question as to whether the "piracy analogy" provides a logically sound genealogy for "modern" instances of universal jurisdiction has not been satisfactorily answered.[36] As such, a fundamental uncertainty remains regarding the history of universal jurisdiction which, in turn, undermines attempts to theorise the principle and justify (or, indeed, reject) its usage. In order to assuage this uncertainty, certain questions ought to be addressed. For example: whether piracy has ever been regarded as genuinely "heinous" in nature (and, if so, on what basis); whether "modern" exercises of universal jurisdiction owe an ancestral lineage to historic actions against pirates; and what the similarities might be between pirates and, for instance, *génocidaires* such as Adolf Eichmann. By examining the relevant histories and linking them to modern day practice, this book intends to address and explain the relationship between historic exercises of universal jurisdiction over piracy and modern universal jurisdiction over "core" international crimes. In turn, the unravelling of these historical and legal problems allows for a more detailed understanding of the nature and pedigree of universal jurisdiction.

---

31 Randall, *supra* no26, 797.

32 Kontorovich, *supra* no19; Harry D, Gould, "Cicero's Ghost: Rethinking the Social Construction of Piracy", in Michael J. Struett, Jon D. Carlson, and Mark T. Nance (eds), *Maritime Piracy and the Construction of Global Governance* (New York: Routledge, 2013) 23, 24; Matthew Garrod, "Piracy, the Protection of Vital State Interests and the False Foundations of Universal Jurisdiction in International Law", 25 *Diplomacy and Statecraft* (2014) 195.

33 Kontorovich, *ibid.;* Anna Petrig, "Piracy" in Donald R. Rothwell, Alex G. Oude Elferink, Karen N. Scott, and Tim Stephens (eds), *The Oxford Handbook of the Law of the Sea* (Oxford: OUP, 2015) 843, 860–861.

34 *Ibid.*

35 As documented *infra*, 8.2.1.

36 As noted by, e.g., Nahal Kazemi, "Justifications for Universal Jurisdiction: Shocking the Conscience is Not Enough" 49 *Tulsa Law Review* (2013) 1, 34, and Johan van der Vyver, "Prosecution and Punishment of the Crime of Genocide" 23 *Fordham International Law Journal* 286 (1999), 321.

1.1 Defining Key Terms

Some consideration of the terms "universal jurisdiction" and "piracy" is first required by way of explanatory prologue.

The precise meaning of the term "universal jurisdiction" is, of course, dependant on the meaning of "jurisdiction". This is, in itself, an ambiguous term that reflects any of several meanings depending on the context in which it is used.[37] An examination of the etymology of jurisdiction reveals that the term is linked with claims to power and authority. It derives from the Roman magisterial power to "*ius dicere*", to determine and apply the applicable law in respect of legal disputes.[38] The modern conjugation of "juris" and "diction" together literally means "speaking law".[39]

In an international law context "jurisdiction" refers to the informal set of rules designed to regulate and restrain States' competence to apply their own laws and legal procedures within a given situation, by identifying "the State or States whose contact with the facts is such as to make the allocation of legislative competence just and reasonable".[40] In so doing, the notion of "jurisdiction" bequeaths (or revokes) legitimacy to State claims to adjudicative power while purporting to protect the fundamental principle of sovereign equality.[41] Indeed, "jurisdiction" and "sovereignty" are closely related concepts, sometimes used interchangeably, although the former term usually describes the State's competence to act in respect of specific legal matters, whereas the latter refers to more general competences.[42]

Jurisdictional competence is generally claimed by States in four key situations, namely: where a suspected offence occurs on a State's territory (the

37 Marko Milanović, "From Compromise to Principle: Clarifying the Concept of State Jurisdiction in Human Rights Treaties" 8 *Human Rights Law Review* (2008) 411; Bill Grantham, "The Man Who Shot Liberty Valance" in Shaun McVeigh (ed.) *Jurisprudence of Jurisdiction* (Abingdon: Routledge, 2007) 225.

38 J. Plescia, "Conflict of Laws in the Roman Empire" 38 *Labeo Rassegna di Diritto Romano* (1992) 30, at 32.

39 Shaunnagh Dorsett & Shaun McVeigh, "Questions of Jurisdiction" in McVeigh (ed.), *supra* no37, 3, 22.

40 Frederick A. Mann, "The doctrine of jurisdiction in International Law" 111 *Recueil des Cours* (1964) 1, 44.

41 *Lotus, supra* no3, 25; Gregor Noll, "Theorising Jurisdiction" in Anne Orford and Florian Hoffmann (eds), *The Oxford Handbook of the Theory of International Law* (Oxford: OUP, 2016) 600.

42 As discussed in James Crawford, "*Brownlie's Principles of Public International Law* (8th ed.) (Oxford: OUP, 2012), 204–206. See also Mann, *supra* no40, 20, and Shaunnagh Dorsett & Shaun McVeigh, "Questions of Jurisdiction" in McVeigh (ed.), *supra* no37, 3, 3.

"territoriality" principle);[43] where it is suspected to have been *committed by* one of the State's nationals (the "nationality" principle); where it *affects* one of the State's nationals (the "passive personality" principle); and where it affects the State's fundamental interests in some way (the "protective" principle). The claim to jurisdiction in each of these circumstances is grounded in the fact that a legitimate State concern is involved.[44] Within these delineating principles a State's jurisdiction may take different forms, such as a jurisdiction to prescribe (*i.e.* to legislate for a given offence), jurisdiction to adjudicate (to pass judgement on the lawfulness of a given act or to interpret the law), and jurisdiction to enforce (to arrest a suspected perpetrator, within a criminal law context). No formal system of jurisdictional demarcation exists, however. Rather, State claims to jurisdiction are traditionally governed by the *Lotus* principle, namely that "[r]estrictions upon the independence of States cannot [...] be presumed"[45] so that whatever is not prohibited by international law must therefore be allowed. In practice, though, States tend to positively justify claims to jurisdiction based on the above principles.[46] Moreover, several areas of international law are governed by subject-specific jurisdictional regimes.[47]

Universal jurisdiction complicates this setup somewhat. From a criminal law perspective, the principle of universal jurisdiction permits States to claim jurisdiction over a suspected offence "based solely on the nature of the crime, without regard to where the crime was committed, the nationality of the alleged or convicted perpetrator, the nationality of the victim, or any other connection to the [prosecuting] State".[48] Universal jurisdiction, then, represents a break from archetypal "State-centred" bases of jurisdiction. Claims to jurisdiction of this kind are predominantly assertions of prescriptive or adjudicatory

---

43 The territorial principle is thought of as overriding and inviolable so that, as a general rule, there ought to be no interference with a State's right to prescribe and enforce laws within its own territory; *Lotus*, *supra* no3, 18; Kelsen, *General Theory of Law and State* (trans. Anders Wedberg) (Cambridge, MA: Harvard University Press, 1949), 212. Territoriality also applies to ships upon the high seas that are registered to the State or carry its flag (*Lotus*, 25).

44 Cedric Ryngaert, *Jurisdiction in International Law* (2nd ed.) (Oxford: OUP, 2015), 38–39, 43; Alejandro Chehtman, The Philosophical Foundations of Extraterritorial Punishment (Oxford: OUP, 2010), Chapter 3.

45 *Lotus*, *supra* no3, 18.

46 Ryngaert, *supra* no44, 29.

47 For instance, the 1996 *Hague Convention on Parental Responsibility and Protection of Children*, articles 5–14.

48 *Princeton* Principle 1, *supra* no26, 28. See also Roger O'Keefe, "Universal Jurisdiction: Clarifying the Basic Concept", 2 *Journal of International Criminal Justice* (2004) 735, 745, suggesting that "universal jurisdiction amounts to the assertion of jurisdiction to prescribe

competence given that claims to enforcement jurisdiction are likely to manifestly contravene the principle of territorial inviolability.[49] The exception to this rule appears to be piracy which, due to its unique *locus delicti* upon the high seas, is frequently and uncontroversially the subject of universal enforcement jurisdiction.[50] Universal jurisdiction is sometimes further separated into "conditional" and "absolute" types, the former dependent on the presence of the suspect on State territory whereas the latter can be exercised at any time regardless of any kind of nexus to the suspect.[51] However the more audacious "absolute" form of universal jurisdiction appears to be a vanishing concept.[52]

The term "piracy" inevitably evokes romance and adventure. It might put us in mind of battle-scarred galleons sporting the skull-and-crossbones of the "Jolly Roger", crewed by rum-guzzling rogues wearing eye-patches and missing limbs. Piracy is deeply engrained in our culture: "talking like a pirate" is a common hobby (even boasting a day of the year dedicated to it),[53] as is dressing up in pirate attire. Most of us will be able to reel off the names of several infamous pirates, and almost everyone will have witnessed piracy in films, television, or books. Our perception of piracy is shaped by such famous works as Lord Byron's *The Corsair* (1814),[54] *Treasure Island* (1883, with a famous Disney film adaptation in 1950),[55] *Peter Pan* (1911),[56]

---

in the absence of any other accepted jurisdictional nexus at the time of the relevant conduct".

49 Lassa Oppenheim, *International Law: A Treatise* (London: Longmans, Green & Co, 1905), Book 1, s. 147; International Court of Justice, *Arrest Warrant, supra* no17, Dissenting Opinion of Judge Van den Wyngaert, 164; O'Keefe, *ibid.*

50 Antonio Cassese, "When May Senior State Officials be tried for International Crimes? Some Comments on the *Congo v Belgium* Case" 13 *European Journal of International Law* (2002) 853, 857–858.

51 As outlined in *Princeton* Principle 1, *supra no26*. See also Antonio Cassese, "Is the Bell Tolling for Universality? A Plea for a Sensible Notion of Universal Jurisdiction" 1 *Journal of International Criminal Justice* (2003) 589, and *Arrest Warrant, supra* no17, Separate Opinion of Judge Guillame, 41, and the Joint Separate Opinion of Judges Higgins, Kooijmans and Buerguenthal, 76.

52 Aisling O'Sullivan, *Universal Jurisdiction in International Criminal Law: The Debate and the Battle for Hegemony* (Oxon: Routledge, 2017), 199; Cassese, *ibid.*; Separate Opinions to *Arrest Warrant, ibid.*

53 Tessa Berenson, "Happy Talk Like A Pirate Day!" *Time Magazine* (website), 19 September 2014.

54 Lord Byron, *The Corsair* (London: John Murray, 1814).

55 Robert Louis Stevenson, *Treasure Island* (Boston: Roberts Brothers, 1884); *Treasure Island* (dir. Byron Haskin, Disney), 1950.

56 JM Barrie, *Peter and Wendy* (Hodder & Stoughton, 1911). The novel originated as the 1904 play, *Peter Pan.*

Pirates of the Caribbean (2003)[57] and the true story of *Captain Phillips* (2013).[58] These romanticised visions are certainly based in factual histories of piracy, albeit possessing certain fantastical embellishment.[59] Yet they reveal, in themselves, inherent complexities about what it means – both socially and legally – to be a pirate. What, exactly, defines a "pirate", and who decides this?

The definition of "piracy" has historically been somewhat amorphous, referring to any number of malpractices united by a common geography: the high seas.[60] In modern international law, however, we do have a generally agreed definition of "piracy" as contained in the 1982 United Nations Convention on the Law of the Sea (UNCLOS). Article 101 of UNCLOS defines "piracy" as "any illegal acts of violence [...] committed for private ends by the crew or the passengers of a private ship [...] and directed [...] on the high seas, against another ship"[61] and provides for universal jurisdiction over such acts.[62] The UNCLOS definition contains several elements that have developed over centuries of refinement, namely: it constitutes an act of violence;[63] originating on one ship and affecting another; perpetrated upon the high seas; by a private (*i.e.* non-State) actor and for private (*i.e.* non-political) motive.[64] This is the general definition that shall be adopted throughout the book. Note that there are several other terms that have historically also been applied to pirates, such as "corsairs" or "buccaneers" – where these terms are used, they will be defined for the reader and any nuances explained.

---

57 *Pirates of the Caribbean: The Curse of the Black Pearl* (dir. Gore Verbinksi, Disney, 2003), plus sequels.

58 *Captain Phillips* (dir. Paul Greengrass, Sony, 2013).

59 See Neil Rennie, *Treasure Neverland: Real and Imaginary Pirates* (Oxford: OUP, 2013) on the blurring of fact and fiction.

60 Alfred P. Rubin, *The Law of Piracy* (Honolulu: University Press of the Pacific, 2006), 1, ascribing six different meanings to the term; Harvard Research in International Law "Draft Convention on Piracy with Comments", 26 *American Journal of International Law* (1932) supplement, 749, 769; Peter MacDonald Eggers QC, "What is a pirate? A common law answer to an age-old question" in Douglas Guilfoyle (ed.), *Modern Piracy: Legal Challenges and Responses* (Cheltenham: Edward Elgar, 2013), 250.

61 Article 101. The act can also be undertaken from or against an aircraft, but must occur in "a place outside the jurisdiction of any State" in order to constitute piracy.

62 Per Article 105, "On the high seas, or in any other place outside the jurisdiction of any State, every State may seize a pirate ship [...] and arrest the persons and seize the property on board. The courts of the State which carried out the seizure may decide upon the penalties to be imposed, and may also determine the action to be taken [...]".

63 The definition is now generally interpreted broadly to cover, per UNCLOS, any "act of violence"; see commentary in Eggers, *supra* no60, 255–258.

64 H.E. José Luis Jesus, "Protection of Foreign Ships against Piracy and Terrorism at Sea: Legal Aspects" 18 *International Journal of Marine and Coastal Law* (2003) 363, 378–379; Clyde H. Crockett, "Toward a Revision of the International Law of Piracy" 26 *DePaul Law Review* (1976) 78, 84–96.

1.2 Understanding the "Piracy Analogy": Core Themes and Questions

Part 1.2 serves three aims, the first (Section 1.2.1) being an examination of how the "piracy analogy" has been invoked historically (since the early 1800s) to justify prosecutions of "core" international crimes. This study is crucial to understanding the influence of piracy (in terms of "why" and "how") on the exercise of universal jurisdiction today. Section 1.2.2 reveals the challenges that universal jurisdiction has been subject to, while Section 1.2.3 discusses why the "piracy analogy" continues to be relevant and establishes the need for a closer analysis of piracy's influence in this regard.

1.2.1 *Beyond Piracy: the Emergence and Growth of "New" Universal Jurisdiction*

Piracy is generally recognised as having been the first (and, for centuries, only) crime subject to universal jurisdiction.[65] Yet by invoking the "piracy analogy" the *Eichmann* case tapped into a trend that by 1961 had already acquired momentum, the analogy gradually gaining influence due to its "rhetorical currency and known connotations"[66] and for enabling jurisdictional workarounds to problematic situations. Attempts were made in the early 1800s, for instance, to analogise piracy to the practice of slavery.[67] The *Lieber Code*, promulgated in 1863 as a prototypical US military field manual (and forerunner of the humanitarian standards set out in the Geneva Conventions),[68] compared irregular combatants (acting "without commission") to "pirates", a comparison designed to deny battlefield obligations.[69] Moving into the twentieth century, the 1922 *Washington Treaty Relating to the Use of Submarines and Noxious Gases in Warfare* invoked "piracy" when it declared that any person flouting its provisions "shall be deemed to have violated the laws of war and shall be liable to trial and punishment *as if for an act of piracy* and may be brought to trial before the civil or military authorities of any Power within the jurisdiction of which he may be found".[70] Thus the notion of pirates as "rightless

65 See *supra* n017.

66 Dino Kritsiotis, "The Contingencies of Piracy", 41 *California Western International Law Journal* (2011) 305, 319.

67 Bassiouni, "The History", *supra* n027, 49–50; Randall, *supra* n026, 797–799; Rubin, *supra* n060, 147–149.

68 Jean-Marie Henckaerts, "Lieber Code" in Antonio Cassese (ed.), *The Oxford Companion to International Criminal Justice* (Oxford: OUP, 2009) 409–410.

69 *Lieber Code* (Instructions for the Government of Armies of the United States in the Field, United States War Sept., General Orders 100, April 24, 1863), Article 82.

70 Article 3; emphasis added.

enemies"[71] already formed the basis for arguments seeking to deny rights to new classes of enemy, over a hundred years prior to the *Eichmann* judgement.

Prior to *Eichmann* the "piracy analogy" proved to be influential in the 1946 trial of twenty-two senior Nazis at the Nuremberg International Military Tribunal (IMT).[72] Robert H. Jackson, prosecuting on behalf of the United States, suggested that "[t]he principle of individual responsibility for piracy [...] is old and well-established".[73] A similar claim was made by Jackson's British colleague Sir Hartley Shawcross.[74] The UN Secretary-General also drew the comparison after the trials, tentatively noting that "the Court considered the crimes under the [Nuremberg] Charter to be, as international crimes, subject to the jurisdiction of every State. The case of piracy would then be the [...] appropriate parallel."[75] The historical allusion to piracy was intended to secure legitimacy for the trials and a firm jurisdictional grounding in a situation where the normal rules of territoriality, nationality and/or passive personality did not obviously apply.[76] The analogy also served a higher purpose by confirming and popularising the notions of individual criminal responsibility and universal jurisdiction over heinous international offences (as epitomised by the actions of the Nazis). The pirate "was suddenly the agent of the political and legal movement",[77] the progenitor of war crimes trials and inspiration for expansive forms of jurisdiction.

71 This term is borrowed from Walter Rech, "Rightless Enemies: Schmitt and Lauterpacht on Political Piracy" 32 *Oxford Journal of Legal Studies* (2012) 235.

72 See, e.g., Telford Taylor, *The Anatomy of the Nuremberg Trials: A Personal Memoir* (New York: Knopf, 1992). The reference to piracy was, however, less of an influence at the Tokyo IMT, where jurisdiction was explicitly ceded by the Japanese government; see Robert Cryer, Håkan Friman, Darryl Robinson and Elizabeth Wilmshurst, *An Introduction to International Criminal Law and Procedure* (3rd ed.) (Cambridge: CUP, 2014), 116.

73 Opening to *Trial against Hermann Wilhelm Göring and Others*; 2 *Trials of the Major War Criminals before the International Military Tribunal*, 149–150.

74 3 *Trials of the Major War Criminals before the International Military Tribunal*, 106.

75 Secretary-General of the United Nations, *The Charter and Judgment of the Nuremberg Tribunal: History and Analysis*, U.N. Doc. A/CN.4/5 (1949), 80. The Secretary-General conceded, however, that he could reach no definite conclusion on the matter.

76 Randall, *supra* no26, 802–803, noting that a universal theory of jurisdiction provided the greatest chance for a successful outcome, and Madeline H. Morris, "Universal Jurisdiction in a Divided World" 35 *New England Law Review* (2001) 337, 345, suggesting that "[b]ecause no specific precedent existed prior to WWII for subjecting war crimes and crimes against humanity to universal jurisdiction, it is unsurprising that the extension of universal jurisdiction to those crimes would have relied in part on analogies to the law of piracy".

77 Daniel Heller-Roazen, *The Enemy of All: Piracy and the Law of Nations* (Brooklyn: Zone Books, 2009), 160.

Three years after the conclusion of the Nuremberg trials, universal jurisdiction (beyond piracy) would find codification in the four 1949 Geneva Conventions governing the humanitarian rules of warfare. A common article written into each of the conventions provides that contracting parties should "search for persons alleged to have committed [...] grave breaches [of the conventions], and shall bring such persons, regardless of their nationality, before its own courts".[78] Alternatively the contracting party must deliver the captured person to another State that is or may be willing to prosecute the individual.[79] These "extradite or prosecute" (*aut dedere aut judicare*) provisions,[80] inspired by the Nuremberg precedent,[81] provided "the first multilateral recognition by States of universal jurisdiction over war crimes".[82]

The *Eichmann* trial thus marked the culmination of over a century of legal reasoning deriving from the "piracy analogy", but was nevertheless a hugely significant development in that it marked the first instance of a State unilaterally exercising universal jurisdiction against a crime other than piracy.[83] Moreover *Eichmann* extended the principle to embrace genocide (in the guise of "crimes against the Jewish people") and crimes against humanity. Significantly no State objected to the trial or to the novel jurisdictional claims contained within it, perhaps given the ubiquity of disgust at the accused's crimes.[84] *Eichmann* signalled a broader application of universal jurisdiction over serious international crimes,[85] setting a precedent for further trials of Nazis in States that bore no obvious connection (in terms of the traditional principles of jurisdiction) to the offences tried.[86]

In 1993 the outbreak of hostilities in Yugoslavia led the UN Security Council (UNSC) to adopt the novel approach of creating the *ad hoc* International

---

78 Article 49/50/129/146 of conventions 1–4 respectively; see *supra* no28.

79 *Ibid.*

80 See International Law Commission Report, *supra* no30.

81 Christopher C. Joyner, "Arresting Impunity: The Case for Universal Jurisdiction in Bringing War Criminals to Accountability" 59 *Law & Contemporary Problems* (1996) 153, 166.

82 Roger O'Keefe, "The Grave Breaches Regime and Universal Jurisdiction" 7 *Journal of International Criminal Justice* (2009) 811, 811.

83 A phenomenon dubbed "new" universal jurisdiction by Kontorovich, *supra* no19.

84 Germany, for instance, welcomed the trial; see Louis Henkin, *How Nations Behave: Law and Foreign Policy* (2nd ed.) (New York: Columbia University Press, 1979), 273.

85 As discussed in Schabas, *supra* no8, 692; Randall, *supra* no26, 809–814; and Reydams, *supra* no26, 161–162.

86 Notable examples include: *Polyukhovich v Australia,* (1991) 172 CLR 501, F.C. 91/026; *R v Finta* [1994] S.C.R. 701 (Canada); *Fédération Nationale des Déportés et Internés Résistants et Patriotes and Others v Barbie* 78 I.L.R. 125 (Fr. Cass. Crim. 1983); and *R v Sawoniuk* (UK, Central Criminal Court 1999) (unpublished).

Criminal Tribunal for the former Yugoslavia (ICTY).[87] The institution was mandated by the UNSC to prosecute suspected perpetrators of genocide, war crimes and crimes against humanity committed within the territory of the former Yugoslavia from 1991.[88] As the first internationally constituted tribunal since the Nuremberg and Tokyo IMTS, the Court confirmed the principle of individual criminal responsibility under international law and promoted, the right of States to exercise universal jurisdiction (via reference to *Eichmann* and the "piracy analogy").[89]

Taking their lead from the ICTY, several European countries (most notably Germany) initiated a fresh wave of universal jurisdiction prosecutions, this time targeting suspects implicated in the atrocities committed in Yugoslavia.[90] A similar pattern of prosecutions followed the UNSC's establishment of a separate International Criminal Tribunal for Rwanda (ICTR) in November 1994.[91] Since 1999, and the high-profile *Pinochet* case in the United Kingdom,[92] universal jurisdiction cases have become more widespread, with officials from the Democratic Republic of Congo, Chile, Argentina, Guatemala, Russia, Uzbekistan, Afghanistan, Iraq, China, Israel, the United States, Chad, and Liberia *inter alia* becoming the subjects of universal jurisdiction proceedings predominantly

---

87 UN Security Council Resolution 827, 25 May 1993.

88 Statute of the ICTY (as amended 7 July 2009 by UNSC Resolution 1877), Articles 2–5, 8.

89 See e.g., *Prosecutor v. Tadić*, "Decision on the Defence Motion for Interlocutory Appeal on Jurisdiction" (Appeals Chamber) 2 October 1995, paras 57–59, and *Furundžija*, *supra* n030, para. 156.

90 Notable examples include: *Tadić*, Federal Supreme Court, 13 February 1994 (Germany; the suspect was extradited to the ICTY); *Djajić*, Judgment, (Higher Regional Court of Bavaria, 23 May 1997); *Jorgić*, Judgment, Higher Regional Court at Düsseldorf, 6 September 1997; *Sokolović*, Judgment, Federal Supreme Court, (Germany) 21 February 2001; *Cvjetković* (Austria), Landesgericht, Salzburg, 31 May 1995; *Knesević*, Supreme Court of the Netherlands, 11 November 1997, translated in 1 *Yearbook of International Humanitarian Law* (1998) 600. On the influential nature of the *ad hoc* tribunals in this respect, see Wolfgang Kaleck, "From Pinochet to Rumsfeld: Universal Jurisdiction in Europe 1998–2008" 30 *Michigan Journal of International Law* (2009) 927, 929, and Kontorovich, *supra* n019, 199.

91 UNSC Res 955, 8 November 1994. Notable cases include *Higaniro et al* ("The Butare Four") (Belgium), Unreported, Cour d'Assises de l'Arrondissement Administratif de Bruxelles-Capital, 8 June 2001. See also: "*Niyonteze v. Public Prosecutor*", 96 *American Journal of International Law* (2002) 231, 231 (Switzerland); FIDH, "Pascal Simbikangwa convicted of genocide and complicity in crimes against humanity" (France), 14 March 2014; and Redress, "Onesphore Rwabukombe convicted of accessory to genocide" (Germany), February 2014.

92 *R* v *Bow Street Metropolitan Stipendiary Magistrate Ex p. Pinochet Ugarte* (No. 3) House of Lords, 24 March 1999; [2000] 1 A.C. 147. For a discussion of the influence of *Pinochet* see O'Sullivan, *supra* n052, 138–157, and Naomi Roht-Arriaza, *The Pinochet Effect: Transnational Justice in the Age of Human Rights* (Philadelphia: University of Pennsylvania Press, 2005).

across European States (including Belgium, France, Switzerland, UK, Netherlands, Scandinavia, Germany, Austria and Spain).[93] The centre of gravity for universal jurisdiction cases is firmly within Europe, although a handful of non-European States (including the US, Argentina and South Africa)[94] are increasingly making use of the principle. In 2016 former Chadian dictator Hissene Habré was found guilty of crimes against humanity, war crimes and torture by the specially constituted African Union backed *Chambres Africaines Extraordinaires* in Senegal.[95] *Habré* was perhaps the most notable universal jurisdiction trial of 2016, yet it forms part of a broader rise in the number of prosecutions: in total there were 47 such cases were open across thirteen different States (four at trial stage),[96] while in 2017 there were 126 ongoing cases across fourteen States (sixteen at trial), figures that indicate constant growth.[97]

International criminal law was given a permanent institutionalised footing in 2002 in the form of the International Criminal Court (ICC), as established by the 1998 Rome Statute.[98] The existence of the ICC does not, however, obviate the need for universal jurisdiction, which still plays a crucial role in situations beyond the Court's territorial or temporal purview, or in prosecuting suspects that the ICC lacks the resources to proceed against.[99] Incidentally, universal jurisdiction was rejected as a jurisdictional basis for the ICC given the opposition of some States (notably the US) to the prospect of an international court with

93 See overview in Kaleck, *supra* no90, 932–958. See also Human Rights Watch, "The Long Arm of Justice: Lessons from Specialised War Crimes Units in France, Germany and the Netherlands", September 16, 2014 (available online), and Olympia Bekou, "Doing Justice for the Liberian Victims of Mass Atrocity NGOs in Aid of Universal Jurisdiction" 13 *Journal of International Criminal Justice* (2015) 219.

94 Most notably the US trial of Charles McArthur Emmanuel ("Chuckie") Taylor for torture committed in Liberia; see BBC, "Taylor's son jailed for 97 years", 9 January 2009 (available online). See Richard Dicker, "A Few Reflections on the Current Status and Future Direction of Universal Jurisdiction Practice" 107 *American Society of International Law Proceedings* (2013) 233.

95 *Chambre Africaine Extraordinaire d'Assises, Ministère Public v Hissein Habré*, Judgement, 30 May 2016. See also Reed Brody, *Victims bring a Dictator to Justice: The Case of Hissène Habré* (2nd ed.) (Berlin: Bread for the World, 2017).

96 TRIAL International, *Make Way for Justice (#3): Universal Jurisdiction Annual Review 2017*, 3.

97 TRIAL International, *Make Way for Justice (#4): Momentum towards accountability: Universal Jurisdiction Annual Review 2018*, 6. See also Maximo Langer, "Universal Jurisdiction is Not Disappearing" 13 *Journal of International Criminal Justice* (2015) 245.

98 UN doc. A/CONF. 183/9, 17 July 1998. At the time of writing, 123 States have ratified the *Rome Statute* (figure taken from ICC Assembly of States Parties website, "The States Parties to the Rome Statute").

99 Mark Chadwick, "Modern Developments in Universal Jurisdiction: Addressing Impunity in Tibet and Beyond", 9 *International Criminal Law Review* (2009) 359, 387–390; Cedric

universal reach.[100] Although a setback for the broader recognition and usage of universal jurisdiction,[101] the political rejection of the principle at the ICC has not dissuaded States from invoking the principle.

By this stage in the evolution of universal jurisdiction, the "piracy analogy" that underwrote Nuremberg and *Eichmann* has arguably become less important in terms of justifying the principle's continued existence and development. Rather than reliance on the "historicity" of universal jurisdiction over piracy, proponents of the principle draw support from applicable treaties or customary international law (though the strength of the customary legal basis is uncertain).[102]

Arguments in favour of universal jurisdiction will often, however, supplant such textual or practice-based observational evidence with theoretical justification that draws on the heinous nature of the "core" international crimes – a "moralist" position which maintains that heinous crimes "affect the whole of mankind and shock the conscience of all nations of the world".[103] This argument often relies on a historical connection with piracy. An alternative theoretical justification proposes that universal jurisdiction plays a necessary "gap-filling" role in cases where there is an "absence or uncertainty of a jurisdiction capable of being effectively exercised over the crime in question",[104] thereby disputing the "moralist" position. Part of the purpose of this book is to address

---

Ryngaert, "Universal Jurisdiction in an ICC Era" 14 *European Journal of Crime and Criminal Justice* (2006) 46, 49–51.

100 Morten Bergsmo, "The Jurisdictional Regime of the International Criminal Court" 6 *European Journal of Crime, Criminal Law and Criminal Justice* (1998) 345, 347–350; Olympia Bekou and Robert Cryer, "The International Criminal Court and Universal Jurisdiction: A Close Encounter?" 56 *International and Comparative Law Quarterly* (2007) 49.

101 O'Sullivan, *supra* no52, 164.

102 Discussed *infra*, 8.2.1.

103 *Tadić* (ICTY), *supra* no89, paras 57 and 59, paraphrasing from *Eichmann*, *supra* no5. Similar arguments can be found in Bassiouni, *supra* no27, Randall, *supra* no26, 788–789, Margaret M. DeGuzman, "Criminal Law Philosophy in William Schabas's scholarship" in Margaret M Deguzman and Diane Marie Amann (eds), *Arcs of Global Justice: Essays in Honour of William A. Schabas* (Oxford: OUP, 2018) 155, 159, the dissenting opinion of Judge van den Wyngaert to *Arrest Warrant*, *supra* no17, 166–167, and the Joint Separate Opinion of Judges Higgins, Kooijmans and Buerguenthal, also to *Arrest Warrant*, 77 and 81. This view appears to have been endorsed by several States; see overview in Kevin Jon Heller, "What is an International Crime? (A Revisionist History)" 58 *Harvard International Law Journal* (2017) 353, 357–358.

104 Christopher Staker, "Jurisdiction" in Malcolm D. Evans, (ed.) *International Law* (4th ed.) (Oxford: OUP, 2014), 309, 322. Several further theories are advanced by Devika Hovell in "The Authority of Universal Jurisdiction 29 *European Journal of International Law* (2018) 427.

the competing arguments for the theoretical justification of universal jurisdiction, via an examination of the original rationale for the principle.

1.2.2 *Questioning Universal Jurisdiction*

Since the early 2000s, and notwithstanding the continued increase in universal jurisdiction cases, the principle has been subject to increased criticism. The hostility to universal jurisdiction is largely based around two main critiques.

The most prominent objection to universal jurisdiction might be thought of as a "formalist" position that challenges "the injustice of politically motivated or 'show' trials, privileging the moral value of maintaining order and stressing state consent to jurisdiction".[105] This approach generally rejects universal jurisdiction due to its perceived interference with the keystone concepts of sovereign equality and non-intervention.[106] Variations on the theme decry universal jurisdiction as judicial neo-colonialism,[107] as "Eurocentric",[108] the "reserve of the privileged few",[109] or as risking "judicial chaos".[110] Such criticisms are often conflated with politicised objections to specific instances of universal jurisdiction. Since 2000, for instance, political pressure (in the guise of legal objection) from the US and China have caused the curtailment of expansive "absolute" universal jurisdiction laws in Belgium[111] and Spain.[112] The African Union has also objected to a perceived abuse of universal jurisdiction as exercised by

105 O'Sullivan, *supra* n052, 115.

106 Reydams, *Universal Jurisdiction, supra* n026, 224–225.

107 Steven R. Ratner, "Belgium's War Crimes Statute: A Postmortem" 97 *American Journal of International Law* (2003) 888, 894; G. Bykhovsky, "An Argument against Assertion of Universal Jurisdiction by Individual States" 21 *Wisconsin International Law Journal* (2003) 161, 177.

108 Henry A. Kissinger, "The Pitfalls of Universal Jurisdiction" 80 *Foreign Affairs* (2001) 86; Rephael Ben-Ari, "Universal Jurisdiction: Chronicle of a Death Foretold?" 43 *Denver Journal of International Law and Policy* (2015) 165, 195–197.

109 Reydams, *Universal Jurisdiction, supra* n026, 224–225.

110 Separate Opinion of Judge Guillame in *Arrest Warrant, supra* n017, 44.

111 A proposed Belgian investigation into the conduct of George HEW Bush and Tommy Franks during the first Gulf War led to US threats to pull funding from NATO's Brussels headquarters; the investigations were promptly abandoned and Belgian universal jurisdiction laws curtailed in 2003. See Ratner, *supra* n0107 and Naomi Roht-Arriaza, "Universal Jurisdiction: Steps Forward, Steps Back", 17 *Leiden Journal of International Law* (2004) 375, 385.

112 Spanish universal jurisdiction laws were heavily curtailed in 2009, and again in 2014, following prolonged pressure from China. The pressure on Spain was linked with Spanish judges' investigation of Jiang Zemin's conduct in Tibet; see Ignacio de la Rasilla del Moral, "The Swan Song of Universal Jurisdiction in Spain", 9 *International Criminal Law Review* (2009) 777; Noora Arajärvi, "Looking Back from Nowhere: Is There a Future for Universal Jurisdiction over International Crimes?" 16 *Tilburg Law Review* (2011) 5, 18; and Amnesty

European States.[113] Division among States over the proper scope of universal jurisdiction is evident from the ongoing debate at the UN General Assembly Legal Committee, which has run for almost ten years at the time of writing.[114] Importantly this line of objection to universal jurisdiction does not, however, question the applicability of the principle to piracy.[115]

The arguments outlined above do not question or negate the underlying "piracy analogy", but a second line of critique has arisen which does object to this foundational theory. By relying on the "piracy analogy", proponents of universal jurisdiction are able to invoke the time-tested historicity of the principle as an inviolable truth that lends support to its continued credibility, regardless of contemporary objections.[116] Any attack, therefore, against the aptness of the "piracy analogy" would also consist of an attack at the historic and theoretical heart of the principle of universal jurisdiction. A key proponent of this line of argumentation, Eugene Kontorovich argues that "piracy cannot serve as a precedent for the new universal jurisdiction [...]. [C]ourts and scholars have accepted the piracy analogy uncritically, thereby allowing [modern universal jurisdiction] to be built on a hollow foundation".[117] The basis of Kontorovich's objection is that modern universal jurisdiction is analogised to piracy on the basis of the supposed "heinousness" of the offence, this being an overly

International, *Spain: Current Human Rights Concerns and a Setback in the Struggle Against Impunity*, Submission to the UN Universal Periodic Review, January 2015.

113 See Martin Mennecke, "The African Union and Universal Jurisdiction" in Charles Chernor Jalloh and Ilias Bantekas (eds), *The International Criminal Court and Africa* (Oxford: OUP, 2017), 10. African Union States have, though, expressed general support for the principle, as indicated by the adoption of an *African Union Model National Law on Universal Jurisdiction over International Crimes* (Doc. EX.CL/731(XXI)c) in 2012.

114 See, e.g., Resolution 71/149 adopted by the General Assembly (Sixth Committee), 13 December 2016 ("*Recognizing* the diversity of views expressed by States and the need for further consideration towards a better understanding of the scope and application of universal jurisdiction"). The Sixth Committee has had universal jurisdiction on its agenda since 2009 but has not, as of November 2018, reached an agreement on either the definition or scope of the principle.

115 Ved Nanda, "Exercising Universal Jurisdiction over Piracy" in Michael P. Scharf, Michael A. Newton and Milena Sterio (eds), *Prosecuting Maritime Piracy: Domestic Solutions to International Crimes* (Cambridge: CUP, 2015) 54, 54.

116 For examples where the piracy analogy has been to support a "historicity" argument in favour of universal jurisdiction see, *e.g.*, Benjamin B. Ferencz, "A Nuremberg Prosecutor's Response to Henry Kissinger", 8 *Brown Journal of World Affairs* (2001) 177, 177; Thomas H. Sponsler, "The Universality Principle of Jurisdiction and the Threatened Trials of American Airmen" 15 Loyola Law Review (1968–69) 43, 47; *Filártiga v Peña-Irala*, 630 F.2d 876 (2d Cir. 1980), 890.

117 Kontorovich, *supra* n019, 186.

convenient comparison that cannot, in his view, be drawn.[118] Indeed, pirates hardly seem comparable, in terms of the severity of their actions, to *génocidaires*, or war criminals,[119] seeming to belong instead to "a lesser, ordinary class of evil".[120] This apparent discrepancy has been reflected, to an extent, in modern practice in relation to piracy; for much of the twenty-first century, States who captured pirates often chosen to release them without charge.[121] Consequently, State practice "appears inconsistent with international norms which classify piracy as a universal crime which all States should take an interest in repressing and deterring",[122] placing it out of sync with suggestions that piracy is a serious menace, and that universal jurisdiction developed as a response to a "heinous" offence. And yet pirates were, historically, claimed to be *hostes humani generis*,[123] the enemies of all mankind, and routinely punished most severely.[124] An impenetrable complexity in the history of piracy appears to be at play, requiring greater attention and scrutiny.

This apparent paradox ought to cause us to question why piracy was historically considered to be so unique as to lead, unanimously and unopposed, to the adoption of universal jurisdiction by States. The rationale for universal jurisdiction over piracy has never been satisfactorily dealt with, despite a range of theories, prompting the need for a focused study to shed light on the link between old and new.

---

118 *Ibid.* Kontorovich's argument is based largely on the historical State practice of privateering; he argues that, as States essentially practiced piracy themselves, it cannot have been considered especially "heinous". See similar claims in Malcolm D. Evans and Sofia Galani, "Piracy and the Development of International Law" in Panos Koutrakos and Achilles Skordas (eds), *The Law and Practice of Piracy at Sea: European and International Perspectives* (Oxford: Hart, 2014) 343, 344–345; Geoffrey Robertson, *Crimes Against Humanity: The Struggle for Global Justice* (3rd ed.) (London: Penguin, 2006), 274; Luc Reydams, "The Rise and Fall of Universal Jurisdiction", Leuven Centre for Global Governance Working Paper No. 37, January 2010, 12; and Hovell, *supra* no104, 442, 443.

119 Kazemi, *supra* no36, 32; Petrig, *supra* no33, 860–861.

120 Kontorovich, *supra* no19, 217.

121 Jack Lang, *Report of the Special Adviser [on legal issues related to piracy] to the Secretary-General on Legal Issues Related to Piracy off the Coast of Somalia*, 25 January 2011, 3, suggesting that nine out of ten captured pirates were being released at this time.

122 Eugene Kontorovich and Steven Art, "An Empirical Examination of Universal Jurisdiction for Piracy", 104 *American Journal of International Law* (2010) 436, 445. Less than 1.5 percent of 1158 reported piracy attacks between 1998 and 2009 resulted in a prosecution based on universal jurisdiction.

123 Lord Coke, *The Third Part of the Institutes of the Laws of England; Concerning High Treason, and Other Pleas of the Crown and Criminal Causes.* (c. 1628), Chapter 49 (p113).

124 Marcus Rediker, *Villains of All Nations* (London: Verso, 2004), 35, detailing the hundreds of hangings that took place in Britain and its colonies in the 1710s and 20s.

1.2.3 *The Continued Relevance of the "Piracy Analogy"*

The "piracy analogy" remains relevant as the historic and theoretical bedrock upon which "new" universal jurisdiction (the post-*Eichmann* phenomenon of prosecuting egregious human rights violations) has been able to evolve, notwithstanding the ambiguous precedent lent to the principle via State practice and scholarly opinion.[125] As Kontorovich insists, if we discard the "piracy analogy" as a historical reference point for "new" universal jurisdiction,

> there may [still] be a plausible account of why heinous crimes should be universally prosecuted. But this argument would no longer have the backing of history. [...] Thus perhaps the principal result of stripping away the piracy analogy is to reveal the untested and fragile nature of modern universal jurisdiction.[126]

Given the purported implications of "stripping away the piracy analogy", a closer examination into this claim is warranted. Why was it that piracy was and remains subject to this unique principle?[127] What historical processes led to the legal state of affairs that pertains today? What was it about pirates that made them "*hostes humani generis*"? Given the dissonance of ideas about the nature of piracy it is imperative to uncover the true legal identity of the pirate (as defined throughout history), how pirates fit into (or outside) the international legal system, and how their successors in "modern" universal jurisdiction (*i.e.* perpetrators of "core" international crimes) relate to them. A cursory examination of these questions reveals an extensive and fascinating history of case law, State practice and scholarly thought regarding the nature of piracy and identity of those who commit it.[128] To date there has not, however, been a thorough historical legal study of piracy that considers whether the analogy to "core" international crimes (and concomitant usage of universal jurisdiction) is indeed a legitimate comparison to draw. A handful of studies of the law of piracy do already exist, most notably Alfred Rubin's largely historical monograph on the

125 1.2.1, *supra*; 8.2.1, *infra*.

126 Kontorovich, *supra* n019, 237.

127 See, e.g., Joshua Goodwin, "Universal Jurisdiction and the Pirate: Time for an Old Couple to Part", 39 *Vanderbilt Journal of Transnational Law* (2006) 973, 987–1002, summarising several extant theories. The "heinousness" of piracy and practical problems related to suppressing crime on the high seas emerge as commonly proposed explanations.

128 Examples of such examinations include Goodwin, *ibid.*, and Tamsin Paige, "Piracy and Universal Jurisdiction" 12 *Macquarie Law Journal* (2013) 131.

topic,[129] but these do not study the development of universal jurisdiction in relation to piracy, or draw conclusions as to the appropriateness of the "piracy do analogy" to the broader contemporary application of universal jurisdiction.[130] A better understanding of the nature, meaning, purpose, and relevance of the "piracy analogy" will allow us a better understanding of the nature of universal jurisdiction, as it applies to piracy specifically and to "core" international crimes more generally.[131]

1.3 Scope, Methodology, and Structure

This book serves two central aims, namely: (i) to ascertain the rationale behind the link between piracy and universal jurisdiction; and (ii) to discern whether, based on this relationship, the "piracy analogy" is a legitimate reference point for "new" universal jurisdiction. It addresses these questions via a comprehensive historical study of the reasons why universal jurisdiction became attached to piracy, a critical consideration of whether the same reason(s) can be applied to jurisdiction for the "core" international crimes, and an analysis of what this means for present conceptions of universal jurisdiction and international (criminal) law more broadly.

The book is structured according to relevant historical periods during which conceptions of piracy, and of jurisdiction *over* piracy, were developed. It traces a line from the Roman revulsion at piracy through to the twenty-first century and the proliferation of offences subject to universal jurisdiction. The narrative presents the core legal components of the study against a backdrop of historical and cultural events that influenced the scholars, jurists, legislators and politicians who, in turn, shaped the legal history of piracy. The importance of

---

129 *Supra* no60. Also worthy of mention are Daniel Heller-Roazen's *The Enemy of All: Piracy and the Law of Nations* (*supra* no77), which examines the evolution of legal thought and political philosophy relating to piracy since Roman times, and Amedeo Policante's *The Pirate Myth: Genealogies of an Imperial Concept* (Abingdon: Routledge, 2015), which adopts a genealogical approach to the question of why and how the pirate became "first enemy of the human race" (Introduction, x).

130 See, e.g., Lauren Benton, "Toward a New Legal History of Piracy: Maritime Legalities and the Myth of Universal Jurisdiction" 23 *International Journal of Maritime History* (2011) 225, 229, suggesting that "[a]n overview of the legal treatment of piracy, and in particular its relation to jurisdictional claims and efforts to construct other prohibition regimes using controls on piracy as a precedent, remains unwritten".

131 A proposal that finds support in, *e.g.*, Michael Davey, "A Pirate Looks at the Twenty-First Century: The Legal Status of Somali Pirates in an Age of Sovereign Seas and Human Rights" 85 *Notre Dame Law Review* (2010) 1197, 1204.

historical influence cannot be overlooked; rather, "the present cannot be properly assessed, nor future projected, without an understanding of the past".[132] The depth of history surrounding these issues is rich and complex, remaining deeply relevant to current legal and political developments.

A doctrinal and evaluative approach is adopted, building an argument from historical perspective that is itself an interdisciplinary engagement with law, sociology, culture, geography, politics and literature that together inform and influence modern day (legal) approaches to piracy and universal jurisdiction. *Context* appears to be the missing element of commentaries on the historical roots of piracy, here forming a fundamental component of the narrative that will develop our historical and contemporary understanding of the universal jurisdiction phenomenon. Law forms as a response to events and to societal needs: it cannot exist in isolation.[133] Studying the events and responses that first shaped the laws we have today therefore forms a lynchpin to a proper, fuller understanding of why we have universal jurisdiction over piracy and, indeed, over "core" international crimes. The narrative therefore ought to inform the decisions that relevant actors take when dealing with the interrelated topics of piracy and universal jurisdiction.

The research draws on legal positivism as the basis for understanding the origins and purpose of universal jurisdiction. This is as opposed to a "naturalist" vein of thought that commonly presents pirates (and, sometimes, the perpetrators of "core" international crimes) unthinkingly as "*hostes humani generis*",[134] a kind of generic "enemy of all mankind". Such an approach struggles for any principled analysis of why, exactly, pirates might have been branded in this way, culminating in a vague approach that allows for the kind of deconstruction of "*hostes humani generis*" such as that undertaken by Kontorovich.[135] A positivist approach, in contrast, allows an examination of the laws and historical or political developments that caused this perception. In other words, "case law and influential scholarship reflect that the establishment of universal jurisdiction is most often centred around an inquiry as to whether the principle exists in positive law, either domestic or international".[136] This is not to say that "natural law" approaches are altogether useless; indeed, Chapter 4 presents a

132 RP Anand, *New States and International Law* (2nd ed) (Gurgaon: Hope India Publications, 2008), 5.

133 See Philip Handler, "Legal History" in Dawn Watkins and Mandy Burton (eds), *Research Methods in Law* (Abingdon, Ox: Routledge, 2013) 85, 95, on the relationship between legal history and broader social, political and cultural studies.

134 See, e.g., Gould, *supra* no32, 24, summarising this position.

135 *Supra* no19.

136 Hovell, *supra* no104, 429.

close investigation of Alberico Gentili and Hugo Grotius' approaches to piracy, which are predominantly set within a natural law paradigm. Nevertheless, their arguments are placed within historical context and their influence checked against positive developments regarding the developing international law of piracy.

The investigation seeks to build from the bottom up and reach logical conclusions based on informed, objective study as opposed to "cherry-picking" facts and arguments that might fit a pre-ordained hypothesis or ideological ambition. Appeals to normative or moralistic explanations for universal jurisdiction hinging on "deductive" reasoning extrapolated from labels such as "*hostes humani generis*" seem counterintuitive, given that they fail to address *why* pirates initially gained the moniker.[137] Conversely, an "inductive" and principled approach that objectively assesses the available evidence and pledges no allegiance to any particular pre-existing theory based will provide a more coherent, logical, and overarching narrative. The book does not claim to represent a full legal history of piracy, instead electing to focus on the theme of jurisdiction. Nor does it claim to provide a definitive "theory" of universal jurisdiction (if one were possible), instead drawing conclusions from a historical study of piracy and establishing how this might assist in understanding the phenomenon.

Research is drawn from primary sources wherever possible: original historical texts, cases, statutes and treaties. It has not always been possible, however, to work directly from primary documents, particularly when studying pertinent developments in ancient Republican Rome. As such, analysis of historical events will also rely on the works of reputable historians, particularly where different accounts agree on given facts. Secondary sources will be used where appropriate to evaluate and understand historical developments, approached critically and allocated a suitable weight.

Four distinct time periods are chosen to facilitate this study, each one representing a significant development in terms of how piracy or universal jurisdiction has come to be defined or understood. Chapter Two chronicles the first of these periods, the Roman Republican era during which universal jurisdiction over piracy and the notion of "*hostes humani generis*" are commonly believed to have originated.[138] The chapter examines the relevant history of the time and the manner in which Rome regarded and dealt with "piracy". The works of the orator and philosopher Cicero are particularly important when looking at this period, given his role in denunciating and dehumanising pirates

137 Kontorovich, *supra* n019, 234.
138 Gould, *supra* n032, 24.

as a ubiquitous menace.[139] It will be shown that these early pirates were in fact organised communities posing a threat to Roman hegemony and that the use of "piracy" as a political term by Cicero assisted the Roman Empire in its eradication of these undesirables. This exploration of early histories uncovers a highly politicised history of piracy, one which formed the basis of later claims to universal jurisdiction (or something similar in spirit) by, for instance, Alberico Gentili, Hugo Grotius, Lord Coke, and, crucially, by national legislatures and courts. Cicero's reproach of piracy created and cultivated the "Ciceronian paradigm"[140] of piracy that that draws a distinction between civilised peoples ("us") and "primordial" interlopers ("them"), a division that helps to explain the development of universal jurisdiction over the latter class of societally displaced "outsiders".

Chapter Three builds on the foregoing by examining how the "Ciceronian paradigm" of piracy, which posits an objective State-centric view of pirates as the enemies of civilised States, has been used (and abused) by historians, legal scholars and States in order to vilify objectionable practices of certain enemies. It looks at the history and (cultural) identity of pirates, examining how the term was used in the sixteenth and seventeenth centuries, and how this informed responses to piracy. Particular emphasis is placed on the works of English judge and jurist Lord Edward Coke, who appears to be the source of the phrase "*hostes humani generis*", despite espousing a definition of piracy that limits his conception of the offence to a domestic law paradigm. Inspired by the "Ciceronian paradigm" of piracy, Coke in turn influenced the development of universal jurisdiction. Another key development during this period was the development and normalisation of privateering, essentially the use and manipulation of piracy by States. The commonplace usage of privateers by States blurs the distinction between lawful and unlawful, private and public, and raises questions about the "heinous" nature of piracy. It is submitted, however, that their nature and purpose is fundamentally different to that of stateless pirates. Given that the correlation of piracy with State-sponsored privateering forms a key element of Kontorovich's dismissal of the "piracy analogy",[141] the chapter places particular focus on the relationship between these two maritime activities.

---

139 Gould, *ibid.*, 25; Rubin, *supra* no60, 83.

140 This term is borrowed from Thomas Heebøll-Holm, *Ports, Piracy and Maritime War: Piracy in the English Channel and the Atlantic, c. 1280 – c. 1330* (Leiden: Brill, 2013), 3.

141 *Supra* no19, 186.

Chapter Four looks at the philosophical foundations of universal jurisdiction as developed through the late sixteenth and early seventeenth century works of Alberico Gentili and Hugo Grotius. Both scholars were deeply influential in continuing the "Ciceronian paradigm" and laying the foundations of universal jurisdiction vis-à-vis piracy. The two scholars approach piracy from a different perspective, however. Gentili's work is largely based within an early formulation of the laws of war and the makeup of the State, so that the meaning of piracy, and responses thereto, are considered within this context. Grotius approaches piracy through the paradigms of both the laws of war and the freedom of the seas, and is the first scholar to closely engage with the problems presented by piracy. Grotius, in turn, lays the ideological bedrock for future claims to universal jurisdiction by States. It will be shown how the two scholars, read together, formulate a conception of piracy that forms the basis for later exercises of universal jurisdiction by rejecting pirates' position in the international order on a twofold basis – as an entity anathema to the State, to the nascent "international community" based around universally shared concepts of morality, and as violators of the consecrated right to free commerce.

The previous chapters together form the background to Chapter Five, charting the practical and theoretical developments that enabled the use of universal jurisdiction to emerge in the late 1600s and early 1700s. The chapter draws on contemporary cases and commentaries (with a particular focus on the exploits of Captain Kidd) to demonstrate how and why universal jurisdiction emerged, principally via British claims to jurisdiction over piracy.

Chapter Six draws on the revolutionary histories set out in Chapter 5 to hypothesise on the various theories behind initial claims to universal jurisdiction over piracy at this time. It does so via three overlapping theoretical approaches, namely: the characterisation of pirates as enemies of commerce and interlopers on the juridified mercantile space of the high seas; the notion of universal jurisdiction as being based on the "heinousness" of piracy; and the idea that universal jurisdiction is based on exceptional policing considerations, given the difficulty of apprehending pirates. Chapter Six concludes that piracy represented a threat to an emergent global community that relied on trade for stability and that several factors unique to the act of piracy justified its designation as a particularly "heinous" offence. This study is carried out in isolation from modern theories on universal jurisdiction so as not to be unduly influenced retrospectively by such philosophies. Instead, the study is juxtaposed against a contemporary historical context.

Ultimately the narrative links to the present and future in Chapters Seven and Eight. Chapter Seven explores how universal jurisdiction over piracy became enshrined in treaty via UNCLOS (by reference to historic precedent) and dissects issues arising from the treaty definition, including problems of jurisdiction. Against the backdrop of twenty-first century "Somali" piracy, the chapter examines the issues inherent in tackling piracy as a contemporary problem, thereby bringing the narrative into the present day.

Chapter Eight examines how the "piracy analogy" has shaped and informed the exercise of universal jurisdiction over "core" international crimes. The first half of the chapter demonstrates that an intrinsic link exists between the exercise of universal jurisdiction over piracy and the "core" international crimes, particularly in terms of how each is perceived to impact upon the "agreed vital interests of the international community",[142] as informed by changing international imperatives. In so doing, it reiterates the central importance of the connection to piracy. The second half looks at the realities of exercising universal jurisdiction in the modern age, providing an overview of present international law on the matter and making recommendations for how the principle might best develop in future, as informed by the pervasive "piracy analogy".

Chapter Nine forms a conclusion, recapping the findings of the previous chapters and summarising the findings. It considers the potential aspirations of universal jurisdiction (as rationalised under the "piracy analogy") and cautions against its limitations.

1.4 On Stranger Tides

The subtitle of the book, *On Stranger Tides*, is borrowed from a 1987 novel of the same name by Tim Powers.[143] The plot revolves around puppeteer John Chandagnac who is pressganged into becoming a pirate and is ultimately caught up in Blackbeard's plot to locate the mysterious "Fountain of Youth", which will – as its name suggests – renew him. This book bears some plot similarities, requiring us (like Chandagnac) to become knowledgeable in piracy and its history, all the while seeking the elusive Fountain – what it is about piracy that explains how and why the phenomenon has become subject to a unique jurisdictional regime. In turn, discovering the Fountain will breathe new life into the debate surrounding the origins and theoretical basis of universal jurisdiction.

142 *Eichmann* (Supreme Court), *supra* n01, para. 12.

143 New York: Ace Books, 1987.

CHAPTER 2

Crime of the Ancient Mariner: Legal and Political Perspectives on Piracy in Antiquity

> Rome, which had conquered the whole world, might have been subdued by a parcel of pirates.[1]

The turbulent era of history that Captain Johnson refers to occurred early in the first century BC, as the Roman Republic came under constant assault from maritime communities operating from bases in the Eastern Mediterranean. Rome suffered frequent grain shortages as a result, while coastal settlements were routinely plundered.[2] The Romans' strategy to contain these bellicose "pirates" manifested in a concerted military effort led by Pompey the Great in 67 BC, backed by a campaign of speeches issued by the orator and philosopher Cicero which cast them as *communes hostes omnium*, "the common foe of all the world".[3] Rome's double-edged response to these communities effectively forms the basis of modern day abhorrence of piracy, their taxonomy as *hostes humani generis,* and their subjection to universal jurisdiction (as developed via the elaborate accounts of Renaissance scholars such as Alberico Gentili and Hugo Grotius).[4] As such these "world-historical events of revolutionary

1 Captain Charles Johnson, *A General History of the Robberies and Murders of the Most Notorious Pirates* (1724) (with an introduction and commentary by David Cordingly) (London: Conway Maritime Press, 1998), 6.

2 Philip De Souza, "Greek Piracy", in Anton Powell (ed.), *The Greek World* (London: Routledge, 1997) 179, 189.

3 Cicero's quote is taken from *De Officiis*, III, s.107 (ed. Walter Miller, with an English Translation; Cambridge, MA: Harvard University Press, 1913). This phrase might alternatively be translated as "the common enemies of all communities", as suggested by Joshua Goodwin, "Universal Jurisdiction and the Pirate: Time for an Old Couple to Part", 39 *Vanderbilt Journal of Transnational Law* (2006) 973, 989.

4 The reference to events in ancient Rome is standardly included in many (legal) histories of piracy, most notably: Alfred P. Rubin, *The Law of Piracy* (Honolulu: University Press of the Pacific, 2006), 3–13; James Kraska, *Contemporary Maritime Piracy: International Law, Strategy, and Diplomacy at Sea: International Law, Strategy, and Diplomacy at Sea* (Santa Barbara, CA: ABC-CLIO, 2011), 10–14; Tamsin Paige, "Piracy and Universal Jurisdiction" 12 *Macquarie Law*

 | DOI:10.1163/9789004390461_003

significance"[5] are where we must begin. We cannot attempt to understand universal jurisdiction today without first deciphering the events of this period.

This chapter examines the apparent division inherent in humanity as proposed by Cicero (and put into effect by Pompey), scrutinising the context and the theory behind the jurist's famous orations. It provides a historical and ideological backdrop to Chapters 3 and 4 which will (*inter alia*) demonstrate the methods by which pirates were displaced from the narrative of international law, itself the tool of "civilised" States, largely by force of rhetoric. As we will see, this was a trend that would ultimately give way to proscriptive domestic and international laws regarding piracy, as chronicled in Chapters 5 to 8. These latter chapters rely on the pre-existence of normative values that formed during the Roman Republican period as a side effect of Roman dominance: the inherent illegality of piracy, the ascendancy of territorial Statehood and the sanctity of free commerce. We may take these principles for granted today, yet this was not the case prior to the events of this period. Of course, if the "pirates" had been victorious against Rome (as Captain Johnson suggests almost happened), the modern political and legal world may be a rather different place.

Part 2.1 investigates how "pirates" forced Rome to the brink of disaster and examines how the Roman response (both military and legal) against the pirates was conceived, with a particular focus on how the enemy was defined and their destruction justified. This historical study is carried out against a context of major shifts in (geo)political ideology occurring at the time – for instance, the increased reliance on trade, the emergence of the territorial State, and Roman attempts to manipulate the *jus gentium*, a ubiquitous natural law purportedly governing all of civilisation.[6] The investigation reveals the existence of an extremely complex political and legal relationship between Rome and the "pirates", a situation that has nevertheless deeply influenced subsequent historical developments. Part 2.2 examines the oratories of Cicero, whose work *De Officiis* is often cited as an influential text in favour of the universal condemnation and outlawry of piracy.[7] Part 2.3 forms a conclusion, looking

Journal (2013) 131, 132–134; Amedeo Policante, *The Pirate Myth: Genealogies of an Imperial Concept* (Abingdon: Routledge, 2015), 3–27; Daniel Heller-Roazen, *The Enemy of All: Piracy and the Law of Nations* (Brooklyn: Zone Books, 2009), 31–68; and M. Cherif Bassiouni, "The History of Universal Jurisdiction and Its Place in International Law" in Stephen Macedo (ed.), *Universal Jurisdiction: National Courts and the Prosecution of Serious Crimes under International Law* (Philadelphia: University of Pennsylvania Press, 2004) 39. The contributions of Gentili and Grotius to this oeuvre are discussed in Chapter 4, *infra*.

5 Carl Schmitt, *The Nomos of the Earth* (1950) (trans. G.L. Ulmen) (New York: Telos Press, 2003), 44.

6 Peter Stein, *Roman Law in European History* (Cambridge: CUP, 1999), 12–13.

7 As noted in, e.g., Harry D. Gould, "Cicero's Ghost: Rethinking the Social Construction of Piracy", in Michael J. Struett, Jon D. Carlson, and Mark T. Nance (eds), *Maritime Piracy and the*

at the implications for practitioners of "piracy", including their subjection to universal jurisdiction.

Studying developments that occurred during the first century BC brings inherent risks of perspective. Given the time gap involved the relevant evidence is primarily textual, while certain terms are likely to have been corrupted in translation. Any conclusions will, by necessity, be influenced and shaped by the works of others, although care is taken to consider the original language and context of relevant scholarship on the subject.

Before proceeding, it will be useful to briefly establish the various Greek and Latin terminology relevant to piracy at this time, as these terms will be referred to throughout the chapter. The English term "pirate" originates from the Greek πειρατής (*peiratēs* in Latin transliteration, the same in both singular and plural)[8] as popularised in around 140 BC by Greek historian Polybius, whose work would later form the basis for historical scholarship in Rome.[9] Polybius applied the term to belligerent communities governed by recognised political leaders,[10] and may have intended it pejoratively.[11] The word derives from *peira*, for a trial, risk or attempt,[12] meaning that a *peiratēs* would have been one who "tests" or "puts to proof".[13] *Peiratēs* were deemed to "put to proof" the ordered territorial civilisations of the time, the response from their enemies being the use of this term as a moral or political judgement aimed at delegitimising their actions.[14] The term "*peiratēs*" will be used throughout this chapter to refer to the maritime communities who preyed upon Rome, particularly during the first century BC. An earlier Greek term also often translated as "pirate" is ληστής (*lēstēs* in Latin transliteration, deriving from *leis*, plunder).[15] The two

Construction of Global Governance (New York: Routledge, 2013) 23, 24–25, Goodwin, *supra* no3, 989, and Thomas Heebøll-Holm, *Ports, Piracy and Maritime War: Piracy in the English Channel and the Atlantic, c. 1280 – c. 1330* (Leiden: Brill, 2013), 2.

8 Translation from Henry Liddell and Robert Scott, *An Intermediate Greek-English Lexicon* (Oxford: Clarendon Press, 1889).

9 Philip de Souza, *Piracy in the Graeco-Roman World* (Cambridge: CUP, 2002), 7; Rubin, *supra* no4, 5–6.

10 Polybius, *The Histories* (c. 150 BC), trans. William R Paton (Cambridge, MA: Loeb Classical Library, 1954) Vol. 2, Book IV, s68 (p461), and Plutarch, *Parallel Lives of Greeks and Romans* (c. 100 AD), transl. Bernadotte Perrin (Cambridge, MA: Loeb Classical Library, 1917) Vol. 5 (*Pompey*), s24. This interpretation is confirmed by Rubin, *ibid.*

11 De Souza in Powell (ed.), *supra* no2, 180.

12 William Morris (ed.), *American Heritage Dictionary of the English Language* (Boston, MA: American Heritage Publishing and Houghton Mifflin, 1969), pp998, 1534; De Souza, *Graeco-Roman, supra* no9, 3. Other English words derived from this root include fear, peril, experience, expert and, empire.

13 Daniel Heller-Roazen, *supra* no4, 35.

14 De Souza, *Graeco-Roman, supra* no9, 42.

15 Greek entry taken from Liddell and Scott, *supra* no8. See also De Souza, *ibid.*, 3.

terms appear to have been used interchangeably, although *lēstēs* more often refers to "brigands" (denoting an armed, perhaps violent, band of robbers)[16] whereas *peiratēs* seems to refer more to organised political units (such as Polybius' "belligerent community" usage).[17] The contexts in which the latter term was used suggest a usage in the context of war rather than law enforcement operations, as seen in both Polybius and Plutarch.[18] The usage is not consistently uniform and it is not possible to definitively untangle the terms and apply exclusive meanings to them.[19] In particular, organised resistance groups were sometimes derided as *lēstēs* in order to demonise them and convert them "into outlaws".[20] We can nevertheless be guided by the contexts and relative consistency with which the terms were used.

There were also several Latin terms for "pirate" in use at the time. The most common, based on surviving texts, was *praedone* (derived from *praeda*, "plunder"),[21] which could refer to either a pirate or a brigand (similar to the Greek *lēstēs*), with context usually required to identify the precise nature of the act – for instance, the qualifier *maritimus*, signifying that the act occurred at sea.[22] For example, Justinian's sixth century *Digest* features two references to *praedones* (usually translated into English as "robbers") where they are explicitly distinguished from *hostes* (recognised "enemies") for the purpose of establishing the rights that are available to them in a conflict situation (such as the right of *postliminium*, which is reserved to recognised *hostes*).[23] Although *praedone* might technically have meant "robber", it appears to have served a dual purpose by identifying "irregular" belligerents who did not qualify for

16 De Souza, *ibid.* See also Willard Cowles "Universality of Jurisdiction over War Crimes", 33 *California Law Review* (1945) 177, defining brigands as "a small, loose, degenerate society, the members having little or no sense of allegiance to any State", (184) broadly correlating the term to the commission of war crimes (198, 200).

17 See references cited *supra* n010.

18 *Ibid.*

19 See, for instance De Souza, *Graeco-Roman, supra* n09, 8–9, preferring to equate the term *peiratēs* with banditry, thereby excluding any kind of political connotation.

20 Ken Dowden, "'But there is a difference in the ends…': Brigands and Teleology in the Ancient Novel" in Michael Paschalis and Stelios Panayotakis (eds), *The Construction of the Real and the Ideal in the Ancient Novel* (Groningen: Barkhuis, 2013) 41, 43.

21 Rubin, *supra* n04, 11; Walter Rech, *Enemies of Mankind: Vattel's Theory of Collective Security* (Leiden, Martinus Nijhoff, 2013), 30; Gould, *supra* n07, 27.

22 See examples in De Souza, *Graeco-Roman, supra* n09, 13, and in Anna Tarwacka, *Romans and Pirates: Legal Perspective* (Warsaw: Wydawnictwo Uniwersytetu Kardynała Stefana Wyszyńskiego, 2009), 19–20.

23 *Digest*, ed. Alan Watson (Philadelphia: University of Pennsylvania Press, 2011) (original Latin available online at thelatinlibrary.com), XLIX.XV.XXIV and L.XVI.CXVIII. *Postliminium* refers to the restoration of any rights or property forfeited during war: Rubin, *supra* n04, 12.

legal protections. Like the Greek *lēstēs*, it was perhaps intended in a disparaging manner.

Less commonly used, at least until the first century BC,[24] was the Latin *pirata* (plural *piratae*),[25] derived from the Greek *peiratēs* (perhaps as a direct transliteration), albeit with no clear distinction in terms of definition from *praedone*[26] – indeed, the two are used interchangeably by Cicero, at one point in consecutive sentences.[27] However, *pirata* is always translated into English as "pirate" (with the maritime aspect implied), as opposed to *praedone* which is variously translated as either "robber" or "pirate". A further term used to apply to "brigands" in a wide range of circumstances was *latrone* (from *latro*, "mercenary").[28] The situation is further muddled by the fact that *pirata*, *praedones* and *latrones* were often used as terms of political insult.[29] These terms should be further distinguished from *rapina*, referring to violent theft at Roman law.[30]

This brief linguistic analysis perhaps presents more confusion than clarity, given the interchangeability of terms and the inclination to apply certain terms pejoratively to organised armed groups, regardless of original meaning. In any case it seems clear that the "Greek and Roman conception of 'piracy' distinguished between robbers, who were criminals at Roman law, and communities called 'piratical' which were political societies",[31] albeit with no

---

24 When it became popularised by Cicero: see Dowden, *supra* no20, 44.

25 Liddell and Scott, *supra* no8; Charlton T. Lewis and Charles Short, *A Latin Dictionary* (Oxford: Clarendon Press, 1879).

26 Gould, *supra* no7, 27; De Souza, *Graeco-Roman*, *supra* no9, 12–13.

27 *De Officiis* Book III, s107: "*Ut, si praedonibus pactum pro capite pretium non attuleris, nulla fraus est, ne si iuratus quidem id non feceris. Nam pirata non est ex perduellium numero definitus, sed communis hostis omnium*", translated as "suppose that one does not deliver the amount agreed upon with *pirates* as the price of one's life, that would be accounted no deception – not even if one should fail to deliver the ransom after having sworn to do so; for a *pirate* is not included in the number of lawful enemies, but is the common foe of all the world" (emphasis added). Original and translation from Miller (ed.), *supra* no3.

28 *Thesaurus Linguae Latinae*, vol. VII, Leipzig 1934, 1014–1017. See also Thomas Grünewald, *Bandits in the Roman Empire: Myth and Reality* (1999), translated by John Drinkwater (London: Routledge, 2004), 5, explaining that "[t]he complete renunciation [by Rome] of her own use of mercenaries, together with a deeply entrenched mistrust of foreign mercenaries, led to a change in the use of the term *latro* in Rome: the original meaning 'mercenary', was displaced in favour of the new, exclusive meaning 'bandit', referring to any sort of extra-legal man of violence".

29 For instance by Cicero (*The Verrine Orations*, 2.1.90 and 2.4.23; *Philipics*, 13th Oration, s18), Julius Caesar (*The Civil Wars*, trans. W.A. McDevitte and W.S. Bohn (Loeb Classical Library, 1917) Book 3, chapter 110; 3.112), and Octavian (*Res gestae Divi Augusti*, (Loeb Classical Library, 1924) s25). See also Brent D. Shaw, "Bandits in the Roman Empire", 105 *Past and Present* (1984) 3, 3 and 23, and Grünewald, *ibid.*, 73–76.

30 Grünewald, *ibid.*, 15.

31 Rubin, *supra* no4, 12.

obvious consistency. An exception to the general theme of ambiguity might be found in the distinction between Greek *peiratēs* and *lēstēs*.[32] The former term referred to certain organised political communities towards which the Greeks or Romans felt contempt while the latter appears to define, fairly consistently, outright bandits or plunderers (albeit with occasional pejorative use in application to groups better branded *peiratēs*).[33] These nuances should be borne in mind in reading the chapter.

2.1 Roman Hegemony and the Downfall of "Piracy"

Within the course of a century, plunder at sea went from being an accepted practice to a dubious enterprise, albeit with exceptions in cases where it was carried out by self-identifying "States" such as Rome. Part 2.1 examines the reasons for this development, and its consequences, in closer detail. Section 2.1.1 introduces the ambiguity with which "pirates" were treated in ancient history, an opacity that gave way to a sterner treatment of maritime robbery at the height of the Roman Republic (during the first century BC) when its rulers denounced the seafaring communities that sustained themselves by plundering others. Sections 2.1.2 and 2.1.3 examine in greater depth the reasons behind this pivotal historical development by considering the role of increased trans-Mediterranean commerce and the historical rise of the territorial State, respectively. Sections 2.1.4 and 2.1.5 respectively examine how these evolutions in political and social theory translated into Roman laws on piracy and Roman "wars" against "pirates" (in particular Pompey the Great's campaign in 67 BC).

2.1.1 *Heroes and Antagonists: Early Histories of "Piracy"*

> [T]he very first time something valuable was known to be leaving a beach on a raft, the first pirate was around to steal it.[34]

Robbery at sea has existed for as long as humans have sailed upon it,[35] but it has not always been an objectionable practice. To the contrary, early sources

32 See references at *supra* n010, and associated text.

33 Rubin, *supra* n04, 5.

34 Jack A. Gottschalk & Brian P. Flanagan, *Jolly Roger With an Uzi: The Rise and Threat of Modern Piracy* (Naval Institute Press, 2008), 1.

35 Angus Konstam, *Piracy: The Complete History* (Oxford: Osprey, 2008), 10; Benerson Little, *Pirate Hunting* (Washington DC: Potomac Books, 2010), 19 (noting that sea travel dates back at least 130,000 years).

suggest that piracy was a "creditable, indeed glorious, means of enrichment"[36] and "as legitimate a means of existence as hunting and fishing".[37] Homer's *Iliad* and *Odyssey*, dating from the seventh or eighth century BC, both express tolerance for piracy (ληστής, *lēstēs*)[38] and even equate it with adventure and heroism.[39] Merchants, on the contrary, were treated with suspicion.[40]

Wandering "sea-peoples" became a common feature of the Mediterranean in the late Bronze Age (c. 1400–1200 BC), driving political change by assailing coastal communities, contributing to the collapse of several empires and probably stalling technological advancement.[41] The region witnessed cycles of growth and destruction whereby outposts of civilisation developed, only to be checked by disparate bands of what Polybius termed *peiratēs*, hostile migratory tribes of "sea-peoples" that sustained themselves on plunder and occasionally even established reasonably sized empires.[42] These groups are in numerous history books denominated "pirates" given that they attacked from the sea and lacked a discernible territorial base, yet their identity is more complex than the term "pirate" warrants, being "not strictly pirates in the true sense, but [...] more like hostile migratory tribes with ships".[43] They might be better defined as maritime communities who sustained themselves by plunder – a fact that, in itself, was unremarkable, given that most (if not all) communities of this age plundered the goods of others.[44]

These plunder-based communities reached apogee with the emergence of the Cilician *peiratēs*, based in the eastern Mediterranean from the latter half of the second century BC. The Cilicians were initially valued by Rome for their

36 Coleman Phillipson, *The International Law and Custom of Ancient Greece & Rome* (London: Macmillan, 1911), 370.

37 Thucydides, *History of the Peloponnesian War*, trans. Charles Foster Smith (Cambridge, MA: Loeb Classical Library, 1928), Book 1, Chapter 5, ss1–3.

38 Shaw, *supra* no29, 24.

39 David Abulafia, *The Great Sea* (Oxford: OUP, 2011), 88; Robert Haywood and Roberta Spivak, *Maritime Piracy* (London: Routledge, 2012), 24–25.

40 *Ibid.*, 63 and 191; De Souza, *Graeco-Roman, supra* no9, 23.

41 R. Drews, *The End of the Bronze Age: Changes in Warfare and the Catastrophe ca. 1200 BC* (Princeton, NJ: 1993), 3; Henry A. Ormerod, *Piracy in the Ancient World* (Baltimore: JHU, 1997), 13–14.

42 Such as the empire of Polycrates, "Tyrant of Samos", who controlled the Aegean in the sixth century BC: Philip Gosse, *The History of Piracy* (1932) (Mineola, NY: Dover Publications, 2007), 332–333.

43 Konstam, *supra* no35, 12. See also De Souza, *Graeco-Roman, supra* no9, 15–16, noting that "[w]arfare and piracy had not come to be differentiated in this early period".

44 Heebøll-Holm, *supra* no7, 5, noting that "[i]n antiquity, the plunder of defeated enemies during war was a perfectly acceptable action".

steady supply of slaves[45] but, from the latter part of the second century BC, they gained in power and began to dominate the Mediterranean. For eighty years they "swept the seas with war like a tempest",[46] "pillag[ing] harbours and entire cities, almost organised as nations",[47] closing down trade and causing widespread famine in the process.[48] The damage caused to Rome's trade routes threatened the Republic's very existence. Grain shortages in 75–73 BC, blamed largely on Mediterranean "piracy", led to large-scale rioting.[49] Plutarch wrote that the Cilician *peiratēs* were "a disgrace to the Roman supremacy" due to their apparent mockery of Rome, this being their "crowning insolence".[50] Plutarch's condemnation of the *peiratēs* is somewhat revealing in terms of what it tells us about Roman pride and sense of moral superiority.[51]

For Rome to sustain its trade links and its place at the apex of Mediterranean geopolitics, the primordial ways of the *peiratēs* required elimination. There were two key factors that the Romans felt set them apart from the troublesome Cilicians, both of which influenced and informed Pompey's subsequent purge – namely, the increasing importance to Rome of trans-Mediterranean trade, and the significance placed on territorial Statehood. These factors, which are significant to understanding key points that will arise later in the book, are now considered in greater detail.

2.1.2 *The Rise of Commerce*

In the early 1600s Hugo Grotius based his epic treatise *De Jure Praedae* around what he called the *libertas commerciorum*, the essential and God-given right

---

45 De Souza, *Graeco-Roman, supra* n09, 98–101; Haywood & Spivak, *supra* n039, 27.

46 Richard Zouche, *An Exposition of Fecial Law and Procedure* (1650), trans. James L. Brierly (Washington, DC: Carnegie Endowment for International Peace, 1911) 1.7, 38, adding that they broke "the treaty of the human species and destroy[ed] commerce".

47 Cassius Dio, *History of Rome* (c. 229 AD), transl. E. Cary (Cambridge, MA: Loeb Classical Library, 1924) Book 36, Chapter 20, paras 3–4 (using the term *lēstēs*). See also Appian, *Roman History: The Mithridatic Wars* (c. 150) (trans. Horace White, New York: Macmillan, 1899) Chapter 9, s. 63, suggesting that the Cilicians resembled "regular fleets rather than robber bands (*lēstēs*)". The Cilicians were loosely united under "pirate king" Mithridates: Plutarch, *supra* n010, 24.

48 Ormerod, *supra* n041, 233; Gosse, *supra* n042, 336–337.

49 De Souza, *Graeco-Roman, supra* n09, 142.

50 Plutarch, *supra* n010, s24.

51 Romans' perceived moral superiority is exemplified by Pliny the Elder's statement that "[d]oubtless it is, and past all question, that of all nations under the sun, the Romans excel and are the only men for all kind of virtues" (*The History of the World* (c. 77–79 AD), trans. Philemon Holland, 1601, Book VII, Chap. XL) and is embodied by the motto "*Moribus antiquis res stat Romana virisque*", "the Roman State survives by its ancient customs and its manhood". Cicero similarly believed Romans to be at the top of a hierarchical order: *De Legibus*, Book I, 23.

of States to engage in trade unhindered, with the freedom of the seas, "*mare liberum*", forming a central aspect of this.[52] Today the principle of the freedom of the high seas, as an enabler of inter-State commerce, is well-established,[53] yet the concept has a lineage that can be traced back to a time much earlier than Grotius. Republican Rome placed a great emphasis on ensuring free trade across the Mediterranean as they sought to rely on an unobstructed trade in slaves (from around 150BC),[54] food,[55] papyrus,[56] and building materials.[57] These requirements were central to the survival of the Roman State.[58] The co-operation and mutual benefit derived from trans-Mediterranean commerce sustained the newly evolved "*homo economicus*"[59] at the expense of plunderous communities of *peiratēs*, whose existence was effectively predicated on plundering the goods of others.[60] The latter represented an abrasive, outmoded model of political and economic aggression that gradually became eclipsed by trade-reliant civilisation.[61] Such groups represented "the parasitical alter ego of international commerce".[62]

This is not to suggest that the frequent acts of plunder carried out by the *peiratēs* were, of themselves, the salient issue. Rome itself continued to plunder others in war (at least until the end of the third century AD),[63] and modern "Westphalian" States continued to do so until 1856.[64] The distinction, however equivocal, between these two "types" of community appears to lie in the reasons for which such polities engaged in conflict or undertook acts of plunder. Rome, for instance, perceived itself as partaking in "communally organized armed conflict, which in principle involved a polity's entire fighting population", intended to secure tangible interests such as territory or to exercise rights

52 Martine Julia van Ittersum, "Introduction" to Hugo Grotius, *Commentary on the Law of Prize and Booty (De Jure Pradae)* (ed. Ittersum) (Indianapolis: Liberty Fund Inc, 2006), xix. See also discussion at 4.1.2, *infra*.

53 United Nations Convention on the Law of the Sea 1982, Article 87.

54 De Souza, *Graeco-Roman, supra* no9, 64; Jeremy Black, *The Atlantic Slave Trade in World History* (NY: Routledge, 2015), 9–10.

55 Abulafia, *supra* no39, 204; Peter Garnsey, *The Roman Empire: Economy, Society and Culture* (Berkeley, CA: University of California Press, 1987), Chapter 5.

56 F. Meijer, *A History of Seafaring in the Classical World* (Beckenham: Croom Helm, 1986), 187–188.

57 Policante, *supra* no4, 5.

58 *Ibid.*, 5–6.

59 Jody Greene, "*Hostis Humani Generis*" 34 *Critical Enquiry* (2008) 683, 696.

60 De Souza, *Graeco-Roman, supra* no9, 23.

61 Rubin, *supra* no4, 10–12; De Souza, *ibid.*, 23.

62 Greene, *supra* no59, 688.

63 Edward Gibbon, *History of the Decline and Fall of the Roman Empire*, Volume I (1776) (London: Penguin, 1985), 199.

64 See 3.1 and 5.1.4, *infra*.

in self-defence.[65] This was as opposed to "privately organised predatory enterprises, smaller in scale, whose primary objective was the acquisition of material gain".[66] The distinction is assisted by Cicero's definition of a State as "an assemblage of people in large numbers associated with respect to justice and a partnership for the common good".[67] Conversely, *peiratēs* were cast as the antithesis to this setup, lacking "the bonding necessary to form a State".[68] They acted, instead "from the passions of the body rather than from the reason that human beings share with the gods".[69] The distinction is similar to Grotius' later theoretical division between communities formed "for the sake of wrongdoing" as opposed to "for the enjoyment of rights".[70] This political typology and the fundamental division of humanity it presents (as influenced by Cicero)[71] forms the basis for Rome's disparate treatment of the troublesome Cilician *peiratēs*.

Claiming control over the *peiratēs* would enable Rome to better ensure the free flow of goods, ostensibly by enforcing their own prototypical principle of *mare liberum* (albeit in apparent contradiction to the possessive characterisation of the Mediterranean as *mare nostrum*, purportedly for the "common good").[72] Later Roman scholars would recognise the sea as being "open to everybody by nature"[73] while Justinian's *Digest* recognised the sea as *res nullius* and free from any claims of ownership.[74] As such the importance of the free sea and of free commerce, as manipulated by Roman claims to authority, emerges from Roman political ideology – with *peiratēs* designated as the enemy to this notion.

This commercial awakening placed the Cilicians in direct opposition to the superior might of Rome.[75] As such, our own conception of history is a subjectively determined view of the war against the plundering *peiratēs* as an

65 Vincent Gabrielsen, "Warfare and the State" in P. Sabin, H. van Wees & M. Whitby (eds), *The Cambridge History of Greek and Roman Warfare* (Cambridge, 2007) 248, 248–249.

66 *Ibid.*

67 Cicero, *De Republica*, (54–51 BC), trans. Clinton Walker Keyes (London: Heinemann, 1928), 65 (Book I, xxv). See also commentary in William E. Conklin, "The Myth of Primordialism in Cicero's Theory of *Jus Gentium*" 23 *Leiden Journal of International Law* (2010) 479, 503.

68 Conklin, *ibid.*, 489.

69 *Ibid.*

70 Hugo Grotius, *The Rights of War and Peace* (ed. Richard Tuck, from the edition by Jean Barbeyrac), (Indianapolis: Liberty Fund, 2005), Book III Chapter III, para II.

71 See *infra*, 2.2.

72 Olga Eveline Tellegen-Couperus, *A Short History of Roman Law* (NY: Routledge, 1993), 32. *Mare nostrum* translates into English as "our sea".

73 Cited in Lassa Oppenheim, *International Law: A Treatise* (1905), Book 1, s248.

74 *Digest*, *supra* no23, I.VIII.II. See also Heebøll-Holm, *supra* no7, 127.

75 Lauren Benton, "Toward a New Legal History of Piracy: Maritime Legalities and the Myth of Universal Jurisdiction", 23 *International Journal of Maritime History* (2011) 225, 228; Rubin, *supra* no4, 12.

objective "enemy", in a narrative written by history's winners.[76] Pompey's campaign to clear the seas of pirates in 67 BC and Cicero's subsequent denouncement of piracy played on this schism. If sea robbery had originally been treated as acceptable to some degree, then by the time of Plutarch's *Parallel Lives*, written in the first century AD, "there was an implication of impropriety to that [...] antiquated way of life in a new commercial and political order that could not countenance interference with trade in the Mediterranean Sea".[77] This statement presumably applies to the *peiratēs* as communities whose *raison d'être* was to plunder, rather than to any community who simply practised plunder on occasion (*e.g.* Rome itself). The term "pirate" has been invoked in this acrimonious way ever since, used as a tool to divide and to castigate.

2.1.3 *The Ascendance of Territory*

There was a further level to the discrimination against the Mediterranean *peiratēs,* linked to an important shift in the geography of Statehood occurring at the time. The territorial nature of the Roman Republic lent it certain advantages that *peiratēs* or other nomadic peoples did not possess, such as a sense of community, reasonably precise geographic definition (these two factors being components of Cicero's definition of a commonwealth),[78] and certain strategic advantages.[79] Indeed, Rome was one of the earliest polities to define itself predominantly in terms of territory rather than purely by personal association.[80] The sea was considered, on the contrary, a chaotic, unconquerable maelstrom.[81] This societal differentiation based on territorial organisation

76 See Philip De Souza, "Piracy in Classical Antiquity: The Origins and Evolution of the Concept" in Stefan E. Amirell and Leos Müller (eds), *Persistent Piracy: Maritime Violence and State-Formation in Global Historical Perspective* (Basingstoke: Palgrave Macmillan, 2014) 24, 27, suggesting that the line between piracy and warfare was essentially a matter of "subjective attribution".

77 Rubin, *supra* n04, 8.

78 Conklin, *supra* n067, 490 and 500.

79 Heller-Roazen, *supra* n04, 17 and 163–164; Jean Gottmann, *The Significance of Territory* (Charlottesville: University Press of Virginia, 1973), 1–2.

80 John A. Agnew, "Timeless Space and State-Centrism: The Geographical Assumptions of International Relations Theory" in Rosow, Inayatullah and Rupert (eds), *The Global Economy as Political Space* (London: Lynne Rienner, 1994) 87, 89. Rome nevertheless placed considerable emphasis on Roman citizenship; for instance, only native Romans fell within the jurisdiction of the prestigious *jus civile* – see, *e.g.*, Hendrik Spruyt, *The Sovereign State and its Competitors: An Analysis of Systems Change* (Princeton NJ: Princeton University Press, 1996), 3.

81 Heller-Roazen, *supra* n04, 163–164. See also, in general, William Langewiesche, *The Outlaw Sea: A World of Freedom, Chaos and Crime* (New York, NY: North Point Press, 2004).

caused a historical distinction to be drawn between territorial and "other" organised polities which, in addition to the commerce thread considered above, contributed to the demise of *peiratēs* as a viable polity.

If we consider the origins of the term "territory", we reach an intriguing conclusion. It is often assumed that "territory" is an extension of the Latin *terra*, meaning earth. Instead, however, the word most likely derives from *terrere*,[82] meaning "to frighten" via *territorium*, "a place from where people are frightened".[83] Thus territory is borne of exclusion – literally of "terrifying" persons from a geographic space, the way the *peiratēs* were "terrified" from Roman waters. "Territory" is thus a claim "of authority, or of resistance to authority, [...] made by particular actors with particular substantive interests to promote".[84] It is also a claim to law.

The Roman shift towards territoriality appears to have been borne out in practice by discrimination against non-territorial nomadic groups. The Roman renegade Tacferinas, for instance, led a coalition of nomadic Berber tribes in a rebellion against Rome in the period 17–24 AD[85] but was denied formal *hostes* status, an acknowledgement which would have recognised his army as "equals" on the battlefield.[86] The Berbers were instead denounced by Emperor Tiberius in Latin as *praedones*.[87] This derogatory classification overlooks the political motivation for Tacferinas' eight-year campaign, itself characterised by Roman historian Tacitus as *bellum* (a recognised state of war).[88] The distinction

82 JA Simpson and ESC Weiner, *The Oxford English Dictionary*, 2nd ed. (Oxford: Clarendon, 1989), vol. XVII, 819. See also Thomas Baldwin, "The Territorial State" in Hyman Gross and Ross Harrison (eds), *Jurisprudence: Cambridge Essays* (Gloucs: Clarendon Press, 1992).

83 Stuart Elden, *Terror and Territory: The Spatial Extent of Sovereignty* (University of Minnesota Press, 2009), xxviiii.

84 Hannah L. Buxbaum, "Territory, Territoriality, and the Resolution of Jurisdictional Conflict" 57 *American Journal of Comparative Law* (2009) 631, 634. This construction of "territory" bears similarities to the moralist claim to authority sometimes asserted by States exercising universal jurisdiction; see, e.g., Policante, *supra* no4, 169–172.

85 Grünewald, *supra* no28, 48.

86 The Latin *hostis* (pl. *hostes*) was originally used in Rome to mean "foreigner" or, more specifically, one with "rights equal to those of Roman citizens", but over time came to refer to an "enemy", specifically a rights-bearing "public" enemy. A *hostis* sought "by legitimate principles" to defend his rights, whereas a private enemy (*e.g. praedones*) "aim[ed] to bring harm to his antagonist": Heller-Roazen, *supra* no4, 94–98. See also Conklin, *supra* no67, 498 (noting that Cicero recognised that *hostis* had evolved to mean "enemy" by the time of *De Officiis*, c. 44 BC), and Schmitt, *supra* no5, 51 (suggesting that "[t]he ability to recognise a *Justus hostis* [just enemy] is the beginning of all international law").

87 Tacitus, *Annals* (trans. J. Jackson) (Loeb Classical Library, 125–1937) 3.73.2 (referring to Tacferinas as "*desertor*", "*praedo*" and "*latro*").

88 Tacitus, *ibid.*, 2.52.1.

between *hostes* and *praedones* is clarified in Justinian's *Digest*, where it is stated that "[t]he enemy (*hostes*) are those on whom the Roman people has publicly declared war [...]; others are termed robbers or brigands (*latrunculi vel praedones*)".[89] In Tacferinas' case this designation is likely to have been at least partly due to a "lack of territorial authority".[90] Tacitus described the Berber nomads as *inconditi* ("tramps") or *vagi* ("drifters").[91] Nomadic Celts, Illyrians and Germans were similarly regarded as primitive barbarians.[92] The consequences of this are a dichotomy, a persistent divide between civilisation (represented by the ordered, roughly territorialised "State") and the stateless, non-territorial "primordial world".[93] The dichotomy would allow *carte blanche* for the displacement not only of *peiratēs* but also any "stateless" peoples.[94] This "territorial imperative"[95] would provide the theoretical basis for Roman conquests of nomadic tribes,[96] as well as later genocidal colonial campaigns against itinerant peoples in Africa and the post-Columbian Americas.[97]

---

89 *Digest*, *supra* no23, XLIX.XV.XXIV, cited in Grotius, *supra* no70, III.IX.XVI. See also Grünewald, *supra* no28, 16 (noting that *hostes* and *latrones* are identical in form, being differentiated only in political terms).

90 Alan K. Bowman, Edward Champlin and Andrew Lintott, *The Cambridge Ancient History (Vol X: The Augustan Empire, 43 BC – AD 69)* (Cambridge: CUP, 1996) 594. Tacferinas would likely have also been despised for being a Roman deserter: Brent D. Shaw, "Fear and Loathing: The Nomad Menace and Roman Africa" 52 *Revue de l'Université d'Ottawa* (1982) 25, 38, and Grünewald, *supra* no28, 50.

91 Tacitus, *supra* no87, 3.21.

92 Edward James, *Europe's Barbarians AD 200–600* (Abingdon: Routledge, 2014), 250; Grünewald, *supra* no28, 50.

93 Conklin, *supra* no67, 500, adding (at 501) that "human beings in the primordial condition were likened to animals", a theme that continued into the eighteenth century vis-à-vis pirates; see 5.1.3, *infra*.

94 Including slave uprisings, generally categorised as instances of *latrocinium*, denoting violence against the State carried out by unrecognised belligerents: see examples in Grünewald, *supra* no28, 80.

95 Dino Kritsiotis, "Public International Law and its Territorial Imperative" 30 *Michigan Journal of International Law* (2009) 547, 548.

96 See examples in Conklin, *supra* no67, 503.

97 Frédéric Mégret, "From 'savages' to 'unlawful combatants': a postcolonial look at international humanitarian law's 'other'" in Anne Orford (ed.), *International Law and its Others* (Cambridge: CUP, 2006), 265. The distinction would become engrained in early conceptions of the laws of war, including a 1914 British military manual co-authored by Lassa Oppenheim (J.E. Edmonds and L. Oppenheim, *Land Warfare: An Exposition of the Laws and Usages of War on Land, for the Guidance of Officers of His Majesty's Arms* (London, 1914), para. 7) and in the *Lieber Code* (Instructions for the Government of Armies of the United States in the Field, United States War Sept., General Orders 100 (April 24, 1863)), articles 24 and 25.

The establishment of Roman supremacy in the Mediterranean constituted a seismic shift in the way authority came to be claimed and organised. State power became monopolised by territorially organised communities, based on principles of collective security and shared morality, as opposed to large-scale plunder.[98] In the case of the Roman Republic (and, later, Empire), a great amount of military power was vested in this proto-State setup, lent a legal legitimacy by Cicero's conception of the *jus gentium* and the exclusion of pirates from its ambit.[99] As Jacques Derrida suggests, "the dominant power is the one that manages to impose and thus, to legitimate, indeed to legalise (for it is always a question of law) on a national or world stage, the terminology and thus the interpretation that best suits it in a given situation".[100] The collapse of "piracy", a formerly legitimate pursuit, was primarily about territory and the power vested therein by Rome (as represented by "law").[101] In this way, territory became a prerequisite to law (and, by extension, claims to jurisdiction),[102] and land-appropriation "the archetype of a constitutive legal process".[103]

These processes shape our contemporary approach to international law and, more specifically, provide a conceptual basis for universal jurisdiction by identifying an "other" who lies beyond the contours of what denotes acceptable society.[104] Thought of in this way, universal jurisdiction effectively works to define the international community, historically and today, by identifying who is *excluded* from that community. It does this by identifying those actors – be they pirates or (*e.g.*) *génocidaires* – who offend intrinsic values common to all States, such as the importance of commerce or the preservation of human diversity, respectively.[105] By reference to Roman "moral territorialism", as

---

98 Alejandro Chehtman, *The Philosophical Foundations of Extraterritorial Punishment* (Oxford: OUP, 2010), 41. The significance of territory is reflected today in the definition of Statehood: see James Crawford, *The Creation of States in International Law* (2nd ed) (Oxford: OUP, 2006), 55–61.

99 Discussed *infra*, 2.2.

100 Giovanna Borradori (ed.), *Philosophy in a time of terror: dialogues with Jürgen Habermas and Jacques Derrida* (University of Chicago Press, 2003) 105.

101 Schmitt, *supra* no5, 44–49.

102 Per Gottmann, *supra* no79, 4, "[t]erritorial sovereignty became an essential expression of the law, coinciding with effective jurisdiction".

103 Schmitt, *supra* no5, 47.

104 Adeno Addis, "Imagining the International Community: The Constitutive Dimension of Universal Jurisdiction" 31 *Human Rights Quarterly* (2009) 129, 160.

105 See, respectively, and from a modern day perspective, UN Security Council Resolution 1816 (2 June 2008), preambular para. 2, and International Criminal Tribunal for the former Yugoslavia, Appellate Judgment in *Prosecutor v Radislav Krstić* , Appeals Chamber, 19 April 2004, para. 36.

devised by Cicero[106] and played out in the various power struggles described in this chapter ("world-historical events of revolutionary significance"),[107] we can identify the origins of this process. Rome "legitimated its hegemony over the Mediterranean with the claim of keeping piracy in check, and championing civilisation, peace and prosperity".[108] In so doing it put in motion a series of events that culminated in the Israeli Supreme Court's holding (in *Eichmann*) that international crimes "constitute acts which damage vital international interests; they impair the foundations and security of the international community; they violate universal moral values and humanitarian principles which are at the root of the systems of criminal law adopted by civilised nations".[109]

2.1.4 *Law on Piracy*

Piracy is, today, outlawed as a domestic offence in many national legal systems.[110] This does not appear to have been the case in ancient Rome, however. Whereas common theft (or "*rapina*")[111] was outlawed, the unique nature of seaborne "piracy", which was treated by the Romans in a conflict paradigm rather than one of law-enforcement, rendered it unsuitable to domestic legal solutions.[112] The few relevant rules in existence appeared to relate to the rights of pirates in conflict situations, and did not distinguish pirates from land-based brigands.[113] For instance, Justinian's *Digest* assimilates pirates with brigands (in Latin, *piratis aut latronibus*), requiring that both should be denied any right of *postliminium* so that "persons who have been captured by pirates and brigands remain legally free".[114] The focus here is on the denial of rights that would normally be bestowed on *hostes* in a conflict situation. Accordingly, captured pirates or brigands do not appear to have been afforded procedural

106 See *infra*, 2.2.

107 Schmitt, *supra* no5, 44.

108 Policante, *supra* no4, 20.

109 Supreme Court of Israel, *Eichmann v. A-G Israel*, 36 *International Law Reports* (1968) 227, para. 11.

110 *Piracy Law Database* maintained by *Oceans Beyond Piracy*, available online. See also discussion in Beatriz López Lorca, "Harmonisation of National Criminal Laws on Maritime Piracy: a Regulatory Proposal for the Crime of Piracy and its Penalties", 23 *European Journal on Criminal Policy and Research* (2017) 115.

111 Grünewald, *supra* no28, 15.

112 Adolph Berger, *Encyclopaedic Dictionary of Roman Law* (Vol 43) (Philadelphia: American Philosophical Society, 1968), 631, noting that no specific laws existed to deal with piracy specifically. Moreover, contemporary jurists did not view it as something to concern themselves with (Grünewald, *ibid.*, 1–2 and 5–6).

113 Tarwacka, *supra* no22, 20–21.

114 *Digest, supra* no23, XLIX.XV.XIX. See also Heller-Roazen, *supra* no4, 97–99.

protections. Rather, private individuals or local militias were legally authorised to capture and kill offenders, while in more severe circumstances Roman legions were dispatched.[115] Those captured could be summarily executed.[116] The account of a young Julius Caesar capturing and crucifying the pirates that had held him captive serves as a famous example of this,[117] blurring the line between law enforcement and military operation.[118] By contrast, crimes such as theft or murder would, at this point in the Republic's history, be tried by a jury of up to seventy-five members, with fixed penalties imposed.[119] Piracy (and land-based brigandage) were not considered in the same context.

Given that piracy was essentially an issue external to the Roman State, efforts to contain it were focused outwards. An attempt to manipulate the situation in the Mediterranean was made in c. 100 BC via an inscription found at both Delphi and Knidos known as the *lex de provinciis praetoriis*.[120] The inscription stipulated that Romans and their allies should be able to navigate the seas in safety.[121] In order to achieve this, the inscription requests neighbouring Mediterranean kingdoms to deny safe harbour to *peiratēs*, imposing fines for non-compliance.[122] The inscription marks the earliest attempt by Rome to attach broad normative principles to the control of piracy and the ideal of the freedom of the seas, "articulat[ing] the Romans' assumption of the right to take aggressive, imperialistic measures in order to counter the threat".[123] It also offers a glimpse of Rome's perception of its own moral superiority and self-defined role as proud guardian of the cosmopolitan *jus gentium* against extraneous marauders,[124] as illustrated by Strabo's claim, at the turn of the millennium, that Roman imperialism represented "a civilising and ordering process for the whole world".[125] Even prior to its *de facto* control of the Mediterranean, Rome

115 See examples in Grünewald, *supra* no28, 100, 131, and 150.
116 Myles Lavan, *Slaves to Rome: Paradigms of Empire in Roman Culture* (Cambridge: CUP, 2013), 90–91.
117 Konstam, *supra* no35, 17.
118 Shaw, *supra* no29, 21; Heller-Roazen, *supra* no4, 98–99.
119 Richard A. Bauman, *Crime and Punishment in Ancient Rome* (London: Routledge, 1996), 17.
120 Stuart H. Jones, "A Roman Law Concerning Piracy", 16 *Journal of Roman Studies* (1926) 155–173; De Souza, *Graeco-Roman, supra* no9, 108 and 111.
121 *Ibid.*
122 De Souza, *ibid.*, 112. There is no evidence that any of these communities took action, though Mediterranean communities appeared to be in favour of the accord – a request from Rhodes may have triggered the pledge (De Souza, 107).
123 *Ibid.*, 113.
124 Gosse, *supra* no42, 336; Policante, *supra* no4, 7–11.
125 Strabo, *Geography*, 5.3.5, paraphrased in De Souza, *Graeco-Roman, supra* no9, 202–203.

felt sufficiently righteous to declare the sea "*mare nostrum*"[126] and to "*ius dicere*" (to "speak the law" or, in a modern sense, to claim jurisdiction) for places where they held no *dominion*.[127] Consequently "[w]ith the establishment of the Roman State and its great system of law, piracy, once admissible and even admired, would have naturally diminished, retreating from all the main channels of the seas to take refuge [...] at the geographic margins of Greco-Roman legality".[128] This situation bears remarkable parallels to State practice regarding later instances of piracy, wherein States claimed moral authority over regions (*viz.* the high seas) where they held no *de facto* control. Like the Cilician *peiratēs*, later Caribbean and Somali pirates similarly fell afoul of stronger claims to moral and legal authority, substantiated with force.[129]

2.1.5 *War on Piracy*

Roman campaigns against Mediterranean *peiratēs* portrayed a level of brutality that corresponded with their abhorrent characterisation and extra-legal treatment. During Servilius Isauricus' campaign in Lycia, 77–75 BC, Roman legions did not hesitate to carry out severe punishment against captured foes, including summary beheadings, crucifixions[130] and, in at least one instance, roasting a "pirate" captain to death over a fire.[131] Similarly, in Metellus' Cretan campaign (67 BC), captured "pirates" were routinely summarily executed.[132] Although opponents in these campaigns constituted well-organised maritime communities, the manner in which the campaigns were conducted suggests they were regarded as brigandish criminal organisations, in line with the geopolitical shift away from "plunder economies" as documented earlier in the chapter.

The most famous and influential of the Roman campaigns against the *peiratēs,* which would ultimately bring the Cilician threat to an end, was conducted rather differently and under unique circumstances. In 67 BC, with

126 See *supra*, n072.

127 J. Plescia, "Conflict of Laws in the Roman Empire" 38 *Labeo Rassegna di Diritto Romano* (1992) 30, 32.

128 Heller-Roazen, *supra* n04, 33–34, citing and translating Yvon Garlan, *La guerre dans l'antiquité* (Paris: Fernand Nathan, 1972), 19.

129 Jarret Berg, "'You're Gonna Need a Bigger Boat': Somali Piracy and the Erosion of Customary Piracy Suppression" 44 *New England Law Review* (2010) 343, 355. These ideas are explored further in Chapter 5, *infra*.

130 Shaw, *supra* n029, 20.

131 Alfred S. Bradford, *Flying the Black Flag: A Brief History of Piracy* (Westport, CT: Greenwood Publishing Group, 2007), 41. Servilius' aggressive approach apparently pleased Cicero.

132 De Souza, *Graeco-Roman, supra* n09, 171; Tarwacka, *supra* n022, 55.

the Republic at crisis point, the Senate took the drastic action of granting the legendary general Pompey The Great an expansive power to rid the Mediterranean of *peiratēs*, a feat that he supposedly achieved in just a few months.[133] The *Lex Gabinia de piratis persequendis* (named for its sponsor, the tribune Aulus Gabinius) granted Pompey "an out-and-out monarchy and [...] power over all men",[134] in reference to the sweeping powers granted (although probably not designed to confer on Pompey an imperial *dominion* over Cilicia).[135]

Written sources suggest that the campaign was characterised as war against a "pirate polity" as opposed to a law enforcement mission.[136] Plutarch, for instance, described the campaign in the context of a formal war,[137] while Velleius (c. 29 AD) defined the campaign as one of "regular warfare"[138] and Cicero described it as a "maritime war" (*maritime bello*).[139] Livy similarly wrote that Pompey "brought the war (*belloque*) against the pirates (*piratis*) to an end in Cilicia".[140] These views offer insights into the way the conflict was perceived and characterised by Rome, by its contemporary leaders and its subsequent historians. Characterising the campaign as such appears to be unique and in contrast, for example, to Servilius Isauricus' earlier Lycian campaign, the slave wars, or Julius Caesar's vengeful crucifixion of his pirate captors.[141] The Cilicians were, though, a more formidable prospect, and were loosely united under a recognised political leader in Mithridates, king of Pontus.[142] A further nuance arises when we consider that Pompey's campaign did not commence with any formal declaration of war (a disparity shared with the campaign fought against Tacferinas),[143] nor was it supposed that the *peiratēs* themselves had made such a declaration.[144] It has been proposed that Rome simply regarded the *peiratēs*

---

133 Ormerod, *supra* no41, 234–235; Max Radin, "The Roman Law of Delphi and the *Lex Gabinia*" 23 *The Classical Journal* (1928) 678.

134 Plutarch, *supra* no10, 177.

135 Heller-Roazen, *supra* no4, 53–54; Rubin, *supra* no4, 7.

136 Gould, *supra* no7, 28.

137 Rubin, *supra* no4, 7.

138 *Historiae Romanae* (ed. Frederick W. Shipley, Cambridge, MA: Loeb Classical Library, 1924), Book II, s 31.

139 *De Imperio Gnaei Pompei* ("On Pompey's Command") (66 BC), Chapter 15, s.44, Latin edition edited by Albert Curtis Clark (Oxford: Clarendon, 1908), English translation by C.D. Yonge (London: Henry G. Bohn, 1856).

140 *History of Rome* (c. 27–25 BC), trans. AC Schlesinger (Cambridge, MA: Loeb Classical Library, 1959) Book 14 (*Periochae*), XCIX.

141 Shaw, *supra* no29, 21.

142 Plutarch, *supra* no10, 24.

143 See *supra*, 2.1.3.

144 Rubin, *supra* no4, 9–10 and 83. Moreover, Pompey was not awarded an official "triumph" following his defeat of the *peiratēs* (Heller-Roazen, *supra* no4, 100).

as being in "in a permanent state of war with all people",[145] though this does not explain why the *Lex Gabinia* was required to seemingly initiate the conflict.

Perhaps "[t]he problem was one of State definition, between those acts against the State that were 'out-law' (that is, against the community but outside the scope of its law) and those which constituted major acts of violence against the whole State as such (that is, wars)".[146] Applying this model of conflict differentiation, the sporadic plunder missions of the Cilician *peiratēs* would generally be classed as "out-law", whereas the scale of Pompey's Cilician campaign arguably placed it in the latter category, even if this characterisation generated unease among classical historians, who were generally reticent to paint the pirate communities as formal *hostes* on an equal footing to Pompey.[147] The inconsistent characterisations of the campaign left the Cilician *peiratēs* in an odd position, legally (or definitionally) speaking. They fell short of being characterised (by Roman historians) as *hostes,* in that they could not be regarded as "equals", with no declaration of war required; yet they were somehow a "more legitimate" enemy than slaves or brigands.[148] The Cilician *peiratēs* were an enemy *sui generis,* unique in nature. Thus even as Cicero placed them beyond the scope of the *jus gentium* and judged them to be "the common enemy of mankind, with whom neither good faith nor a common oath should be kept",[149] Pompey concluded treaties with their leaders and gave rewards of land in return for peaceful surrender.[150] This apparent contradiction presents no easy conclusion regarding Rome's approach to piracy, given the complex nature of the conflict and the variables with which historians characterised it. Pompey's campaign marks the start of an age-old problem in understanding how to define piracy in terms of whether it is better defined as a criminal offence under domestic law or an act of belligerence by a quasi-State polity.[151] It may be that the Cilician campaign was in itself a unique war against a unique opponent,

---

145 Rubin, *ibid.*, 12.

146 Shaw, *supra* n029, 21.

147 Phillipson, *supra* n036, 375.

148 Rubin, *supra* n04, 9–10; Gould, *supra* n07, 26–27.

149 Cicero, *De Officiis, supra* n03, Book III, s.107.

150 De Souza, *Graeco-Roman, supra* n09, 170–171 and 175–177; Haywood & Spivak, *supra* n039, 26.

151 See, e.g.: Eric A. Heinze, "A Global War on Piracy? International Law and the Use of Force against Sea Pirates" in Struett *et al, supra* n07, 47, 57–62; Eugene Kontorovich, "A Guantánamo on the Sea: The Difficulty of Prosecuting Pirates and Terrorists", 98 *California Law Review* (2010) 243, 259–262; Michael H. Passman, "Protections Afforded to Captured Pirates Under the Law of War and International Law", 33 *Tulane Maritime Law Journal* (2008) 1; Alexander Proelss, "Piracy and the Use of Force" in Panos Koutrakos and Achilles Skordas (eds), *The Law and Practice of Piracy at Sea: European and International Perspectives* (Oxford: Hart, 2014), 53; Heller-Roazen, *supra* n04, 176–177; and Thilo Marauhn,

itself much removed from the isolated and apolitical bands of sea-robbers we call "pirates" today.

The conclusion of Pompey's "war" forms the backdrop for the subsequent historical subdual of piracy. With control over the entire Mediterranean, Rome was able to put contemporary "piracy" to rest and guarantee the safety of the seas.[152] Pompey was subsequently portrayed as abolishing a "formerly legitimate lifestyle" that had become "anachronistic in the modern commercial world that was ancient Rome".[153] This perception would later be reinforced by Cicero, whose oratories form the historic basis for universal jurisdiction over piracy today. We now turn to an analysis of Cicero's work and legacy.

2.2 The "Ciceronian Paradigm" of Piracy

> They paint the world full of shadows and then tell their children to stay close to the light. Their light. Their reasons, their judgments. Because in the darkness, there be dragons.
>
> CAPTAIN FLINT, *Black Sails*[154]

The fictional Captain Flint suggests that pirates have, since time immemorial, been cast as the villains to "their" civilisation, hypothetical "dragons" lying wait in the "painted shadows". The claim is remarkably perceptive, drawing on a long line of history by which pirates have been forcibly condemned as anarchical villains to "civilised" society. Though what counts as "civilised" in any given context will, of course, be largely relativistic, defined by those with the power to do so.

Marcus Tullius Cicero must take a large share of the credit for "painting the shadows" inhabited by the draconic pirates. A lawyer, public speaker, Roman consul and onetime governor of Cilicia (51–50 BC), Cicero is sometimes credited with introducing the notion of *hostes humani generis* in response to the threat of piracy.[155] In fact Cicero did not coin this phrase (which instead finds

"Counter-piracy Operations and the Limits of International Humanitarian Law", also in Koutrakos and Skordas (eds), 67.

152 Abulafia, *supra* n039, 199–201.

153 Goodwin, *supra* n03, 978.

154 Episode "XXXVIII" (dir. Jonathan E. Steinberg, 2017). *Black Sails* acts as a loose prequel to Robert Louis Stevenson's *Treasure Island* set in and around Nassau, Bahamas, c. 1715, featuring both literary and real-life pirates.

155 See, e.g., Bassiouni, *supra* n04, 47.

its origins 1300 years later in the writings of Bartolus of Saxoferrato),[156] although his speeches and writings have retained a powerful influence in terms of the historical marginalisation of pirates. Here we focus on the speeches made by Cicero following the conclusion of Pompey's campaign, the rhetoric of which substantiates the foregoing practice and forms the theoretical basis for the treatment of piracy (sowing the seeds of universal jurisdiction) going forward. Note that although we have already touched upon the works of Cicero insofar as they are relevant to the "territorial imperative", here we address his approach to "piracy" more directly.

Cicero *did* use the phrase "*communes hostes omnium*" ("the enemies of all communities") to describe what he termed, in Latin, *piratae* (the plural of *pirata*, derived from the Greek *peiratēs*).[157] The term was initially used in Cicero's prosecution of corrupt Sicilian governor Gaius Verres in 70 BC,[158] three years before the passing of the *Lex Gabinia*. Cicero preyed on public fears and prejudices by comparing Verres to a pirate, referring to him as both *praedoni* and *piratae* (interpreted in the English translation as "robber and pirate"),[159] with the intention of humiliating him.[160] In making the comparison, Cicero describes pirates as "the bitterest and most dangerous enemy of the Roman people, or, rather the common enemy of all peoples"[161] and emphasises their "lust for plunder and disregard of proper behaviour", drawing on contemporary concerns about the threat posed to Rome.[162] His intention appears to be to portray pirates (designated as either *praedones* or *piratae*) in as bad a light as possible so as to strengthen his prosecution of Verres. We see an interesting parallel, here, to the twentieth century invocation of the "piracy analogy" wherein the negative perception of piracy and its subjection to universal jurisdiction was

156 Bartolus of Saxoferrato, "De Captivis et Postliminino Reversis Rubrica", in *Apostilla domini Bartoli Saxoferato super secunda parte DIgeti novi* (Milan: Johannes Antoni de Donato, 1486), discussed in Heller-Roazen, *supra* no4, 103. The phrase was nevertheless used in alternative contexts during Roman times: Pliny the Elder used it to refer to Nero, while Emperor Constantine referred to magicians by the same. Lactantius and John Chrysostom used it to refer to the Devil: see Rech, *supra* no21, 35–36, and Gould, *supra* no7, 25.

157 See *supra* no25.

158 Cicero, *Verrine Orations* (original Latin in William Peterson (ed.), Oxford: Clarendon, 1917) II.IV.XXI, containing the variation "*hostes communes sint omnium*". English translation by C.D. Yonge, London: George Bell & Sons, 1903).

159 Cicero, *ibid.*, II, 4, 23.

160 Rech, *supra* no21, 29; De Souza, *Graeco-Roman, supra* no9, 152–157.

161 Cicero, *Verrine Orations, supra* no158, II, 5.76; De Souza, *ibid.*, 132.

162 Haywood and Spivak, *supra* no39, 8; De Souza, *ibid.*, 157.

extended to other offences.[163] By this time the ill-feeling towards "primordial" "plunder economies" was well engrained enough to apparently sustain Cicero's analogy in targeting Verres.

Cicero's later treatise on moral duties, *De Officiis*, has become more influential as a historical precedent for the abhorrent nature of piracy. In it Cicero outlines his notion of the ubiquitous *jus gentium*, conceived as a universal law embracing "all members of the human race" united by common values (such as respect for trade),[164] but excluding those who endangered that unity.[165] Described by Cicero as a response to the "degradation of social mores",[166] the nature of the *jus gentium* was such that certain acts were punishable under the law of nature, binding all members of the *societas omnium inter omnes* regardless of written law.[167] Pirates (here *piratae*) were inherently opposed to this formulation (they "destroy the universal brotherhood of mankind")[168] and instead formed part of the external "primordial world".[169] Their ill-effects on commerce were a key factor in this, as Cicero's formulation of the *jus gentium* required respect for natural resources such as the high seas.[170] Accordingly, a "pirate (*pirata*) is not included in the number of lawful enemies, but is the common foe of all the world; and with him there ought not to be any pledged word nor any oath mutually binding".[171] Thus,

> The pirate (*pirata*) escapes not one but all the circles of responsibility drawn in the Roman work. "The common enemy of all", he cannot be considered a criminal, because he does not belong to the city-state; yet he also cannot be counted among the foreign opponents of war, since he

163 See summary *supra*, 1.2.1.

164 *De Officiis, supra* no3, I, L. Per Jeremy Waldron, "Foreign Law and the Modern Ius Gentium", 119 *Harvard Law Review* 129 (2005-06), 132, "*jus gentium*" is often equated with the term "international law" today, but which "once had a broader meaning, comprising something like the common law of mankind, not just on issues between sovereigns but on legal issues generally – on contract, property, crime, and tort".

165 *Ibid.*, III.CVII. See also Policante, *supra* no4, 11–12, and M. Cherif Bassiouni, *International Criminal Law: Sources, Subjects and Contents* (Leiden: Brill, 2008), 129–130.

166 Rafael Domingo, *The New Global Law* (Cambridge, CUP, 2011), 7, citing *De Officiis, ibid.*, III.LXIX. Domingo, however, notes that "[n]owhere in Cicero's many works does he clearly define *jus gentium*" (6).

167 *Ibid.*

168 Cicero, *De Officiis, supra* no3, III.VI.

169 Conklin, *supra* no67, 500.

170 Policante, *supra* no4, 11-1.

171 Cicero, *De Officiis, supra* no3, III.CVII.

> cannot be "included in the number of lawful enemies". He moves [...] in a region in which duties no longer hold.[172]

Cicero appears to affirm the conception of the pirate as a *sui generis* enemy whose liminal, double-negative status is substantiated to an extent by the events of Pompey's Cilicia campaign.[173] Consequently the pirate is cast as the "evil" antithesis to civilised Statehood and the original target of a universal condemnation that would later manifest as universal jurisdiction.[174]

We have the foundations of the "piracy analogy" here, then, in Cicero's manipulation of the status of *piratae*, his handling of the *jus gentium*, and the dividing line drawn between "us" and "them".[175] Cicero's legacy is, however, complicated by numerous factors such as the dubious precedential value of *De Officiis*,[176] within which Cicero makes only a passing reference to piracy in the context of an abstract work concerned more with morality and political philosophy.[177] Cicero likely intended his anti-pirate diatribes and original terminology to be memorable, but his statements were not substantiated with evidence and were likely to be intended as rhetorical (in support, for instance, of the post-Pompey Roman dominance of *mare nostrum*). Interestingly, the arch-pirate Mithridates supposedly referred to the Romans in turn as "pirates",[178] demonstrating the subjective and pejorative nature of the term. The identity of Cicero's *piratae* is also an issue, as it seems likely that the Cilician "pirates" were largely demonised for being a particularly troublesome group of maritime and nomadic tribes, making it difficult to apply his writings to piracy in a more general sense. The Cilician pirates bear little resemblance to the Somali pirates of the twenty-first century, for example. The confusion over the legal classification of the Cilician wars exacerbates the problem.

---

172 Heller-Roazen, *supra* n04, 16.

173 This is notwithstanding the peaceful manner in which Pompey concluded the "war", by forging peace treaties and overseeing exchanges of property with defeated *peiratēs*, in contrast to those carried out by, e.g., Metellus; see *supra*, 2.1.5.

174 Addis, *supra* n0104, 160.

175 De Souza in Amirell and Müller, *supra* n076, 39.

176 Gould, *supra* n07, 25. Cicero's logic was criticised by Grotius: *supra* n070, Book II, Chapter 13, s15. The closest another Roman writer came to Cicero's rhetoric is possibly Florus, in his claim that Cilicians broke the *foedere generis humani*, the "peace of the world": *Epitome of Roman History*, Book 1, XLI, III, 6 (trans. E.S. Forster) (Loeb Classical Library, 1929).

177 As affirmed in, *e.g.*, Rubin, *supra* n04, 10, and Heller-Roazen, *supra* n04, 101.

178 De Souza, *Graeco-Roman*, *supra* n09, 134; Avi Avidov, "Were the Cilicians a Nation of Pirates?" 12 *Mediterranean Historical Review* (1997) 5, 46.

The Roman age may have established that "pirates" are "evil, dishonourable people who are not worthy of respect",[179] yet this seems to be of little precedential or theoretical value given the deep confusion over the identity of that enemy.[180] Yet Cicero nevertheless left a powerful legacy by way of the "us" and "them" dichotomy: the "Ciceronian paradigm" of piracy.[181]

2.3 Roman Legacies: Conclusions from the Original Annihilation of Piracy

The ancient vintage of universal jurisdiction is often traced to the actions of Pompey, Cicero, and the campaign against the Cilician *peiratēs*.[182] As this chapter has demonstrated, however, this connection is an over-simplification and the true situation far from straightforward. To better capture some of the intricacies and dilemmas presented in this chapter, the conclusion will be separated into two sections: 2.3.1 examines the ideological split that occurred at this time, between civilised States and piratical "others", whereas 2.3.2 focuses more closely on the conclusions we can draw as regards the origins of the "piracy analogy".

2.3.1 *History's Battle Lines*

Piracy has existed in some form ever since mankind took to the sea, manifesting either as opportunistic raids organised by private, apolitical individuals or as communal ventures organised in furtherance of economic gain for a political community as a whole.[183] In either case there was, initially, no institutionalised objection to the practice. Plunder was commonly accepted as a method of economic accumulation, and plunderers often idolised.[184]

Such a *modus vivendi* proved antithetical, however, to the emergence of maritime trade and its benefactor, *homo economicus*.[185] The new norm of pacific mercantilism came to be represented by hegemonic Rome, itself reliant on free

179 De Souza, *ibid.*, 150.

180 Per Gould, *supra* no7, 29–30, "[t]he idea that an individual or a group could be the common enemy of humanity was clearly in evidence in classical thought. What was emphatically not in evidence, however, were any of the conclusions we draw as to the consequences of falling into that category".

181 Heebøll-Holm, *supra* no7, 3–5.

182 As noted in, e.g., Gould, *supra* no7, 24–25, and Heebøll-Holm, *ibid.*, 2.

183 *Supra*, 2.1.1.

184 *Ibid.*

185 *Supra*, 2.1.2; Abulafia, *supra* no39, 204; Greene, *supra* no59, 696.

maritime traffic for the import of slaves, grain, papyrus, and other goods.[186] As the Roman monopoly over the Mediterranean region became consolidated it was clear that history could only take one route, so that the testing *peiratēs* had to be eliminated. A key flaw of these communities (in the eyes of Rome) was not their "piracy" as such, given that plunder was a common feature of warfare as practiced by all polities of the age; rather, the issue appeared to be the communities' "primordial" geographic and societal setup, their continued mainstreaming of violent plunder as an economic device as opposed to pacific trade and, importantly, their antagonism towards trade-hungry Rome.[187] The combined circumstances present a set of reasons as to why these "pirate states" ultimately failed. Their persecution and ultimate destruction marked a critical turning point for human civilisation and the early development of international law.

Rome's destruction of these groups was based on brute force paired with a claim to moral superiority. Pompey's celebrated campaign represented the final victory for the ostensibly civilised territorial State, a polity that valued trade and would engage in war only for political purposes rather than for private gain. Cicero's magniloquence played a central role in this narrative, through his of idolising Pompey and vilification of what he termed *piratae*. Cicero's speeches became a dominant aspect of the anti-pirate narrative, partly because of his influential position and use of memorable axioms, but also because his claims were roughly supported by historical fact. It matters not that Mithridates and other Roman enemies used the same term (*piratae*) to refer to Rome. Given the defeat and demise of Rome's enemies, these statements are valueless. Having established dominance (militarily and morally) over the known world, Rome had won the right to dictate history from its own perspective.[188] Cicero espoused a caricature of the *piratae* designed to suit his own ends and those of the Roman Republic. The might of Rome as manifested through Pompey's campaign – together with the political rhetoric of Cicero, the rise of territorialism and the increased reliance on trade – altered the course of global events by redefining geopolitical ideologies. "Pirates" (or their pre-modern ancestors) represented the negative, exclusionary aspect of this ideology. The "pirates" of old might therefore be described as "being in a state of perpetual war with society, rather than as criminals to be punished by force of law".[189]

186 *Supra*, 2.1.2.

187 *Ibid.*

188 Martin Murphy, "Petro Piracy: Predation and Counter-Predation in Nigerian Waters" in Douglas Guilfoyle (ed.), *Modern Piracy: Legal Challenges and Responses* (Cheltenham: Edward Elgar, 2013) 61, 68.

189 Haywood & Spivak, *supra* n039, 7.

The destruction of these proto-State pirate-like groups "came to represent the paradigm of an imperial form of discriminatory violence".[190] Thomas Heebøll-Holm characterises this discriminatory view of piracy as the "Ciceronian paradigm", wherein pirates become depoliticised and objectively criminal, "a category created by a hegemonic and durable regime in a region with the power to define right and wrong and where the pirate is cast as the enemy of the commonality".[191] Accordingly the principal consideration in terms of determining "legitimacy" is not whether a practice conforms to "rational or ethical behaviour" but, rather, where the balance of power is located.[192] It is a situation that has echoed through the ages ever since: Cicero's claims at the time of Rome's emerging hegemony are roughly paralleled by those of Gentili and Grotius during the emergence of European empires in the sixteenth and seventeenth centuries, with the rhetoric used as a tool of political and economic expansion.[193] Ultimately "the thoughts of these philosophers, in combination with the increasing strength of the State, became the norm for the view on pirates. In this view pirates are parasites on the international trade".[194]

In an anecdote recounted by Saint Augustine in the fifth century, Alexander the Great asks a pirate "what he meant by keeping hostile possession of the sea", to which the pirate proudly answered "[w]hat thou meanest by seizing the whole earth; but because I do it with a petty ship, I am called a robber, whilst thou who dost it with a great fleet art styled Emperor".[195] The parable forms the ideological basis of the alternative "Augustinian paradigm" of piracy, recognising that the vilification of "piracy" was never as clear-cut as "us versus them" and suggesting that the term is subjective and serves the powerful purpose of

190 Policante, *supra* no4, 15.

191 Heebøll-Holm, *supra* no7, 3–5.

192 *Ibid.*, 4. See also Shaw, *supra* no29, 44, noting that "[i]n story and legend [...] conflicts of authority are symbolized as scenes of contact between the holders of legitimacy and those who threatened their claim".

193 Heebøll-Holm, *ibid.*, 2–3; Policante, *supra* no4, 28.

194 Heebøll-Holm, *ibid.*, 3.

195 Augustine, *The City of God* (5th Century AD) (ed. RW Dyson, Cambridge: CUP, 1998), 4.4. Augustine adds that if a criminal gang wins recruits, acquires territory and subdues peoples, it will eventually "attain impunity" and become a "kingdom". In a similar vein, Alexander the Great has himself been described as a "plunderer of the first magnitude" (Captain Alexander Smith, introduction to *A General History of the Lives and Adventures of the Most Famous Highwaymen*, London, 1719) and Louis XIV of France a "Monster, whom we dignify with the title of hero: conqueror and emperor, but yet no other than a more splendid sort of highwayman" (Cotton Mather, *Instructions to the Living, from the Condition of the Dead*, Boston, 1717, 44).

denouncing and denying rights to an enemy.[196] As such "[i]t is not only that piracy is the secret name of Empire and the pirate is [...] the mirror image of the most powerful emperor, [but] even more radically the pirate wants us to question many of the certainties on which the very structure of our contemporary society is based".[197]

Nevertheless, it is the contrary "Ciceronian paradigm", a dehumanising epithet that casts the pirate beyond the embrace of the *jus gentium*, that has become the accepted standard for piracy, informing later rules and triggering the development of universal jurisdiction.[198] Accordingly, "[t]he pirate is defined not so much by what he does but by who he stands in opposition to, whose claim to exclusivity he challenges".[199] In other words, pirates represent the *wrong kind* of power.[200]

2.3.2 *A Roman Conception of Universal Jurisdiction?*

The international law prohibition of piracy (and the origin of universal jurisdiction) is often traced to the works of Cicero and actions of Pompey in the first century BC; "this, so the story goes, was the beginning".[201] It is not clear, however, that Roman notions of "piracy" were at all analogous to the modern meaning of what we mean by the same term. The reference points (or "contingencies") by which we define piracy (*i.e.* privately motivated acts of violence, occurring on the high seas)[202] did not form part of the Roman definition, while the words *peiratēs, praedones* or *piratae* seem to have been largely intended as a pejorative used to denigrate communities dissimilar to Rome (on several levels).

Ancient allusions to universal jurisdiction are difficult to accept, given that the suppression of piracy was characterised more as a nuanced version of war rather than a criminal process, while the fact of Rome's hegemony makes it difficult to argue in favour of a "universal" jurisdiction when politics and legal process was dominated by a single entity.[203] The evidence actually militates

196 Heebøll-Holm, *supra* no7, 3–5.

197 Amedeo Policante, "The New Pirate Wars", 3 *Global Discourse* (2013) 52, 54.

198 See Chapter 5 *infra*.

199 Mikkel Thorup, "The horror of the 'enemy of humanity' – on pirates, terrorists and states", presentation at "Fear, Horror & Terror", 1st Global Conference, Mansfield College, Oxford, September 10–12, 2007, 7.

200 Bruce Buchan, "Anarchism and Liberalism" in Nathan J. Jun (ed.), *Brill's Companion to Anarchism and Philosophy*, 51, 66–67, referencing the works of John Locke.

201 Gould, *supra* no7, 25.

202 UNCLOS, Article 101; Dino Kritsiotis, "The Contingencies of Piracy", 41 *California Western International Law Journal* (2011) 305.

203 Rech, *Enemies of Mankind, supra* no21, 32; Randall Lesaffer, "Roman Law and the Intellectual History of International Law" in Anne Orford and Florian Hoffmann (eds), *The Oxford Handbook of the Theory of International Law* (Oxford: OUP, 2016) 38, 39.

against the existence of universal jurisdiction, as suggested by the fact that Mediterranean satellite communities failed to take any action against pirates following the issuance of the Delphi/Knidos inscription, paired with the fact that *peiratēs* were sheltered and supported elsewhere in the region.[204] Perhaps a more suitable term for the pirate would have been "*hostes Romani generis*".[205]

This is not to deny the foundational importance of the events considered in this chapter. Despite the ambiguity of the "pirate" menace in Rome, the influence of this period (for the purposes of the argument laid out in this book, at least) lies in the lasting influence of Cicero's claim that pirates were "the enemies of all", as supported by a set of histories that effectively "prove" that this was the case. This claim forms the basis for future claims to universal jurisdiction over pirates and, indeed, later adversaries of "the international order".[206] The story *does* begin here, insofar as it lays the groundwork for universal jurisdiction. Cicero would be cited by, for instance, Alberico Gentili,[207] Hugo Grotius[208] and Lord Coke[209] as they grappled with the problematic identity of the "pirate".[210] It is these later echoes of Cicero that form the rudimentary basis for universal jurisdiction over piracy.

The legacy of Cicero and the events surrounding Pompey's eradication of the *peiratēs* (or *piratae*) have influenced later thought on the topic and ultimately inform the application of universal jurisdiction as a response to "core" international crimes today.[211] Our identification of certain actors as "evil others"[212] deserving the condemnation of all civilised States is derived from the "Ciceronian paradigm", an idea consequently propagated throughout history. The

204 Most notably by Mithridates; see Rech, *ibid.*, 31.

205 See Rech, *ibid.*, 31, and Heebøll-Holm, *supra* no7, 7, disputing the existence of universal jurisdiction at this time.

206 Rosalyn Higgins, *Problems & Process: International Law and How We Use It* (Oxford: Clarendon, 1995), 58.

207 *De Jure Belli Libri Tres* (1589) (trans. John C. Rolfe) (Oxford: Clarendon Press, 1933), 22.

208 *Supra* no70, II.XIII.XV.

209 *The Third Part of the Institutes of the Laws of England; Concerning High Treason, and Other Pleas of the Crown and Criminal Causes.* (c. 1628), Chapter 49.

210 Per Gould, *supra* no7, 23, "Roman legal practice was used to legitimate Renaissance and early modern practice. The fact that *actual* Roman practices did not match later claims about them was not important to the development of the new practices. What mattered was that agents accepted those claims as legitimizing the new practices that were being advocated".

211 Higgins, *supra* no206, 58. See also Menno T. Kamminga, "Lessons Learned from the Exercise of Universal Jurisdiction in Respect of Gross Human Rights Offenses" 23 *Human Rights Quarterly* 940, 943, noting that universal jurisdiction developed in response to an enemy who "offen[ds] against the conscience of the civilized world".

212 Addis, *supra* no104, 159.

renewed application of Cicero by Coke is discussed in Chapter 3,[213] and his invocation by Gentili and Grotius in Chapter 4.[214] The implications for our modern day conception of "international community", based on certain universally accepted standards of morality and behaviour, are considered in Chapter 6.[215]

213 *Infra*, 3.3.

214 Chapter 4, *infra*, in general.

215 *Infra*, 6.2.1.

CHAPTER 3

Dimensions of Piracy: States, Privateers and *Hostes Humani Generis*

The Roman histories explored in Chapter 2 suggest that a distinction was drawn between "civilised" Rome and "primordial" *peiratēs* (or *piratae*), communities who fell short of the expectations of the universally applicable *jus gentium*. As a result these outsiders were rendered *communes hostes omnium*, denounced by Cicero and warranting extermination at the hands of Pompey.[1] A close investigation of the relevant events of this period, however, does not provide us with a clear definition of "piracy" given the apparently ambiguous nature of the *peiratēs*.[2] Rather, the definition of "piracy" became wrought with an ambiguity that would not be clearly resolved until the formalisation of a specific definition in the 1958 Geneva Convention on the High Seas.[3] The situation became more complex over the intervening centuries as the term "piracy" was applied to a broad range of different maritime actors, complicating the identity of the "pirate" and creating issues for any straightforward exposition of Kontorovich's "piracy analogy". These different actors include privately motivated sea-robbers ("pirates" in the traditional sense), rudimentary polities (the latter-day equivalent of the Cilician *peiratēs*) and State-sponsored "privateers".

"Privateering" refers to the common tendency among States (from at least the thirteenth century)[4] to engage in plunder *by proxy* via licenses issued to privately funded mariners. Privateering was identical to piracy in every way

1 *Supra*, 2.1.5.

2 *Ibid.*

3 Article 15, providing that "Piracy consists of any [...] illegal acts of violence, detention or any act of depredation, committed for private ends by the crew or the passengers of a private ship or a private aircraft, and directed: (a) On the high seas, against another ship or aircraft, or against persons or property on board such ship or aircraft; (b) Against a ship, aircraft, persons or property in a place outside the jurisdiction of any State". This definition, reproduced in Article 101 of the 1982 United Nations Convention on the Law of the Sea, remains somewhat problematic; discussed *infra*, 7.1.

4 The earliest privateering commissions were issued in England by Henry III in 1243, containing instructions to "annoy our enemies by sea or by land"; see Theodore M. Cooperstein, "Letters of Marque and Reprisal: The Constitutional Law and Practice of Privateering", 40 *Journal of Maritime Law and Commerce* (2009) 221, 223.

 | DOI:10.1163/9789004390461_004

except that the plunderer had obtained State authorisation for their actions.[5] A privateering commission (or "letter of marque") would permit the plunder of merchantmen belonging to an identified State (or States) or, in some cases, allow the holder to attack and suppress suspected pirates.[6] Yet privateers often operated on the edge of legality, pushing the terms of their commissions to their limits.[7] Conceptions of "good" States versus "evil" pirates merged into a grey area where maritime plunder became the norm.[8] Yet even while States openly and commonly engaged in plunder, stateless pirates remained the subject of disdain and abhorrence, in keeping with the divisive rhetoric of Cicero.[9] These issues are part of the broader problem of piratical *identity*, this being the overarching theme of this chapter.

The histories outlined in Chapter 2 and the later prevalence of privateering suggest that there is something inherent in the underlying *nature* of piracy that renders it opprobrious as opposed to, simply, the act of plunder. This chapter explores this problem of identity (or "nature") through two related subjects. The first of these is the practice of privateering, the common occurrence of which appears to create some difficulty regarding the definition of and perceived "heinousness" of piracy.[10] Understanding this phenomenon is an important part of understanding the relationship between States and pirates as well as between piracy and universal jurisdiction. Eugene Kontorovich,

5 Eugene Kontorovich, "The Piracy Analogy: Modern Universal Jurisdiction's Hollow Foundation" 45 *Harvard International Law Journal* (2004), 183, 210–223.

6 Cooperstein, *supra* no4.

7 Lauren Benton *A Search for Sovereignty: Law and Geography in European Empires, 1400–1900* (Cambridge: CUP, 2010), 113. What is not clear is the exact point at which a "privateer" becomes a "pirate". Clearly he would need to exceed the terms of his commission (with Captain Kidd an archetypal case in point, see 5.2, *infra*). However, the League of Nations Committee of Experts for the Progressive Codification of International Law, *Questionnaire No. 6* adopted January 1926 (reproduced in 20 *American Journal of International Law* (1926) 222, 227) notes that "although the object of the privateersman is to take the property of others, [he possesses] a legal standing as regards nationality; at the same time it places responsibility upon the nation whose flag he flies, and thereby excludes any idea of piracy".

8 On the prevalence and past acceptability of State-sponsored plunder see: Thomas Heebøll-Holm, *Ports, Piracy and Maritime War: Piracy in the English Channel and the Atlantic, c. 1280–c. 1330* (Leiden: Brill, 2013), 5; Hugo Grotius, *The Rights of War and Peace* (ed. Richard Tuck, from the edition by Jean Barbeyrac), (Indianapolis: Liberty Fund, 2005), Book III, Chapter V ("Of Spoil and Rapine in War"); and Philip De Souza, "Piracy in Classical Antiquity: The Origins and Evolution of the Concept" in Stefan E. Amirell and Leos Müller (eds), *Persistent Piracy: Maritime Violence and State-Formation in Global Historical Perspective* (Basingstoke: Palgrave Macmillan, 2014) 24, 24 and 27.

9 See *infra*, 3.2.2.

10 Particularly as explored in Kontorovich, *supra* no5.

for instance, relies heavily on the correlation between piracy and privateering to demonstrate his claim that piracy could never have been considered to be particularly "heinous" if States were commonly engaged in the same practice, so that the "heinousness" connection between piracy and crimes against humanity, as invoked in *Eichmann*, is based on a fallacy.[11] However, the key to understanding this distinction surely lies in the question of identity and authority: whereas privateers represented States, pirates lay altogether outside this system.[12] Closer investigation into Kontorovich's theory is required, alongside a historical analysis of the distinction between privateering and piracy.

The second issue dealt with is the nature of piracy *stricto sensu* (*i.e.* in its archetypal "sea-robber" form, as defined in the 1982 UN Convention on the Law of the Sea).[13] It considers how States defined and dealt with piracy at this time (including a consideration of how State jurisdiction was interpreted and applied), and what piracy represented both for the State and for the pirates themselves. This analysis reveals much about the inherent *nature* of pirates beyond simply the *actus reus*. The British approach to piracy, in particular, is investigated via the work of Lord Coke, whose designation of pirates as *hostes humani generis* suggests a continuation of Ciceronian rhetoric. Analysis of the meaning and intention behind this remarkably pervasive term is required.[14]

The issues considered are broadly contemporaneous, so that a focus on the sixteenth and seventeenth centuries enables the chapter to consider and juxtapose issues with privateering and State responses to piracy (including discussion of Lord Coke's contribution to the oeuvre). There is also a structural reason for the content and placement of this chapter, namely that the issues herein require due consideration prior to entering into an analysis of piracy as it appears in the works of Alberico Gentili and Hugo Grotius, this being the remit of Chapter 4. Both Gentili and Grotius rely on and perpetuate the distinction between piracy and Statehood, so that this chapter forms an important background and context to their writing.[15]

This chapter is structured into three parts. Part 3.1 examines how privateering influenced and complicated responses to piracy. The writing engages with

11 *Ibid.*, 210–223.

12 Gerry Simpson, "Piracy and the Origins of Enmity", in Matthew Craven, Malgosia Fitzmaurice and Maria Vogiatzi (eds), *Time, History and International Law* (Leiden: Martinus Nijhoff, 2007) 219, 226.

13 Article 101; see *supra* 1.1.2.

14 As suggested in, *e.g.*, Jody Greene, *"Hostis Humani Generis"*, 34 *Critical Inquiry* (2008) 683.

15 Per Simpson, *supra* n012, 219, "[b]y the time that Gentili came to write his *Three Books on the Laws of War* in 1589, dealing for the first time with the international legal problems of piracy, a historic tradition was already well in place".

Kontorovich's claim that the historical prominence of privateering effectively displaces the idea that universal jurisdiction over piracy can be based on a "heinousness" rationale. This discussion of privateering must precede the later analysis of piracy *stricto sensu* as it allows us to (roughly) locate the threshold between piracy and state-sponsored acts. Part 3.2 examines instances of piracy "proper" prior to the emergence of universal jurisdiction in the late 1600s, how States struggled to define and contain it according to the law, and why its perpetrators became known as *hostes humani generis*, by reference to the works of Lord Coke. Part 3.3 forms a conclusion which, based on the foregoing, summarises several key issues that will be carried forward to later chapters.

3.1 *Authorised Plunder*: Deconstructing the "Privateer"

> Man's greatest good fortune is to chase and defeat his enemy, seize his total possessions, leave his married women weeping and wailing, ride his gelding, use the bodies of his women.
>
> GENGHIS KHAN[16]

Plunder formed a common and accepted aspect of inter-State warfare until relatively recently.[17] Throughout most of history it was routine to appropriate the goods of the opposition in the course of hostilities, a situation that only changed with the international outlawing of privateering at the 1856 Declaration of Paris[18] and subsequent outlawing of "pillage" ("wilful and unlawful appropriation of property during armed conflict")[19] under the 1907 Hague Conventions and 1949 Geneva Conventions.[20] Hugo Grotius affirmed in 1625 that "every man

---

16 Cited in Mike Edwards, "Lord of the Mongols", *National Geographic*, December 1996.

17 See, *e.g.*, Jean-Denis G.G. Lepage, *Medieval Armies and Weapons in Western Europe: An Illustrated History* (Jefferson, NC: McFarland, 2014), 120, and D.P. O'Connell, *The Influence of Law on Sea Power* (Manchester: University of Manchester Press, 1975), Chapters III-VII.

18 Declaration of Paris, April 16, 1856, reproduced in Adam Roberts and Richard Guelff, *Documents on the Laws of War* (3rd ed.) (Oxford: OUP, 2000), 48–49.

19 James Stewart, "Pillage", in Antonio Cassese *et al* (eds), *The Oxford Companion to International Criminal Justice* (Oxford: OUP, 2009), 454–455.

20 In the Annex to the Hague Convention (IV) Respecting the Laws and Customs of War on Land, 1907 ("The Hague Regulations"), Article 23 outlaws the seizure of enemy property on land, subject to military necessity, while Article 28 forbids "pillage" and Article 47 forbids pillage in the context of an occupation. Article 7 of the Hague Convention (IX) Concerning the Bombardment of Naval Forces in Time of War prohibits pillage in the context of coastal attack. Article 33(2) of Geneva Convention IV (1949) prohibits all forms of pillage, subject to military necessity (Article 53), while Article 4(2)(h) of Protocol II additional

in a solemn war acquires the property of what he takes from the enemy",[21] while in 1758 Emmerich de Vattel wrote that "the sovereign may grant the troops what share of the booty he pleases. At present most nations allow them whatever they can make on certain occasions when the general allows of plundering".[22] The ubiquity of plunder (both State-sponsored and otherwise) suggests that it was the underlying identity of the actor rather than his actions that were important in determining what constitutes "piracy".[23]

Francis Drake was already an experienced sailor when, in 1570, he was granted a privateering commission by Elizabeth I authorising him to attack Spanish merchant shipping (though England and Spain were technically at peace until 1585).[24] Privateering commissions provided a mechanism by which monarchs could engage private individuals into serving the interests of the State,[25] entitling them to seize goods belonging to specified enemies or, in some instances, neutrals.[26] Drake proved himself a highly successful privateer, taking many richly-loaded Spanish treasure galleons.[27] In March 1579, for instance, Drake apprehended the treasure galleon *Cacafuego* near Panama, destroying the

---

to the Geneva Conventions (1977) outlaws the pillage of private property in non-international armed conflicts. The prohibition does not extend to "booty of war" (public property belonging to the enemy and part of the war effort). "Pillage" is also criminalised as a war crime under Rome Statute, Articles 8(2)(b) (xvi) and 8(2)(e)(v). According to the Rome Statute definition the "pillage" must be carried out "for private or personal use" and must not be for military necessity. An anomaly remains, however, in maritime combat, as private enemy vessels and cargoes may be taken as prize, a distinction that remains in place to allow the seizure of potential contraband being imported by the enemy state. There is a rebuttable presumption that cargoes on enemy vessels have "enemy character"; see 1994 San Remo Manual on International Law Applicable to Armed Conflicts at Sea (reproduced in Roberts & Guelff, *supra* no18, 573), Articles 135–139. See, further, James Kraska, "Prize Law" in *Max Planck Encyclopaedia of Public International Law* (available online).

21 *Supra* no8, III.VI.II.

22 *The Law of Nations* (trans. Charles G. Fenwick) (Washington, DC: Carnegie Institution of Washington, 1916), Book 1, Chapter 9, s 164.

23 Simpson, *supra* no12, 226.

24 Angus Konstam, *Piracy: The Complete History* (Oxford: Osprey, 2008), 54.

25 The term "privateering" was not in fact coined until the mid-seventeenth century (David Childs, *Pirate Nation: Elizabeth I and her Royal Sea Rovers* (Barnsley: Seaforth, 2014), 10), but will be utilised throughout the book to describe practice fitting the general definition.

26 See, e.g., F.M. Kert, "Cruising in Colonial Waters: The Organisation of North American Privateering in the War of 1812" in David John Starkey, Jaap de Moor and E.S. van Eyck van Heslinga (eds), *Pirates and Privateers: New Perspectives on the War on Trade in the Eighteenth and Nineteenth Centuries* (Exeter: University of Exeter Press, 1997) 141, 145. For an example see *English Letter of Marque Against Pirates*, issued to Captain William Kidd by King William III of the Third of England, 1695; available at www.constitution.org.

27 Konstam, *supra* no24, 54.

ship's mast with cannon-fire and seizing cargo to the value of £200,000 (roughly half the Crown's annual income).[28] His actions are indiscernible from a pirate attack; for example, an extract from Captain Johnson's *General History of* [...] *Pirates* reveals how, on spotting the *Pearl* near Jamaica, the pirate Captain Charles Vane "hoisted the black flag and fired three guns each at the *Pearl*. She struck and the pirates took possession".[29] The accounts are interchangeable.

In terms of his actions, then, Drake was a pirate (indeed, the Spanish regarded him as such).[30] Yet, in terms of identity, he was a privateer, his actions recharacterised under a "veneer of legal cover".[31] Drake's actions represent only the tip of an iceberg, for privateering was rife throughout the Mediterranean in the sixteenth and seventeenth centuries[32] and continued into the American colonies well into the nineteenth century.[33] Plundering alongside the English "Sea Dogs"[34] were, *inter alia*, the North African "Barbary Corsairs",[35] the Dutch "Sea Beggars",[36] and privateers operating on behalf of the Spanish,[37] Portuguese,[38] French,[39] Florentines,[40] Genoese[41] and the Sovereign Military Order of Malta.[42]

---

28 Recounted *ibid.*, 58–60.

29 Captain Charles Johnson, *A General History of the Robberies and Murders of the most notorious Pirates* (1724) (with an introduction by David Cordingly; London: Conway Maritime Press, 1998), 108. The conduct described took place in December 1718.

30 Walter Rech, *Enemies of Mankind: Vattel's Theory of Collective Security* (Leiden, Martinus Nijhoff, 2013), 40. Moreover, Elizabeth I reportedly referred to Drake as "my pirate": Konstam, *supra* no24, 61.

31 Jon Latimer, *Buccaneers of the Caribbean: How Piracy Forged An Empire 1607–1697* (Cambridge, MA: Harvard University Press, 2009), 13.

32 Christopher Harding, "*Hostis Humani Generis* – The Pirate as Outlaw in the Early Modern Law of the Sea" in Claire Jowitt (ed.), *Pirates? The Politics of Plunder, 1550–1650* (Basingstoke: Palgrave Macmillan, 2007) 20, 25; Philip Gosse, *The History of Piracy* (1932) (Mineola, NY: Dover Publications, 2007, 111.

33 Peter Earle, *The Pirate Wars* (New York: Thomas Dunne Books, 2003), 212–214 and 231–247; Alfred P. Rubin, *The Law of Piracy* (Honolulu: University Press of the Pacific, 2006), 157–162.

34 Latimer, *supra* no31, 12. Other famous "Sea Dogs" included Walter Raleigh, John Hawkins and Martin Frobisher.

35 Gosse, *supra* no32, 10–47. "Corsair" is a Mediterranean term for privateer or pirate: Earle, *supra* no33, 39.

36 Virginia W. Lunsford, Piracy and Privateering in the Golden Age Netherlands (Gordonsville, VA: Palgrave Macmillan, 2005).

37 Adrian Tinniswood, *Pirates of Barbary* (London: Vintage, 2011), 28.

38 Gosse, *supra* no32, 266.

39 *Ibid.*, 97–98.

40 Alberto Tenenti, *Piracy and the Decline of Venice 1580–1615* (London: Longmans, 1961), Chapter 3.

41 Gosse, *supra* no32, 10–11.

42 *Ibid.*, 33–36; Tenenti, *supra* no40, Chapter 3.

Sub-contracting the State in this way bore several advantages: it offered a cheaper alternative to fully constituted navies,[43] harnessed the talents of established sailors,[44] bolstered the economy by establishing a market in seized goods[45] and enabled the State to deny responsibility by disputing any connection, if questions were to be raised about the actions of commissioned privateers.[46] It also kept pirate numbers down by securing work for them.[47] Despite the apparently fine line between State-sponsored privateering and autonomous piracy, the former practice "was not blemished in the public mind by the ruthlessness and indiscriminacy of pirates who used violence for private purpose without rules or restriction".[48] On the contrary, privateers were routinely hero-worshipped as soldiers of empire[49] and the morally grey areas they inhabited overlooked in favour of the military advantages they brought.[50]

The conflagration of piracy with delegated State belligerence creates some challenges in terms of investigating the origins of universal jurisdiction over piracy. Most notably it challenges perceptions that piracy was ever considered a particularly "heinous" crime, with consequences for the "heinousness" theory of universal jurisdiction.[51] For instance, Kenneth Randall argues that an "accurate rationale for not limiting jurisdiction over pirates to their state of nationality relies on the fundamental nature of piratical offenses. Piracy may comprise particularly heinous and wicked acts of violence or depredation, which are often committed indiscriminately against the vessels and nationals of numerous states".[52] The commonplace and accepted historical practice of privateering presents a problematic obstacle to this approach, given that "[t]he side-by-side coexistence within the same international legal order of legal privateering and universally punishable piracy undermines the theory that

43 Clive Senior, *A Nation of Pirates: English Piracy in its Heyday* (Newton Abbot: David & Charles, 1976), 7.

44 Michael Davey, "A Pirate Looks at the Twenty-First Century: The Legal Status of Somali Pirates in an Age of Sovereign Seas and Human Rights" 85 *Notre Dame Law Review* (2010) 1197, 1201.

45 Claire Jowitt, *The Culture of Piracy, 1580–1630: English Literature and Seaborne Crime* (Farnham: Ashgate Publishing, 2010), 7 and 35.

46 Janice E. Thomson, *Mercenaries, Pirates and Sovereigns* (Princeton, New Jersey: Princeton University Press, 1994), 21.

47 Konstam, *supra* no24, 34.

48 Ruth Wedgwood, "The Revolutionary Martyrdom of Jonathan Robbins", 100 *Yale Law Journal* (1990) 229, 240.

49 Jowitt, *Culture of Piracy, supra* no45, Chapter 2.

50 See, e.g., Grotius, *supra* no8, II.XVII.XX.

51 As argued by Kontorovich, *supra* no5. See the discussion *supra*, 1.2.2.

52 Kenneth Randall, "Universal Jurisdiction under International Law", 66 *Texas Law Review* (1987–88) 785, 793.

piracy was regarded as a wildly depraved practice entirely outside the bounds of civilized conduct".[53] This is an important point – the *actus reus* of privateering and piracy are identical, and privateering could in certain instances be equated, in terms of "heinousness", with piracy.

This argument, however, overlooks a key element in what it means to be a pirate. Central to the pursuit of privateering was the role of the State in giving its blessing to an act (or series thereof) that would otherwise be piracy.[54] The mutually recognising club of "peer polities" that formed Europe's States at this time effectively decided what was acceptable and, inversely, what was piracy.[55] Thus, what pirates really represented was the *absence* of *recognition* and *authority* (an "un-political entity")[56] rather than the actual act of plunder.

A plunderer would thus be denounced as a "pirate" if he did not have a sovereign commission or if the licensing "authority" was not recognised as a sovereign State. This meant that plunderers acting on behalf of unrecognised polities were routinely branded pirates – the Vikings,[57] for instance, and the Dalmatia-based sixteenth century Uskoks were derided as such,[58] even if both might have been able to put forward a case for "Statehood". This derogatory use of the term "pirate" occasionally found application between States – for instance, the Spanish branded Drake a "pirate" despite his being a licensed

53 Kontorovich, *supra* no5, 222.

54 See, e.g., *United States v. Ambrose Light*, 25 F. 408, 412 (S.D.N.Y. 1885), and Lauren Benton, "Legal Spaces of Empire: Piracy and the Origins of Ocean Regionalism" 47 *Comparative Studies in Society and History*" (2005) 700, 704.

55 See Daniel Heller-Roazen, *The Enemy of All: Piracy and the Law of Nations* (Brooklyn: Zone Books, 2009), 42, noting that "political authority [is] a power that decides on the rightful use of forceful capture, thereby judging a single activity – pillaging – to be alternately licit and illicit, imperative and forbidden, depending on the setting". Admittedly, this does not bring us closer to determining what constituted a "State" or "political authority" at this time, though this was in any case a problematic notion; see, e.g., Joseph H. Strayer, *On the Medieval Origins of the Modern State* (Princeton, NJ: Princeton University Press, 1970), 20, suggesting that "what we are looking for is the appearance of political units persisting in time and fixed in space, the development of permanent, impersonal institutions, agreement on the need for an authority which can give final judgements, and acceptance of the idea that this authority should receive the basic loyalty of its subjects".

56 Carl Schmitt, "The Concept of Piracy (1937)", 2 *Humanity: An International Journal of Human Rights, Humanitarianism and Development* (2011) 27, 28.

57 Although "pirate-like" in their actions, the Norsemen operated in accordance with political ambitions and were only retrospectively branded "pirates": Neil Price, "Ship-Men and Slaughter-Wolves: Pirate Polities in the Viking Age" in Amirell and Müller (eds), *supra* no8, 51, 53.

58 The Uskoks were a small Christian military collective who turned against Venice in the 1590s, leading to retaliation against these "[r]obbers, a tribe of ruffians, iniquitous rogues": Tenenti, *supra* no40, 3.

privateer,[59] and the Dutch were termed "pirates" in a Mughal-Portuguese treaty of 1615[60] whereas, conversely, the aggressively larcenous Barbary Corsairs were commonly perceived as serving the Ottoman Empire and, therefore, as legitimate plunderers.[61] These characterisations suggest a certain stigmatism to the term. Indeed, categorising an enemy as "piratical" went further than simply discrediting them, being intended to "represent an assertion of one law's legitimacy over another"[62] and as a claim to legal and/or moral superiority.

Operating outside the system of State sanction, unaffiliated "pirates" represented the statelessness and lawlessness of the sea, interlopers on a world stage that was otherwise roughly under the proxy control of mutually recognising "peer polities",[63] sailing "to challenge assertions of sovereignty with counter-assertions of independent polity".[64] These notions are reminiscent of the origin of the term "pirate" as one who "puts to proof" or challenges the authority of the State.[65] In contrast to the seaborne anarchy of the pirate ship,[66] privateering vessels were "islands of law [...], representatives of municipal legal authorities – vectors of crown law thrusting into ocean space",[67] however irregularly and poorly applied that portable "law" was. The oceans became not so much *terra nullius* as a dynamic legal space, "a complex tangle of [legal] strategies" designed, in part, to stem the lawlessness of piracy.[68] This fragmentation at sea in turn sharpened desires for the creation

59 Rech, *supra* no30, 40.

60 Michael Kempe, "'Even in the Remotest Corners of the World': Globalised Piracy and International Law, 1500–1900", 5 *Journal of Global History* (2010) 353, 361.

61 Jean Bodin, *Six Livres de la Republique*, 1576, Book 1, Chapter 1, reproduced in Rech, *supra* no30, 49; Gentili, *De Jure Belli Libri Tres* (orig. 1589) (trans. John C. Rolfe) (Oxford: Clarendon Press, 1933), Book 1, 113; Cornelius van Bynkershoek, *Two Books of Questions of Public Law*, trans. Tenney Frank (Washington, DC: Carnegie Endowment for International Peace, 1930), 99; *Southern v Howe*, 2 Rolle 5 (1617).

62 Emily Sohmer Tai, "The Legal Status of Piracy in Medieval Europe", 10 History Compass (2012) 838, 840.

63 Tai, *ibid.*, 838; Heebøll-Holm, *supra* no8, 245.

64 Emily Sohmer Tai, "Marking Water: Piracy and Property in the Pre-Modern West", presentation at *Seascapes, Littoral Cultures, and Trans-Oceanic Exchanges*, Washington, DC, 12–15 February 2003, available online.

65 Heller-Roazen, *supra* no55, 35; Chapter 2 (introduction), *supra*.

66 Bruce Buchan, "Anarchism and Liberalism" in Nathan J Jun (ed.), *Brill's Companion to Anarchism and Philosophy* (Leiden: Brill, 2017) 51, 57.

67 Benton, "Legal Spaces", *supra* no54, 704. See also Amedeo Policante, *The Pirate Myth: Genealogies of an Imperial Concept* (Abingdon, Ox: Routledge, 2015), 61.

68 Benton, *Search for Sovereignty, supra* no7, 104–141.

of an international legal (and mercantile) order among European States,[69] a conceived project that pitted autonomous pirates as a universal villain: *hostes humani generis*.[70]

Separating public from private acts in this context is inevitably unlikely to be straightforward, leading to issues in defining and recognising piracy *stricto sensu*.[71] Nevertheless the distinction between the two will always exist in principle, so that State authorisation completely transforms the legal nature of the act.[72] Kontorovich's "heinousness" criterion is based on a straightforward formula of how much damage the pirate (or privateer) causes, to which sovereign approval makes no difference. Assessed in this way it would be reasonable to conclude that "sea robbery was historically not seen as an inherent wrong [...], as is clear from the issuance by every maritime nation of licenses to engage in sea robbery".[73] While we can unequivocally accept that a crime such as genocide, for instance, is inherently wrong and universally condemnable (at least by any civilised standard of morality),[74] the same is not necessarily true of piracy, particularly when we consider that plunder was historically acceptable *if* authorised. However to properly consider the distinction between privateer and pirate, we have to consider what the "pirate" stood for: he did not represent the State system but was instead utterly outside it, a threat to the vital and exclusive right of the State to engage in maritime commerce.[75] The privateer, conversely, when acting within his commission, was part of the system, however imperfect that system might have been. This idea of the pirate as "outsider" is key to understanding the origins of universal jurisdiction. Early conceptions of exclusive politics and "peer polity" relations form the overriding factor in determining the existence of "piracy", a conclusion that fits the narrative of the Cilician *peiratēs* and the "Ciceronian paradigm".[76]

This presents us with an inherent legal and political divide between mutually recognising "peer polity" States (to whom privateers could be assimilated) and unauthorised pirates. Part 3.2 now investigates the nature of pirates *stricto*

---

69 Kempe, *supra* no60, 359.

70 Jason Power, "Maritime Terrorism: A New Challenge for National and International Security" 10 *Barry Law Review* (2008) 111, 113.

71 Thomson, *supra* no46, 117.

72 See, e.g., Matthew Garrod, "Piracy, the Protection of Vital State Interests and the False Foundations of Universal Jurisdiction in International Law", 25 *Diplomacy and Statecraft* (2014) 195, 200.

73 Kontorovich, *supra* no5, 223.

74 John Rawls, *The Law of Peoples* (Cambridge, MA: Harvard University Press, 1999) 79.

75 Power, *supra* no70, 113.

76 2.2, *supra*.

sensu on the opposite side of this equation, examining their identity, motives, and the manner in which States initially sought to contain them.

3.2 *Beyond the State*: Defining and Responding to Piracy

Defined by their lack of institutionalised character, pirates by definition directed their actions indiscriminately and worked towards private motives as opposed to the public/political motives of States and agented privateers.[77] Part 3.2 looks in greater detail at the identity of the "pirate" and initial State attempts to curtail the phenomenon. This analysis is, in turn, central to understanding the reasons why pirates were originally dubbed *hostes humani generis* and became subjected to universal jurisdiction. Section 3.2.1 provides a political and sociological examination of pirates themselves. Having established that pirates operate in opposition to the State,[78] it will be useful to understand who they are and what ideologies they represent. Section 3.2.2 analyses early State responses to piracy until the late 1600s, this being the point at which universal jurisdiction over piracy began to take shape (as detailed in Chapter 5). This study will provide an indication of the manner in which States initially regarded pirates and the struggles encountered in subjecting them to legal process. Section 3.2.3 focuses specifically on the influential work of English judge and jurist Lord Edward Coke, whose contribution to the oeuvre – most notably the phrase *hostes humani generis* – requires closer analysis.

3.2.1 *Pirate Politics and Society*

Piracy flourishes wherever trade thrives but State influence falters, a "parasitical alter ego of international commerce"[79] sustained by vacuums of effective

---

77 The modern-day definition of piracy includes only private acts, so that politically motivated actions cannot qualify as "piracy". UNCLOS, Article 101, defines piracy as "any illegal acts of violence [...] *committed for private ends* [...]" (emphasis added). This definition may, however, create a grey area regarding what is and is not "private" or "political"; see Samuel P. Menefee, "Piracy, Terrorism, and the Insurgent Passenger: A Historical and Legal Perspective", in Natalino Ronzitti (ed.), *Maritime Terrorism and International Law* (Dordrecht: Martinus Nijhoff, 1990) 43, 60; and H.E. José Luis Jesus, "Protection of Foreign Ships against Piracy and Terrorism at Sea: Legal Aspects" 18 *International Journal of Marine and Coastal Law* (2003) 363, 378–379.

78 3.1, *supra*.

79 Jonathan Ignarski, "Terrorism in a Maritime Context: Law, Insurance, and the Legal Implications of Armed Merchant Ships", in Brian A.H. Parritt (ed.) *Violence at Sea: A Review of Terrorism, Acts of War and Piracy, and Countermeasures to Prevent Terrorism* (Paris, 1986), 183, 183.

power. Its effects can be seen in all parts of the world and from all periods in history: examples include the Japanese "*Wōkòu*" who thrived in Chinese estuaries from the thirteenth to sixteenth centuries;[80] the Channel Islander "Eustace the Monk" who terrorised French and English shipping in the thirteenth century;[81] the seventeenth century Jacobean pirates who thrived in British waters;[82] the eighteenth century genre-defining pirates of the Caribbean;[83] the scattered Pacific pirates of the early nineteenth century;[84] or indeed the twenty-first century "pirates of Somalia".[85] Everywhere they form "the shadow of commerce, an unceasing form of guerrilla warfare, a frontier of opportunity for the upwardly mobile, the crusades at a grassroots level, a kind of kidnapping or mugging, and a routine investment".[86]

From the privileged standpoint of the "Ciceronian paradigm" of piracy (the predominant historical narrative)[87] pirates are depicted as the scourge of humanity, a subsection of society that fell short of the expectations of Grotian civilisation with its humanist ends and peaceful mercantilism. Hugo Grotius (whose work will be examined in greater detail in Chapter 4) decreed that "a company of pirates and robbers [is not] to be reputed a State [...]. For [pirates] are associated on the account of their crimes", as opposed to States, which "associate for the peaceable enjoyment of their own rights".[88] This trope portrays the pirate as a motiveless devil figure whose sole *raison d'être* is to make life difficult for merchants.

This one-dimensional perspective overlooks the complex ideologies, identities and structures of pirate crews. Pirates often had a common background and motivation for their actions; by way of example, Marcus Rediker relates the life story of "typical" pirate Walter Kennedy (c. 1695–1721):

80 Ivy Maria Lim, "From *Haijin* to *Kaihai*: The Jiajing Court's Search for a *Modus Operandi* along the South-eastern Coast (1522–1567)", 2 *Journal of the British Association for Chinese Studies* (2013) 1, 1.

81 D.A. Carpenter, "Eustace the Monk" in *Oxford Dictionary of National Biography* (OUP) (available online); Konstam, *supra* no24, 34.

82 Gosse, *supra* no32, 122–146; Neville Williams, *Captains Outrageous: Seven Centuries of Piracy* (London: Barrie and Rockliff, 1961), 89–90.

83 Johnson, *supra* no29; Konstam, *supra* no24, 150–248.

84 Gosse, *supra* no32, 325–326.

85 For an overview see, *e.g.*, Jay Bahadur, *Deadly Waters: Inside the hidden world of Somalia's pirates* (London: Profile, 2011).

86 Robert I. Burns, "Piracy as an Islamic-Christian Interface in the Thirteenth Century", 11 *Viator* (1980) 165, 165.

87 Heebøll-Holm, *supra* no8, 3–5. See also *supra*, 2.3.1.

88 *Supra* no8, III.III.II.

> [Kennedy] was born into poverty in a port city; he was experienced in the rough conditions of life at sea, in both the navy and the merchant service; he was apparently unmarried; and he was in his mid-twenties. These traits served as bases of unity with others when, in search of something better, he decided to become a pirate. And yet he, like the others, was not merely escaping oppressive circumstances. He was escaping *to* something new, a different reality, something alluring about which he had heard tales in his youth.[89]

This statement tells us a lot about the identity of the pirates of the time. Apart from the captains (who were likely to have served as privateers or in the regular navy), pirate crews were generally drawn from the lower social classes[90] and had little prospect for finding suitable work.[91] For them, piracy was often the best (or only) way of making a decent wage[92] (and, in any case, "hanging could be little worse" than starving).[93] Most were former naval recruits escaping poor working conditions,[94] severe punishment for transgression,[95] low pay,[96] and little prospect for career advancement.[97] Others fled abject situations at home, escaping debtors,[98] prisons or the slave trade.[99] Still others came aboard out of greed or for sheer adventure.[100]

Motivated by modest backgrounds, pirates tended to view themselves as champions of social justice.[101] They were anarchists, insofar as they challenged "[t]he exploitation of the poor by the rich, of the powerless by the powerful, or of women by men".[102] They detested authority figures and tortured or executed captains they considered to be particularly cruel, or governors who

89 Marcus Rediker, *Villains of All Nations* (London: Verso, 2004), 59.

90 *Ibid.*, 62; Lunsford, *supra* no36, 105.

91 Rediker, *ibid.*, 50.

92 *Ibid.*, 57.

93 *Ibid.*, 71.

94 See Tinniswood, *supra* no37, 20, providing a vivid description of conditions aboard a Jacobean naval vessel.

95 *Ibid.*, 20–21; the usual punishment for a misdeed was a "thrashing" with a "cat-o-nine tails".

96 *Ibid.*

97 Williams, *supra* no82, 90.

98 Rediker, *supra* no89, 56.

99 *Ibid.*, 58. Pirate crews often became ethnically diverse as a result.

100 *Ibid.*, 57–59; Williams, *supra* no82, 90.

101 Marcus Rediker, "The Seaman as Pirate: Plunder and Social Banditry at Sea" in C.R. Pennell, *Bandits at Sea: A Pirates Reader* (NYU Press, 2001) 139, 142.

102 Buchan, *supra* no66, 58. See also P.T. Leeson, "An-*aargh*-chy: The Law and Economics of Pirate Organisation" 115 *Journal of Political Economy* (2007) 1049.

played a part in hanging their brethren.[103] The justice they administered was a distinctive "class justice", targeted at the norms of established European power politics.[104] Indeed they sought to "negate all the values – discipline, reason and order – celebrated by European civilisation".[105] The infamous black flags of the pirates, often embellished with a motif (such as the skull and crossbones) intended to intimidate others into prompt surrender, were designed to mock the flags of States and proclaim that the pirates had no master but themselves.[106]

Despite harbouring agents of anarchy, the pirate ship was a place of rules and principles. Strict rules proscribed misconduct such as keeping secrets, stealing, or "meddling with prudent women".[107] The same rules often set allowances for compensation should a crewman be wounded in battle, with the precise amounts depending on the extent of the injury (hence the trope of the peg-legged or eye-patched pirate).[108] Pirate ships were defiant kingdoms unto themselves, floating hydrarchies[109] or, depending on perspective, abortive States.[110] The pirate ship was, in this way, a "world turned upside down",[111] the physical refutation of *State*-made discipline and law, in favour of self-organising anarchy.[112] Yet in many respects the (post)medieval pirate ship was decades ahead of Europe's feudal monarchies, espousing Rousseauian natural law concepts of "liberty, equality and community" centuries prior to the French Revolution.[113] They were among the world's first true democracies.[114] Pirates were "not simply the enemies of mankind because they attack

103 Rediker, *Villains, supra* no89, 33.
104 *Ibid.*, 93–96.
105 Policante, *supra* no67, 93.
106 Rediker, *Villains, supra* no89, 164–165.
107 See, e.g., Gosse, *supra* no32, 190, detailing the rules of John Philips' vessel *Revenge*, in the early 1700s.
108 *Ibid.*, and Rediker, *Villains, supra* no89, 34.
109 Douglas R. Burgess, Jr., "Hostis Humani Generi: Piracy, Terrorism and a New International Law", 13 *University of Miami International & Comparative Law Review* (2006) 293, 304.
110 Stefan Eklöf Amirell and Leos Müller, "Introduction: Persistent Piracy in World History" in Amirell and Müller (eds), *supra* no8, 1, 5–6. See also John Locke, *Two Treatises of Government* (1690), ed. P Laslett (Cambridge: CUP, 1998) II, s176, 385, suggesting that "Robbers and Pyrates have a Right of Empire over the whomsoever they have force enough to master".
111 Rediker, *Villains, supra* no89, 61.
112 *Ibid.*, 62; Leeson, *supra* no102.
113 Chris Land, "Flying the Black Flag: Revolt, Revolution and the Social Organisation of Piracy in the 'Golden Age'", 2 Management and Organisational History (2007) 169.
114 Gabriel Kuhn, *Life Under the Jolly Roger: Reflections on Golden Age Piracy* (Oakland, CA: PM Press, 2009), Chapter 4.

the interests of the ruling classes but also because they offer ideological opposition by living a counter-life".[115]

This helps to explain why pirates are so popular today, of course – they "rejected the constraints of a law-abiding society, lived life to the full, sailed to exotic destinations, took whatever they wanted – everything that the average book reader might have dreamed about, but was never going to do".[116] As such their "elusiveness, the powerful metaphor of the ship and the sea, the exotic location of [their] tales, the ideals of equality and democracy that [they] represent" have enabled pirates to become "a sort of archetypical bandit, a social or primitive rebel who almost all of us, in some way, can relate to and find sympathy with".[117] The fascination is not a new one; throughout much of history, representations of pirates have treated them as curiously enthralling creatures of ambiguous morality.[118] Shakespeare's *Hamlet* (c. 1603), for instance, features a band of pirates in a small yet crucial plot point. In Act IV, the title character is sent to England by Claudius, ostensibly for Hamlet's protection whereas in fact Claudius intends for the protagonist to be executed upon his arrival. Hamlet boards a ship for England, but he never arrives. Recounting his time at sea (as relayed in a letter read out by Horatio), Hamlet recalls that:

> Ere we were two days old at sea, a pirate of very warlike appointment gave us chase. Finding ourselves too slow of sail, we put on a compelled valour: and in the grapple I boarded them: [...] so I alone became their prisoner. They have dealt with me like thieves of mercy: but they knew what they did: I am to do a good turn for them.[119]

Hamlet is henceforth able to return to England, escape death, and plot his bungled revenge against Claudius. This *deus ex machina* appears to be a remarkably fortuitous event, one that was perhaps premeditated.[120] In any case the pirates are perceived as a force for good and Hamlet's attitude towards them is sympathetic, which is unsurprising given that they effectively saved his life. Through this brief passage, which in a few words conveys a thrilling maritime world of romance and adventure, Shakespeare uses the topical issue

115 Simpson, *supra* no12, 220.
116 Konstam, *supra* no24, 318.
117 Kuhn, *supra* no114, 125.
118 Jowitt, *Culture of Piracy*, *supra* no45, Chapter 2.
119 William Shakespeare, *Hamlet* (1603) (ed. Neil Taylor & Ann Thompson, London: Puffin, 2006), IV, vi, 14–20.
120 Lois Potter, "Pirates and 'turning Turk' in Renaissance Drama", in Jean-Pierre Maquerlot and Michèle Willems, *Travel and Drama in Shakespeare's Time*, 124, 124.

of piracy to invoke interest and provoke debate.[121] The "good turn" offered by Hamlet refers to the practice, common at Shakespeare's time, of obtaining a royal pardon for the pirates.[122] Shakespeare's *Hamlet* gives us a glimpse of the romanticised anti-heroic handling that pirates received in the writing of later authors. For instance Lord Byron's 1814 poem *The Corsair*, romanticising the tale of a young sailor ostracised from his community, proved popular,[123] while Sir Walter Scott's 1822 novel *The Pirate*[124] and Giuseppi Verdi's Byron-inspired 1848 opera *Il Corsaro* also provided "a sanitised, rose-tinted view of the pirate world, in which pirates were romantic heroes and rebels against authority rather than simply a bunch of unwashed cutthroats".[125] Byron and others pioneered the romantic "piracy" genre that would be perfected in 1883 by Robert Louis Stevenson's *Treasure Island*, the novel that allowed pirates the foothold from which they have so thoroughly penetrated and inhabited the collective consciousness.[126] Jack Sparrow is only the latest in a long line of endearing rebels.[127]

Pirates existed, then, in a close and reciprocal relationship with the State and with the public in general, representing both popular heroes and anarchic villains. They were foils to authority and redistributors of wealth, the seaborne equivalent of Robin Hood, "Prince of Thieves".[128] The tremendously successful eighteenth century pirate "Black" Sam Bellamy once proclaimed that between pirates and States,

> there is only this difference: [States] rob the poor under the cover of law [...], and we plunder the rich under the protection of our own courage [...]. I am a free prince and I have as much authority to make war on the whole world as he who has a hundred sail of ships at sea.[129]

121 Potter, *ibid.*, 125.

122 Earle, *supra* no33, 61.

123 Byron, *The Corsair* (London: John Murray, 1814).

124 Walter Scott, *The Pirate* (Edinburgh: Archibald Constable, 1822).

125 Konstam, *supra* no24, 311–312.

126 *Ibid.*, 312, noting that "Stevenson introduced all those other elements of piracy that have now become the bedrocks of pirate mythology".

127 *Pirates of the Caribbean: The Curse of the Black Pearl* (dir. Gore Verbinksi, Disney, 2003).

128 *Robin Hood: Prince of Thieves* (dir. Kevin Reynolds), 1991.

129 Cited in C.R. Pennell, "Introduction – Brought to Book: Reading about Pirates" in Pennell (ed.), *supra* no101, 3, 9. See also Johnson, *supra* no29, 37, suggesting that "if power and command be the thing which distinguish a prince, these ruffians had all the hallmarks of royalty".

In making this claim Bellamy invoked the apparently subjective division between civilised "States" and anarchic "pirates", echoing Saint Augustine's similar fifth century anecdote.[130] To Saint Augustine and Sam Bellamy, States and pirate ships were similar constructs. Both were associations of peoples governed by rules, and both attacked and plundered others.[131] From an "Augustinian" perspective,[132] therefore, the situation was one of inequality; pirates were discriminated against because they did not conform to the standards of States (for Cicero, these standards were about territorial institutionalisation and the disavowal of plunder for its own sake).[133]

Unfortunately for pirates, the contrary "Ciceronian paradigm" has gained ascendancy, made reality by the military might of States, in turn allowing them to claim a Weberian "monopoly of the legitimate use of physical force".[134] Sam Bellamy may have declared himself a "free prince", but to State power-brokers he was "the enemy of the human species" and catalyst for the development of international law.[135] Indeed, Bellamy's contemporary, Howel Davies, once proclaimed that that hoisting the black flag meant "a declaration of war against the whole world".[136]

Thus pirates' "rejection of law and the exercise of their will against the interests of society firmly placed them in the class unto themselves that Cicero had long ago identified".[137] They did not simply endanger the commercial relations of the State, but they actively opposed its existence, and the structured societal values it stood for. The pirate's cynicism rendered him diametrically opposed to the State-sponsored privateer, even if their actions were identical. Pirates might be better understood less as "enemies of mankind" but rather as enemies of the *State*.[138] This sociological analysis goes a long way to transforming the erroneous preconception that "[t]he crime of piracy consists of

130 Augustine, *The City of God* (5th Century AD) (ed. RW Dyson, Cambridge: CUP, 1998), 6.3.15; discussed *supra* 2.3.1.

131 See, e.g., Rediker, *Villains, supra* no89, Chapters 4 and 5.

132 *Supra*, 2.3.1.

133 These themes are carried through, largely intact, by Alberico Gentili and Hugo Grotius, as discussed *infra*, Chapter 4.

134 Max Weber, "Politics as a Vocation" in Hans Gerth (ed.) *From Max Weber: Essays in Sociology* (1948), 1991 reprint (Abingdon, Ox: Routledge, 1991), 78. See also *supra*, 2.1.3.

135 Heller-Roazen, *supra* no55, 160.

136 Johnson, *supra* no29, 134.

137 Davey, *supra* no44, 1201.

138 Mikkel Thorup, "The horror of the'enemy of humanity' – on pirates, terrorists and states", presentation at "Fear, Horror & Terror", 1st Global Conference, Mansfield College, Oxford, September 10–12, 2007, 11.

nothing more than robbery at sea".[139] This much was recognised by Cicero,[140] as it would also be by Gentili and Grotius.[141]

3.2.2 *Responding to Piracy: Law beyond Territory*

The unique nature of piracy has proved to be a perpetual problem for State legislatures and courts. Given its uniquely extraterritorial nature and similarity to belligerent State-sponsored plunder, early legal responses to piracy were often disarrayed. This section reveals some of the issues faced by States prior to the common acceptance of universal jurisdiction as a tool for suppressing piracy, a process that only began to occur in the late 1600s.[142] The section provides a necessary background to the later histories of universal jurisdiction by exploring some of the obstacles to prosecuting pirates under pre-existing traditional claims to jurisdiction.

Sources reveal very few instances of piracy prosecutions prior to the late 1600s, and even in these cases it is not always possible to separate out acts of piracy from other crimes for which the accused was tried (robbery at land and sea were rarely distinguished).[143] As a general rule States tended not to meddle in the affairs of marine merchants[144] and, in any case, State intervention would have been difficult in such a "judicial no-man's land".[145] Assertions of State jurisdiction were generally restricted to claims based on feudal allegiance (the precursor of nationality-based jurisdiction).[146] For instance, an English statute of 1414 stated that piratical depredations committed by the king's subjects in times of peace "brought great dishonour upon his name" and were considered to be acts of high treason.[147] Moreover, sixteenth century captures and punishments of pirates were limited to English pirates working close to English coasts, thereby avoiding potential jurisdictional pitfalls or diplomatic upsets.[148]

---

139 Kontorovich, *supra* n05, 191.

140 *Supra*, 2.2.

141 *Infra*, 4.1.2. Grotius would emphasise the State's divine right to engage in commerce upon the seas, this being an existential right being denied by the pirate.

142 Discussed *infra*, Chapter 5, in general.

143 Heebøll-Holm, *supra* n08, 238–240; Williams, *supra* n082, 20.

144 Heeboll-Holm, *ibid.*, 128–134.

145 *Ibid.*, 230.

146 Cedric Ryngaert, *Jurisdiction in International Law* (2nd ed.) (Oxford: OUP, 2015), 51–54. This form of proto-nationality jurisdiction predated territory-based jurisdiction as the usual link by which a sovereign would claim the right to act as judge. On the later emergence of territoriality as the dominant form of jurisdiction see, e.g.: Stuart Elden, *The Birth of Territory* (Chicago: University of Chicago Press, 2013).

147 Edward Lewis, "Responsibility for Piracy in the Middle Ages", 19 *Journal of Comparative Legislation and International Law* (1937) 77, 85.

148 Rubin, *supra* n033, 36.

The evidence suggests that England, at least, generally only claimed jurisdiction over "its own" pirates and, then, generally charged them with treason, based on the vitiation of feudal responsibilities.[149] This situation presented some difficulty, however, given that pirates, upon being captured at sea, could fall into the hands of *any* State.[150] For a capturing non-national State to prosecute would have raised issues regarding the jurisdictional competency from which they were entitled to act.

Any instances of cross-jurisdictional punishment would have been complicated by unpredictable policy among the European powers. Elizabeth I's reign, for instance, was notable for a somewhat lax approach towards pirates (who were, after all, privateers in waiting), earning England a dubious designation as "a nation of pirates".[151] Many aristocratic families made a healthy living from sponsoring piracy, which "has always benefited from the support of unscrupulous great men, only too happy to receive bribes and cheap pirated goods at no risk to themselves".[152] Elizabeth's successor, James I, adopted a tougher stance on pirates, judging them to be "the enemies of God and man",[153] yet the difficulties involved in their apprehension meant that they were often pardoned.[154] Dutch practices were similar, with several accounts of infamous pirates receiving pardons.[155] In 1651 the Dutch States-General issued a statement pardoning *all* Dutch pirates, describing it as an "unusual mercy".[156]

As piracy was generally treated as treason, then, and in any case was frequently pardoned, it was rare for States to capture and prosecute a pirate of different nationality. Nevertheless accounts do exist of foreign pirates being tried and executed in the Dutch Republic.[157] These were almost exclusively Dunkirkers, a group of pirates or privateers technically in the employ of Spain who frequently troubled Dutch shipping. Flushing (Vlissingen) served as the venue for several such trials and executions, notably that of Jacques Colaert,

---

149 Lewis, *supra* no147, 77–87. "Piracy" and "treason" were conflated until at least 1694, as documented in the trial of several English privateers commissioned by the exiled James II; see Sarah Craze, "Prosecuting privateers for piracy: How piracy law transitioned from treason to a crime against property" 28 International Journal of Maritime History (2016) 654.

150 *Ibid.*, 89.

151 Senior, *supra* no43. See, however, Earle, *supra* no33, 18, describing this phrase as being "somewhat exaggerated and [...] really just a way of being rude to the English".

152 Earle, *ibid.*, 20–21.

153 Tinniswood, *supra* no37, 87.

154 Jowitt, *Culture of Piracy, supra* no45, 152–159; Tinniswood, *ibid.*, 66–69.

155 See examples in Lunsford, *supra* no36, 141, 172, 175.

156 Lunsford, *ibid.*, 160–161.

157 LHJ Sicking, *Neptune and the Netherlands: State, Economy and War at Sea in the Renaissance* (Brill, 2004), 480.

captured and hanged alongside thirty-seven of his crew in 1600.[158] The trial and execution of the Dunkirkers raises an important question of whether they were tried and convicted as pirates, or simply executed as particularly troublesome belligerents, given their links with Spain.

A further curious exception to the general lack of pirate prosecutions occurred in Venetian Zante in 1603. Two pirates of English origin were captured by Venice, leading to some uncertainty as to how they ought to be dealt with. Venice contacted Elizabeth I directly, requesting that the "villains" be punished by "a severe sentence against them",[159] though it is not clear what response (if any) was received from England. Tired of awaiting a satisfactory reply, Venice eventually took matters into its own hands – a despatch from the Governor of Zante to the Venetian Doge, dated May 28 1603, informs him that

> I had in my hands two English Corsairs. They freely confessed their crime, and were, moreover, identified by the Captain, the crew, and the merchant on board the plundered ship, [...]. Convicted and confessed as guilty of this crime, I, with my Council, condemned them to be hung by the neck [*sic.*], and the sentence was carried out on a high tower of this castle.[160]

News of these executions was received "in appearance, at least, with much satisfaction by the English; but in reality not without some regret for the large gains made that were reaped from the booty [...] [and the belief] that their men were not to be beaten".[161] This revelation suggests that England did not consider it prudent to protest the executions, preferring to disown any association with the captured pirates and, *prima facie*, favouring the Venetians' course of action. As might be expected given the Elizabethan attitude to piracy, however, the events appear to have been met with furtive dissatisfaction. In any case the episode reveals much about claims to jurisdiction over pirates, with States of the time apparently preferring not to punish captives who bore no feudal (or national) allegiance to them and, then, only doing so as a reluctant last resort. Such cautious deferral bears resemblance to the modern day trend of "subsidiarity", in the context of "core" international crimes, whereby an

158 *Ibid.*, noting also that several Dunkirkers who had confessed to acts of piracy were executed in Flushing (Vlissingen) in 1548 "to serve as an example to everyone".

159 Calendar of State Papers Relating to English Affairs in the Archives of Venice, Volume 9 (1592–1603), 15 Feb 1603.

160 *Ibid.*, Volume 10 (1603–1607), 18 May 1603.

161 *Ibid.*, 28 May 1603.

interested State (such as the territorial or nationality State) the opportunity to try a suspect prior to any assertion of universal jurisdiction.[162]

This historical overview reveals the difficulties States would have faced in implementing a system based on "universal jurisdiction" at a time when society (and jurisdiction) was based on restrictive conceptions of allegiance and feudalism.[163] Beyond this, the lack of necessary arrangements or understandings between States made "international" prosecutions problematic. Permissions had to be obtained and diplomatic tightropes walked. The requisite shared political mindset for such an internationalised form of jurisdiction, in an insular (post)medieval world, simply did not exist. Moreover pirates were notoriously difficult to capture: they generally knew the seas better than State navies and were better equipped. A shift in attitude (and a boost in tangible strength) would be needed if the nascent project of international law, the final triumph of the State over the pirate, was to be realised.[164]

There are nevertheless glimmers, from this time, of a broad "universal" jurisdiction. As the Venetian example demonstrates, there was a certain convenience to suppressing a foreign perpetrator when the feudal "home" State is unprepared to act. There are also suggestions from around this time that piracy was considered to be a particularly heinous act – several States had made it a capital offence from the 1300s[165] and in England, the 1536 *Offences at Sea Act* expressed reluctance in its preamble at "pirates, robbers and murders upon the sea" having previously "escaped unpunished".[166] We find further claims regarding the serious nature of piracy in the works of Lord Coke (discussed below, 3.2.3), who nevertheless insisted on treating the problem via a treason paradigm, based on feudal allegiance.[167] The developments recounted suggest a slowly building appetite among European States to become more closely involved and cooperative in controlling piracy. Change was afoot: a catalytic sea-change in State attitudes towards piracy would be brought about in the early 1600s when interstate trade became an important concern of States, as

162 Discussed *infra*, 8.2.2.

163 Lewis, *supra* no147, 89.

164 Per Earle, *supra* no33, 55, "until States were absolutely determined to eradicate piracy and were prepared to devote considerably increased numbers of ships and men to such a policy, little would be achieved".

165 Examples include Genoa and Venice, as discussed in Emily Sohmer Tai, "Restitution and the Definition of a Pirate: The Case of Sologrus de Nigro" 19 *Mediterranean Historical Review* (2004) 34, 44, and Ruthy Gertwagen, "Venice, Genoa and the Fights over the Island of Tenedos (Late Fourteenth and Early Fifteenth Century) 67 *Studi Veneziani* (2013) 35, 68.

166 Pickering, *The Statutes at* Large (1763), 348–349; reproduced in Rubin, *supra* no33, 36.

167 *The Third Part of the Institutes of the Laws of England; Concerning High Treason, and Other Pleas of the Crown and Criminal Causes* (c. 1628), 111–113.

vocalised and aggressively asserted by Hugo Grotius[168] and built upon in State policy.[169]

3.2.3 *Lord Coke and* "Hostes Humani Generis"

Lord Edward Coke was one of the most influential jurists of his age, partly due to his role in several prominent cases, but also due to his anti-establishment stance which saw him work to erode the Crown's influence over the English legal system.[170] Born in 1552, Coke became a well-regarded barrister during the 1580s.[171] He went on to serve as Attorney-General from 1594 until 1606, heading up a string of high profile prosecutions including those of Walter Raleigh (for treason, 1603) and the Gunpowder Plot conspirators (1606).[172] He became Chief Justice of the Common Pleas (with jurisdiction over *inter partes* actions that did not involve the King) from 1606 to 1613 and, ultimately, Chief Justice of the King's Bench (with jurisdiction *inter alia* over any cases which did concern the King) from 1613 until 1616, from whence he presided over a string of cases that dealt with the identity of pirates and the applicability of relevant laws.[173]

In *R v Marsh* (1615)[174] Coke made the historic revelation that "a pirate *est hostis humani generis*" ("enemy of all mankind") with the effect that he forfeited the right of *habeas corpus*. He further established that in order to be tried for piracy (over which the Admiralty Court possessed jurisdiction),[175] the suspect had to be a royal subject, failing which the incident fell outside the remit of the legal system (Coke equated piracy to "treason").[176] This appears to present something of a contradiction. The limitations inherent in English jurisdiction appear to have been an overriding concern for Coke, whose narrow jurisdictional approach corresponds with contemporary practice suggesting

168 *Infra*, 4.1.2.

169 *Infra*, 5.2.

170 John Baker, *An Introduction to English Legal History* (Butterworths, 2002), 167 and 183; John Hostettler, *Sir Edward Coke: A Force for Freedom* (Chichester: Barry Rose Law Publishers, 1997), 106.

171 Allen D. Boyer, *Sir Edward Coke and the Elizabethan Age* (Palo Alto, CA: Stanford University Press, 2003), 115 and 125–133.

172 See 1 *Criminal Trials* (1850) 400, 400–511 and Humphry William Woolrych, *The Life of the Right Honourable Sir Edward Coke* (London: J & WT Clarke, 1826), 70).

173 Most notably *R v Marsh,* (1615) 3 Bulstrode 27, 81 E.R. 23, and *Hildebrand, Brimston, & Baker's Case* (1 *Rolle* 285 (1615), King's Bench, Hilary Term).

174 *R v Marsh, ibid.* The case saw the arrival of the term "pirate" in common legal usage: Rubin, *supra* no33, 44.

175 As affirmed in *Scadding's Case,* 1 January 1608, 80 *E.R.* 91, and *Re Admiralty*, (1610) 12 Coke Reports 79, 77 E.R. 1357, both presided over by Lord Coke.

176 *Hildebrand, supra* no173.

that States were reluctant to prosecute "foreign" pirates.[177] The equation of "piracy" with "treason" rested on the ancient feudal notion that the accused is bound in loyalty to his monarch, so that the illegality of "piracy" flowed from a breach of that loyalty.[178] Coke apparently intended to characterise piracy as essentially a criminal act subject to domestic jurisdiction as opposed to any form of political act of belligerence or subversion that might warrant a different response.[179] Arguably such a characterisation of piracy deprived pirates of "both the majesty and menace traditionally accorded them under the law",[180] yet we must reconcile Coke's strict jurisdictional approach with his momentous description of pirates as "*hostes humani generis*". Coke apparently deemed the phrase to be self-explanatory, and offered no further explanation as to why pirates should forfeit the right of *habeas corpus*.

Greater detail regarding Coke's views on piracy can be gleaned from his celebrated *Institutes of the Laws of England* (c. 1628),[181] written by Coke in his retirement. Here Coke repeats his treason conception of piracy and affirms that "*pirata est hostis humani generis*" and should be "drawn and hanged".[182] Coke adds that if the perpetrator were not an English subject, he would still be *hostis humani generis*, although he would not commit treason under English law. The logic behind this is not clear, although presumably the pirate would be *hostis humani generis* for having broken the loyalty of his home State. This would have placed him outside the allegiance of the State and thus, "at war [with] the whole world".[183] The claim also indicates that any State could look on a pirate as having committed a grave sin indeed, notwithstanding whether he owed them allegiance. Thus the origins of universal jurisdiction begin to

177 *Supra*, 3.2.2.

178 Per Rubin, *supra* no33, 66, "common law judges in England thought municipal concepts of jurisdiction the essence of the situation and traced jurisdiction to the legal powers of the sovereign in England over his subjects and his territory".

179 In *R v Marsh* (*supra* no173) Coke recounted a case where he dealt with one Samuel Pelagii, a Moroccan subject who had plundered a Spanish ship and found himself in an English jail (*Pelagii v. The Spanish Ambassador*, Bulstrode 27). Coke reasoned that Pelagii could not be tried in England (under Spanish authority) given that Spain and Morocco "are enemies, and […] open hostility is between them, and therefore this taking from an enemy in this manner by the other, is not in judgement of law *spoliatio sed legalis captio*: and if an enemy do take goods of another, this is not felony". The Pelagii case was better dealt with in a context of belligerence (the suspect being a State agent) rather than criminality.

180 Douglas R. Burgess, "Piracy in the Public Sphere: The Henry Every Trials and the Battle for Meaning in Seventeenth-Century Print Culture", 48 *Journal of British Studies* (2009) 887, 902.

181 *Supra* no167.

182 *Ibid.*, 111–113.

183 Johnson, *supra* no29, 134.

take shape. It is likely that, in making this claim, Coke drew on the confusing palette of discussions concerning "enemies of mankind" that originated with Cicero and were built upon, with additional layers of argument, in later years.[184] The phrase itself, a variant on Cicero's *communes hostes omnium*,[185] originated with fourteenth century Italian jurist Bartolus of Saxoferrato[186] and was later adopted by Sir Francis Bacon in a 1622 declaration that pirates were *communes humani generis hostes* (lent an air of authenticity by being formulated in Latin),[187] "whom all nations are to prosecute, not so much in the right of their own fears, as upon the band of human society".[188] The phrase was also used by Pliny the Elder, Constantine, Lactantius and John Chrysostom to refer, variously, to tyrants, magicians, or the Devil.[189] Even if the term is intended to be a paraphrase borrowed from Cicero, the pirates that Coke intended to refer to, "rovers and robbers upon the sea", did not compare to the Cilician *peiratēs*, groups of considerable size and organisation whose "raid mentality" had placed them in a continuous war with all around them, forcing them to clash with purportedly civilised Roman culture.[190] Nevertheless given the essentially subversive attitude of many pirates and their attitudes towards the hegemony of States, the comparison seems rather apt (notwithstanding the arguably inappropriate designation of pirates as "*hostes*").[191]

Provenance aside, Coke's invocation of the rhetorical phrase "*hostis humani generis*" would become synonymous with the exercise of universal jurisdiction by British courts in the late 1600s and early 1700s, when the threat of piracy

184 See, e.g., Rech, *supra* n030, 36, noting that "[t]he convergence of theological, philosophical, and juridical elements used with discriminatory function had repercussions for the modern vision of piracy, beginning from the first definition of the pirate as a *hostis humani generis* in sixteenth century admiralty law – a definition resorted to by Sir Edward Coke in his *Institutes*". This is despite the Latin meaning of *hostis* as a legally constituted enemy: see 2.1.3, *supra* (footnote 86).

185 Cicero, *Verrine Orations*, II.IV.XXI (original Latin in William Peterson (ed.), Oxford: Clarendon, 1917; see also *supra*, 2.2.

186 Bartolus of Saxoferrato, *De Captivis et Postliminio Reversis Rubrica* in *Apostilla domini Bartoli de Saxoferato super secunda parte Digesti novi* (Milan: Johanes Antoni de Donato, 1486).

187 Harry D, Gould, "Cicero's Ghost: Rethinking the Social Construction of Piracy", in Michael J. Struett, Jon D. Carlson, and Mark T. Nance (eds), *Maritime Piracy and the Construction of Global Governance* (New York: Routledge, 2013) 23, 24.

188 "An Advertisement Touching An Holy War" (1622) in Spedding, Ellis, and Heath, eds., *The Works of Francis Bacon* v. XIII. (Boston: Houghton Mifflin, and Co., 1900), 212–213. Bacon appears to be strongly influenced by the relevant Roman histories.

189 Rech, *supra* n030, 35–36; Kempe, *supra* n060, 356.

190 2.1.5, *supra*. See also Joshua Goodwin, "Universal Jurisdiction and the Pirate: Time for an Old Couple to Part", 39 *Vanderbilt Journal of Transnational Law* (2006) 973, 990.

191 2.1.3, *supra* (footnote 86).

to American colonies had become severe.[192] Both Coke and Hugo Grotius are cited extensively in *Bonnet's Trial*, for instance, in 1718 in which the Admiralty Court held that

> As to the heinousness or wickedness of the offence [of piracy], it needs no aggravation, it being evident to the reason of all men. Therefore a pirate is called *hostis humani generis*, with whom neither faith nor oath is to be kept.[193]

This view seems to correspond to Coke's usage of the term to convey a sense of seriousness. In modern legal process, the phrase is sometimes manipulated to invoke a sense of heinousness, having been used by courts and scholars to equate other serious offences with the supposed severity of piracy.[194] In the US case *Filártiga v Peña-Irala*, for instance, the Court of Appeals for the Second Circuit confirmed that "the torturer has become like the pirate and slave trader before him *hostis humani generis*, an enemy of all mankind".[195] The claim was cited and repeated at the International Criminal Tribunal for the former Yugoslavia in the *Furundžija* case, in the context of war crimes (torture and rape).[196]

In reality, though, the term is nothing more than "mere embellishment",[197] a "rhetorical invective"[198] designed to disparage piracy. This has made the phrase a handy reference point for other crimes also considered to be "heinous", such

192 Harding, *supra* no32, 22.

193 *Bonnet's Trial*, 15 State Trials (Howell) 1231 (Am. Vice Adm. 1718), 1235. See also similar holdings in *Kidd's Trial*, 14 Howell's State Trials 123 (1701), *Quelch's Trial*, 14 Howell's State Trials 1067 (1704), *Re Tivnan* 122 E.R. 971 (1864), *US v Harmony*, 43 U.S. (2 How.) 210, 232 (1844), *Brig Malek Adhel*, 43 U.S. (2 How.) 210 (1844) and *In re Piracy Jure Gentium* [1934] AC 586.

194 See, *e.g.*, Randall, *supra* no52, 794, and Tullio Treves, "Piracy, Law of the Sea, and Use of Force: Developments off the Coast of Somalia", 20 *European Journal of International Law* (2009) 399, 400.

195 *Filártiga v Peña-Irala*, 630 F.2d 876, 890 (2d Cir. 1980).

196 *Prosecutor v Anto Furundzija*, Judgment of 10 December 1998, para. 147.

197 *The Ambrose Light*, *supra* no54.

198 Matthew Tindall, *An Essay Concerning the Laws of Nations and the Rights of Soveraigns* (1694) 25–26. See also Harvard Research in International Law, "Draft Convention on Piracy with Comments", 26 *American Journal of International Law* (1932) 749, 803 (noting that the term "is an ancient verbal condemnation of the conduct of a pirate and a figurative epitome of the common war against him"), Gould, *supra* no187, 33 (noting that *hostes humani generis* is a self-sustaining idea; "if someone or something is the enemy of all humanity, then it is a matter of the utmost concern. But this tells us nothing") and Kontorovich, *supra* no5, 234 (describing the term *hostis humani generis* as an "ominous-sounding epithet").

as (*inter alia*) slavery, torture, war crimes and genocide – a litany of offences that *prima facie* bear no discernible connection with piracy.[199] The term's heightened use in early eighteenth century piracy cases, at a time when piracy had overrun colonial life, substantiates this notion.[200] "*Hostis humani generis*" became the language of the courts in order to justify the use of universal jurisdiction, the argument being that if a pirate was indeed "the enemy of all mankind", then all States surely possessed an interest in suppressing him.[201] This argument is explored in detail in Chapter 5, which examines the increasingly systematic invocation of universal jurisdiction by eighteenth century courts and scholars. It is nevertheless necessary to discuss the issue here to juxtapose this later exploitation of the term against Coke's original take on jurisdiction over piracy (itself defined by contemporary conceptions of State jurisdiction, delimited by feudal proto-nationality).[202] Coke seemingly did not intend to equate the notions of *hostis humani generis* and universal jurisdiction, rather anticipating that the former would, by reference to ancient tradition, merely emphasise his abhorrence of piracy.

Coke's invocation of the term "*hostis humani generis*" nevertheless retains considerable significance. All coastal nations suffered pirates, and their extraterritorial nature bestowed upon them a mysterious, anarchic quality. As residents of the high seas, the usual State-centric bases of jurisdiction could not compel them to act according to State-made laws. They were a class apart from landlubbing criminals such as thieves and murderers, even if their crimes were *prima facie* no worse; attacking from the sea, they resembled an invasion force without being one, their purposes purely malevolent and militarily purposeless (except at a subversive anarchic level). As such, although "*hostis humani generis*" is an empty term in terms of technical quality, it is a deeply purposive and meaningful term, intended to shock and to stir debate. As Jody Greene eloquently summarises,

> In its self-appointed task of speaking for the civilised and the human, international law has been unable to move beyond categories like *hostis humani generis*, even though in using them it founds what some still

199 The hypothesised "heinousness" of piracy is discussed *infra*, 5.2.2, and its relationship to crimes under "new" universal jurisdiction is discussed *Infra*, 6.2.1.

200 See examples cited *supra*, no193.

201 Kontorovich, *supra* no5, 234–235 and Gould, *supra* no187, 41.

202 Saskia Sassen, *Territory, authority, rights: from medieval to global assemblages* (Princeton, NJ: Princeton University Press, 2006) 32–33, and Thomson, *supra* no46, 116.

want to believe is a genuine legal science on a legal fiction, a fiction that nonetheless retains the power to haunt us.[203]

3.3 Conclusion

Everyone is a monster to someone. Since you are so convinced that I am yours, I will be it.

CAPTAIN FLINT, *Black Sails*[204]

By the late sixteenth century "piracy" had become a focal point for discussion about the scope and remit of international law,[205] a system policed by a mutually recognising society of territorial States (or "peer polities")[206] with the pirate representing those who were outside the system, a "*hostis humani generis*" from the "primordial world" beyond.[207] The pirate was the "constitutive exception", the exceptional figure against which the international community was able to define itself[208] (including, later, via the use of universal jurisdiction).[209] Yet the pirate was a dichotomous menace, "both cunning thief and generous lord of the sea, anarchist and nation builder, destructive demon and pioneer of commerce".[210]

Central to the issue over the pirate's identity is the problem of *authority* which manifests itself through the distinction between privateer and pirate. The former represented State law and sovereignty, the latter a servant of lawlessness. Yet the variable and fluid nature of State sanction made it near-impossible to tell with much certainty who was a pirate and who was a privateer; as such, "a simple binary, appropriate for famous Golden Age figures like Blackbeard, distorts

203 Greene, *supra* no14, 703.

204 Episode "XVIII" (dir. Steve Boyum), 2015.

205 Antony Anghie, *Imperialism, Sovereignty and the Making of International Law* (Cambridge: CUP, 2005), 3.

206 Tai, "Legal Status of Piracy", *supra* no62, 838.

207 Randall Lesaffer, "Alberico Gentili's *ius post bellum* and Early Modern Peace Treaties", in Benedict Kingsbury and Benjamin Straumann (eds), *The Roman Foundations of the Law of Nations* (Oxford: OUP, 2010) 210, 211; William E. Conklin, "The Myth of Primordialism in Cicero's Theory of *Jus Gentium*" 23 *Leiden Journal of International Law* 479, 500.

208 Simpson, *supra* no12, 223 ("It may be that the international legal order's own ambitions rest on the presence of outsiders like pirates"). See also Policante, *supra* no67, 87 and 133–136.

209 Greene, *supra* no14, 695.

210 Joel H. Baer, "'The Complicated Plot of Piracy': Aspects of English Criminal Law and the Image of the Pirate in Defoe", 23 *The Eighteenth Century* (1982) 3, 26.

the complexity and ambivalence of Renaissance depictions of 'pirates'".[211] The problem was complicated further by the ambiguous presentation of pirates in contemporary culture and reception in the public mindset. Nevertheless, the division between pirate and State-sponsored privateer existed *in principle* and as such marks a theoretical schism between the civilised and the uncivilised (the latter "*hostes humani generis*"). As such it would be inapposite to draw conclusions about the nature of piracy based on the practice of States (via privateers). The (not so) simple distinction between State and pirate, moreover, fails to consider the voluntary war that pirates elected to fight against the stifling control of Europe's burgeoning sovereign States, a battle that pitted them as antagonists to the civilising project of international law. There is more to draw out of this issue, and to this extent Chapter 4 will discuss the influential works of Alberico Gentili and Hugo Grotius, insofar as they examine the nature of piracy (particularly as compared with sovereign States).

A further issue is the development of a trans-national jurisdictional system (or lack thereof) suitable for enforcing internationally agreed norms against the pirate interlopers. Claims to jurisdiction were, in general,[212] strongly tied to feudal allegiances, yet such a system was hardly conducive to the effective suppression of "high seas" piracy. A broad base of shared jurisdiction would seem to be the sensible option, although some rationale would be required to overhaul the feudal/nationality system. Contemporary practice among European States suggests a more limited jurisdictional principle. Lord Coke, while taking steps to signal the heinousness of piracy via the epithet of "*hostis humani generis*", also approached the subject within this strict jurisdictional paradigm.

We now turn to an examination of how international scholars Alberico Gentili and Hugo Grotius sought to overcome these problems, sowing the seeds of universal jurisdiction in so doing.

---

211 Jowitt, *Culture of Piracy, supra* n045, 9.

212 See exceptions *supra*, 3.2.2.

CHAPTER 4

The Philosophical Foundations of Universal Jurisdiction: Piracy in the Works of Alberico Gentili and Hugo Grotius

The story of universal jurisdiction began with Cicero, inasmuch as his ideologies formed the foundation for a world order that placed "piracy" (an admittedly vague concept in Cicero's time) in opposition to civilised Roman Statehood.[1] This is not to say that Rome actually adopted and endorsed the practice as a way of handling the threat of the Cilician *peiratēs* (or *piratae*). Indeed, the principle did not emerge as a fully realised concept until the late seventeenth century.[2] Later assertions of universal jurisdiction owed a debt to the influential works of late sixteenth century Italian academic Alberico Gentili and early seventeenth century Dutch scholar Hugo Grotius. Both were central to the early development of international law which, drawing on Cicero's doctrines, they based firmly around the conception of the sovereign State. In defining the State, the identity of the "pirate" was simultaneously negatively determined, so that the pirate's fate was interminably linked with the definition and rise of Statehood, as expressed through the formative ideologies of international law. This anti-Statist and extralegal designation of piracy would, in turn, influence the application of universal jurisdiction to universally condemnable perpetrators of "core" international crimes.[3]

The rhetoric of excluding certain actors from the remit of international law had reappeared several times since Cicero's lifetime. In the late twelfth century Italian jurist Azzo of Bologna distinguished "*hostes*" (recognised enemies) from extralegal "*latrones*" ("brigands") and *latrunculi* ("robbers"),[4] maintaining the Roman distinction of equal "enemies" and undeserving "others".[5] Fourteenth century Italian scholar of Roman law Bartolus of Saxoferrato confirmed that "enemies (*hostes*) are not to be compared to pirates (*pyrates*)" who were

1 2.2, *supra*.

2 5.2, *infra*, in conjunction with the historical background described at 3.2.2, *supra*.

3 Amedeo Policante, *The Pirate Myth: Genealogies of an Imperial Concept* (Abingdon, Ox: Routledge, 2015), 169–172. Discussed further at 8.1, *infra*.

4 Azzo of Bologna, *Summa Codicis* (c. 1210) 1; discussed in Bruno Paradisi, "International Law and Social Structure in the Middle Ages", 2 *Indian Year Book of International Affairs* (1964) 154–161.

5 As described in Justinian's *Digest*, ed. Alan Watson (Philadelphia: University of Pennsylvania Press, 2011) (original Latin available online at thelatinlibrary.com), XLIX.XV.XXIV.

 | DOI:10.1163/9789004390461_005

"*hostes humani generis*".[6] Several sixteenth century scholars elaborated on this general theme; French philosopher Jean Bodin, for instance, conceived a distinction between the "well-ordered government" and its antithesis, the "pirate state".[7] Pierino Belli, a military adviser to Spain and the Holy Roman Empire, claimed that "pirates (*piratae*) are wholly outside the pale of the law" so that "it should be permissible for anyone to attack them".[8] And Flemish scholar Balthasar de Ayala wrote that a band of pirates, being associated together "with wrong-doing and dishonesty for its object, [...] cannot proceed under the laws of war [...]; but all the modes of stress known to the laws of war may be employed against them".[9] With subtle variation, the consensus regarding pirates was clear – they were "an especially abominable enemy with no rights whatsoever".[10] These scholars, though, added little to the debate about the identity of pirates and their treatment at the hands of States, acting instead as rigid conduits of Cicero.

In contrast, Gentili and Grotius devoted large swathes of their influential theses – *De Jure Belli Libri Tres* (the Laws of War in Three Books, 1589)[11] and *De Jure Belli ac Pacis* (The Laws of War and Peace, 1625)[12] respectively – to the act of piracy, in turn crafting their own influential archetypes of the phenomenon in substantial detail. Both were deeply influenced by the political intrigues of their own time and their works are, in part, a response to contemporaneous events. Outbreaks of Mediterranean piracy coincided with an emerging debate about the jurisdictional space of the sea, a discussion driven by the exponential growth of maritime trade between European States and the scramble for empire.[13] As the European powers expanded into the New World, "piracy

6 Bartolus of Saxoferrato, *De Captivis et Postliminio Reversis Rubrica* in *Apostilla domini Bartoli de Saxoferato super secunda parte Digesti novi* (Milan: Johanes Antoni de Donato, 1486); translated in Daniel Heller-Roazen, *The Enemy of All: Piracy and the Law of Nations* (Brooklyn: Zone Books, 2009), 103.

7 *Six Livres de la Republique,* (1576), Book 1, Chapter 1, translated in Walter Rech, *Enemies of Mankind: Vattel's Theory of Collective Security* (Leiden: Martinus Nijhoff, 2013), 51.

8 *De Re Militari et Bello Tractatus* (1563) (trans. Herbert C. Nutting) (Oxford: Clarendon, 1936), 83.

9 *Three Books on the Law of War and on the Duties Connected with War and on Military Discipline* (1582), ed. John Westlake (Washington DC: Carnegie, 1912), 11–12, 59 and 66.

10 Thomas Heebøll-Holm, *Ports, Piracy and Maritime War: Piracy in the English Channel and the Atlantic, c. 1280 – c. 1330* (Leiden: Brill, 2013), 14.

11 Alberico Gentili, *De Jure Belli Libri Tres* (trans. John C. Rolfe) (Oxford: Clarendon Press, 1933).

12 Hugo Grotius, *The Rights of War and Peace* (ed. Richard Tuck), (Indianapolis: Liberty Fund, 2005).

13 P.W. Birnie, "Piracy: Past, Present and Future", 11 *Marine Policy* (1987) 163, 164; Lauren Benton, "Toward a New Legal History of Piracy: Maritime Legalities and the Myth of Universal Jurisdiction", 23 *International Journal of Maritime History* (2011) 225, 225.

was never far behind, a persistent irritant snapping at the heels of legitimate commerce and snatching what takings it could".[14] Just as ancient Rome had responded to crippling trade stagnation and subsequent grain famine, so history repeated itself. Fresh ideas were required for the containment of the old menace – an adage that, incidentally, rings equally true for modern day piracy.[15]

Alberico Gentili's background placed him in a unique position to contemplate the "pirate problem". Italian by birth (San Ginesio, 1552), Gentili took a professorship at Oxford in 1587 and later practised as a Spanish advocate to the English Admiralty Court.[16] Gentili was a major contributor to the emergence of the law of nations as a scholarly discipline and has since proved to be deeply influential in terms of his scholarly contribution to the debate on piracy.[17] His work has faced critiqued, however, for being heavily reliant on Roman sources (making frequent reference to Cicero) and neglecting contemporary thought and practice, having "no desire to discuss questions of fact".[18] Nevertheless, Gentili's "mistakes about Roman beliefs and practices became our starting points and our commonplaces", while his account is "standardly included in the account of how we have come to understand pirates as the enemies of all humanity".[19]

Working roughly thirty years later than Gentili, Leiden-born Hugo Grotius (b. 1583) is today regarded as "the father of international law" for his original

---

14 David Cordingly and John Falconer, *Pirates: Fact & Fiction* (London: Collins & Brown Ltd, 1992), 67.

15 Discussed *infra*, 7.2.

16 Benedict Kingsbury and Benjamin Straumann, "Introduction" in Kingsbury and Straumann (eds), *The Roman Foundations of the Law of Nations* (Oxford: OUP, 2010), 1, 5.

17 As recognised in, e.g.: Alfred P. Rubin, *The Law of Piracy* (Honolulu: University Press of the Pacific, 2006), 28; M. Cherif Bassiouni, "The History of Universal Jurisdiction and Its Place in International Law" in Stephen Macedo (ed.), *Universal Jurisdiction: National Courts and the Prosecution of Serious Crimes under International Law* (Philadelphia: University of Pennsylvania Press, 2004) 39, 47; Harry D, Gould, "Cicero's Ghost: Rethinking the Social Construction of Piracy", in Michael J. Struett, Jon D. Carlson, and Mark T. Nance (eds), *Maritime Piracy and the Construction of Global Governance* (New York: Routledge, 2013) 23, 30–31; Theodor Meron, "Common Rights of Mankind in Gentili, Grotius and Suarez", 85 *American Journal of International Law* (1991) 110, 116; and Lauren Benton, *A Search for Sovereignty: Law and Geography in European Empires, 1400–1900* (Cambridge: CUP, 2010), 124–126.

18 Gentili, *supra* no11, 21. See also Andreas Wagner, "Lessons of Imperialism and of the Law of Nations: Alberico Gentili's Early Modern Appeal to Roman Law", 23 *European Journal of International Law* (2012) 873, suggesting that Gentili "relied very much on mechanisms, arguments, and analogies from Roman civil law, and there is not the slightest hint of a possible check of their being in the general, i.e. global or universal, interest".

19 Gould, *supra* no17, 30–31.

formulation of international law,[20] even if his "work bristles with borrowings" from Cicero and the Roman notion of the *jus gentium*.[21] Like Gentili before him, Grotius has also had a lasting influence in terms of expositing piracy and, in particular, its subjection to universal jurisdiction.[22] His work regarding piracy stems from a request made to him by the *Vereenigde Oostindische Compagnie* (Dutch United East India Company, "VOC") to write a report justifying the seizure of the richly laden Portuguese vessel *Santa Catarina* by the VOC in the Strait of Singapore in 1603.[23] The seizure, by a Dutch merchant, was viewed as retaliation for several Portuguese transgressions against the Dutch in southeast Asia, for instance the 1602 sacking of the Dutch-held "Spice Islands" (today part of Indonesia) and, later the same year, the execution of seventeen Dutch sailors for mistakenly entering the harbour at Macau.[24] The resulting text, *De Jure Praedae* ("The Law of Prize and Booty", c. 1604),[25] was a remarkably expansive analysis of State relations via international law, as part of which Grotius characterised the right to trade as an immovable, God-given entitlement.[26] Perhaps counter-intuitively, then, Grotius' "defence of an act of piracy turned out to be the starting point for modern international maritime law".[27] *De Jure Praedae* was never published (at least until its rediscovery in the nineteenth

20 Hamilton Vreeland, Jr, *Hugo Grotius: The Father of the Modern Science of International Law* (Oxford: OUP, 1917).

21 Edwin DeWitt Dickinson, "The Analogy between Natural Persons and International Persons in the Law of Nations" 26 *Yale Law Journal* (1917) 564, 568.

22 Grotius has often been cited to justify claims to universal jurisdiction; see, e.g., *A-G Israel v. Eichmann* (1961) (District Court), 36 *International Law Reports* (1968), para, 14; In re *Piracy Jure Gentium* [1934] AC 586 (UK); *Bonnet's Trial*, 15 State Trials (Howell) 1231, 1235 (Am. Vice Adm. 1718) (UK); *United States v Smith*, 18 US 5 Wheat 153 (1820), 163–166; International Court of Justice, Case Concerning the Arrest Warrant Of 11 April 2000 (*Democratic Republic of the Congo v. Belgium*) (2002), Dissenting opinion of Judge van den Wyngaert, para. 59 (p154); *Seychelles v. Mohamed Ahmed Ise & Four Others* (June 30, 2011); *Seychelles v Houssein Mohammed Osman & Ten Others* (October 12, 2011); Maria Gavouneli, *Functional Jurisdiction in the Law of the Sea* (Leiden: Martinus Nijhoff, 2007), 20; Meron, *supra* n017, 112; Eric A. Heinze, "A Global War on Piracy? International Law and the Use of Force against Sea Pirates" in Struett *et al* (eds), *supra* n017, 47, 49.

23 Stephen C. Neff, "Introduction" in Hugo Grotius, *On the Law of War and Peace*, (ed. Neff) (Cambridge: CUP, 2012) xv.

24 Martine Julia van Ittersum, "Introduction" in Hugo Grotius, *Commentary on the Law of Prize and Booty De Jure Praedae* (ed. Ittersum) (Indianapolis: Liberty Fund Inc, 2006), xix.

25 *De Jure Praedae*, *ibid.*

26 Ileana M. Porras, "Constructing International Law in the East Indian Seas: Property, Sovereignty, Commerce and War in Hugo Grotius' *De Iure Praedae*, or 'On how to Distinguish Merchants from Pirates'", 31 *Brooklyn Journal of International Law* (2005–06) 741, 755.

27 William Langewiesche, *The Outlaw Sea: A World of Freedom, Chaos and Crime* (New York, NY: North Point Press, 2004), 36.

century) as it was deemed too inflammatory, the Dutch fearing that it would stoke tensions with the Portuguese.[28] The twelfth chapter of the text, however, was repurposed and published anonymously, in 1609, as *Mare Liberum* ("The Free Sea"), a seminal redefining of the high seas as a "common good" accessible to all.[29]

Grotius' later life, however, was an unhappy one. He was imprisoned in 1618 for his part in a *coup d'état* and, though he later escaped, he was forced to live the remainder of his life in exile.[30] He remained productive, though; exiled in Paris, Grotius wrote his most influential work, *De Jure Belli ac Pacis*, a thesis on the laws of war that, *inter alia*, denounced the pirate as a threat to civilised Statehood and the common inheritance of the free sea.[31]

This chapter studies and compares the relevant works of Gentili and Grotius insofar as they relate to piracy and universal jurisdiction more generally. The two scholars were unique in terms of their approach to these topics. Gentili, for instance, was primarily concerned with defining Statehood and elaborating the right to "just" war, with piracy posited as a peripheral activity with no place in the system. Grotius built upon these arguments, being more concerned with mainstreaming the right to trade and the crucial role of the free sea in ensuring this right, with pirates cast as antagonists to a mercantile utopia. These scholarly works are analysed against the historical context provided in Chapter 3 and juxtaposed with Lord Coke's alternative domestic viewpoint.[32] Part 4.1 introduces and compares each scholar's *conception* of piracy – its definition and its place within the international legal system – while Part 4.2 examines the consequences of drawing this distinction, discussing each writer's conception of jurisdiction over piracy. Part 4.3 provides a conclusion to the findings in the chapter, looks at the legacies left by Gentili and Grotius, and assesses their overall contribution to the development of universal jurisdiction. This study forms a critical philosophical backdrop to the emergence of universal jurisdiction over piracy in the late seventeenth and early eighteenth centuries, as examined in Chapter 5.

---

28 Martine Julia van Ittersum, "Preparing *Mare Liberum* for the Press: Hugo Grotius' Rewriting of Chapter 12 of *De iure praedae* in November-December 1608" in Hans W. Blom (ed.), *Property, Piracy and Punishment: Hugo Grotius on War and Booty in De Iure Praedae: Concepts and Contexts* (Boston, MA: Brill, 2009) 246, 251.

29 Hugo Grotius, *Mare Liberum 1609–2009* (ed. Robert Feenstra) (Leiden: Brill, 2009).

30 Jonathan M. Israel, *The Dutch Republic: Its Rise, Greatness, and Fall, 1477–1806* (Oxford: Clarendon, 1995), 433–449.

31 Discussed *infra*, 4.1.3.

32 3.2.3, *supra*.

As always, a certain amount of caution is required when reading these works, given that "[w]e can only guess at the motivations of the actors and at the association of ideas which coloured their understanding of what they were 'up to'".[33] With this in mind, references to the relevant works are set within their broader context throughout.

4.1 Defining the Pirate

> When a king brands us pirates, he doesn't mean to make us adversaries. He doesn't mean to make us criminals. He means to make us monsters. For that's the only way his God-fearing, taxpaying subjects can make sense of men who keep what is theirs and fear no one.
>
> CAPTAIN FLINT, *Black Sails*[34]

The fictional Captain Flint provides a fair assessment of how State governments sought to portray pirates from the early 1600s onwards. It was a characterisation deliberately intended to dehumanise, to provoke disgust and to justify destroying the pirate way of life. The besmirching of pirates in this way was intended to ensure the supremacy of the State over those who sought to subvert it. This "monstrous" archetype of piracy permeates the works of Grotius and Gentili (indeed, Captain Flint keeps a copy of Grotius' *De Jure Belli ac Pacis* in his cabin, this being perhaps the source of his concerns).[35]

Defining "piracy", though, was no straightforward task. State-sponsored privateers existed alongside stateless pirates, the two largely identical except for the identity of their patrons.[36] Even the term "pirate" had no agreed definition; according to Cicero, the pirate represented an outmoded form of society and politics that did not correlate with civilised Statehood[37] whereas sixteenth and seventeenth century domestic legal approaches characterised pirates more concretely as treasonous "robbers upon the sea" punishable by their home State.[38] Often, though, the term was intended simply as a pejorative, devoid of legal purpose.[39]

33 Porras, *supra* no26, 747.
34 Episode "I" (2014, dir. Neil Marshall).
35 *Ibid.*
36 3.1, *supra*.
37 2.2, *supra*.
38 3.2.2, *supra*. See also Rubin, *supra* no17, 66.
39 See examples at 3.1, *supra*.

Although defining "piracy" appears to be a Sisyphean task, there appeared to be general agreement on what the pirate was *supposed* to represent: namely, the subversion of Statehood (or of recognised political authority), a figure that civilisation could unite against and, inversely, define itself. We meet this theme of division again with Gentili's *de Jure Belli Libri Tres*, as detailed in Section 4.1.1. We then turn to Grotius' definition of piracy (which posits the piracy as an enemy of inter-State trade), as outlined in his books *De Jure Praedae* and *De Jure Belli ac Pacis*, in Sections 4.1.2 and 4.1.3 respectively.

4.1.1 *The Pirate and the State in Gentili's* De Jure Belli Libri Tres

> [T]he power of the sword not being committed into your hands by any lawful authority, you were not empowered to use any force.[40]
>
> JUDGE NICHOLAS TROTT, *Bonnet's Trial*

Alberico Gentili was the first scholar to develop a systematic concept of piracy as part of an international law framework,[41] dealing with it as an aside to the main theme of his thesis, namely, the laws of war, both *ad bellum* and *in bello*.[42] By focusing on the nature of the State, Gentili defined the pirate by what it *was not* than by what it *was*.

Gentili uses "*piratis*" throughout *De Jure Belli Libri Tres* to refer to "pirate(s)" (as it is always interpreted in the English translation).[43] It is not possible to discern exactly who Gentili intended to apply the term to, particularly as examples throughout his thesis are scarce. The term could have been intended to apply to "raiding communities" akin to the Cilicians or, conversely, to the "sea-robber" pirates that had by this time become a serious problem off the English coasts. Gentili's intended target is, for his purposes, largely unimportant given his intention to broadly distinguish "States" from unacceptable "others". His employment of the term "*piratis*" could therefore effectively embrace any non-State actor engaged in plunder (including the different conceptions of "pirates" just described), thereby falling outside the protective embrace of Gentili's developmental international law.

40 *Bonnet's Trial, supra* n022.

41 Michael Kempe, "'Even in the Remotest Corners of the World': Globalised Piracy and International Law, 1500–1900", 5 *Journal of Global History* (2010) 353, 355.

42 Gentili believed himself the originator of the laws of war; see Randall Lesaffer, "Alberico Gentili's *ius post bellum* and Early Modern Peace Treaties", in Kingsbury and Straumann (eds), *supra* n016, 210, 211–212.

43 *Supra* n011.

The principal manner in which Gentili distinguishes "pirates" from "States" (or, in his own terms, "sovereigns") is through his claim that "war is [only] waged by sovereigns".[44] This is because *only* sovereigns, as the manifestation of civilised society, possess no "earthly judge" to settle disputes between them.[45] Pirates and brigands ("*piratis et latrunculis*" in Gentili's original Latin),[46] in contrast, fall under the earthly power and jurisdiction of States and therefore claim no independent right to settle disputes by war ("the arbitrage of Mars").[47] Under this analysis pirates were sovereign subjects.[48] Logically, then, Gentili's negative definition of the pirate ought to be dependent on a positive definition of the "sovereign" State (such as "wholly free Venice", offered as a sole example).[49]

Gentili's definition of the sovereign State is, however, not straightforward. Various attributes indicating sovereign Statehood are scattered throughout his thesis. For instance, Gentili appears to require a certain level of organisation ("a senate, a treasury, united and harmonious citizens, and some basis for a treaty of peace")[50] and a "just motive" for war.[51] The latter criterion is a variable dependent on the relevant "cause" for war, so that "[t]he claim to the title of general will be justified, not so much by the command of a regular army or by the capture of cities [...] as by the assumption of a public cause".[52] We can discern from Gentili's 1599 history of Rome, *De Armis Romanis*, that the "public cause" criterion required wars to be fought with "valour", "virtue" and "justice".[53] Gentili provides a rare example to clarify his point regarding "virtue" by referencing the history of the Roman foe Viriathus, leader of the Lusitanian people from around 147 to 139 BC. The Romans' initial attempt to take Lusitania (roughly synonymous with modern day Portugal) ended in a humiliating defeat which in turn forced them into a treaty. Viriathus was subsequently declared an ally of Rome, leading Roman historian Cassius Dio to praise Viriathus

44 This is the title of Chapter 3 of Gentili's *De Jure Belli Libri Tres*, *ibid.*

45 *Ibid.*, 15–17, elaborating that "[w]ar is made against those who cannot be controlled by the laws, but judicial decisions are rendered in the case of private citizens" (22).

46 Gentili, *ibid.*, 20.

47 *Ibid.*, 15 and 20. To do so was punishable by death (20).

48 *Ibid.*, 15 and 22.

49 *Ibid.*, 21.

50 *Ibid.*, 25. Gentili's language is an echo of Cicero's claim that a commonwealth (or *res publica*) should possess an *imperium* (executive), *consilium* (a council to advise on policy) and *libertas* (freedom for the citizen); Cicero, *De Republica*, (54–51 BC), trans. Clinton Walker Keyes (London: Heinemann, 1928) Book 1, ss 41 and 69, Book 2 ss 56–57, 69.

51 Gentili, *ibid.*, 25.

52 *Ibid.*

53 Diego Panizza, "Alberico Gentili's *De Armis Romanis:* The Roman Model of the Just Empire" in Kingsbury and Straumann (eds), *supra* no16, 53, at 54–60.

for having fought with honour and for his people rather than for the spoils of war.[54] According to Gentili, Viriathus "turned from private brigandage to the defence of his country's cause, became a general instead of a brigand, and may be said to have waged war. The Roman people accordingly made a treaty of peace with him".[55] The evolution of Viriathus' status appears to have been provoked by his successful resistance to the Roman advance, so that his appraisal was likely intended as a propaganda exercise designed to save embarrassment. Having been pushed back by the Lusitanians, it suited the Roman cause to entreat with them, necessitating Viriathus' elevation in stature.

If we apply this logic, the assumption of "just motive" (and, consequently, Statehood) appears to be a subjective variable determined by established States to further their own designs. In Gentili's example it was left to Rome to characterise the legal nature of Viriathus' wars against them. His characterisation of "just motive" is to be judged by those who hold the sway of power, *viz.* Rome in ancient times and (to cite Gentili's only example), Venice in the late sixteenth century.[56] The approach is one of "legality over legitimacy"[57] or "prescription [over] description"[58] with the result that "a single ruler could, by fiat, decide which enemies were legitimate representatives of a State and which, by contrast, were mere 'bandits'".[59] Under this analysis pirates became a political creation and, moreover, "an incredibly charged tool, because once an enemy was denied access to international law, he was severely discriminated against and could be dealt with accordingly".[60] The account of Viriathus appears to validate this claim, as do the relevant histories charted in Chapter 3, wherein the Statehood of polities such as the Barbary States were shown to hinge on their political recognition by existing "peer polity" States.[61] The consequence is that "[t]he international body of law concerning universal jurisdiction is, then,

54 Cassius Dio, *History of Rome* (c. 229 AD), transl. E. Cary (Cambridge, MA: Loeb Classical Library, 1924), Book XXII (Chapters 73–78).

55 Gentili, *supra* n011, 24–25. See Thomas Grünewald, *Bandits in the Roman Empire: Myth and Reality* (1999), translated by John Drinkwater (London: Routledge, 2004), Chapter 2, describing Viriathus' characterisation as a "noble bandit" in contrast to Tacferinas, the renegade Berber (discussed *supra* 2.1.3).

56 Gentili, *ibid.*, 21.

57 Rech, *supra* n07, 54.

58 Philip J. Stern, *The Company State: Corporate Sovereignty & the Early Modern Foundations of the British Empire in India* (Oxford: OUP, 2011), 9.

59 Heller-Roazen, *supra* n06, 109.

60 Peter Schröder, "Vitoria, Gentili, Bodin: Sovereignty and the Law of Nations" in Kingsbury and Straumann (eds), *supra* n016, 163, 178.

61 3.1, *supra*. For instance, Gentili considered the Barbary States to be "States" despite disapproving of their raids; *supra* n011, Book 1, 113.

perhaps paradoxically, a body of law propounded by civilised nations designed to address those who do not deserve to be protected by the laws of civilised nations",[62] a model that is "putatively universal but profoundly exclusive".[63] Through Gentili's reasoning we see a clear continuation of the Ciceronian distinction between "civilised" and "primordial" polities.[64] The distinction is also broadly synonymous with the modern ideal of the "international community" based around common notions of universal morality.[65]

There is an extra level of complexity, however, to Gentili's definition of the "State". The idea of "virtue", while ultimately being a subjective construct, is nevertheless based on an objective assessment of the community in question. The example of Viriathus would seem to suggest that "rebels", while not meeting the standard of a fully constituted Gentilian "sovereign", could nevertheless be honoured as civilised *hostes* if pursuing a "just" or "virtuous" cause. Broadly speaking, Gentili confirms that rebels "who have proved false to friendship, to a treaty, or even to voluntary dependence" can nevertheless retain the rights of war and the other privileges of the law of nations if they retain this "virtuous" aspect to their campaigns.[66] Pirates and brigands, on the contrary, were effectively "rebels without a cause". Put another way, "[i]t is impossible to pretend that acts which are done for the purpose of setting up a legal state of things [...] are piratical for want of an external recognition of their validity".[67] As expressed by Balthasar de Ayala, a community of pirates associated together "with wrongdoing and dishonesty for its object"[68] as opposed to the "virtuous" ends of the civilised "Ciceronian" State, associated "for the peaceable enjoyment of their own rights".[69] We can attach labels, then, to the sovereign State and the antithetical pirate – but those labels can only be attached by those with "lawful authority" to do so, those "holding the sword" (to borrow from Judge Trott's analogy in the *Bonnet* case).[70]

---

62 Jody Greene, "*Hostis Humani Generis*" 34 *Critical Enquiry* (2008) 683, 700.

63 Frédéric Mégret, "From 'savages' to 'unlawful combatants': a postcolonial look at international humanitarian law's 'other'" in Anne Orford (ed.), *International Law and its Others* (Cambridge: CUP, 2006) 265, 312.

64 Cicero, *De Officiis*, III, s.107 (ed. Walter Miller, with an English Translation; Cambridge, MA: Harvard University Press, 1913); discussed *supra*, 2.2.

65 Policante, *supra* n03, 169–172. See also *infra*, 8.1.

66 *Supra* n011, 24.

67 William E. Hall, *International Law*, 8th ed. (Oxford: Clarendon, 1924), 310–311.

68 *Supra* n09.

69 Grotius, *Belli ac Pacis, supra* n012, III.III.II. See also 4.1.3, *infra*.

70 *Supra* n040 and accompanying text.

Gentili took up Cicero's theme of universal enmity towards the ill-defined "*piratae*" and "endowed [it] with greater precision",[71] reintroducing it for a new audience that needed a line of separation, particularly given the prevalence of privateers and existence of quasi-State polities such as the Uskoks.[72] He sought to portray a neatly divided world of lawfully existing States and "outsiders", the latter being non-State "systemic enemies"[73] who did not fit the ideals of the system. The taxonomy allowed Gentili to incriminate "pirates" while sparing privateers (or regular naval forces) who also engaged in freebooting.[74]

Gentili's strict delineations are misleadingly absolutist in a world of fluid political systems, "defined not by singular, sovereign monocracies but intersecting empires, pluralistic legal cultures, and a variety of shapes and forms of hybrid and competing jurisdictions".[75] The elusive nature of the Barbary States,[76] the competing principalities of the Holy Roman Empire,[77] and the "spiritual" jurisdiction of the Pope over much of Europe[78] bear historical witness to this geo-political smorgasbord. *De Jure Belli Libri Tres* represented an idealistic world of clearly defined States and subjects, an oversimplification that betrays, perhaps, an anxiety that in fact the perfect sovereign State did not (yet) exist.[79]

Gentili's strict separation of "sovereign State" from "pirate" nevertheless forms a central component of the identity of the pirate today. Judge Moore, in his dissenting opinion to the *Lotus* case, reflected this in his claim that:

---

71 Kempe, *supra* no41, 356.

72 Alberto Tenenti, *Piracy and the Decline of Venice 1580–1615* (London: Longmans, 1961), 3. See also 3.1, *supra*.

73 Policante, *supra* no3, 134.

74 Regarding privateering, Gentili states that a privateer may be regarded as part of a sovereign State "from letters of their king" (*supra* no11, 26). Discussed at 3.1, *supra*.

75 Stern, *supra* no58, 9.

76 The Barbary States have variously been described as vassal States of the Ottoman Empire, sovereign States in their own right, or "pirate States"; see Janice E. Thomson, *Mercenaries, Pirates and Sovereigns* (Princeton, New Jersey: Princeton University Press, 1994), 45, and Rech, *supra* no7, 44–46.

77 See, e.g., William E. Conklin, *Hegel's Laws: The Legitimacy of a Modern Legal Order* (Stanford, CA: Stanford University Press, 2008), 16.

78 Anne Orford, "Jurisdiction Without Territory: From the Holy Roman Empire to the Responsibility to Protect" 30 *Michigan Journal of International Law* (2009) 981, 984–988; Stuart Elden, *The Birth of Territory* (Chicago: University of Chicago Press, 2013), 180–210.

79 Per Lesaffer, *supra* no42, 215, "the State itself had not yet set itself up as an externally or internally sovereign body politic holding exclusive jurisdiction over its territory and monopolising its external relations".

> acts of piracy by law of nations [...] are done under conditions which render it impossible or unfair to hold any State responsible for their commission; [...] a pirate either belongs to no State or organized political society, or by the nature of his act he has shown his intention and his power to reject the authority of that to which he is properly subject.[80]

Judge Moore drew on Gentili's basic argument in suggesting that pirates seek to subvert State authority and the idealistic Ciceronian commonwealth upon which this is based.[81] Because the pirate effectively challenged the orthodoxies and expectations of civilised Statehood, with its "associat[ion] for the peaceable enjoyment of [individual] rights",[82] it represented the antithesis of the State, a larcenous society that stole from others purely for private gain.

In summary, Gentili suggested that the designation of "pirate" is effectively decided by whoever "holds the sword".[83] The pervasive, neo-Ciceronian logic espoused by Gentili has proved deeply influential in terms of how we view piracy today and has moulded the basic principles of modern international law. It forms the basis for the use of universal jurisdiction in terms of identifying those who may be subjected to it. Consequently,

> the old antagonist – criminal and enemy – stepped forward in a new and unfamiliar light. His former insignificance now concealed an unexpected relevance. On account of the indeterminate hostility that defined him as "the enemy of the human species", the pirate was suddenly the agent of the political and legal movement.[84]

4.1.2 *Piracy, Commerce and the Free Sea in Grotius'* **De Jure Praedae**

If Alberico Gentili presented a rudimentary characterisation of piracy defined as a foil to the "sovereign State", then Hugo Grotius added substance to that proposition. The first of Grotius' major works, *De Jure Praedae*, presented pirates as adversaries to the universally applicable ideal of the free sea. Inter-State trade and communication occurred almost exclusively by way of the sea,

80 Permanent Court of International Justice, *The Case of the S.S. Lotus*, 1927, dissenting opinion of Judge Moore, 69, para. 5, internal quotation marks omitted.

81 Gerry Simpson, "Piracy and the Origins of Enmity", in Matthew Craven, Malgosia Fitzmaurice and Maria Vogiatzi (eds), *Time, History and International Law* (Leiden: Martinus Nijhoff, 2007), 219, 228.

82 Grotius, *Belli ac Pacis*, *supra* no12, III.III.II.

83 To paraphrase from *Bonnet*, *supra* no22.

84 Heller-Roazen, *supra* no6, 160.

so that piracy posed a genuine threat to the emerging international economy.[85] An act of similar gravity today might consist in shutting down the Internet, a disaster that would likely set civilisation back by decades. Thus, the content of *De Jure Praedae*, originally intended as a comment on a single hostile act in a faraway sea (the *Santa Catarina* seizure),[86] became a deeply relevant comment on the character of the pirate, recasting him as the archvillain of the age.

Grotius employs the terms "*piratae*" and "*praedones*" when describing pirates in the original Latin of *De Jure Praedae*, although he apparently intends subtly different meanings.[87] "*Piratae*" are specifically described as individuals "who despoil others through privately exercised force and without urgent reasons to do", whereas "*praedones*" appears to refer to "persons who without any legitimate cause usurp authority to wage public war", with the example of Cilicians and Normans given.[88] The difference between the two terms thus appears to relate to the intentions of the group being described when carrying out acts that resemble piracy. The identification of "*praedones*" with Cilician pirates or Normans suggests that Grotius intended to apply this term to highly organised societies bearing a resemblance to or claiming to be States ("public" piracy), whereas "*piratae*" appears to be more closely matched to the modern definition of pirate as "sea-robber" ("private" piracy).[89] Both terms are translated into the English version as "pirate" or sometimes "freebooter".

The free sea represented, for Grotius, a natural law right that had subsisted since time immemorial,[90] "a primary rule or first principle [of the law of nations], the spirit of which is self-evident and immutable"[91] and an essential

85 Kenneth Randall, "Universal Jurisdiction under International Law", 66 *Texas Law Review* (1987–88) 785, 793–794.

86 Neff, *supra* no23, xv.

87 Latin original text (Leiden: Martinus Nijhoff, 1868), 308. Conversely, the two terms appear to be used interchangeably by Cicero: *Verrine Orations*, II, 4.23 (original Latin in William Peterson (ed.), Oxford: Clarendon, 1917); English translation by C.D. Yonge, London: George Bell & Sons, 1903). See also 2.2, *supra*.

88 *De Jure Praedae*, *supra* no24, 447.

89 See Michael Kempe, "Beyond the Law: The Image of Piracy in the Legal Writings of Hugo Grotius" in Blom (ed.), *supra* no28, 379, 382, suggesting that "Grotius distinguishes [...] between private sea-robbery by *piratae* and public sea-robbery by *praedones*". No explicit distinction is made by the author in the later *De Jure Belli ac Pacis*.

90 Jeroen Vervliet, "Introduction" to *Mare Liberum*, *supra* no29, xv-xviii. On the chequered history of the law of the sea since Roman times see R.P. Anand, *Origin and Development of the Law of the Sea* (The Hague: Martinus Nijhoff, 1983), Chapter 2. Curiously, Grotius considered the Mediterranean to be a "mere gulf" (as opposed to a "vast maritime tract") which *could* be claimed as territory by the Genoese and Venetians; *Mare Liberum*, 49–50.

91 *Mare Liberum*, *ibid.*, 7.

component of the universally applicable *jus gentium*.[92] Grotius conceived of the sea as a jurisdictional void (or "state of nature"),[93] where "the situation becomes very much what it was before States and courts of justice were established"[94] and, accordingly, "the private actor returned to his original sovereignty and could engage in just war" without requiring the authority or encountering the judgement of the State.[95] Just as Julius Caesar had captured and crucified the pirates who held him hostage,[96] so the right to exact one's own personal retribution lay in *every* human being when removed from the apparatus of the State.[97]

The notion of the "free sea" (and associated "private war") formed, for Grotius, part of the larger principle of "*libertas commerciorum*", the universal right to unhindered trade, itself a divine and inalienable right of States.[98] Interference with trade, Grotius reasoned, was a universal offence, there being "no stronger reason underlying our abhorrence of robbers and pirates than the fact that they besiege and render unsafe the thoroughfares of human intercourse".[99] The claim mirrored Roman concerns about the disruption of trade by pirates, a threat to the dominant "sub-species" of human, "*homo economicus*".[100] It was interference with this universal right that made pirates such heinous and hateworthy beings (the archenemy of *homo economicus*) and granted States the right to retaliate[101] (including, ultimately, via the collective right of universal jurisdiction). The central importance of trade as a right of States was not a

92 *Ibid.*, 12.

93 Per Carl Schmitt, *The Nomos of the Earth* (1950) (trans. G.L. Ulmen) (New York: Telos Press, 2003), 43, "[t]he sea has no *character*, in the original sense of the word, which comes from the Greek *charessein*, meaning to engrave, to scratch, to imprint".

94 *De Jure Praedae*, *supra* no24, 138.

95 Porras, *supra* no26, 788–789, explaining that "when judicial means for the attainment of his rights proved defective, the individual was in Grotius' view still privileged to execute his own rights. [...] [I]ndividuals are returned to their original state before civil law and are freed to become judges and executors in their own case, or, in other words, to engage in just private war in response to an injury". Grotius clarifies that for "war" to be "just" "one must consider the causes involved [:] defence, recovery, punishment [and] whenever obligations are not duly discharged" (*ibid.*, 105). Action against pirates likely falls under a "defensive" cause (see, e.g., *United States v. Ambrose Light*, 25 F. 408, 413 (S.D.N.Y. 1885)).

96 See 2.1.4, *supra*.

97 Though as we will see, Grotius favoured the delegation of this private "vendetta" back to the State: *infra*, 4.2.2.

98 Ruth Lapidoth, "Freedom of Navigation – its Legal History and its Normative Basis" 6 *Journal of Maritime Law & Commerce* (1975) 259, 271.

99 *De Jure Praedae*, *supra* no24, 220.

100 Greene, *supra* no62, 696.

101 Gould, *supra* no17, 34.

new notion; Spanish theologian Francisco de Vitoria, for instance, had written that the right to trade was grounded in natural law, and that in certain circumstances the frustration of trade could provide sufficiently just cause for war.[102] Yet the right to trade, and to an untempered "free" sea upon which this could occur, was pertinent for renewed discussion given its increasing importance to emerging Westphalian States, fuelled by their commercial dealings with each other.[103] Grotius capitalised on the established "Ciceronian paradigm" of piracy to promote his own agenda of advancing the *libertas commerciorum*.[104]

By placing strong emphasis on the "free sea" norm and underlining its historic and universal pedigree, Grotius intended to highlight the fundamental importance of the "wrong" done to the Dutch by the Portuguese in the East Indies, providing a moral and legal basis for the subsequent seizure of the *Santa Catarina*.[105] When set against the context of Gentili's discourse on piracy, Grotius' claim that Portugal itself could be "piratical" seems anomalous,[106] though it is likely Grotius intended to illustrate the perceived wrong done by the Portuguese by branding them, pejoratively, as "pirates".[107]

With the free sea and the *libertas commerciorum* established as the normative basis for his work, Grotius went on to define piracy as an opposing force, characterising it as "dishonourable [despoliation of] others through privately exercised force and without urgent reasons for so doing", upon the high seas.[108] Grotius clarified that one could judge whether a suspected pirate possessed "honour" by establishing "the end sought"[109] – a position reminiscent of Gentili's example of Viriathus and the idea that war could be "just" if fought for honourable reasons (subject to the endorsement of sovereign State power

102 *De Indis*, 1532; discussed in Alex J. Bellamy, *Just Wars: From Cicero to Iraq* (Cambridge: Wiley, 2006), 51.

103 Benedict Kingsbury and Adam Roberts, "Grotian Thought in International Relations", in Hedley Bull, Benedict Kingsbury and Adam Roberts (eds), *Hugo Grotius and International Relations*, (Oxford: OUP, 2002), 1.

104 2.3.1, *supra*.

105 Porras, *supra* no26, 788.

106 Grotius described the Portuguese as "not very different from pirates. For if the name of 'pirate' ("*piratis*") is appropriately bestowed upon men who blockade the seas and impede the progress of international commerce, shall we not include under the same head those persons who forcibly bar all European nations [...] from the ocean [?]": *De Jure Praedae*, *supra* no24, 449.

107 Porras, *supra* no26, 788; The accusation of piracy was used equally by the Portuguese against the Dutch: Kempe, "Beyond the Law", *supra* no89, 385–386.

108 *De Jure Praedae, supra* no24, 447.

109 *Ibid.*, 455.

brokers).[110] Grotius added that "dishonourable" despoilers "incur universal detestation, since by audacious but unwarlike devices they turn public loss into private gain, a course of conduct clearly incompatible not only with justice but also with fortitude, the virtue wherein legitimate enemies vie with one another".[111] An attack made by pirates "neither weakens the enemy to any appreciable extent nor advances the interests of his own side"[112] so that it is meaningless, devoid of "fortitude", as defined here by Grotius.

We are provided, then, with a more elaborate analysis of how, exactly, pirates are distinguished from States. Whereas both engage in plunder, the motivation of the pirate is "private gain" as opposed to the "fortitudinous" (or "virtuous") appropriation carried out by the State. Grotius' position relies heavily on the "Ciceronian paradigm",[113] adding to the rich history of discussion that went before, whereby the pirate was said to be "beyond the pale" of civilisation.[114] It nevertheless also adds texture to the basic Ciceronian or Gentilian position by positing the pirate as an endemic threat to the sacrosanct right to trade. Through this analysis the defining feature of the pirate shifts from the stateless status of the offender (*per* Cicero, Gentili) to an identity that combines status with purpose. In so doing, Grotius takes us towards the commonly accepted modern-day definition of piracy, as set out in the 1982 United Nations Convention on the Law of the Sea (UNCLOS): "acts of violence or detention, or any act of depredation, committed for private ends by the crew or the passengers of a private ship".[115] The definition requires a specific *act* by a specific *actor*.

Although *De Jure Praedae* was never published (at least until its nineteenth century rediscovery), the twelfth chapter of the treatise was published anonymously in 1609 as *Mare Liberum*, which the Dutch government considered a sufficiently concise and objective treatise on the VOC's right to trade and navigate freely in the East Indies.[116] That Grotius approached the subject from a position of some partiality is not in doubt, the intention of the State-commissioned *De Jure Praedae* and the watered down *Mare Liberum* being, in effect, "a political tract advancing monopoly claims involving unimpeded Dutch access to Asian

110 4.1.1, *supra*. See also Michael Kempe, "Beyond the Law", *supra* no89, 380–381, suggesting that pirates serve to distinguish right from wrong in Grotius' works.

111 *De Jure Praedae, supra* no24, 449.

112 *Ibid.*

113 2.1.3, *supra*.

114 Belli, *supra* no8, 83.

115 Article 101.

116 Ittersum, "Introduction" to *De Jure Praedae, supra* no24, xxi; David Armitage, "Introduction" in Hugo Grotius, *The Free Sea* (trans. Richard Hakluyt, ed. David Armitage) (Indianapolis: Liberty Fund, 2004), xv-xx.

trade" as opposed to "a legal treatise about the freedom of the seas".[117] Nevertheless, despite an initial negative response to *Mare Liberum*,[118] the freedom of navigation upon the high seas would gradually come to be accepted as a fundamental principle of international law from the second half of the seventeenth century onwards.[119] The Dutch authorities were among those who outwardly supported and promoted Grotius' views; a government proclamation from 1645 read "the entire existence and welfare, as well as the fame of the United Provinces, depends upon its shipping, and foreign trade, and commerce".[120] The publication concretely established the perception of the pirate as a thief not only of property but of a universal and sacrosanct right subsisting in the *res nullius* (or, better, *res communis*) of the high seas.

4.1.3 *"Confederated only to do Mischief": The Pirate in Grotius'* De Jure Belli ac Pacis

> What were these villains after but money? What do they care for but money? For what would they risk their rascal carcasses but money?
>
> SQUIRE TRELAWNEY, *Treasure Island*[121]

Squire Trelawney's account of the pirate mind is a caricature, an oversimplified perception of who pirates were and what they stood for (he would later be proved wrong, to an extent, by the ambiguous morality of Long John Silver). Yet his statement could easily substitute for Grotius' conceptualisation of piracy as fleshed out in his *magnum opus*, *De Jure Belli ac Pacis*. Grotius completed the work in exile from the Dutch Republic following his involvement in

117 Christopher R Rossi, *Sovereignty and Territorial Temptation* (Cambridge: CUP, 2017), 49.

118 The treatise was initially protested against by England and Scotland (Vervliet, *supra* n090, xx; Armitage, *ibid.*, xi) and in texts by the British writers William Welwood (*An Abridgement of All Sea Laws*, 1615), John Selden (*Mare Clausum*, "The Closed Sea", 1635), and Portuguese priest Seraphim de Freitas (*De Iusto Imperio Lusitanorum Asiatico*, 1625). These refutations of Grotius appeared to reflect actual practice: throughout the seventeenth century claims to "closed" seas were advanced by Denmark, Spain, Turkey, Portugal, Genoa, Tuscany, Venice, the Papacy and the Dutch (especially in the East Indies); see Israel, *supra* n030, 934–956, and WE Butler, "Grotius and the Law of the Sea" in Bull *et al* (eds), *supra* n0103, 209, 211–212.

119 See Anand, *supra* n090., 3, praising Grotius as "the first to proclaim the freedom of the seas by elaborate argument, which later came to be accepted as an unchallenged doctrine of international law". On the modern position see 1982 United Nations Convention on the Law of the Sea, Article 87, declaring that "the high seas are open to all States".

120 As reproduced in Virginia W. Lunsford, *Piracy and Privateering in the Golden Age Netherlands* (Gordonsville, VA: Palgrave Macmillan, 2005), 179.

121 Robert Louis Stevenson, *Treasure Island* (Boston: Roberts Brothers, 1884), 48.

an attempted *coup d'état*, freeing him from the overt political influence found in his earlier works. Grotius' approach to piracy in this work took him closer to Gentili's notion that pirates were set in opposition to civilised Statehood while simultaneously elaborating on the idea that pirate communities were intrinsically iniquitous,[122] a point developed in *De Jure Praedae*. At the core of Grotius' (re)conceptualisation is his assertion that

> a company of pirates and robbers [is not] to be reputed a State, though perhaps they may observe some kind of equity among themselves [...]. For [pirates] are associated on the account of their crimes; but [States], though sometimes not wholly guiltless, do associate for the peaceable enjoyment of their own rights, and to do right to foreigners, if not in all things according to the law of nature.[123]

Grotius adds that there is a great difference "between a nation, however wicked, and those who, not making a body of people, are confederated only to do mischief",[124] the latter having "no right of nations belonging to them".[125] The difference between "pirate" and "State", then, lies in their intrinsic nature, their *raison d'être*, a conceptualisation that builds upon the "fortitude" or "virtue" distinction drawn in *De Jure Praedae*.[126] Thus the pirate's persecution was not *simply* based on their tendency to attack ships and violate the sanctity of the free sea. Grotius' conceptualisation went further by incriminating the very nature and purpose of piratical communities, which were "associated on the account of their crimes".[127] Given the reasons for their association, their plunder could only be for their own private gain. To cite again from *De Jure Praedae*, "piratical" plunder "neither weakens the enemy to any appreciable extent nor advances the interests of his own side".[128] It serves no virtuous purpose. A "State", on the contrary, being associated "for peaceable enjoyment of

---

122 See Laurens Winkel, "Problems of Legal Systematisation from *De Iure Praedae* to *De Iure Belli ac Pacis*" in Blom (ed.), *supra* no28, 61, for an exploration of how Grotius' themes shift.

123 Grotius, *Belli ac Pacis, supra* no12, III.III.II.

124 *Ibid.* Pirates, Grotius confirms, are "notoriously wicked": III.XIX.III.

125 *Ibid.*, II.XVIII.II.

126 4.1.2, *supra*.

127 *Belli ac Pacis, supra* no12, III.III.II.

128 *De Jure Praedae, supra* no24, 449. Grotius added that that "Statehood" can additionally be measured by the possession of certain qualities, such as a "government of public Affairs, a public Council, a Treasury, the right of commanding the people by virtue of their consent and union, [and] the power of making peace and war": *ibid.*, III.I.I.

[individuals'] rights",[129] would remain a State even if "not wholly guiltless", suggesting that it could permissibly commit acts resembling piracy (as was indeed the case).[130] The presumption is that when States plunder the property of others, they do so in furtherance of a public cause. Once again, Grotius' argument is heavily indebted to Cicero's formulation of the *jus gentium*, inasmuch as he sought to distinguish "civilised" States from primordial piratical "others", depending on their core values (such as respect for commerce).[131] Empowering the latter would normalise and condone plunder economies, a course that would arguably lead to a "perpetual state of nature".[132]

Through his denunciation of piracy in *De Jure Belli ac Pacis*, Grotius helped to consolidate the archetypal view of the pirate as the "monsters" defined self-referentially by Captain Flint and the kleptomaniacs described by Squire Trelawney. Grotius helped to shape concepts of Statehood and international relations at a time (the Thirty Years War) when ideas about sovereignty were a violent flashpoint. He helped to develop the idea that States were fully independent and existed in an inclusive international society governed by moral dictates,[133] ideas that would in turn influence the terms of the 1648 Peace of Westphalia.[134]

When read together, Gentili and Grotius deliver a compound theory for why pirates came to be considered *hostes humani generis* and, ultimately, subject to universal jurisdiction. For Gentili this was about *authority* (or "who holds the sword") and *virtue*, a dual solution that hinged on subjective recognition by existing "peer polities". Grotius lent an abstract empiricism to the debate by insisting that the intrinsic nature or *raison d'être* of the polity was the key

129 *Belli ac Pacis, supra* n012, III.III.II.

130 Per Jan Klabbers, "Piracy in Global Law and Global Governance" in Panos Koutrakos and Achilles Skordas (eds), *The Law and Practice of Piracy at Sea: European and International Perspectives* (Oxford: Hart, 2014) 329, 330, "Grotius astutely noted that States too sometimes engage in uncommendable activities, rendering the distinction between States and pirates into one of degree rather than one of kind".

131 2.2, *supra*.

132 To borrow from Immanuel Kant, *The Metaphysics of Morals* (1797) s60, reproduced in HS Reiss, *Kant: Political Writings* (Cambridge: CUP, 1991). Kant is, here, concerned with the actions of the "unjust enemy", an actor whose "expressed will [...] displays a maxim which would make peace among nations impossible and would lead to a perpetual state of nature if it were made into a general rule". The crew of a democratically governed pirate ship might, nevertheless, consider themselves to be above this primordial natural state: Peter Hayes, "Pirates, Privateers and the Contract Theories of Hobbes and Locke" 39 *History of Political Thought* (2008) 461, 462.

133 See, e.g., G.I.A.D. Draper, "Grotius' Place in the Development of Legal Ideas about War" in Bull *et al* (eds), *supra* n0103, 177, 204–205.

134 Hedley Bull, "The Importance of Grotius in the Study of International Relations", in Bull *et al, ibid.*, 65, 75–76.

factor – pirates "turn public loss into private gain"[135] and exist *only* to plunder, as opposed to States, which exist to facilitate the rights of individuals.[136] Although States did engage in plunder they nevertheless did so for reasons that Gentili termed "just",[137] or that Grotius believed possessed "fortitude" or "virtue".[138] Together the scholars built upon and perpetuated the predominant "Ciceronian paradigm" of piracy.

It may seem counterintuitive that the "heinousness" of piracy is largely an issue of identity and constitution rather than of action. This is in contrast to modern examples of universal jurisdiction over "core" international crimes such as genocide, crimes against humanity or war crimes, *et cetera*, where the identity of the perpetrator is unimportant to determining whether a crime has been committed.[139] The issue of identity-based criminality has to be understood by reference to the nature of international law and politics such as it existed at the time. Ever since Cicero, States sought to consecrate their own position in the legal order at the expense of piratical intruders whose existence threatened to undermine civilised political order that, at its heart, was based on principles of peaceful coexistence and mercantilism.[140] Conversely the pirate ship represented a "primordial" model for society that a generally pacific world could not, ultimately, sustain.

The fundamental assertions about the nature and status of piracy established herein form, crucially, the backbone of a consolidated response to piracy, as manifested through States. This communal response would, over time, develop into universal jurisdiction. Part 4.2 now considers the responses that Gentili and Grotius considered ought to be taken against the pirates they had described, thus setting the philosophical and theoretical origins of this principle.

---

135 *De Jure Praedae, supra* n024, 449.

136 As per Thomas Hobbes' notion of the State in his 1651 work *Leviathan: or, the Matter, Forme, & Power of a Commonwealth Ecclesiasticall and Civill*, the State represents the "collective interest" of all persons present via a "social contract", providing protection from the lawless "state of nature" that would otherwise exist. John Locke would later warn that legitimate governments could nevertheless *become* "pirates" if they violated the social contract and entered a state of war with their people: *Two Treatises of Government (1690)*, ed. P Laslett (Cambridge: CUP, 1998), II, ss196–208.

137 *Supra* n011, 25.

138 *De Jure Praedae, supra* n024, 449.

139 For instance, Article 27 of the *Rome Statute of the International Criminal Court* notes that "[t]his Statute shall apply equally to all persons without any distinction based on official capacity".

140 See Chapter 2, *supra*, in general.

4.2 Responding to Piracy

Part 4.1 sought to establish the identity of the "pirate" as proposed by influential Renaissance scholars Alberico Gentili and Hugo Grotius. This analysis of identity is integral to informing responses to piracy, including via universal jurisdiction, as exercised by States. We turn, now, to the responses to piracy proposed by Gentili and Grotius, in sections 4.2.1 and 4.2.2, respectively. A particular focus will be placed on the idea of universal jurisdiction and the manner in which it was influenced by these works.

4.2.1 *"The Common Enemies of all Mankind": Implementing the "Gentili Divide"*

Alberico Gentili, as we have seen, adopted a definition of piracy based on its differentiation from the State.[141] It was a designation determined, in effect, on the consensus of self-identifying "peer polity" States, placing the "pirates" who opposed them outside the civilising embrace of the Ciceronian *jus gentium*.

The consequences of exclusion were dire. For Gentili, pirates were "the common enemies of all mankind (*piratae omnium mortaliu hostes sunt communes*)" so that "the laws of war cannot apply to them".[142] Further, because pirates "clearly sin against the laws of nature and mankind, [...] any one whatsoever may check such men by force of arms. [...] [B]ecause in the violation of that law we are all injured, and individuals in turn can find their personal rights violated".[143] Based on Gentili's strict retaliation approach, any State may "effectively extend [their] jurisdiction anywhere into ocean space to punish offenders after declaring their sponsors illegitimate",[144] a claim that resembles the formulation of universal (enforcement) jurisdiction over the high seas as found in UNCLOS, which provides that "[o]n the high seas, or in any other place outside the jurisdiction of any State, every State may seize a pirate ship [...], and arrest the persons and seize the property on board".[145] Based on Gentili's reasoning, universal jurisdiction over piracy would appear to be based on the inherent misdeed of the pirate, who through his intolerable identity "clearly sin[s] against the laws of nature and mankind".[146] In this way, Gentili plays a role in signalling the "march to criminalisation" of piracy.[147] It is clear that the

141 4.1.1, *supra*.
142 *Supra* no11, 22, citing Cicero, *Verrine Orations*, VI.V.XXX.
143 *Ibid.*, 122.
144 Benton, *Search for Sovereignty*, *supra* no17, 130.
145 Article 105.
146 *Supra* no11, 122.
147 Robert Haywood and Roberta Spivak, *Maritime Piracy* (Oxford: Routledge, 2012), 9.

basic divisive narrative proposed by Gentili remains pervasive, particularly in informing the "piracy analogy" as invoked in *Eichmann*.[148]

Gentili became a central figure in the marginalisation and punishment of piracy.[149] Through his works we find an updating of Cicero and a restatement of the liminal nature of pirates during the formative years of international law. The Roman hegemon had effectively reappeared in the guise of cooperating and mutually reinforcing European States, and Cicero's rhetoric became more relevant than ever. Gentili lent definition to the community of States, a construct that would find greater coherence through Grotius' *De Jure Belli ac Pacis* and the Peace of Westphalia,[150] allowing it as a collective to recognise and take action against those falling outside the community.[151] This is essentially the same "community" that, today, defines the scope and the moral imperative of international law today and determines the exceptive distinction between accepted State subjects and those "others" (such as pirates or *génocidaires*) who fall outside it.[152]

4.2.2 *Hugo Grotius and the Philosophical Underpinnings of Universal Jurisdiction*

The definition of the pirate as established by Grotius in *De Jure Praedae* and, later, *De Jure Belli ac Pacis*, reveals important inroads into the logic of universal jurisdiction. By setting the debate about piracy in *De Jure Praedae* within the context of the oceanic "state of nature", Grotius draws a distinction between crimes committed within a State-governed territorial jurisdiction and those which occur in "desert places" such as on the high seas. In the latter scenario, the offender does not break the law of any single *specific* State but instead commits an objective, inherent and universally condemnable wrong, based on his or her interference with the universally applicable right to navigate freely upon the high seas (in addition, presumably, to breaking the bond of feudal allegiance with his or her State of nationality). A useful parallel may be drawn with the notion of "*mala in se*",[153] universally recognised offences "that address fundamental

148 Chapter 1 (introduction), *supra*.

149 Heller-Roazen, *supra* no6, 105.

150 Bull, *supra* no134, 75–76.

151 Heller-Roazen, *supra* no6, 160.

152 Paul W. Kahn, "Speaking Law to Power: Popular Sovereignty, Human Rights, and the New International Order" 1 *Chicago Journal of International Law* (2000) 1, 4; Adeno Addis, "Imagining the International Community: The Constitutive Dimension of Universal Jurisdiction" 31 *Human Rights Quarterly* (2009) 129, 144–145; Simpson, *supra* no81, 224.

153 Hans Kelsen, *General Theory of Law and State* (trans. Anders Wedberg) (Cambridge, MA: Harvard University Press, 1949), 51–52; William A. Schabas, *Unimaginable Atrocities: Justice, Politics, and Rights at the War Crimes Tribunals* (Oxford: OUP, 2012), 34.

human values, whose perpetration is viewed as naturally or inherently evil"[154] and whose effects permeate all of human society, rather than being limited to a single State. To borrow from Enlightenment philosopher John Locke, the commission of such "trespass[es] against the whole species" help to distinguish and define, in opposition, the "great and natural community" of civilised mankind.[155] From a familiar Ciceronian perspective, such actions separate ordered civilisation from the primordial or piratical "other".[156]

De Jure Belli ac Pacis places the onus of punishment for acts of piracy firmly on States, for "since the establishment of States and communities, it is judged reasonable to transfer this right to the respective States or their sovereigns, according to whose discretion all faults, as do properly concern them, are to be punished or remitted".[157] Moreover, the "State where the [...] offender lives or has taken shelter, should, upon application being made to it, either punish the demanded person [...] or else deliver him up to be treated at the discretion of the injured party".[158] Although Grotius intimated in *De Jure Praedae* that on the lawless space of the high seas "the private actor returned to his original sovereignty and could engage in just war",[159] here he adds that this right had since been delegated back to the State of which the "private actor" was a part. Thereby States become the ultimate enforcers of natural law, with the right to enforce being dependant only on the presence of the accused, regardless of any other connecting "links" to the offence. On a related note, regarding the right to punish "suppliants" (refugees), Grotius maintains that they could be prosecuted in the State they have fled to, but only for crimes that either "affect the State, or are of a very heinous and malignant nature".[160] Based on Grotius' claims that pirates were "notoriously wicked"[161] and offenders against natural law, they would seem to fit this category of villains. Here we find the strongest

154 Schabas, *ibid.*

155 Locke, *supra* no136, s8.

156 2.2, *supra*.

157 *Supra* no12, Book II.XXI.III.

158 *Ibid.*, II.XXI.IV. This position appears to reflect the modern-day principle of "extradite or prosecute", as found in several treaties (including the 1949 Geneva Conventions), permitting the use of universal jurisdiction where applicable; discussed in Amnesty International, *International Law Commission: The Obligation to Extradite or Prosecute* (2009), 32.

159 Porras, *supra* no26, 788–789.

160 *Supra* no12, II.XXI.V. Grotius adds that "[a]s for lesser faults it has been the custom to connive at them, unless by the articles of treaty it has been particularly agreed on to the contrary", noting also that this represents a European custom "for some ages last past". Grotius clearly perceived different levels of seriousness in offences, although it is not clear how he measured this. The argument is akin to that of "no safe haven" in the context of modern claims to universal jurisdiction; see Devika Hovell, "The Authority of Universal Jurisdiction 29 *European Journal of International Law* (2018) 427, 439–441.

161 *Ibid.*, III.XIX.III.

resemblance, in terms of Grotius' works, of something resembling "universal jurisdiction": the power of the State to prosecute *any* offence against natural law and/or which may have been "very heinous and malignant" – subject only to the prosecuting State claiming custody of the accused.

These claims in turn complement Grotius' oft-cited proposal that

> Kings [...] have a right to exact punishments, not only for injuries committed against themselves, or their subjects, but likewise, for those which do not peculiarly concern them, but which are, in any persons whatsoever, grievous violations of the law of nature or nations. [...] Nay, it is so much more honourable, to revenge other peoples' injuries rather than their own.[162]

This quote is often regarded as an unequivocal statement condoning universal jurisdiction in relation to (in Grotius' words) "grievous violations of the law of nature or nations".[163] The conduct to which Grotius refers is not made clear, although his description of piracy as "notoriously wicked" would seem to make it a likely contender. The extract should be treated with some caution, however, insofar as Grotius' concern here appeared to be with the conditions for "just war", as suggested by the title of the section within which the quote appears: "Whether it be lawful for Kings and States to make War upon such as violate the Law of Nature".[164] Supporting this interpretation, Grotius adds that "war may be justly undertaken [...] against those who practise Piracy", for "of such barbarians, and rather beasts than men, [...], war against such is natural" and, further, "the justest war [*sic.*] is that which is undertaken against wild rapacious beasts".[165] The language used here is reminiscent of Cicero, and finds Grotius at his linguistic limits in terms of expressing his contempt for pirates. The wording blurs the line between criminal prosecution and military action, rendering

162 *Ibid.*, II.XX.XL.

163 See, e.g., *Eichmann* (District Court), *supra* n022, para. 14; *Arrest Warrant*, *supra* n022, separate opinion of President Guillaume, 37; Alexis Blaine and Benedict Kingsbury, "Punishment and the *ius post bellum*" in Kingsbury and Straumann, *supra* n016, 241, 253; Ryan Rabinovitch, "Universal Jurisdiction *In Absentia*" 28 *Fordham International Law Journal* (2005) 500, 516; Mark S. Zaid, "Will or Should the United States Ever Prosecute War Criminals?: A Need for Greater Expansion in the Areas of both Criminal and Civil Liability" 35 *New England Law Review* (2001) 447, 449; and Gavouneli, *supra* n022, 20.

164 *Supra* n012, II.XX.XL.

165 *Ibid.* Grotius also includes, among this number, "those who are inhuman to their parents" and "those who eat human Flesh". Grotius adds that the power to punish in this way is "a right that most allow of, and the practice of all nations confirms", but does not provide any sources for his empirical claim.

it of dubious worth to any argument in favour of universal jurisdiction. Nevertheless Grotius closes this section with a valuable statement, clarifying that the power of "punishing" individuals derives not from any "civil jurisdiction" claimed by the State but, rather, from "the law of nature [...], that natural right which was [...] before the foundation of governments".[166]

In making these claims, namely the right to punish "suppliants" suspected of "heinous crimes" and the right of kings to "punish [...] grievous violations of the law of nature or nations" (albeit, perhaps, in a retaliatory *ad bellum* sense), Grotius conveys the same sense of universal morality shared by his predecessors Cicero and Gentili.[167] This same theory of universal morals would be repeated again over three hundred years later by the Israeli Supreme Court in *Eichmann*.[168] These sources all conceive of a certain class of offences that offend against civilisation as a whole, that "affect the whole of mankind and shock the conscience of all nations of the world".[169] To repeat the forceful rhetoric of the *Eichmann* case, such offences "damage vital international interests; they impair the foundations and security of the international community; they violate universal moral values and humanitarian principles which are at the root of the systems of criminal law adopted by civilized nations".[170] How Grotius understood this to operate in practice, though, is not made clear; in common with Gentili, he worked at a theoretical level and, for the main part, chose not to draw on contemporary real world events. In any case there would be obstacles to overcome before moving beyond restrictive seventeenth century conceptions of State jurisdiction,[171] and universal jurisdiction in practice would not be realised for almost another century,[172] yet the principle was effectively formulated for the first time in these passages.[173] Grotius was thus instrumental in developing the idea of the pirate as a universally punishable "outlaw".[174]

Universal jurisdiction, as exercised by States today, appears to be the logical endpoint for the merging of Grotius' separate conceits of: (i) the "state of nature"

166 *Ibid.*

167 *Supra*, 2.2 and 4.1.1.

168 Supreme Court of Israel, *Eichmann v. A-G Israel*, 36 *International Law Reports* (1968) 227, para. 11.

169 *Prosecutor v. Tadić*, ICTY Appellate Judgement, 10 August 1995, para. 142. See also 1.2.1, *supra*.

170 *Eichmann* (Supreme Court), *supra* no168, para. 11.

171 3.1.2, *supra*.

172 5.2, *infra*.

173 See *supra* no22 for citations of Grotius as a precedent for the use of universal jurisdiction.

174 John Kavanagh, "The Law of Contemporary Sea Piracy", 5 *Australian International Law Journal* (1999) 127, 136.

or *res nullius/communis* scenario, as applied to the high seas; (ii) the idea that the freedom of the sea (or of commerce) is a universal right, the violation of which is grievous and affects all States, and (iii) the affirmation that States ought to punish rapacious non-State transgressors of such a norm.[175] That the *locus delicti* of piracy occurs on the high seas is important to Grotius' thesis, as only from this fluid geographic space can the universally applicable *libertas commerciorum* be violated. Only in this non-space can robbers become "pirates", the enemies of *all* mankind, as opposed to those of a single society. When read together these strands combine different theories as to why universal jurisdiction applied to pirates, for instance the idea that it solves the problem of a jurisdictional void (*i.e.* the high seas) and that it is exercisable in response to a "heinous" offence. Both these theories are true – indeed, they are inextricably connected.

4.3 Conclusion

> [M]y heart was sore for him, wicked as he was, to think on the dark perils that environed and the shameful gibbet that awaited him.
>
> JIM HAWKINS, *Treasure Island*[176]

Young Jim Hawkins, the narrator of Treasure Island, is conflicted in his feelings for Long John Silver. The old pirate saved his life and, yet, he was still a pirate, for whom the noose was inevitable. The statement stands in contrast to the tone of this chapter, which is essentially an analysis of cold, dehumanised, legal-political rhetoric denouncing the threat that piracy posed to the world of civilised, State-organised peoples. There is no room in Gentili or Grotius for comparative morality; there is only room for the taciturn, hard illegality of piracy. As if in a historical twist of fate, Silver would redeem himself and eventually disappear, presumably to a life of further misadventure. This too is symbolic (for our purposes), a hint that the age of the pirate was not over quite yet.

This chapter documents a pivotal point in the history of universal jurisdiction, in which past State practice and scholarly writings are synthesised by the colossi of international law into hyperbolic treatises, ripe with memorable

175 See, e.g., Marek St. Korowicz, "The Problem of the International Personality of Individuals", 50 *American Journal of International Law* (1965) 533, 534, on Grotius' contribution to the theory of individual criminal responsibility in international law.

176 *Supra* n0121, 246.

axioms and influential enough to shape the future course of history. The academic histories documented herein form a filter through which the elusive history of piracy (and responses thereto) flows, only to be revised as an internationally condemnable wrong, based on a reappraisal of the pirate's identity and a discernible need for coordinated response.[177] Gentili and Grotius borrowed from the ancient histories of piracy (and the repression thereof), invoking them piecemeal to apply to situations that were not wholly equivalent. Yet the political situation was closely analogous to the Roman yesteryear, wherein the rhetoric of Cicero ran parallel to a military backlash against troublesome external raiders. Just as Rome formed a Mediterranean hegemony that warranted the demise of the primordial *peiratēs*, so the sixteenth and seventeenth century European "peer polity" States rounded on the trade-troubling pirates. Ultimately, "the thoughts of these philosophers, in combination with the increasing strength of the State, became the norm for the view on pirates. In this view pirates are parasites on the international trade".[178] Such is the historical heft contained in these works.

The enduring theme (re)introduced in this period is the divisive narrative of pirates as *hostes humani generis*, "the common enemies of all". The pirate is attributed the dubious aim of waging "war" against all of the civilised world, placing him outside the scope and protection of international law, an anomalous figure whose existence ought not to be tolerated.[179] *Subversion* is the overarching, defining notion of piracy, to which other "contingencies" of piracy are connected – the ideas that the pirate cannot, by definition, represent a State in the proper sense, that he acts for selfish, private gain (needlessly disrupting trade in so doing), and that he acts upon the fluid *res communis* of the high seas.[180]

Alberico Gentili was instrumental in developing the distinction between pirates and civilised society (represented by States) and thereby affirming piracy's subservience (as well as legal and moral subjection) to Statehood. This is an international perspective that consecrated State destruction of piracy, either by force or by law, at a time of apparent confusion over how to apprehend such a menace. Theodor Meron has suggested that "Gentili was an original, enlightened and eloquent writer who has not been given as much credit as his works clearly deserve".[181] This is doubtlessly true; as an originator of the

177 See Gould, *supra* no17, 33.

178 Heebøll-Holm, *supra* no10, 2.

179 Addis, *supra* no152, 159.

180 Dino Kritsiotis, "The Contingencies of Piracy", 41 *California Western International Law Journal* (2011) 305.

181 Meron, *supra* no22, 116.

law of nations Gentili's influence is beyond question. On the specific topic of universal jurisdiction, however, Gentili arguably contributes little, his main input being the idea that pirates are "not sovereigns" and so can be treated as State subjects. Otherwise, Gentili's work in this area serves as little more than a restatement of Cicero. Nevertheless Gentili fulfilled a crucial role in building our perception of what pirates are (and by consequence what *States* are) and why they deserve contemptuous treatment. Moreover, Gentili can be seen as a forerunner to Hugo Grotius' more composite theories on piracy.

Grotius' scholarship, in turn, was shaped by the exigencies of the time. For his first major work, *De Jure Praedae*, Grotius was played as a political pawn. While being primarily intent on promoting Dutch trade and colonial expansion (to the detriment, specifically, of the Portuguese), Grotius effectively opened the book on universal jurisdiction by hypothesising about the empty juridical space of the high sea, where jurisdictional claims were problematic and uncertain. The right to pursue and punish pirates upon this vacuous space was underwritten by the idea that pirates were universally abhorrent, "notoriously wicked" beings.[182] The Grotian analysis established the pirate as a tangible violator of commerce (a categorisation that appeared to include the Portuguese) as opposed to Gentili's somewhat abstract identity-based "enemy" and "subject" of the State.

Grotius' exile from the Dutch Republic largely released him from political influence for the publication of *De Jure Belli ac Pacis*. His stance shifted (under influence from Gentili and the convoluted factional fighting of the Thirty Years War) from the politically-driven view of the pirate as a hindrance to trade and commerce to his conception in *De Jure Belli ac Pacis* of an outlaw community "confederated only to do mischief". This model of the pirate shared two roles: a universal criminal offending against a shared *jus gentium* derived from natural law rather than "civil jurisdiction" and, simultaneously, an illegal combatant fighting all civilised States.[183] Different tracts of *De Jure Belli ac Pacis* appear to authorise their destruction by force of (natural) law or by way of military retaliation, the novel former approach proving critical to the future development of universal jurisdiction. The text became an enduring work that simultaneously built upon and reconceived the ideas that came before it, bringing greater clarity to the debate by seeking out an objective, universal way to define the pirate, transcending those that had gone before. Grotius' legacy is almost certainly down to the sanctity with which both *Mare Liberum* and *De Jure Belli ac Pacis* have been received subsequently, in tandem with his efficient management of

182 *Supra* n012, III.XIX.III.

183 Grotius was close to the truth of how pirates viewed themselves: 3.2.1, *supra*.

the publication process.[184] The book espoused rules of international relations at a time when Europe needed them most, at the height of the Thirty Years' War.[185]

Contemporary municipal law was not yet ready for the revelation of Grotius' work, however. For instance, even while Lord Coke denounced the pirate as *hostes humani generis* he remained insistent that Admiralty prosecutions for piracy could be of English nationals only.[186] Although Gentili and Grotius wrote about, and reinforced, the demise of the pirate, their theories remain exactly that – philosophical suggestions about the nature of piracy and grandiose suggestions for its suppression. Their works are at no point empirical; they are never discussed in the context of ongoing threats of piracy occurring at this time. That was never the point, of course; the texts were intended to suit political machinations and State desires to keep certain undesirables at bay and are, for the most part, restatements of Roman jurisprudence. Yet the pervasiveness of piracy in these works suggests something about the perceived threats of the age, threats that are "simultaneously constitutive and expressive of the international community at given historical moments".[187] International law was constructed around the pirate threat in a similar manner to Cicero's manipulation of the *jus gentium*. This same reactive approach to international law might be applied, today, in the context of genocide or war crimes, for example. There appears, already, to be a common theme to universal jurisdiction: States construct it and use it as a response, set within an international legal context, to a shifting "rogue's gallery" of universal offenders, those whose crimes transcend purely domestic justice.

The enforcement of these theories could of necessity only occur at a domestic level. It would be left to State legislators and judiciaries to flesh out the jurisprudence of Gentili and Grotius, united towards the eradication of piracy. This is not to detract from the important precedential value of these works, for through them we see the origins of international outlawry.[188] We witness the evolution of State jurisdiction, flowing from feudal bond, through claims to territoriality, and beyond, towards a broader foundation based on shared moral or economic principles rather than on power, allegiance, or pure pragmatism.[189]

184 Michael P. Scharf, *Customary International Law in Times of Fundamental Change: Recognizing Grotian Moments* (Cambridge: CUP, 2013), 17.

185 Bull, *supra* no134, 74–75.

186 3.2.3, *supra*.

187 Addis, *supra* no152, 132.

188 Simpson, *supra* no81, 223.

189 Arthur Taylor von Mehren, "Adjudicatory Jurisdiction: General Theories Compared and Evaluated", 63 *Boston University Law Review* (1983) 279, 285.

This debate is today being argued anew in the modern age of cyber-jurisdiction, with the internet the modern-day substitute for free sea lanes, in the form of information rather than goods.[190]

The developments charted in this chapter lie firmly in the world of academia: ideas, reasons and possibilities. A universal jurisdiction over piracy cannot be said to have originated at this time. If anything did emerge, it was an agreement over the serious, *subversive*, nature of piracy, linked with its damage to inter-State commerce at a time when the sea lanes were the only method of communication, trade and empire-building, albeit tempered by ambiguity over the role of privateers. The potential policies inherent in these works were yet to be put into action. It is to this subsequent period of enlightenment that we shall now turn.

---

190 See, e.g., Jack Goldsmith and Tim Wu, *Who Owns the Internet?* (Oxford: OUP, 2006), and Dan Jerker B Svantesson, *Solving the Internet Jurisdiction Puzzle* (Oxford: OUP, 2017).

CHAPTER 5

The Ballad of Captain Kidd: the Fall of Piracy and Rise of Universal Jurisdiction (1625–1856)

My name was William Kidd,
God's laws I did forbid
And so wickedly I did, when I sailed.

I'd a Bible in my hand
By my father's great command,
And sunk it in the sand when I sailed.

I'd ninety bars of gold
And dollars manifold
With riches uncontrolled as I sailed.

We taken were at last
And into prison cast:
Now, sentence being past, we must die.

To the Execution Dock
While many thousands flock,
But I must bear the shock, and must die.

Take a warning now by me
And shun bad company,
Let you come to hell with me, for I must die.[1]

The Ballad of Captain Kidd was intended to serve as a poetic warning to anyone seeking to follow in the stead of this rogue privateer and his romanticised outlaw lifestyle. Yet a closer examination of the context surrounding Captain

1 *The Ballad of Captain Kidd* (selected verses), anon, 1701.

 | DOI:10.1163/9789004390461_006

Kidd's arrest (in 1699) and trial (1701) reveals that he was probably innocent of piracy.[2] Rather, Kidd was a scapegoat for the English,[3] executed to appease their allies and showcase a renewed intolerance of piracy. His death was symbolic, then, but nevertheless marked a crucial turning point in terms of policy towards pirates, signalled by communal suppression in a new era of State relations and untempered commerce.[4] At last, "[l]egal recognition of pirates as criminals emerged from centuries of intermittent cooperation and conflict".[5]

This "age of intolerance" towards piracy was born of necessity. The post-Columbian era of colonial discovery signalled the start of a famous new age of piracy, with sea-robbers spreading beyond the crime-ridden crucible of the Mediterranean to the unruly Caribbean and the American mainland "beyond the line".[6] Here they established bases far from the governments, laws, and navies of Europe, finding ample prey amongst the new-found wealth of the colonies and, often, acquiescence in their deeds.[7] As the colonial powers began to rely increasingly on trade, however, the tide began to turn against the pirates who preyed upon it. Captain Kidd's 1701 trial marked something of a turning point in terms of governmental response to the pirates who so hampered commerce. With so many pirate captains in the region being of British origin,[8] an implicit onus fell on the British governments to implement more effective legal provisions and procedures. A law-driven approach was developed, based on statute and judicial precedent, providing a more concrete and (in theory)

2 David Harpham, "The case of Captain William Kidd – a 300 year old miscarriage of justice?" 3 *New Histories* (July 2012), available online.

3 Given that the union of England and Scotland did not occur until 1707, it is appropriate to refer to the two States separately in reference to events before that date; "Britain" or "The United Kingdom" as a political unit only existed afterwards.

4 See, e.g., A.T. Whatley, "Historical Sketch of the Law of Piracy" 3 *Law Magazine and Review* (1874) 618, 639.

5 Joaquín Alcaide Fernández, "*Hostes humani generis:* Pirates, Slavers and Other Criminals" in Bardo Fassbender and Anne Peters (eds), *The Oxford Handbook of the History of International Law* (Oxford: OUP, 2012) 120, 123.

6 The phrase refers to the longitudinal line (c. 46° west) drawn in the 1494 Treaty of Tordesillas, granting Spain and Portugal exclusive possession of all lands to the west. See Angus Konstam, *Piracy: The Complete History* (Oxford: Osprey, 2008), 38.

7 See, e.g., David J. Starkey, "A Restless Spirit: British Privateering Enterprise, 1739–1815" in David J. Starkey, E.S. van Eyck van Heslinga and J.A. de Moor (eds), *Pirates and Privateers: New Perspectives on the War on Trade in the Eighteenth and Nineteenth Centuries* (Exeter: University of Exeter Press, 1997) 126, 127.

8 David Cordingly, in *Life Among the Pirates: The Romance and the Reality* (London: Abacus, 1995), 15, lists the nationality of pirates "who terrorised the Caribbean from around 1715 to 1725", as being 35 per cent "native Englishmen", 25 per cent "born in the American colonies", 20 per cent "from the West Indian colonies" (mostly Jamaica, Barbados and the Bahamas), 10 per cent Scottish, 8 per cent Welsh, and 2 per cent other Europeans (Swedish, Dutch, French, Spanish and Portuguese).

objective response to piracy than Gentili's status-based distinction or Grotius' "high policy decision".[9] Navies were boosted, anti-pirate laws became stricter and more extensive,[10] and courts became more effective.[11] This tough stance on piracy only dealt with part of the problem, however, as privateers were still allowed to thrive during periods of war between nations. Accordingly State-sponsored plunder remained largely unchecked, allowing piracy to flare up in times of peace. Privateering would endure as a problematic practice of States until the 1856 Declaration of Paris.[12]

Universal jurisdiction gained traction as an applied concept throughout this period, albeit in a scattershot manner. Its advent seems to have been directly connected to the exploits of the unfortunate Captain Kidd (hence his central placement in the chapter) whose own calamitous misadventures ran against the grain of inter-State cooperation and trade.[13] Kidd's denouncement instigated a historic trend whereby pirates became perceived by States (in addition to several scholars) as a threat to the free sea and to the freedom of commerce upon it. Their actions were increasingly considered "heinous"[14] and an intrinsic threat to "all mankind".[15] They became "*hostes humani generis*" and the "constitutive exception" to an international community based on diplomacy and pacific mercantilism.[16] The concept of the "universal offender" would become key to the "piracy analogy" claim made in *Eichman* in the context of genocide (and, by extension, other "core" international crimes), a connection that is examined in greater detail in Chapter 8.[17]

This chapter charts the legal and historical developments surrounding piracy from the late 1600s until the mid-1800s, picking up from Gentili's and Grotius' explications of the "Ciceronian paradigm" of piracy, as described in the previous chapter, and concluding with the outlawing of privateering in 1856. In so doing it demonstrates how the influential critiques of piracy espoused by

9 Alfred P. Rubin, *The Law of Piracy* (Honolulu: University Press of the Pacific, 2006), 68–69.

10 Most notably, in the UK, *An Act for the more effectual Suppressions of Piracy*, 1698, discussed at 5.2, *infra*.

11 As discussed throughout the chapter, esp. 5.2, *infra*.

12 Declaration of Paris, April 16, 1856, reproduced in Adam Roberts and Richard Guelff, *Documents on the Laws of War* (3rd ed.) (Oxford: OUP, 2000), 48–49.

13 See, generally, Robert C. Ritchie, *Captain Kidd and the War Against the Pirates* (Cambridge, MA: Harvard University Press, 1986).

14 See, e.g., *Tryal of Captain Thomas Green and his crew*, 14 Howell's State Trials 1199 (1705).

15 See, e.g., *Kidd's Trial*, 14 Howell's State Trials 123 (1701).

16 Jody Greene, "*Hostis Humani Generis*", 34 *Critical Inquiry* (2008), 695; Amedeo Policante, *The Pirate Myth: Genealogies of an Imperial Concept* (Abingdon: Routledge, 2015), 133–136; Adeno Addis, "Imagining the International Community: The Constitutive Dimension of Universal Jurisdiction" 31 *Human Rights Quarterly* (2009) 129.

17 *Eichmann v. A-G Israel* (Supreme Court), 36 *International Law Reports* (1968) 227; 8.1, *infra*.

these scholars were ultimately put into practice. The history explored herein elucidates the threat that States were being forced to contend with and the political forces that drove universal jurisdiction to emerge as a legal tool in the fight against piracy. It considers and examines how and why legislators, courts and legal scholars conceived of and framed the concept of jurisdiction over pirates. The focus is primarily on English colonial cases, these being the most relevant due to piracy's prevalence in Caribbean and North American waters.[18] An examination of the Captain Kidd episode provides, in miniature, a study of the political and legal influences behind the strong anti-piracy laws and rhetoric. The chapter does not claim to be a comprehensive study of all relevant history and cases from this era[19] but, rather, picks up on themes and threads that run through the cases and commentaries, insofar as they introduced, influenced and reinforced the concept of universal jurisdiction.

Part 5.1 looks at the phenomenon of "buccaneering" whereby English colonial governors licensed privateers to attack Spanish interests in the Caribbean. This policy was ultimately brought to an end by the Treaty of Madrid in 1670, marking a turning point in how pirates came to be perceived by the European powers. A brief exposé of this period is required in order to demonstrate the change in attitudes surrounding piracy at this time, which began to shift post-Madrid, as exemplified by the 1675 *Cusack* case. Part 5.2 provides the chapter's centrepiece, examining the momentous circumstances surrounding the apprehension and trial of Captain Kidd and the catalytic effect this had for later piracy trials (notably that of Thomas Green) and the development of universal jurisdiction. Part 5.3 chronicles the legal developments that occurred during the infamous "golden age" of piracy in the early eighteenth century, when piracy in the Americas reached its peak.[20] The 1713 Treaty of Utrecht is shown to be a foundational moment in the suppression of piracy and development of universal jurisdiction, while several relevant British cases are cited to show how universal jurisdiction gained ground in this respect. Throughout this period we begin to see the *rationale* for universal jurisdiction develop and emerge, a theme that will be fully developed in Chapter 6. Part 5.4 picks up after the suppression of piracy during the "golden age", documenting how the backlash against piracy was cemented into later eighteenth century and early

18 Although this analysis might seem skewed, Britain was historically the State most affected by piracy so that, out of necessity, it was forced to innovate in terms of law and applicable jurisdiction.

19 Rubin, *supra* n09, provides an in-depth study.

20 The period c. 1714–1725 is often described as the "golden age" of piracy due to its pervasive nature and (in)famous characters (particularly around the Americas); see, e.g., Konstam, *supra* n06, 150–248.

nineteenth century scholarly works and transatlantic caselaw, with universal jurisdiction becoming accepted as a vital part of the trans-Atlantic legal armoury. Part 5.5 examines the developments leading up to the 1856 Declaration of Paris and the outlawing of privateering, insofar as they are relevant to the broader suppression of piracy. Finally, Part 5.6 forms a conclusion to the chapter, recapping the key developments and charting the overall development of universal jurisdiction throughout this pivotal period. The legal trends emerging throughout the chapter are analysed and discussed in Chapter 6.

5.1 Piracy "beyond the Line": the Age of the Buccaneers (1625–1690)

> Wherefore should the King keep costly ships to guard his western outposts, when we o' the Brotherhood ha' ever been stout bulwarks 'gainst the greed o' Spain?
>
> "BLACK" BILBO, *The Pyrates*[21]

By the late seventeenth century the majority of European pirates had found themselves a new home in the Americas, far from the power centres of the "Old World". Spanish and Portuguese shipping was the main target of this new breed of piracy. Under the cover of the Treaty of Tordesillas,[22] the Iberian powers had claimed an exclusive right to an entire continent (a claim that their European rivals disputed)[23] and any interlopers venturing west of the Azores were automatically branded "*piratas*".[24]

The first wave of pirates in the region were the "buccaneers": a combination of erstwhile Atlantic pirates, dispossessed natives and escaped slaves.[25] From bases in Hispaniola, Tortuga and, later, Jamaica, they preyed on the steady stream of Spanish shipping, a course of action that was legitimised and normalised by the acquiescence of England and France.[26] The resulting situation was uncertain and dynamic; "whether the buccaneers' activities constituted privateering or piracy was sometimes vague, as the status of peace, war and

---

21 George MacDonald Fraser, *The Pyrates* (1983) (London: HarperCollins, 1996), 354.

22 See *supra* n06.

23 Clive Senior, *A Nation of Pirates: English Piracy in its Heyday* (Newton Abbot: David and Charles (Publishers) Limited, 1976), 44.

24 Neville Williams, *Captains Outrageous: Seven Centuries of Piracy* (London: Barrie and Rockliff, 1961), 117.

25 Marcus Rediker, *Villains of All Nations* (London: Verso, 2004), 39.

26 See, e.g., Robert C. Ritchie, "Government Measures against Piracy and Privateering in the Atlantic Area, 1750–1850" in Starkey *et al*, *supra* n07, 10, 11.

alliance among European players in the Caribbean was fluid",[27] though the English, French and Dutch "all adopted the expedient policy that, while wars might come and go between their powers, the Spanish would always remain the enemy".[28]

A formal truce between England and Spain, enshrined in the 1670 Treaty of Madrid, spelled an unofficial end to governmental acquiescence in piracy and violent privateering.[29] The Treaty, premised on mutual respect for colonial possession and safe trade, provided for "a universal peace, and true and sincere amity [between] Spain and Great Britain",[30] and required the signatories to "take care that their subjects abstain from all violence and injury, and [...] revoke all commissions and letters containing powers either of reprisal or marque".[31] Madrid marked a turning point regarding the manner in which piracy was perceived, on paper at least. Rather than presenting States with a dubious opportunity for waging proxy war, or a reservoir of potential privateers, piracy became recognised as a scourge that deleteriously affected the trade of *all* States. Implementing Madrid was problematic, though, given that State navies remained weak, colonial legal systems were ill-equipped,[32] and sympathy for the buccaneers persisted amongst English colonisers.[33] Moreover, the news that the treaty had been signed was slow to reach the colonies, so that some of the greatest excesses of the buccaneers actually occurred in the early 1670s, most notably Captain Henry Morgan's violent assault on Panama City in early 1671.[34]

The 1675 trial of Irish pirate George Cusack exemplifies the policy shift towards suppression.[35] The anonymous author of the trial report initially laments

27 Joseph Gibbs, *On the Account in the "Golden Age": Piracy and the Americas, 1670–1726* (Brighton: Sussex Academic Press, 2014), 1.

28 Konstam, *supra* n06, 108.

29 Treaty of Madrid, 1670, reproduced in Frances Gardiner Davenport (ed.), *European Treaties bearing on the History of the United States and its Dependencies, Volume II (1650—1697)* (Washington, DC: Carnegie Institution of Washington, 1929), 187. See also Konstam, *ibid.*, 99.

30 Treaty of Madrid, *ibid.*, Clause 2.

31 *Ibid.*, Clause 4.

32 As described in Peter Earle, *The Pirate Wars* (New York: Thomas Dunne Books, 2003), 135–146. Nevertheless, English trade in the Atlantic tripled between 1660 and 1670 (Earle, 147).

33 See, e.g., Earle, *ibid.*, 145, and Ritchie, *Captain Kidd*, *supra* n013, 142.

34 The event precipitated a political crisis, leading to Morgan's arrest and deportation to London. He was later returned as governor of Jamaica with an order to eradicate Caribbean piracy: Williams, *supra* n024, 128.

35 Anon, *The Grand Pyrate: Or, the Life and Death of Capt. George Cusack the Great Sea-Robber* (London: Jonathan Edwin, 1676).

that while accounts of robbers and highwaymen "hath long entertained [the world]",[36] factual instances of piracy were not that well-documented.[37] This statement in itself is somewhat telling, revealing an erstwhile muted attitude towards piracy, unsurprising given that governments would have wished to keep quiet due to their close involvement with pirate/privateer captains.[38] In this instance, however, the trial reporter's revelation of Cusack's crimes and account of his subsequent trial evidences an accessible approach to piracy trials, designed to raise public awareness and shift opinion against the accused. The unnamed presiding judge in the trial is described as "acquainting [the pirates] with his Majesty's right of sovereignty over the British seas; even to the very shores of his neighbours" and reminding them that the monarch's jurisdiction

> extends to punish all outrages, violences and offences whatsoever, committed thereupon, by any persons, (whether his subjects, or strangers) upon ships, persons, or goods, of our own nation; or others in amity with us. Then he shewed the heinousness of the crime of piracy; that it was against the law of nations [and] destructive to commerce.[39]

Piracy is then described by the judge as "the worst of all crimes", "destructive to [...] society" and its perpetrators deemed "*humani generus hostes*, whom everyone was obliged to oppose and destroy".[40] In a departure from Coke's "allegiance" approach to jurisdiction over piracy (though England could likely have claimed a "feudal" proto-nationality jurisdiction over Cusack at a time when the English and Irish thrones were united),[41] the law is stated to be applicable to *any* person who attacks English (or allied) subjects upon "British seas". The reference to "British seas" is a questionable claim that appears to assert a form of territorial jurisdiction over the crimes of the accused, as opposed to a Grotian construct that might have enabled a satisfactory jurisdictional claim

---

36 *Ibid.*, 3.

37 Records of Admiralty trials had not previously been made readily available; see Douglas R. Burgess, "Piracy in the Public Sphere: The Henry Every Trials and the Battle for Meaning in Seventeenth-Century Print Culture", 48 *Journal of British Studies* (2009) 887, 906.

38 As much is suggested in *Cusack*: *supra*, n035, 3. See also Richard Frohock, "The Word and the Grand Pirate, Captain George Cusack" 42 *Early American Literature* (2007) 263, 265.

39 *Cusack*, *ibid.*, 28–29.

40 *Ibid.* The term is a variant on the more familiar "*hostes humani generis*".

41 *The Third Part of the Institutes of the Laws of England; Concerning High Treason, and Other Pleas of the Crown and Criminal Causes* (c. 1628), 113; discussed *supra*, 3.2.3.

over the high seas as "*res communis*". This reluctance may have been due, in part, down to a hesitancy to renounce any territorial claim at a time when the ownership of the high seas had not been decisively settled.[42] In any case the jurisdictional claim over Cusack's acts of piracy is powerfully stated, intended to restore "State authority and just religious and civil order [...], dramatis[ing] the State's powerful assertion of its own linguistic authority while enacting the final containment and dismantling of the pirate's unruly word".[43] This claim to power, through jurisdictional assertion and legal language, tells us much about how the courts, as a branch of the State, were beginning to perceive and deal with piracy (or, at least, it tells us the image they were attempting to convey). The language perpetuates, again, the "Ciceronian paradigm"; the judge's words are the contemporary equivalent of Cicero's divisive oratories, with English law enforcing the *jus gentium*[44] against what might be termed "piracy *jure gentium*", being against the "law of nations".[45] This is a strikingly important development, an indication of a move towards practical claims of universal jurisdiction based on the persuasive but gelded rhetoric that had preceded it, the realisation of an exclusive "universal morality" template for peaceful international co-existence.

42 The term was understood to apply to all waters to "the very shores or ports of [...] neighbouring sovereigns": John Selden, *Mare Clausum* (1635) cited in Thomas Wemyss Fulton, *The Sovereignty of the Sea* (Clark, NJ: The Lawbook Exchange Ltd, 1911) 374. Britain had claimed sovereignty over neighbouring seas since the publication of *Mare Clausum* in 1636, leading to a series of wars with the Netherlands; see Ruth Lapidoth, "Freedom of Navigation – its Legal History and its Normative Basis" 6 *Journal of Maritime Law & Commerce* (1975) 259, 267. This position began to shift to an acceptance of the Grotian *mare liberum* following these conflicts, in the latter half of the seventeenth century: D.P. O'Connell, *The Influence of Law on Sea Power* (Manchester: University of Manchester Press, 1975), 17.

43 Frohock, *supra* no38, 264 and 274–275. The anonymous biographer emphasises Cusack's symbolic act of throwing a Bible overboard, as if repudiating God and creating his own moral order, "like Milton's Satan" (influencing, perhaps, the similar content of *The Ballad of Captain Kidd*).

44 2.2, *supra*.

45 Piracy as an offence under international law as opposed to municipal definitions of the same; see Harvard "Draft Convention on Jurisdiction with Respect to Crime", 29 *American Journal of International Law* (1935) supplement, 435, 751.

Academic literature from the era supported the same trend, with scholars such as Richard Zouche,[46] Samuel Pufendorf,[47] and Henry Molloy[48] all adding to the legacy of Gentili and Grotius with similar but nuanced additions to the oeuvre. Perhaps the greatest seventeenth century academic contribution (post-Grotius) came from jurist and Admiralty lawyer Leoline Jenkins. In a 1668 statement to the Admiralty Courts, Jenkins advocated a prototypal form of universal jurisdiction in advocating that, in respect of piracy, the Crown possessed "[p]ower and jurisdiction [...] in those remoter parts of the world, [...] in concurrence with all other sovereign princes that have ships and subjects at sea".[49] This was so given the Crown's supposedly selfless "concern and authority [...] to preserve the public peace, and to maintain the freedom and security of navigation all the world over".[50] Seven years before Cusack's trial, Jenkins' progressive statement represents an important extension of Grotius' *libertas commerciorum*, an elaboration which recognises a positivist State jurisdiction to maintain the peremptory principle of free commerce and deviates from the Dutchman's largely "natural law" approach.[51] Jenkins does not provide any reasons for his broad jurisdictional claim, though his suggestion that the claim existed "in concurrence with all other sovereign princes" hints at a conceived shared space, a *res communis*, where jurisdiction is shared equally between all States. This approach does not seem to have been adopted wholesale in *Cusack*, however, which preferred the restrictive notion of "sovereignty over the *British* seas".[52] The issue may have been one of expression when tasked with describing a novel concept, whilst simultaneously avoiding the concession of political claims over the seas.

In any case Jenkins' rhetoric, paired with Cusack's trial, evidenced a "fundamental shift [...] occurring in the law, from the laissez-faire attitudes of

46 *Iuris et Iudicii Fecialis* (1650) (trans. JL Brierly, 1911), discussed in Daniel Heller-Roazen, *The Enemy of All: Piracy and the Law of Nations* (Brooklyn: Zone Books, 2009), 112.

47 *De jure naturae at gentium* (1672), trans. Oldfather and Oldfather, 1934) (Oxford : Clarendon, 1934). Pufendorf stayed close to Cokean feudal conceptions of jurisdiction; discussed in Walter Rech, *Enemies of Mankind: Vattel's Theory of Collective Security* (Leiden, Martinus Nijhoff, 2013), pp. 70–85.

48 *De Maritimo et Navali: or, a Treatise of Affairs Maritime and of Commerce* (1707), vol. I.

49 Charge given to an Admiralty Session within the Cinque Ports, 2 September 1668; reproduced in William Wynne, *The Life of Sir Leoline Jenkins* (1724), xc-xci; discussed in Heller-Roazen, *supra* no46, 113–114.

50 *Ibid.*

51 *Supra* 4.2.2. See also Tamsin Paige, "Piracy and Universal Jurisdiction" 12 *Macquarie Law Journal* (2013) 131, 138.

52 *Supra* no35.

Elizabethan privateering to a renaissance of *hostis humani generis*".[53] The gears of justice had begun to grind. Change was afoot.

5.2 Captain Kidd and the Anti-piracy "Revolution" of the 1690s

> [W]ith what face could wretches who had ravaged and made so many necessitous, look up for relief; they had to that moment lived in defiance of the power that now alone they must trust for their preservation.
>
> Captain CHARLES JOHNSON[54]

This quote from Captain Johnson's influential *General History of* [...] *Pirates* suggests a shift in the fortunes of pirates as States attempted to take control of the seas and eradicate the ancient roguish custom. Captain Kidd's capture, trial and execution marked a defining moment in the shift from acceptance to antipathy at a governmental level and in the popular psyche. *The Ballad of Captain Kidd*, portraying its protagonist as a heinous, irreligious villain rather than a romantic anti-hero, is intentionally symptomatic of the shift.[55]

William Kidd was already an experienced privateer when, in New York in 1695, he was approached by a private consortium (personally endorsed by William III) and provided with funding to captain an Indian Ocean pirate-hunting expedition.[56] Kidd was granted a royal commission to seize and apprehend all "pirates, free-booters and sea-rovers, being our subjects, or of other nations associated with them", these being offenders "against the law of nations".[57] In addition, Kidd was permitted to attack French vessels (England had been at war with France since 1689) but was expressly prohibited from attacking the King's "friends or allies, their ships or subjects, by colour or pretence of these presents, or the authority granted".[58] For a year Captain Kidd roamed the oceans in the *Adventure Galley* without making a single capture. His luck

53 Douglas R. Burgess, "*Hostis Humani Generi*: Piracy, Terrorism and a New International Law" 13 *University of Miami International & Comparative Law Review* (2006) 293, 312.

54 Captain Charles Johnson, *A General History of the Robberies and Murders of the most notorious Pirates* (1724) (with an introduction by David Cordingly; London: Conway Maritime Press, 1998), 188–189.

55 See 3.2.1, *supra*, on the ambiguous manner in which piracy was treated in Elizabethan and Jacobean literature.

56 Richard Zacks, *The Pirate Hunter: The True Story of Captain Kidd* (London: Review, 2003), Chapter 1.

57 Cited in Harpham, *supra* n02.

58 *Ibid.*

turned in January 1698 when he captured the *Quedagh Merchant*, seizing some £75,000 worth of prize.[59] The *Quedagh* seizure marked the start of Kidd's real problems, however, because although the ship had passed itself off as French (which would have made it acceptable prize)[60] it actually belonged to the Mughal Empire, a close ally and trading partner of the English.[61] The Mughal Emperor, Aurangzeb, was incensed. On his arrival in Boston in 1699, Captain Kidd was promptly thrown in jail.[62]

Captain Kidd had become the scapegoat for English failures to tackle their own piracy problem. Aurangzeb had become increasingly frustrated with seizures of his merchant ships, particularly by the English "King of Pirates" Henry Avery (sometimes spelled "Every").[63] England was determined to put Avery on trial to ease Aurangzeb's concerns and demonstrate, to the world in general, a renewed commitment against piracy.[64] Combating piracy would not only allow it to assuage allies but also to enforce "fundamental distinctions between just and unjust behaviour at sea[,] to insist upon the efficacy of its ships, passes, and law across oceanic space".[65] Kidd's arrest and scapegoating (*in lieu* of Avery, who would never be found) was a direct result of this ideological upheaval, and his trial coincided with a period of reform in English governance and legal process. Constitutional reforms in England at the close of the seventeenth century allowed for greater flexibility and democracy in the legal system. Parliamentary supremacy, established with William III's Glorious Revolution in 1688, allowed for more rapid and responsive legislation.[66] For the first time in history, "[a]mple opportunity [was] afforded for all the legislation

59 *Ibid.*

60 It was a common tactic for ships to carry multiple letters of self-conduct, enabling them to claim the protection of a range of sponsors in order to "guarantee an ally"; see Zacks, *supra* no56, 25. The *Quedagh* would have opted to present a French pass in response to Kidd flying French colours, apparently as a ruse (Zacks, 148–150).

61 Harpham, *supra* no2; Zacks, *ibid.*, 151.

62 Zacks, *ibid.*, 204, and 242.

63 In 1695 Avery had seized the largest of the Mughal fleet, the *Ganj-I Sawal*, reportedly carrying the Mughal's own daughter in addition to great riches; see Burgess, "Piracy in the Public Sphere", *supra* no37, 887.

64 Burgess, *ibid.*, 905, suggests that "[a] successful trial would serve as a counterweight to accusations of pirate brokering in the colonies, as well as the more serious charge from Emperor Aurangzeb that the crown itself looked the other way", this being an issue particularly as William III himself had backed Kidd's venture.

65 Philip J. Stern, *The Company State: Corporate Sovereignty & the Early Modern Foundations of the British Empire in India* (Oxford: OUP, 2011), 136.

66 Frederick W. Maitland and Francis C. Montague, *A Sketch of English Legal History* (New Jersey: The Lawbook Exchange, 2010) 147.

demanded by public opinion",[67] while the streamlining of central government allowed it to reign in local powerbrokers who for so many centuries had made fortunes out of corrupt practices (often through piracy).[68] In 1696 the Board of Trade replaced the Lords of Trade as the dominant power on colonial affairs, a move that introduced technocracy into colonial governance,[69] and an attorney-general and Admiralty judge were installed in every colony, replacing corrupt governors.[70] The Navy was strengthened and a more tangible control proclaimed over the fragmented colonies.[71]

Burgeoning industry drove friendly diplomacy, stirring a "new internationalism" aimed at facilitating trade and maintaining wealth, with the harmonious principle of *mare liberum* at its core.[72] Commerce replaced war and systematic plunder as the prevailing economic driver of State growth, with piracy intrinsically linked (albeit inversely) to the development of the global market. Pirate attacks were no longer the audacious exploits of quaint folk heroes but instead an obstacle to stable commerce and "a serious embarrassment to the State".[73] Inter-State relations and international law (as pioneered by Gentili and Grotius)[74] were increasingly taking root, with diplomacy displacing war as the preferred method for settling disputes.[75] Building ordered relations and strong commercial ties became a political priority; under William III, England appointed an unprecedented eighty ambassadors to maintain friendly relations.[76] Unpredictable privateers were increasingly reined in, coming

67 *Ibid.*, 148.

68 Policante, *supra* no16, 89.

69 Burgess, "Piracy in the Public Sphere" *supra* no37, 891.

70 Ritchie, *Captain Kidd*, *supra* no13, 150.

71 *Ibid.*, 157; Stern, *supra* no65, 140.

72 Theodore F.T. Plucknett, *A Concise History of the Common Law* (Indianapolis: Liberty Fund, 2010 (reprint of 1956 edition)) 68–69.

73 Burgess, "Piracy in the Public Sphere" *supra* no37, 912. See also Tamsin Paige, "The Impact and Effectiveness of UNCLOS on Counter Piracy Operations" 22 *Journal of Conflict & Security Law* (2017) 97, 117, arguing that "what removed piracy from the Caribbean theatre in the 18th century was not criminal law, but rather economic development of the colonies to a point where piracy was less beneficial than legal trade".

74 Hedley Bull, "The Importance of Grotius in the Study of International Relations" in Hedley Bull, Benedict Kingsbury and Adam Roberts (eds), *Hugo Grotius and International Relations*, (Oxford: OUP, "New Edition", 2002) 65; see also Chapter 4, *supra*, generally.

75 Ritchie, *Captain Kidd*, *supra* no13, 149.

76 *Ibid.*, 148.

under ever-tighter regulation and scrutiny,[77] with "legitimate" violence gradually becoming centralised in State navies and militaries.[78]

Political reform, though, could only go so far towards controlling piracy and sending a staunch message to would-be freebooters. An effective piracy law was also required, one which could be applied to the overwhelmed colonies. In fact, the introduction of a new piracy law was already in discussion in the English Parliament in the late 1690s,[79] although it did not arrive in time for the landmark case of *Rex v Dawson*, held in London (at the Old Bailey) in 1696 for several crewmembers of the elusive Henry Avery.[80]

Rex v Dawson appears to mark the earliest actual endorsement of universal jurisdiction (or something resembling it) in court, even if the active base of jurisdiction in the case was derived from the nationality of the accused. Opening the trial, prosecutor Robert Newton suggested that piracy:

> so much exceeds theft or robbery at land; as the interest and concerns of kingdoms and nations, are above those of private families, or particular persons: for suffer pirates, and the commerce of the world must cease, which this nation has deservedly so great a share in, and reaps such mighty advantage by.[81]

Newton's statement plays heavily upon the perceived "heinousness" of piracy, noting its effects not merely on individuals but on States as a whole due to its endangerment of international commerce. Newton's statement might be seen as a combination of Cicero's and Gentili's "stateless" definition of piracy with Grotius' "*libertas commerciorum*" angle.[82] The potential harm to the State itself is cast as a greater sin than any harm that might be incurred upon individuals (though by extrapolation, any harm to the "State" will also harm those individuals that comprise it). Newton's claim also distinguishes the evil of piracy from

77 See, e.g., Ritchie, "Government Measures", *supra* n026, 18–19. For instance, the 1708 Prize Act created a uniform system of prize adjudication and forced privateers to post expensive bonds. Spain and France were also constantly tightening restrictions: Gonçal López Nadal, "Mediterranean Privateering between the Treaties of Utrecht and Paris, 1715–1856: First Reflections", in Starkey *et al, supra* n07, 106 at 112.

78 See, generally, Janice E. Thomson, *Mercenaries, Pirates and Sovereigns* (Princeton, New Jersey: Princeton University Press, 1994).

79 Ritchie, *Captain Kidd, supra* n013, 152–154.

80 13 *Howell's State Trials* 451 (1696).

81 *Ibid.* Newton's statement is all that remains of the original trial. Curiously, the prosecutor shares the same name as actor Robert Newton, who famously portrayed "Long" John Silver in Disney's 1950 adaptation of Treasure Island.

82 See Chapter 4, *supra*, in general.

State-sponsored privateering, the latter of which would threaten only specific States, within the context of conflict, as opposed to endangering "the world".[83]

Notwithstanding Newton's efforts, the jury acquitted the defendants, exasperating British and allied stakeholders committed to curtailing piracy.[84] A retrial was hastily conducted, with every effort taken to ensure a conviction.[85] At the retrial, the prosecution reiterated that piracy was a "crime against the laws of nations, and worse than robbery on the land", the explanation being that "in the case of a robbery on the land, we know who is to pay for it; but in a robbery at sea, it often happens that innocent persons bear the loss of what these men do".[86] This statement suggests an alternative reason as to why piracy might be considered more serious, namely that it is harder to contain, and perpetrators difficult to apprehend. Judge Hedges, in turn, appealed to the jurors to maintain "by the administration of equal justice, the discipline of the seas, on which the good and safety of this nation entirely depends".[87] For our purposes the nuances of jurisdiction are the most interesting aspects of the trial, particularly when juxtaposed against the claims of Newton and Judge Hedges regarding the inherently serious nature of piracy. On this point Hedges held, in an apparent abrogation of Coke's "treason" construction of piracy, but as an expansive variant on *Cusack*,[88] that:

> The king of England hath not only an empire and sovereignty over the British seas, but also an undoubted jurisdiction and power, in concurrency with other princes and States, for the punishment of all piracies and robberies at sea, in the most remote parts of the world.[89]

The judge's claim goes beyond that in *Cusack* by extending jurisdiction even beyond "British seas". *Dawson* marks a defining moment by invoking universal jurisdiction (albeit in an ambitious and rhetorical sense), providing something of a foothold for later expansive ideologies of jurisdiction that would become fully realised in future piracy cases. From a political perspective, and more

83 As discussed in Policante, *supra* no16, 169–172.

84 See Burgess, "Piracy in the Public Sphere" *supra* no37, 900, suggesting that this "indicated that something was seriously misaligned in English attitudes toward piracy". Alternatively, of course, the jury simply might not have been convinced by the evidence presented to them.

85 Ritchie, *Captain Kidd, supra* no13, 135–137. "A stellar cast of legal talent" was attached to the case.

86 *Rex v Dawson, supra* no80.

87 *Ibid.*

88 *Supra* no35 and associated text.

89 *Rex v Dawson, supra* no80.

importantly for England, the trial "put the colonies on notice of a hardening of attitudes" against piracy and satisfied the demands of Emperor Aurangzeb.[90]

Following the fiasco of *Dawson*, the *Act for the More Effectual Suppression of Piracy*[91] was promptly passed and "the empire had its first meaningful legislation on piracy".[92] The legislation established special piracy courts comprised of seven of the pirates' "peers" (usually naval officers) that could convene anywhere. The omission of a jury was deemed an acceptable compromise when dealing with pirates,[93] even if it gave the appearance that piracy trials were designed to convict.[94] Nevertheless, the *Act* affirmed governmental resolve to deal with offenders by trial (however flawed) rather than resort to summary execution. Although pirates might have been regarded for rhetorical or ideological reasons as being "wholly outside the pale of the law",[95] they were nevertheless legal subjects and (nominally) protected by it in terms of procedural guarantees, however minimal. There were no major revelations in the *Act* concerning jurisdiction,[96] save for the expansion of Admiralty jurisdiction to the colonies. Rather, the "universalised" approach was apparently an innovation of the English courts rather than the legislature.[97] Moreover universal jurisdiction does not appear to have been in use in the laws of other States at this time.[98]

---

90 Burgess, "Piracy in the Public Sphere", *supra* n037, 911–912, adding that "both as a precedent for the crown's use of print culture and a marker for the seismic shift in its antipiracy policy, the Avery case is crucial indeed".

91 *Supra* n010.

92 Ritchie, *Captain Kidd*, *supra* n013, 153–154.

93 Peter T. Leeson, "Rationality, Pirates and the Law: A Retrospective", 59 *American University Law Review* (2010) 1219, 1222. Trials held in England itself retained juries.

94 Historical accounts of piracy trials of this era treat them as having been, effectively, decided beforehand; see, e.g., Joel H. Baer, "'The Complicated Plot of Piracy': Aspects of English Criminal Law and the Image of the Pirate in Defoe", 23 *The Eighteenth Century* (1982) 3, 6.

95 Pierino Belli, *De Re Militari et Bello Tractatus* (1563) (trans. Herbert C. Nutting) (Oxford: Clarendon, 1936), 83.

96 The 1700 *Act* limited its scope to "any of His Majesty's natural born subjects or denizens of this kingdom [who] commit any piracy [...] against other [of] His Majesty's subjects".

97 On this see Rubin, *Ethics and Authority in International Law* (Cambridge: CUP, 2007), 84, noting that it is "difficult to view this [Act] as codifying a 'universal' offence, although it could be supposed that the framers of the statute thought that all civilised States made such acts criminal [...]. There is no evidence that such a view influenced the actual wording, passage or interpretation of the legislation".

98 See "Draft Convention on Jurisdiction", *supra* n045, 563–565, listing relevant legislation; only "Great Britain" is noted to have relevant laws dating back to this era, with *Rex v Dawson* specifically cited. See also "Draft Convention on Piracy with Comments", 26 *American Journal of International Law* (1932) supplement 749, 763, suggesting that the origins of universal jurisdiction lay in "Anglo-American" law.

Captain Kidd had returned, then, to a drastically altered political and legal climate to that which he had left behind four years prior. Following his arrest in Boston, Kidd was transferred to London for trial (meaning that the 1700 *Act* effectively had no palpable effect on the outcome, as jury trials were retained in England). The transcript of his trial is filled with much the same rhetoric as *Dawson*, being designed, again, to appeal to England's Mughal allies. The prosecution denounced piracy as "the growing trouble, disturbance and mischief of the trading world, and the peaceable part of mankind", claiming that "all mankind equally and justly detest and abhor" it.[99] Judge Turton noted that "pirates are called *hostes humani generis*, the enemies to all mankind, but [...] especially so to those that depend upon trade. And these things that they stand charged with, are the most mischievous and prejudicial to trade that can happen".[100] The freedom of commerce was repeatedly promoted as a key value that pirates served to disrupt. No elaborate argument was advanced regarding jurisdiction, however, as it was straightforwardly noted that Kidd was "within the jurisdiction of the Admiralty of England".[101] Having been found guilty of separate charges of piracy and murder (Kidd had swung an iron-rimmed bucket at crewman William Moore in a fit of rage, fracturing his skull and killing him),[102] Kidd was executed at Wapping on 23 May 1701 with a Mughal delegate present to verify his demise.[103]

As with *Rex v Dawson*, Kidd's trial was geared to convict, a political tool disguised as legal process rather than a genuine invocation of natural law ideologies.[104] There is nevertheless significant value to be found in the two cases which, along with the revised 1700 *Act*, can be read together as concrete manifestations of the government-sponsored clampdown against piracy, evidencing a key historical turning-point. The cases vocalised what the *Act* did not, namely the position that pirates were "a systemic enemy of the entire international system of States".[105] With the conclusion of the trials came the realisation of Coke's notion of "*hostes humani generis*"[106] and the ideologies advanced by Cicero, Gentili and Grotius.[107]

---

99 *Kidd's Trial*, 14 Howell's State Trials 123 (1701).

100 *Ibid.*

101 *Ibid.*

102 Zacks, *supra* no56, 144.

103 Stern, *supra* no65, 139.

104 See Williams, *supra* no24, 140 describing the trial as "judicial murder" given the lack of procedural protections.

105 Policante, *supra* no16, 85.

106 Institutes, *supra* no41, 113; discussed *supra*, 3.2.3.

107 Chapter 4, *supra*, in general.

Kidd's execution was followed by a string of fierce anti-piracy operations in the Americas, with over a hundred pirates captured and tried between 1700 and 1704,[108] "a nice turnaround from the position only a little earlier in English history when piracy had been condoned as a promoter of the expansion of trade".[109] Domestic prosecutions were, of course, the end-point, the enforcement tool, for all preceding anti-pirate theory. *Houghling's Trial*, held in Virginia in 1700, invoked both *Dawson* and *Kidd* in affirming that

> Piracy is the worst of crimes and pirates the worst of men. Nay, by these base actions they degrade themselves below the rank of men and become beasts of prey, and are worse than the worst of enemies, for they are governed by no laws of nations of or arms. They [...] are enemies of all mankind.[110]

In the 1704 *Quelch* trial, the first held in the colonies under the authority of the 1700 *Act*, the Attorney-General suggested that piracy was "the worst and most intolerable of crimes that can be committed by men. A pirate was therefore justly called by the Romans *hostis humani generis*".[111] Both *Houghling* and *Quelch* suggest a strong stance on piracy among colonial courts, seeking to justify and exploit their newfound judicial powers. They also suggest the permeation of Ciceronian and Grotian ideology into domestic law,[112] albeit in a haphazard manner.

---

108 Philip Gosse, *The History of Piracy* (1932) (Mineola, NY: Dover Publications, 2007), 209–212.

109 Earle, *supra* n032, 147.

110 *Houghling's Trial*, related in Williams, *supra* n024, 134. The quote may have been inspired by John Locke's similar claim that the criminal, "having quitted reason [...] and so revolting from his own kind to that of beasts [...] renders himself liable to be destroyed by the injured person, and the rest of mankind": *Two Treatises of Government* (1690), ed. P Laslett (Cambridge: CUP, 1998) II, s172.

111 14 *Howell's State Trials* 1067 (1704). The prosecution further suggested that pirates could be immediately punished by their captors, "a sign of [piracy's] being of a very different and worse nature than any crime committed upon the land". The extent to which this actually occurred is not clear; Benerson Little writes that "[p]irates were usually returned for trial, although they might be hanged at sea if the commander had the authority and inclination": *The Sea Rover's Practice: Pirate Tactics and Techniques, 1630–1730* (Lincoln, NE: Potomac Books, 2005), 204. Baer, *supra* n094, 6, notes that summary execution may have justifiably occurred in regions "remote from courts of Admiralty" but would have become largely unnecessary following the proliferation of colonial courts.

112 Rubin, *Piracy, supra* n09, 79.

The first instance of a case where universal jurisdiction played an active role was the 1705 Scottish Admiralty *Tryal of Captain Thomas Green and his crew*.[113] Green, the English captain of a Scottish-registered ship, possessed a pirate-hunting commission issued by English authorities. He was arrested in Edinburgh accused of plundering a vessel carrying English and Scottish passengers near India, murdering all on board.[114] Although the court could have made reference to the Scottish connection in respect of either the ship registration or the victims, the prosecution reasoned instead that

> tho' the competency [is] ordinarily said to be found either *in loco delicti* or *in loco domocilii* of the delinquents, or *in loco originis*, yet there is a superior consideration; and that is the *locus deprehensionis*, where the criminal is found and deprehended, which doth so over-rule in this matter [...]. And so it is, that here the [suspects] were and are deprehended, which happening in the case of piracy, a crime against the law of nations, and which all mankind have an interest to pursue, wherever the pirates can be found, the [prosecutor's] interest to pursue is thereby manifest.[115]

The Court accepted this argument, seemingly adopting universal jurisdiction on the basis that that instances of piracy are indeed "crime[s] against the law of nations, and which all mankind have an interest to pursue" (a variant on the common rhetorical denomination, *hostes humani generis*) so that, in turn, all States can respond to any instance of piracy. The overlap of different jurisdictional possibilities appears to have been an important factor in the Court's reasoning. The claim that the "*locus deprehensionis*" is the "superior consideration" is of itself a dubious claim given that, in the context of the modern jurisdictional regime, extradition to a more interested State (such as the territorial State, in instances of "core" international crimes) would in most cases be the preferable option.[116] The justification in this case, in the context of piracy specifically, seems to be largely based on the unique *locus delicti* of piracy which, occurring on the high seas and indiscriminately targeting passing trade, *ipso facto* poses a threat to *all* States. In acting upon the high seas, pirates do not incur injury against any particular State more than any other, nor do they

113 *Supra* n014.

114 See Rubin, *Piracy, supra* n09, 93. A contemporary ballad immortalised Green as "the basest and bloodiest [of all the pirates]", though the evidence against him was actually very thin.

115 *Supra* n014.

116 See, e.g., Antonio Cassese, "Is the Bell Tolling for Universality? A Plea for a Sensible Notion of Universal Jurisdiction" 1 *Journal of International Criminal Justice* (2003) 589, 593–594.

become subject to a particular exclusive jurisdictional claim at the expense of any other. Rather, "*all* mankind have an interest to pursue" pirates. The Court went on to clarify that "it is obvious how heinous [pirates] are", being "in a perpetual war with every State, [...]. They are worse than ravenous beasts, in as far as their fatal reason gives them a greater faculty and skill to do evil. [...] Pirates extinguish humanity in themselves, and prey upon men only, especially upon traders, who are the most innocent".[117] Again, the importance of commerce forms a key component of the analysis, backed by rigorous dehumanising rhetoric. This is in spite of the resolve to actually put pirates on trial, a process that, in itself, recognises them as rights-bearing beings.

Here we find the tentative origins of universal jurisdiction, coalescing around requirements of political expediency and finding tentative legal justification via the claim that piracy affects all States equally. Trials such as *Green* demonstrate the realisation of the divisive ideologies espoused by Cicero, Gentili and Grotius, tangibly expressed via universal jurisdiction. However, given that universal jurisdiction was being crafted and applied domestically and on an *ad hoc* basis, with little cross-communication between States, it developed sporadically and subject to the whim of whichever court happened to be applying it. Moreover, claims to universal jurisdiction did not figure as decisive aspects of any of the cases considered so far (with the possible exception of *Green*). Pirates were predominantly captured and tried by their own countrymen, with States apparently remaining reluctant to allow others to claim jurisdiction over their subjects.[118] As such, universal jurisdiction took on a subsidiary role that saw little formal application. The resultant situation is one of tentative positivism rather than acceptance of Grotian naturalism, but this is not to deny its theoretical existence, as supported in the English courts. Importantly, moreover, piracy was being dealt with in a criminal rather than *in bello* paradigm and, despite the heavy rhetoric being used by courts to express their abhorrence at pirates, they were treated at trial as rights-bearing human beings.

---

117 *Supra* n014. Compare the statement with Grotius' claim that pirates are "wild rapacious beasts": *The Rights of War and Peace* (ed. Richard Tuck, from the edition by Jean Barbeyrac), (Indianapolis: Liberty Fund, 2005), II.XX.XL.

118 See, e.g., 1876 case *R v Keyn* 2 Ex D 63 in which Sir Robert Phillimore stated "I am not aware of any instance, none was cited to us, of the existence of criminal jurisdiction over a foreign vessel for an offence committed when she was not within a port or harbour of the inland". See also Rubin, *Piracy, supra* n09, 317 acknowledging only three "known" instances of universal jurisdiction over piracy between 1705 and 1931 (*Green, supra* n014; *People v Lol-Lo and Saraw*, 43 Philippine Islands 19 (1922); and *In re Piracy Jure Gentium* [1934] AC 586).

5.3 The "Golden Age" of Piracy (1700–1730)

> But 'twas all in vain, they were now told, it was their business to turn their minds to another world, and sincerely to repent of what wickedness they had done in this.
>
> Captain CHARLES JOHNSON[119]

If the 1690s and early 1700s finally saw political opinion turn conclusively against pirates, the advent of piracy's "golden age" in the 1710s and 1720s saw this attitude harden into strict policies designed to destroy it completely. The pirates of this era were firmly at ease with their criminality and usually chose their targets indiscriminately, so that British vessels (as well as any those of any other State) commonly came under attack from British-born pirates.[120] The "golden age" pirates are among history's most memorable, with such infamous folk heroes as Blackbeard, "Black" Bart Roberts, Charles Vane, "Calico" Jack Rackham, Anne Bonny and Mary Read branding their disreputable deeds onto the pirate mythos.[121] Today's swashbuckling representation of those figures does not come close, however, to capturing the terror and chaos of that age. The pirates' fierceness was matched (and probably influenced) only by the ferocity of the State campaign to suppress them.[122]

The "golden age" was directly preceded by the 1713 pan-European *Peace of Utrecht*, which formed a critical moment in the development of State control of the seas (and of pirates), at the expense of subcontracted privateers.[123] European States shifted their ongoing relationship from one of almost constant conflict to one of relative peace,[124] a condition that, in turn, allowed

---

119 Johnson, *supra* n054, 17.

120 See Earle, *supra* n032, 170, noting that swells in piracy accompanied Jacobite insurgencies in 1715–16 and 1719, fuelling traitorous sentiment. The pirate captain Benjamin Hornigold is notable for having been the exception to this rule, having refused to attack British shipping throughout the "golden age", causing mutiny among his crew: see Rediker, *supra* n025, 36.

121 See Neil Rennie, *Treasure Neverland: Real and Imaginary Pirates* (Oxford: OUP, 2013).

122 Lauren Benton, "Toward a New Legal History of Piracy: Maritime Legalities and the Myth of Universal Jurisdiction", 23 *International Journal of Maritime History* (2011) 225, 232.

123 As documented in Carl Schmitt, *The Nomos of the Earth* (1950) (trans. G.L. Ulmen) (New York: Telos Press, 2003), 180–181, and D.C. North, "Sources of Productivity Change in Ocean Shipping, 1600–1850" 76 *Journal of Political Economy* (1968) 953, 954.

124 The 1717–1720 War of the Quadruple Alliance being a notable exception, finding Spain in conflict with a four-way alliance between Britain, France, the Holy Roman Empire and the Dutch Republic. The conflict was mainly fought in Europe, with some smaller clashes in Florida and around the Caribbean in 1719. See David Marley, *Wars of the Americas: a chronology of armed conflict in the New World, 1492 to the Present* (Santa Barbara: ABC-CLIO,

them to turn their mutual attentions to the issue of piracy. The *Peace*, consisting of several constituent treaties,[125] required signatories to commit to "a universal perpetual peace, and a true and sincere friendship" and moreover that they should "wholly refrain and desist from all plundering, depredation, harm-doing, injuries, and annoyance whatsoever as well by land, as by sea".[126] The constituent *Treaty of Navigation and Commerce* between Great Britain and France required "a reciprocal liberty of navigation and commerce, which ought to be [...] the principal fruit of an establishment of peace", and further required that "subjects [...] shall receive no patent, commission, or instruction, for arming and acting at sea as privateers, nor letters of reprisal".[127] Crucially (for our purposes) the treaty also required that signatories "shall [...] cause all [...] pirates and sea-robbers [...] to be apprehended and punished as they deserve, for a terror and example to others".[128] The *Treaty* is therefore definite about piracy and privateering; State-sponsored (or acquiesced-in) plunder would become "an outmoded form of accumulation",[129] with peaceful trade the way of the future. The terms of the peace should, in theory, have enabled any State who arrested a pirate to claim a certain moral high-ground, insofar as piracy would not be a course of action befitting a sovereign.

Any positive effects of the *Peace* were, however, forestalled by the subsequent explosion in piracy caused by the revocation of privateering commissions.[130] By 1716 Nassau, on the Bahaman island of New Providence, had effectively become a "pirate republic"[131] overrun and under the *de facto* control of Benjamin Hornigold and Henry Jennings, though the inhabitants (the "Brethren of the

1998), 242–244. "Global" war would erupt again in 1756, with the commencement of the Seven Years' War between Britain and France (and their respective allies), fought across five continents.

125 There are eleven constituent bilateral treaties to the Peace (the parties being Britain, France, the Netherlands, Savoy, Prussia, Portugal and the Holy Roman Empire) plus several related treaties signed at the same time; for a full list see Randall Lesaffer, "The Peace of Utrecht and the Balance of Power", available online through *Oxford Historical Treaties*.

126 *Treaty of Peace and Friendship between France and Great Britain,* signed at Utrecht, 11 April 1713 (27 CTS 475), Articles I and II.

127 *Treaty of Commerce and Navigation between France and Great Britain,* signed at Utrecht, 11 April 1713 (28 CTS 1), Article III. Peacetime "letters of reprisal" were largely abandoned following Utrecht, a significant development in the State's monopolisation of violence; see Ritchie, "Government Measures", *supra* no26, 12.

128 *Ibid.,* Article XXXV.

129 Policante, *supra* no16, 82.

130 Ritchie, "Government Measures", *supra* no26, 19.

131 David F. Marley, *Pirates: Adventurers of the High Seas* (London: Arms and Armour Press, 1997), 139.

Coast") were never recognised as formal insurgents.[132] The effects were devastating: the British economy flat-lined between 1715 and 1728, between two periods of extensive growth.[133] The pirates represented "a threat to property, the individual, society, the colony, the empire, the Crown, the nation, the world of nations, and indeed all mankind. His villainy was complete".[134]

Based on the ideals of Utrecht and the *Dawson/Kidd* precedents, colonial governors fought to retain control, a slow process achieved by prosecuting as many pirates as possible and making a public spectacle of it.[135] At a public hanging in 1717, Boston minister Cotton Mather proclaimed that: "[a]ll nations agree to treat your tribe as the common enemies of mankind, and [to] extirpate them out of the world".[136] Mather's prophetic statement initiated a trend, as colonial governments began issuing similar anti-piracy propaganda and newspapers increasingly carried accounts of ruthless and barbarous acts. Pirates were routinely denounced as "wild and savage beast[s]"[137] (referencing Grotius' denouncement of pirates as "wild rapacious beasts")[138] and as enemies of Christianity.[139] They were habitually portrayed as incomprehensible, lawless, inhuman beings. Trials became increasingly procedurally lopsided; less a matter of justice, they were became part of the larger campaign "of anti-piratical propaganda, deterrence and retribution"[140] though pirates were, as a

132 Konstam, *supra* no6, 156–157; Colin Woodard, *The Republic of Pirates: Being the True and Surprising Story of the Caribbean Pirates and the Man who Brought Them Down* (London: Pan Macmillan, 2016).

133 *Boston Newsletter*, April 16, 1722; December 2 and 16, 1717; January 16–24, 1724. Reproduced in Rediker, *supra* no25, 31–35.

134 Rediker, *ibid.*, 129.

135 James Kraska, *Contemporary Maritime Piracy* (Santa Barbara, CA: Praeger, 2011), 30–31.

136 Cotton Mather, *Instructions to the Living, From the Conditions of the Dead* (Boston, 1717), 17; reproduced in Rediker, *supra* no25, 127. Mather is perhaps better known for his influential role in the Salem Witch Trials; in his 1693 work *The Wonders of the Invisible World (Being an account of the Tryals of Several Witches lately executed in New England)* (Boston & London: John Dunton, 1693), Mather proclaims, in comparable language, that "all nations had provided laws against [witches]" (119) and moreover that "Devils and witches [are] common enemies of mankind, and set upon mischief" (221–222).

137 *The Trial of Eight Persons Indicted for Piracy* (concerning the crew of "Black" Sam Bellamy), Boston, 1717 (cited in Baer, *supra* no94, 8).

138 See *supra* no117.

139 Rediker, *supra* no25, 127–128, 132, and 151–153. Many of the motifs appearing on pirate flags were appropriated from Christian imagery, and perverted accordingly (Rediker, 167), while Blackbeard apparently stylised himself in Satan's image and once stated that "he came from Hell". The pirates' mockery of Christianity is perhaps unsurprising given the close relationship between Church and State at this time.

140 Konstam, *supra* no6, 205.

general rule, placed on trial nevertheless.[141] Subjecting pirates to judicial process (as opposed to extra-judicial extermination) was intended to establish pirates' subservience to the State and appeal to the legitimacy of State-made law or, at a larger level, to the righteousness of the "international community" of States.[142]

In July 1718 erstwhile buccaneer Woodes Rogers arrived in Nassau to re-establish government rule. He promptly succeeded in clearing the Bahamas of around a thousand pirates (largely by granting royal pardons),[143] though many simply took their proud depredation elsewhere.[144] Among these fugitives was "Gentleman Pirate" Stede Bonnet,[145] whose 1718 trial marked something of a breakthrough in terms of unifying the application of universal jurisdiction with the influential rhetoric of Cicero, Gentili, Grotius and Coke. The commerce angle was re-emphasised, with Judge Trott describing piracy as "an offence that is destructive of all trade and commerce between nation and nation" and adding that, in consequence, "it is in the interest of all sovereign princes to punish and suppress the same".[146] He echoed the *Dawson* trial (in turn inspired by *Cusack*) in adding that "the King of England hath [...] an undoubted jurisdiction and power, in concurrency with other princes and States, for the punishment of all piracies and robberies at sea, in the most remote parts of the world".[147] Citing directly from Coke and Grotius, Trott added that "[a]s to the heinousness or wickedness of the offence, it needs no aggravation, it being evident to the reason of all men. Therefore a pirate is called *hostis humani generis*, with whom neither faith nor oath is to be kept".[148] As one of the earliest "golden age" trials, *Bonnet* provides a template for later trials, combining the most extreme elements of previous statements on piracy. It refines the "badness" of piracy into a succinct but comprehensive statement and promotes a "trade interference"

141 See references *supra*, n0111.

142 Erica Burleigh, "Coercion, Conviction, Conversion: Sovereign Selves and Interior States in Colonial Piracy Trials and Narratives", 24 *Law & Literature* (2012) 151, 155; Frohock, *supra* n038, 274–276.

143 David Cordingly, *Spanish Gold: Captain Woodes Rogers & the Pirates of the Caribbean* (London: Bloomsbury, 2011), 151–171. The motto of the Bahamas became *Expulsis Piratis, Restituta Commercia.*

144 See, generally, Johnson, *supra* n054.

145 Bonnet had, unusually, left a wealthy lifestyle in Barbados to go "on the account", a circumstance he may have been driven to "by some discomforts he found in a married state" (Johnson, *ibid.,* 63).

146 15 *Howell's State Trials* 1231 (Am. Vice Adm. 1718).

147 *Ibid.*

148 *Ibid.*

rationale for universal jurisdiction.[149] It is however necessary to account for the assertion made by Trott, when sentencing Bonnet, that "to theft, you have added a greater sin, which is murder", in reference to the eighteen men who were killed in the act of capturing Bonnet.[150] This claim, perhaps intended in a religious rather than legal sense (the use of "sin" rather than "crime" being relevant), should not be read as negating Trott's strong views on piracy. Both offences carried the death penalty.[151]

As with the earlier *Kidd* and *Dawson* trials, however, the invocation of "universal jurisdiction" in *Bonnet* was actually unnecessary given the premise of a British court sitting in judgement of a British colonial subject. There are nevertheless some interesting cases from this time (in addition to the aforementioned *Green*)[152] that do invoke aspects of extraterritorial (or extra-national) jurisdiction. One such is the 1722 hanging in Jamaica of the Italian Mathew Luke, who had attacked British shipping (killing the entire crew of four merchant vessels) with a Spanish-issued commission.[153] Luke was subsequently captured, tried and executed by the British, alongside 41 crew. However, the case against Luke is likely to have been intended as a warning to the Spanish against violating the terms of the Anglo-Spanish peace established under the Madrid and Utrecht treaties, so that "piracy" as such was probably not the underlying issue.[154] Also of interest is the execution of thirty-eight crewmembers of the pirate ship the *Flying King*, the majority of whom were British (including

149 The 1722 trial of 267 of "Black" Bartholomew Roberts' crew at British-administered Cape Coast Castle (modern day Ghana) similarly emphasised that piracy is aggravated by its commission in "remote and distant parts" and moreover that "[t]o a trading nation, nothing can be so destructive as piracy, or call for more exemplary punishment; besides the national reflection it infers, it cuts off the returns of industry"; reproduced in George Henry Borrow (ed.), *Celebrated Trials and Remarkable Cases of Criminal Jurisprudence*, Volume IV (London: Knight and Lacey, 1825), 38.

150 Johnson, *supra* no54, 76–77.

151 Cordingly, *Romance and Reality*, *supra* no8, 266–267. This penalty for piracy remained in place in the UK until 1998.

152 *Supra* no14.

153 Johnson, *supra* no54, 18.

154 A letter of 26 January 1721 to the Spanish *Alcaldes* (governor) of Trinidad from British governor of Jamaica Sir Nicholas Laws regarding the use of commissioned "*guardacostas*" laments that such actions "are not only a breach of the law of nations, but must appear to the world of a very extraordinary nature, when considered that the subjects of a Prince in amity and friendship, with another, should give countenance to and encourage such vile practices". A reply from the Spanish, dated February 20, states that "If you treat the Spaniards, you happen to take, as pyrates, I will do the same by every one of your people I can take up: I will not be wanting to good manners, if you will do the same. I can likewise act the soldier, if any occasion should offer that way". Reproduced in Johnson, *ibid.*, 19–21.

the captain, Robert Sample), in Portuguese Brazil in 1719.[155] To add to these examples, eighteen Frenchmen among the captured crew of Welshman "Black" Bart Roberts were charged with piracy by the English at Cape Coast Castle (modern day Ghana), though ultimately all were acquitted given that they had been "used like prisoners".[156] These episodes suggest that States generally considered the nationality (or "allegiance") of a captured pirate to be no obstacle to trial and execution.

5.4 Defeating Piracy: the Legacy of Captain Kidd (1730–1855)

> But now our sun is setting, night comes in, the watery wilderness ore which we raign'd, proves in our ruins peaceful.
>
> *"Purser", Fortune by Land and Sea*[157]

The "golden age" is generally thought to have come to an end with the hanging of Frenchman Olivier Levasseur (nicknamed "La Buse") by the French in Réunion in 1730.[158] In the aftermath of the "golden age" and the cleaning up operation in the Caribbean, antagonism towards piracy became normalised via a series of scholarly works published in the latter half of the eighteenth century. German philosopher Christian von Wolff, for instance, influenced by existing case law and scholarly accounts, asserted in his 1747 work *The Law of Nations Treated According to a Scientific Model*[159] that pirates "destroy the security of all

155 Johnson, *ibid.*, 83. Robert Southey, in *History of Brazil, Part III* (London: Longman, Hurst, Reed and Orme, 1819), 152–153, refers to, in 1719, "the arrest of a crew of pirates, who, after having long infested the coast of the Rio, were wrecked upon the beach at Macape, where forty-eight were apprehended by the country people and brought prisoners to Bahia. [...] [T]wenty-seven in number, were hanged, as they well deserved". A letter from the Governor-General of Brazil to King John V of Portugal, dated 26 August 1721, appears to refer to the execution of twenty-two "foreign" pirates captured in Rio de Janeiro: document AHU_ACL_CU_005, Cx 15, D1248, archived in the *Arquivo Hisrtórico Ultramarino*, Lisbon. Whether these events are related (or, even, one and the same) is unclear. See also Earle, *supra* no32, 206, noting that several pirate trials and executions in the late 1720s were conducted by the French, Dutch, Portuguese and Spanish.

156 *Supra* no149, 37.

157 Taken from the final speech by the pirate *Purser* in Thomas Heywood and William Rowley, *Fortune by Land and Sea,* originally performed c. 1607. Reproduced in Lois Potter, "Pirates and 'Turning Turk' in Renaissance Drama" in Jean-Pierre Maquerlot and Michèle Willems (eds), *Travel and Drama in Shakespeare's Time* (Cambridge: CUP, 1996), 127.

158 Earle, *supra* no32, 206.

159 Wolff, *The Law of Nations Treated According to a Scientific Model* (1747) (trans. Joseph H. Drake) (Washington DC: Carnegie Endowment for International Peace, 1934).

nations [...], [t]herefore the right to punish them belongs to all nations, and by this right they can remove from their midst those wild monsters of the human species".[160]

Influenced by Wolff,[161] Swiss jurist Emmerich de Vattel wrote the following paragraph in his 1758 work *Droit des Gens* (Law of Nations):

> although the justice of each nation ought in general to be confined to the punishment of crimes committed in its own territories, we ought to except from this rule those villains, who, by the nature and habitual frequency of their crimes, violate all public security, and declare themselves the enemies of the human race. [...] Thus, pirates are sent to the gibbet by the first into whose hands they fall.[162]

Vattel places a degree of importance on "home justice", then, with the preference being that the territorial State take precedence in the prosecution of crime generally.[163] Vattel advocates exceptions to the rule, however, so that it can be set aside when dealing with "villains who [...] violate all public security".[164] The rationale for this exception appears to be based on a Grotian "natural law" position[165] combined with the position adopted by the English Admiralty court in *Dawson* that piracy threatens States as a whole rather than merely individuals.[166] Elsewhere Vattel advocates Spain's right to destroy the "pirate" towns of Africa, "those nests of pirates, that are continually molesting their commerce and ruining their subjects",[167] thereby also weaving in a commerce commentary on piracy. Vattel's statements appear to affirm the seriousness with which piracy was commonly regarded and the desire for swift punishment of their actions by the first power to capture an offender.[168] In all he adds little, however, to the debate on how pirates should be apprehended

160 *Ibid.*; the cited phrase is an amalgamation of Book 6, s627 and Book 7, s778.

161 Vincent Chetail, "Vattel and the American Dream: An Inquiry into the Reception of the *Law of Nations* in the United States" in Pierre-Marie Dupuy and Vincent Chetail (eds), *The Roots of International Law* (Leiden: Martinus Nijhoff, 2013) 251, 288.

162 *The Law of Nations* (1758) (trans. Charles G. Fenwick) (Washington, DC: Carnegie Institution of Washington, 1916), Book I, ch. XIX, ss 232–233.

163 *Ibid.*

164 *Ibid.* Vattel includes in this list "poisoners, assassins and incendiaries", apparently on the basis that they are also a form of "pirate".

165 4.2.2, *supra*.

166 5.2, *supra*.

167 *Supra* no162, Book III, Chpt IX, s 167.

168 See, Rech, *supra* no47, 28, noting that the "heinousness" of piracy was the main reason for Vattel to advocate for universal jurisdiction.

and punished.[169] This is not to deny his influential impact on the shaping of international law more generally.[170]

In 1769 Oxford professor, judge and Member of Parliament Sir William Blackstone published his influential *Commentaries on the Laws of England*,[171] in which he declared that

> the crime of piracy, or robbery and depredation on the high seas, is an offence against the universal law of society; a pirate being, according to Sir Edward Coke, *hostis humani generis*. As therefore he has [...] reduced himself afresh to the savage state of nature by declaring war against all mankind, all mankind must declare war against him: so that every community hath a right, by the rule of self-defence, to inflict that punishment on him.[172]

Blackstone's "social contract naturalism"[173] placed pirates in a perpetual war with organised society, offending against the universally applicable laws of civilisation, their suppression intrinsically linked to "the peace of the world".[174] Blackstone echoes Grotius in suggesting that "in all marine causes [...], there is no other rule of decision but this great universal law collected from history and usage, and such writers of all nations and languages as are generally approved and allowed of",[175] suggesting not so much a lack of domestic law over the high seas but rather the pre-existence of natural law, binding on pirates (as perpetrators of a "*malum in se*" committed in a "state of nature")[176] and

169 See also criticisms of Vattel's contribution in Eugene Kontorovich, "The Piracy Analogy: Modern Universal Jurisdiction's Hollow Foundation" 45 *Harvard International Law Journal* (2004) 205, 231–232 and Luc Reydams, "The Rise and Fall of Universal Jurisdiction", Leuven Centre for Global Governance Working Paper No. 37, January 2010, 35.

170 See, e.g.: Rech, *supra* no47, 223; Kontorovich, *ibid.*, 230; and Frank S. Ruddy, *International law in the Enlightenment: the background of Emmerich de Vattel's Le Droit Des Gens* (New York: Oceana Publications, 1975) 281–310.

171 Sir William Blackstone, *Commentaries on the Laws of England: In Four Books* (ed. George Sharswood) (Philadelphia: J.B. Lippincott Company, 1893).

172 *Ibid.*, Book IV (Volume 2), 70. Blackstone added two further categories of "offences against the law of nations", namely "violation of safe-conducts" and "infringement of the rights of ambassadors", although there was no corresponding "international law" to support these assertions; see Georg Schwarzenberger, "The Problem of an International Criminal Law" 3 *Current Legal Problems* (1950) 263, 267–268.

173 Rubin, *Piracy, supra* no9, 110, referring to the apparent merging of domestic and natural law in Blackstone's theory, the former taking the form of a "social contract" between government and governed.

174 *Supra* no171, 67.

175 *Ibid.*

176 4.2.2, *supra.*

enforceable by States ("every community") via positive jurisdictional claims.[177] Like others before him, Blackstone was attempting to bridge the gap between Roman-type belligerent treatments of piracy, Ciceronian and Grotian natural law paradigms, and more modern, European positivist criminal procedure – though his "simple language [...] disguise[d] the legal complexities really involved without giving any orientation that would help lawmakers or attorneys find their way through the thickets of the law".[178] Blackstone was repeating a similar heavy rhetoric to that of British courts at around the same time, generally in order to ensure that pirates were denigrated in the strongest light possible, designed perhaps as part of a strategy for deterrence or for the appeasement of political or commercial allies. In so doing, Blackstone may be added to the list of proponents for universal jurisdiction, a contemporary manifestation of Ciceronian thought, who supplemented the old paradigm with a touch of legal contemporaneity. He adds a touch of subtlety and nuance to the discourse of the time, much of which consisted of increasingly inventive insults devised by English prosecutors and judges.

At the other side of the Atlantic Ocean, meanwhile, "piracy" was helping to define an entire nation. In 1787 the founding fathers of the United States considered piracy a serious enough issue to include a clause in the Constitution empowering Congress to "define and punish piracies and felonies committed on the high seas and offences against the law of nations".[179] There is no clear reason given as to why the definition of piracy happened to be left to Congress rather than being reserved to the founding American States. James Madison justified the decision by suggesting that "[t]he definition of piracies might perhaps without inconveniency, be left to the law of nations; though a legislative definition of them, is found in most municipal codes",[180] perhaps indicating that a centralised legislator would be better placed to handle an international issue (as per treaty-making powers and ambassadorial duties). It may be that, as an extraterritorial offence, piracy was considered to be a collective threat to the States as a whole and, as such, better left to federal Congress to deal with on the States' behalf as a defence matter (alongside declaring war, granting letters of marque and reprisal, raising armies and maintaining navies).[181] Piracy is

177 With States taking the place of private individuals in natural law theory; see *supra* 4.1.2 and 4.2.2.

178 Rubin, *Piracy, supra* no9, 110.

179 *The Constitution of the United States,* 1787, Article 1(8), 10. See Rubin, *ibid.*, 122–127, on the drafting history of this provision.

180 Alexander Hamilton, James Madison, and John Jay (eds), *The Federalist Papers* (1788), (New York: New American Library, 1961), 265–266.

181 *US Constitution, supra* no179, 1(8), 11–13.

one of only two offences specifically criminalised in the Constitution itself, the other being "counterfeiting the securities and current coin".[182]

US courts, however, were initially reluctant to deal with piracy as a crime under the "law of nations" as they felt that to do so would effectively be to legislate for the entire world.[183] As such, universal jurisdiction was specifically excluded, as demonstrated in the 1818 case *US v Palmer*, in which the Supreme Court held that any act of "piracy" that had no connection to the US "is not piracy within the meaning of [US law] and is not punishable in the courts of the United States".[184] The US courts struggled to grapple with the contradictions inherent in reconciling "natural law" with European legal positivism.[185] Claims to jurisdiction based on "natural law" could only be asserted when there were gaps in the system, such as in the 1820 case *US v Klintock* in which the Supreme Court accepted jurisdiction over piracy in limited circumstances over "persons on board of a vessel not at the time belonging to the subjects of any foreign power [...] and acknowledging obedience to no government whatsoever".[186] This early jurisprudence runs aground on a clear friction between Grotian "natural law" approaches to piracy and European legal positivism, the latter constrained by the Cokean concern that offenders should only be answerable to their State,[187] despite Blackstone's efforts (half a century earlier) at reconciling the two strands of legal theory. Universal jurisdiction was available as a device to "fill the gap", but only where there was one.[188] This was more than a century after the Scottish Admiralty court had apparently approved the use of universal jurisdiction based on the heinousness of piracy in *Green*, and evidence of applied universal jurisdiction had emerged in other parts of the world.[189]

The issue appeared to be resolved by the about-turn of the Supreme Court in the 1820 case *US v Smith*,[190] issued in response to a revised definition of piracy put forward by Congress in the 1819 *Act to Protect the Commerce of the United States and Punish the Crime of Piracy*. The 1819 Act read:

182 *Ibid.*, 1(8), 6.

183 Rubin, *Ethics and Authority*, *supra* n097, 73–74. See also Henry Wheaton, *Elements of International Law* (1836) (ed. Richard Henry Dana and George Grafton Wilson) (Oxford: Clarendon, 1936), 162.

184 *US v Palmer* 16 U.S. (3 Wheat) 610 (1818), 643.

185 Rubin, *Piracy, supra* n09, 143.

186 18 US (5 Wheat) 144 (1820).

187 Rubin, *Piracy, supra* n09, 143.

188 *Ibid.*

189 *Supra* 5.2, 5.3.

190 *US v Smith* 18 US (5 Wheat) 20 (1820).

> If *any person or persons whatsoever*, shall, on the high seas, commit the crime of piracy, as defined by the law of nations, and such offender or offenders shall afterwards be brought into, or found in, the United States, every such offender or offenders shall, upon conviction thereof, [...] be punished with death.[191]

Assessing the constitutionality of the *Act* Justice Story, for the Court, drew directly on Coke, Grotius, Jenkins and Blackstone, as well as citing from *Dawson, Kidd* and *Green* in asserting that

> There is scarcely a writer on the law of nations, who does not allude to piracy as a crime of a settled and determinate nature [...]. [R]obbery or forcible depredations upon the sea, *animo furandi*, is piracy. [...] The common law, too, recognizes and punishes piracy as an offence, not against its own municipal code, but as an offence against the law of nations, [...] as an offence against the universal law of society, a pirate being deemed an enemy of the human race. [...] And the general practice of all nations in punishing all persons, whether natives or foreigners, who have committed this offence against any persons whatsoever, [...] is a conclusive proof that the offence is supposed to depend [...] upon the law of nations, both for its definition and punishment.[192]

The problematic counterpoints of "natural law" and positivism were adjudged to be reconciled, freeing up the federal courts to deal with a logjam of subsequent piracy cases.[193] The reasoning is a combination of Blackstone's notion of "natural law" as a residual mechanism (positively enforceable by States) and actual State practice to date. Story's judgement became the authoritative US position on piracy *jure gentium* (and jurisdiction thereover) until the 2012 case *US v Dire*.[194]

The British position, meanwhile, was "precisely the mirror image of the logic of the United States: the spread of British jurisdiction by the assertion of Parliament without regard to the international legal order".[195] This broad position was particularly evident in the 1873 Privy Council case, *A-G of Hong Kong v Kwok-A-Sing*, in which the court had no qualm establishing jurisdiction over

191 Act of Mar. 3, 1819, s5.3, emphasis added.

192 *Supra* no190, 161.

193 Rubin, *Piracy, supra* no9, 146.

194 US Court of Appeals, 4th Circuit, 23 May 2012. *Dire* adopted the definition contained in Article 101 of the 1982 *United Nations Convention on the Law of the Sea* (UNCLOS) over that set out in *Smith*.

195 Rubin, *Piracy, supra* no9, 239.

a Chinese national suspected of mutiny on a French ship, with *Rex v Dawson* cited as precedent.[196]

Still, actual assertions of universal jurisdiction, over situations that fell outside "ordinary" jurisdictional grounds, remained very rare.[197] Nevertheless it had clearly become "the Anglo-American view [...] that piracy [was] a special basis of jurisdiction to prosecute and to punish foreigners, although the offence was committed in a place and under circumstances that did not subject it to the state's authority on any ordinary ground".[198] The theoretical groundwork had been laid, to different extents and at different levels by the scholars considered thus far, and the practice (albeit sparse) supported it.

5.5 The Demise of Privateering

The decline of piracy[199] can be inextricably linked to the demise of privateering, with war increasingly becoming "an affair of Governments"[200] via the formation and maintenance of regular navies.[201] Lord Nelson wrote, in 1801, that

> Respecting privateers, [...] I am decidedly of the opinion that [...] they are a disgrace to our country; and it would be truly honourable never to permit them after this war. Such horrible robberies have been committed by them in all parts of the world, that it is really a disgrace to the country which tolerates them.[202]

Queen Victoria similarly scorned privateering as being "a kind of piracy which disagrees with our civilisation", adding that "its abolition throughout the world

196 [1873] LR 5 PC 179; see also commentary in Rubin, *ibid.*, 240–242.

197 As indicated by the Harvard Research group in 1932, "Draft Convention on Piracy", *supra* n098, 756.

198 *Ibid.*, 887.

199 Piracy was considered to be obsolete as an offence by the 1920s; see Edwin D. Dickinson, "Is the Crime of Piracy Obsolete?", 38 *Harvard Law Review* (1925) 334, and Harvard "Draft Convention on Piracy", *ibid.*, 764. This is notwithstanding resurgences in the early nineteenth century, on which, see Earle, *supra* n032, 212–214.

200 Secretary William L. Marcy, quoted in Sir Francis Piggott, *The Declaration of Paris, 1856: A Study, Documented* (London, 1919), 397. See also, generally, Thomson, *supra* n078.

201 Anne Pérotin-Dumon, "The Pirate and the Emperor: Power and the Law on the Seas, 1450–1850" in C.R. Pennell, *Bandits at Sea: A Pirates Reader* (NYU Press, 2001) 25, 44–45.

202 *Piracy in the Levant, 1827–8: Selected from the Papers of Admiral Sir Edward Codrington, KCB* (1934) (Volume 72 of the Navy Records Society), xviii-xix; reproduced in Rubin, *Piracy, supra* n09, 216.

would be a great step in its advance",[203] suggesting an emerging consensus about the detestable nature of privateering and its close links with piracy. James Buchanan, US ambassador to Britain, announced that it would further the progress of friendly civilisation to "abolish war against private property upon the ocean".[204] Nineteenth century wars already relied less on the use of privateers,[205] with major maritime states having developed substantial navies,[206] greater state regulation in place,[207] and several bilateral treaties arising blocking the practice between specific states.[208]

The ambition of eliminating privateering was finally realised in the 1856 *Declaration of Paris*, at the close of the Crimean War.[209] The Declaration stated at the outset that "privateering is and remains abolished" and provided for "recognition of shared guilt and a promise that the behaviour of States which produced the problem will not be repeated" as well as guaranteeing neutral rights to trade undisturbed. The Declaration proved to be a "decisive turning point in the ambivalence of States towards piracy, and to affirm a universal prohibition. It also seemed to lay to rest any previously harboured selfish interest on the part of States to utilize piracy".[210] Piracy became easier to identify and condemn, given that State-sponsored plunder became legally indefensible.[211] Pirates could no longer hide behind State sponsorship, becoming divorced from internationally accepted legal and moral dictates.[212]

The abolition of privateering marked the moment at which the "heinousness" of piracy could be linked directly to its frustration of trade, without having to invoke a convoluted argument to deal with the problem of why

---

203 H.W. Malkin, "The Inner History of the Declaration of Paris" 8 *British Yearbook of International Law* (1927) 1, 30.

204 *British and Foreign State Papers, 1855–1856* (London, 1856), vol. 46, 831–832.

205 See John M. Golden, "Patent Privateers: Private Enforcement's Historical Survivors" 26 *Harvard Journal of Law and Technology* 545, 571, citing the example of the Napoleonic Wars.

206 Theodore M. Cooperstein, "Letters of Marque and Reprisal: The Constitutional Law and Practice of Privateering" 40 *Journal of Maritime Law & Commerce* (2009) 221, 244.

207 F.M. Kert, "Cruising in Colonial Waters: The Organization of North American Privateering in the War of 1812" in Starkey *et al* (eds), *supra* n07, 141, 147.

208 Bryan K. Doeg, "PMCs on the High Seas: the Solution to Somali Piracy or a Failure to Learn from History?" 1 *University of Miami National Security & Armed Conflict Law Review* (2011) 139, 153. Examples include the *Treaty of Amity, Commerce, and Navigation* (between Britain and the US), signed in London, November 19, 1794 (the "Jay Treaty"), Articles 19 and 20.

209 Declaration of Paris, *supra* n012. See, further, Malkin, *supra* n0203.

210 Lawrence Azubuike, "International Law Regime against Piracy" 15 *Annual Survey of International and Comparative Law* (2009) 43, 46.

211 Benton, "Toward a New Legal History", *supra* n0122, 238.

212 Jan Martin Lemnitzer, *Power, Law and the End of Privateering* (London: Palgrave Macmillan), 9–10.

States *can* plunder yet pirates cannot (a distinction that, as we have seen, was based on identity and authority).[213] "Pirate-like" plunder committed by States was now *also* inherently wrong,[214] though motive would remain relevant for the purpose of identifying privately motivated "piracy".[215]

5.6 Conclusion

> *Farewell, the raging main, to Turkey, France, and Spain,*
> *I shall never see you again, For I must die.*[216]

Captain Kidd's plight symbolised a reversal in fortune for piracy and the oppositional rise of the State, a renewed institution determined to promote and derive wealth from friendly commerce. Working on a draft "Convention on Piracy" in 1932, the Harvard Research Group considered the eighteenth and nineteenth centuries a key period in terms of the development of both the definition of piracy and the scope of applicable jurisdiction.[217] It was "a period when piratical depredations were a very real menace to all water-borne commerce and traffic",[218] leading to a burst in legislative activity, jurisprudence and scholarship, in turn based on the building blocks laid by Gentili, Grotius and Lord Coke. The suppression of piracy shifted from an unrefined Ciceronian idea of pirates as a common enemy of all mankind, to an applied "positivist" legal approach that branded pirates as criminals subject to State-made laws and State jurisdictions, in part inspired by pre-existing notions of "natural law". Underlining the new positivism were insistent and consistent claims about the deep-seated serious nature of piracy, a criminal practice that, on the surface level, threatened trade between States and, at a more abstract level, "rent at the fabric of the prevailing economic and political order", presenting "a revolutionary threat to the early modern *status quo*".[219] All this was driven by a subtle undercurrent of *realpolitik*, a desire not only for peaceful seas but

213 3.1 and 4.1.1, *supra*.

214 Seizing enemy goods nevertheless remains permitted in certain situations; 3.1, *supra* (footnote 22).

215 Article 101 of UNCLOS (*supra* no194) defines piracy as "illegal acts of violence or detention, or any act of depredation, committed for private ends by the crew or the passengers of a private ship [...]", thereby excluding acts of State or political acts generally.

216 Excerpt from *The Ballad of Captain Kidd*, *supra* no1.

217 *Supra* no98, 852.

218 Harvard "Draft Convention on Jurisdiction", *supra* no98, 566.

219 Virginia W. Lunsford, Piracy and Privateering in the Golden Age Netherlands (Gordonsville, VA: Palgrave Macmillan, 2005), 137.

also for expansion and the elimination of troublesome opponents who could conveniently (but sometimes dubiously) be classed as "pirates".[220]

By becoming an ever-increasing scourge of an increasingly commercialised global society, pirates ultimately engineered their own downfall. Though it may seem vaguely painful to recognise it now, the forebears of the roguish Jack Sparrow[221] or the bumbling Captain Pugwash[222] were hunted to extermination by a vengeful State collective, a project fuelled by commerce and politics and fought on legal and propagandist battlefields. We see the legal battle fought through such landmark cases as *Cusack, Dawson, Kidd, Green* and *Bonnet* from which universal jurisdiction gradually emerges: a realised, tangible legacy of Gentilian and Grotian thought on the subject of "the common enemies of all mankind". Like the works of Gentili and Grotius, the oratory of the courts seemed doused in rhetoric, their language overbearing to the point of caricature, pirates "savage beasts" who possessed no place in the global order. Looking beyond the rhetoric and overegged claims to legitimacy we see a genuine monster lurking, "a physical and ontological threat" to civilisation justifying a universal legal response.[223]

The histories documented herein form the heart of the "piracy analogy" and the stepping stone for the legal developments of the twentieth century as we begin to see a rudimentary form of universal jurisdiction begin to take shape, moulded by a vehement response to the new threats presented by the ancient enemy. Though the practical application of universal jurisdiction to piracy remained unclear and unprincipled throughout this period (and may have been "honoured more on paper than in practice")[224] we can nevertheless discern a garbled but forceful reasoning behind it, brought to life by the powerful statements of courts, governments and contemporary scholars, all of whom acquiesced in the principle of where they did not actively invoke it.

This chapter forms an essential backdrop for what is to follow, as Chapter 6 now proceeds to dissect its key themes, drawing on the relevant histories to reach conclusions concerning the original rationale for the exercise of universal jurisdiction.

---

220 Rubin, *Piracy, supra* n09, Chapter IV.

221 *Pirates of the Caribbean: The Curse of the Black Pearl* (dir. Gore Verbinksi, Disney, 2003).

222 See David Cordingly and John Falconer, *Pirates: Fact & Fiction* (London: Collins & Brown Ltd, 1992), 113, on the incompetent captain of *The Black Pig*.

223 Andrew Dilts, "To Kill a Thief: Punishment, Proportionality and Criminal Subjectivity in Locke's Second Treatise" 40 *Political Theory* (2012) 58, 60.

224 Eugene Kontorovich, "A Positive Theory of Universal Jurisdiction", Bepress Legal Series, Working Paper 211 (2004), 5; see also references cited *supra* n0118.

CHAPTER 6

Rationalising Universal Jurisdiction: the Provenance of the "Piracy Analogy"

Understanding the original rationale for the exercise of universal jurisdiction is critical to understanding its proper place today.[1] Yet there is a deep divide in the literature regarding the reason *why* universal jurisdiction first developed as a response to piracy. The proclaimed "heinousness" of piracy as a rationale for universal jurisdiction is an old and popular theory, stipulating that it is the serious nature of piracy that warrants the equal attention and concern of *every* State and which warrants the displacement of established jurisdictional bases.[2] Drawing on the dialogue of disdain established in the late seventeenth and early eighteenth century (as catalogued in Chapter 5), proponents of this line of reasoning suggest that the rationale for universal jurisdiction over pirates "relies on the fundamental nature of piratical offenses. Piracy may comprise particularly heinous and wicked acts of violence or depredation".[3] The bloody histories of the previous chapter would seem to support this point, providing a handy historical connection for "new" universal jurisdiction, itself based on a perception that the "core" international crimes "affect the whole of mankind and shock the conscience of all nations of the world".[4] This claim underlies the invocation of the "piracy analogy" in *Eichmann* and provides a historical backbone for the exercise of universal jurisdiction over, *inter alia,* genocide, crimes against humanity, war crimes, and (by some accounts) torture and aggression.[5]

This traditional position has come under increasing scrutiny, however, as several scholars have disputed the historical presumption that piracy was indeed a particularly "heinous" crime, thereby threatening to undo the historical

1 See 1.2.3, *supra.*

2 See *e.g.*: *Eichmann v. A-G Israel (Supreme Court)*, 36 *International Law Reports* (1968), para. 11; Permanent Court of International Justice, *The Case of the S.S. "Lotus"*, September 7th, 1927, Dissenting opinion of Judge Moore, 70–71; Principle 2 of *The Princeton Principles on Universal Jurisdiction* (Princeton University, 2001), 29.

3 Kenneth Randall, "Universal Jurisdiction under International Law", 66 *Texas Law Review* (1987–88) 785, 795.

4 *Prosecutor v. Tadić*, ICTY Appellate Judgement, 10 August 1995, paras 57 and 59, paraphrasing from *Eichmann, supra* n02.

5 1.2.1, *supra.*

 | DOI:10.1163/9789004390461_007

basis of the "piracy analogy".[6] The repudiation of the "heinousness" theory is supported by analogies to privateering and the claim that universal jurisdiction is better justified solely by reference to the unique *locus delicti* of the offence (making it a "transnational" rather than a genuinely "international" crime).[7] The provenance of the piracy analogy, and the nature of universal jurisdiction, is thus under attack. To resolve this dispute is to resolve the suitability of the "piracy analogy" and (dis)establish the foundations of modern international criminal law.

Using the previous chapter as factual background, Chapter 6 will examine these conflicting claims in greater detail, using an inductive empirical approach to ascertain the rationale(s) behind universal jurisdiction, as it emerged at this time, and linking the emerging rationales to the ideologies explored in previous chapters. The study herein will, in turn, provide a backdrop for assessing in the suitability and sustainability of the "piracy analogy" as a precedent for "new" universal jurisdiction over "core" international crimes.[8] It avoids an exhaustive consideration of *existing* theories of universal jurisdiction, as the intent is to consider how the principle emerged from a historical perspective as opposed to considering justifications offered for its advent and development in retrospect. Eugene Kontorovich writes, for instance, that "[t]he modern argument for universal jurisdiction sees the historic treatment of piracy as evidence of an exception to standard jurisdictional limitations based on the 'outrageousness' or 'heinousness' of the crime. In the ["new" universal jurisdiction] theory, heinousness is the common denominator of piracy and the new universal offenses: these are crimes that are profoundly despised throughout the world".[9] Kontorovich uses this basic presumption in order to demolish the usefulness of the "piracy analogy" by demonstrating that piracy was never, in fact, conceived of as particularly "heinous". Yet in this approach, "heinousness" is conceived of in terms of what it means in respect of offences

6 Eugene Kontorovich, "The Piracy Analogy: Modern Universal Jurisdiction's Hollow Foundation" 45 *Harvard International Law Journal* (2004) 205; Harry D, Gould, "Cicero's Ghost: Rethinking the Social Construction of Piracy", in Michael J. Struett, Jon D. Carlson, and Mark T. Nance (eds), *Maritime Piracy and the Construction of Global Governance* (New York: Routledge, 2013), 24; Matthew Garrod, "Piracy, the Protection of Vital State Interests and the False Foundations of Universal Jurisdiction in International Law", 25 *Diplomacy and Statecraft* (2014) 195; Nahal Kazemi, "Justifications for Universal Jurisdiction: Shocking the Conscience is Not Enough" 49 *Tulsa Law Review* (2013) 1; Tamsin Paige, "Piracy and Universal Jurisdiction" 12 *Macquarie Law Journal* (2013) 131, 148–151; Alejandro Chehtman, *The Philosophical Foundations of Extraterritorial Punishment* (Oxford: OUP, 2011), 92–93.

7 Paige, *ibid.*

8 8.1, *infra.*

9 Kontorovich, *supra* no6, 205.

today and then applied retrospectively to piracy – an approach that necessarily involves imposing modern rationales for universal jurisdiction or preconceived conceptions of "heinousness" to an altogether different era. This pitfall might be avoided by studying the original rationales for universal jurisdiction over piracy, excluding reference to modern day justifications for universal jurisdiction over "core" international crimes. The uncorrupted findings from this study can then be applied, comparatively, to broader modern-day assertions of universal jurisdiction.[10]

Part 6.1 considers the perceived "heinousness" of piracy from several angles, namely: its frustration of the *libertas commerciorum* (freedom of commerce), the freedom of States to engage in trade upon the high seas; its indiscriminate effect; the fact that it occurs beyond State borders; and the fact of consensus among States regarding its prohibition (and the use of universal jurisdiction as a result). Part 6.2 then considers two counter arguments: firstly the idea of "reverse heinousness", the idea that universal jurisdiction was attached to piracy as a way of highlighting the *faux* seriousness of it, rather than the other way around; secondly, the notion of *forum conveniens* – the idea that universal jurisdiction over piracy might, alternatively, be better justified by practical considerations, given its usefulness as a "gap-filling" tool on the territorial vacuum of the high seas. Part 6.3 serves as a conclusion, suggesting that the "heinousness" argument can be sustained when framed in the correct way. It draws conclusions for the suitability of the "piracy analogy" as a means of sustaining universal jurisdiction today.

6.1 Piracy as a "Heinous" Offence

> I shall shew you the nature of the offence, and the heinousness thereof.
>
> JUDGE NICHOLAS TROTT, *Bonnet's Trial*[11]

The key to understanding the true nature of piracy lies not so much in the deeds of the pirate but in his *identity*.[12] Pirates have always presented something of an anomaly for an international jurisdictional system that takes, as its starting point, the State's right to claim authority over an event with which it

10 8.1, *infra*.

11 *Bonnet's Trial*, 15 State Trials (Howell) 1231 (Am. Vice Adm. 1718).

12 Adeno Addis, "Imagining the International Community: The Constitutive Dimension of Universal Jurisdiction" 31 *Human Rights Quarterly* (2009) 129, 139 ("it was not the nature of the act but the nature of the actor that mattered").

has a tangible connection (territoriality, or perpetrator nationality, for instance).[13] Representing both a universally belligerent quasi-political force and a *sui generis* criminal operating beyond all borders, it was difficult to know how best to deal with them.[14] Even after the renewed legal and political campaign against pirates in the 1700s,[15] with pirates now effectively classed as *sui generis* extraterritorial criminals rather than as rights-less belligerents,[16] courts struggled to identify who exactly these outlaws were, what laws they were breaking, and how to claim jurisdiction over events that had occurred thousands of miles away, beyond the borders of any State.

This much is clear: piracy is not merely robbery at sea. The effects of piracy, underwritten by its subversive ideals, ran far deeper than the acts of territorially based criminals such as highwaymen. In terms of its effects, it had the potential to bring down Westphalian civilisation ("for suffer pirates, and the commerce of the world must cease"),[17] impacting indiscriminately on all States. This is as opposed to a land-based robber, the effect of whose actions will generally be contained to a single jurisdiction. The *locus delicti* of the offence also made it difficult to counter; to borrow again from Robert Newton (the prosecutor of *Rex v Dawson* as opposed to the *Treasure Island* actor), "in the case of a robbery on the land, we know who is to pay for it; but in a robbery at sea, it often happens that innocent persons bear the loss of what these men do".[18] Moreover it would be erroneous to suggest piracy's relative acceptability by correlation to the State-sponsored mirror practice of privateering.[19]

Yet even if we could consider piracy as being particularly "heinous", this cannot *per se* justify bypassing the usual jurisdictional bases and claiming an immediate right to universal jurisdiction. All legal systems agree, for instance, that murder is a serious offence,[20] but it is not recognised as being subject to universal jurisdiction.[21] Accordingly there must be something more specific about piracy that allows universal jurisdiction to "bite". Some deconstruction is necessary. Here we consider, in turn: the importance to States of the *libertas*

13 1.1, *supra*.

14 3.2.2, *supra*.

15 5.2, 5.3, *supra*.

16 See, *e.g.*, Douglas Guilfoyle, "The Laws of War and the Fight Against Somali Piracy: Combatants or Criminals?" 11 *Melbourne Journal of International Law* (2010) 1.

17 *Rex v Dawson*, 13 *Howell's State Trials* 451 (1696).

18 *Ibid.*

19 See discussion at 3.1, *supra*.

20 See, e.g., John Mikhail, "Is the Prohibition of Homicide Universal? Evidence from Comparative Criminal Law" 75 *Brooklyn Law Review* (2009) 497.

21 Though murder on a massive scale could, depending on the circumstances, qualify as crimes against humanity or genocide which, under customary international law, may be subject to claims of universal jurisdiction.

commerciorum, the sacrosanct right to trade; the indiscriminate nature of piracy; its extraterritorial *locus*; and State consent regarding its heinousness and subjection to universal jurisdiction. These subsections overlap to a large degree, and so cannot be read in isolation.

6.1.1 Libertas Commerciorum: *Universal Jurisdiction, Piracy and the Commercial Imperative*

The *libertas commerciorum*, or freedom of commerce, formed a central component of Hugo Grotius' denunciation of piracy.[22] Pirates were enemies of commerce and trade between States to an extent that, according to Grotius, "no stronger reason underlying our abhorrence of robbers and pirates than the fact that they besiege and render unsafe the thoroughfares of human intercourse".[23] As such the pirate became subject to the wrath of States, as expressed predominantly via prosecutors and judges in seventeenth and eighteenth century courtrooms.[24] The holding of the English Admiralty court in *Cusack provides a prime example*, via its claim that the offender had "shewed the heinousness of the crime of piracy; that it was against the law of nations [and] destructive to commerce".[25] As trade between nations gained ground and became commonplace, so the pirate was adjudged to have violated a central tenet of civilised society, making him subject to a nascent international law and, therefore, punishable under it, regardless of the capturing State.

The increasingly cordial politics, growth in industry, burgeoning commercial relations and growing wealth of the later 1600s and early 1700s demanded the punishment of piracy, an obstructive anachronism that had outstayed its dubious welcome.[26] Captain Kidd's trial, and the circumstances surrounding it, epitomised this trend. Given that the vast bulk of trade occurred over the seas,[27]

22 4.1.2, *supra*.

23 *De Jure Praedae* (trans. Martine Julia van Ittersum) (Indianapolis: Liberty Fund, 2006), 220.

24 5.2, 5.3, *supra*.

25 Anon, *The Grand Pyrate: Or, the Life and Death of Capt. George Cusack the Great Sea-Robber* (London: Jonathan Edwin, 1676), discussed *supra*, 5.1. For a more contemporary take see Robert Haywood and Roberta Spivak, *Maritime Piracy* (Oxford: Routledge, 2012), 35, noting that, left unchecked, "piracy can have an enormous impact on legitimate trade and even State power".

26 See 5.2, *supra*, and also Jason Power, "Maritime Terrorism: A New Challenge for National and International Security" 10 *Barry Law Review* (2008) 111, 113, confirming that "[t]he condemnation of piracy, was based on the consolidation of State sovereignty, the rise of mercantilist economic theories, and developments in international laws and diplomacy between the countries that were once the target of pirates".

27 Randall, *supra* n03, 793–794; Georg W F Hegel, *Elements of the Philosophy of Right* (1820), ed. Allen W. Wood (Cambridge: CUP, 1991), 247 (suggesting that the sea is "one of the chief means of culture, and in it, too, trade acquires a world-historical significance").

pirates' actions indiscriminately impacted the global market and, in turn, a core interest of the international community of States.[28] They caused "severe economic and diplomatic damage in a way that threatened all States" and destabilised the international order.[29] Universal jurisdiction, then, was arguably conceived as a way of addressing the balance.[30] Any State may respond to piracy on behalf of *all* States, each of which is equally affected. To cite Blackstone, "every community hath a right, by the rule of self-defence, to inflict that punishment on [a pirate]".[31] Blackstone conceived of a pre-existing "natural law" in such circumstances (a concept originating with Cicero) that might legitimately be applied by any State, as indeed it had since the early 1700s.[32] Although initially pioneered by States (such as Britain) that had the most to gain by safeguarding the free use of the seas, universal jurisdiction came to be acknowledged by all States "with an acquiescence of the commercial interests which needed protection against those dangerous common enemies".[33] A prosecution undertaken by, e.g., Britain under this principle would effectively be on behalf of "all civilized States",[34] vindicating an "agreed vital interest of the international community",[35] so that exclusive State claims to jurisdiction could be bypassed.

The start of this trend might be traced to Grotius' elucidation of the *libertas commerciorum*, the recognition of a universal right to commerce, this being a key part of the makeup of States and a concept that, in turn, rendered pirates the enemies of the civilising project of international law.[36] This assertion should be read in conjunction with the notion explored in Chapter 4 that pirates differed fundamentally from States in terms of *raison d'être*, a distinction that

28 See, *e.g.*, Georges Abi-Saab, "The Proper Role of Universal Jurisdiction", 1 *Journal of International Criminal Justice* (2003) 597, 599; *United States v. Yousef*, 327 F.3d 56 (3d Cir. 2002), 80–81; Harvard Research in International Law "Draft Convention on Piracy with Comments", 26 *American Journal of International Law* (1932) supplement, 749, 788; Harvard "Draft Convention on Jurisdiction with Respect to Crime", 29 *American Journal of International Law* (1935) supplement, 435, 566; and Clyde H. Crockett, "Toward a Revision of the International Law of Piracy" 26 *DePaul Law Review* (1976) 78, 81.

29 Anthony J. Colangelo, "The New Universal Jurisdiction: *In Absentia* Signaling Over Clearly Defined Crimes" 36 *Georgetown Journal of International Law* (2005) 537, 580.

30 Maria Gavouneli, *Functional Jurisdiction on the Law of the Sea* (Leiden: Martinus Nijhoff Publishers, 2007), 26.

31 Sir William Blackstone, *Commentaries on the Laws of England: In Four Books* (ed. George Sharswood) (Philadelphia: J.B. Lippincott Company, 1893), Book IV (Volume 2), 70.

32 Discussed *supra*, 5.4.

33 "Draft Convention on Piracy", *supra* no28, 764–765.

34 Sheldon Glueck, *War Criminals: Their Prosecution and Punishment* (New York: A.A. Knopf, 1944), 100.

35 *Eichmann, supra* no2, para. 12.

36 4.1.2, *supra*.

allows us to overcome the historical problem that States themselves *also* negatively impacted trade by licensing privateers to plunder goods from others.[37] In any case, the fact that the abolition of privateering was driven by its negative impact on newly realised ideals of inter-State commerce supports the claim that maritime plunder in all its forms (excepting legitimate seizure during war)[38] was considered to be a problematic and serious issue.[39]

No concrete action was taken towards enforcing the *libertas commerciorum* specifically, however, until England's response, under duress, to the Captain Kidd episode.[40] The motives for England's subdual of its pirates were twofold, the immediate intent being to reconcile with their Mughal allies, with the long-term intention being to secure a future without such strained ties and, further, one in which States were supreme upon the seas and could secure the free trade that they both desired and needed. England's actions were universally condoned, for the pirates served no State, yet threatened all.[41] Other States began to construct their own anti-piracy legislation in order to both lend agreement and contribute to the communal project of eradication.[42] Universal jurisdiction arose organically, then, as the universal expression of all States uniting behind a common agenda (what might be defined as an expression of Grotian and Blackstonian "natural law").[43] In turn, universal jurisdiction served to define the international community of States according to the "Ciceronian paradigm".[44] Its exercise appeared "as a constitutive moment in the transition to an ordered system of capital accumulation on a global scale".[45] The fact that prosecutions of pirates did not, by definition, implicate States provides a key reason why universal jurisdiction was allowed to emerge and

37 4.1.1 and 4.1.3, *supra*, by reference to the works of Gentili and Grotius.

38 3.1, *supra*, footnote 22.

39 5.5, *supra*.

40 5.2, *supra*.

41 Even States that do not directly trade upon the sea will be affected by the effects of piracy on the cost of commodities. For instance, when a Saudi oil tanker was hijacked by pirates in 2008, oil prices rose globally: Raissa Kaslowsky & Simon Webb, "Somali Pirates Seize Saudi Tanker Carrying $100 Million in Oil", *Washington Post*, Nov. 17, 2008. See also Joseph M. Isanga, "Countering Persistent Contemporary Sea Piracy: Expanding Jurisdictional Regimes", 59 *American University Law Review* (2010) 1267, 1273–1274, noting that "piracy cause[s] substantial disruption and loss to the world economy, which is heavily reliant on maritime shipping, it also leads to escalating costs associated with increasingly steep ransom demands and higher insurance premiums".

42 "Draft Convention on Jurisdiction", *supra* no28, 563–565, listing relevant legislation.

43 5.4, *supra*.

44 2.2, *supra*.

45 Amedeo Policante, *The Pirate Myth: Genealogies of an Imperial Concept* (Abingdon: Routledge, 2015), 90; see also Addis, *supra* no12.

flourish.[46] By comparison, the application of universal jurisdiction to "core" international crimes (*i.e.* genocide, crimes, against humanity, war crimes, aggression) frequently creates political disagreement given that suspects are often closely linked to State power structures.[47]

The claims to jurisdiction over the high seas meant the reconceptualisation of the maritime space into an accessible, "juridified" space rather than an indomitable wilderness ruled over by pirates.[48] A unique legal space was created "in which various sovereign nations operated in tension with one another without interfering in each other's rights to travel and trade freely",[49] tensions which consolidated themselves into international customs and conventions.[50] The seas were *territor*ialised (in the original Latin sense of that term)[51] to provide an avenue for safe trade, while those who opposed it would have to face the consequences (enforceable by universal jurisdiction) of being in opposition to the project of friendly civilisation. The system resembled a novel take on the *Pax Romana*, with Roman hegemony substituted for that of Westphalian States.[52] In this way, navies and merchants disseminated and applied municipal laws across the high seas, creating a communal quasi-territorial order that *complemented* the existence of Westphalian Europe by reaching into geographic zones that standard jurisdictional bases (territoriality, nationality, *et cetera*) could not.[53] "Universal" jurisdiction in this sense, then, might be seen as a patchwork of exoteric territorial jurisdiction, the result of all States' desires to protect what belongs to them in common, "*terror*fied" against pirates, the nationality of whom became unimportant. Pirates effectively shaped the world order, catalysing the project of international law, forcing commonality of action, and transforming the ocean into a global commons, "a different kind

46 Eugene Kontorovich, "A Positive Theory of Universal Jurisdiction", Bepress Legal Series, Working Paper 211 (2004), 14; Madeline H. Morris, "Universal Jurisdiction in a Divided World" 35 *New England Law Review* (2001) 337, 339.

47 Discussed *infra*, 8.2.2.

48 Policante, *supra* no45, 78 and 129, paraphrasing Michel Foucault, *The Birth of Biopolitics: Lectures at Collège du France, 1978–79* (New York: Palgrave Macmillan), 176.

49 James Muldoon, "Who Owns the Sea", paper presented at the conference "Sea Changes: Historicizing the Oceans", Universitat Greifswald, July 2000; cited in Lauren Benton, "Legal Spaces of Empire: Piracy and the Origins of Ocean Regionalism", 47 *Comparative Studies in Society and History* (2005) 700, 706.

50 Donald R. Rothwell and Tim Stephens, *The International Law of the Sea* (Oxford: Hart, 2010), 4.

51 2.1.3, *supra*.

52 See A. Parchami, *Hegemonic Peace and Empire: The Pax Romana, Britannica and Americana* (London: Taylor & Francis, 2009), 61, on the "reincarnation" of the *Pax Romana* as the *"Pax Britannica"*.

53 Policante, *supra* no45, 170.

of bounded legal space".[54] Through their demise pirates became the original martyrs to international law; this is Captain Kidd's full legacy.

This is surely one of the great triumphs of international law,[55] one from which all States stood to benefit. The idea of piracy affecting such an "agreed vital interest"[56] is of central importance to understanding the inherently serious nature of piracy and the relevance of the "piracy analogy" for the broader scope of universal jurisdiction.

6.1.2 *Piracy's Indiscriminate Effect*

The notion that piracy is a genuinely indiscriminate offence provides a further viable explanation for the invocation of universal jurisdiction. Pirates display "an antagonism that cannot be defined as that of one individual with respect to another or of one political association with respect to another. Such an antagonism [...] appears not as particular but as general; it is often represented as 'universal'".[57] *All* States have an interest in maintaining the free space of the sea and are affected by the endangerment of that principle.[58] By definition, pirates target their victims indiscriminately, so that politically-motivated attacks against selected States are not generally conceived as piratical,[59] and crimes committed within territorial waters also do not, generally, qualify as piracy *jure gentium*.[60]

54 Benton, "Legal Spaces", *supra* no49, 723–724.

55 See, *e.g.*: Benton, *ibid.*, 706; Policante, *supra* no45, 82; Carl Schmitt, *The Nomos of the Earth* (1950) (trans. G.L. Ulmen) (New York: Telos Press, 2003), 44, and Haywood and Spivak, *supra* no25, 56.

56 *Eichmann*, *supra* no2, para. 12.

57 Daniel Heller-Roazen, *The Enemy of All: Piracy and the Law of Nations* (Brooklyn: Zone Books, 2009), 11.

58 See, *e.g.*, *Harmony v. United States* 43 U.S. (2 How.) (1844), 232; Randall, *supra* no3, 793; Dino Kritsiotis, "The Contingencies of Piracy", 41 *California Western International Law Journal* (2011) 305, 322; Joshua Michael Goodwin, "Universal Jurisdiction and the Pirate: Time for an Old Couple to Part", 39 *Vanderbilt Journal of Transnational Law* (2006) 973, 1001; and Barry H. Dubner, *The Law of International Sea Piracy* (The Hague: Martinus Nijhoff, 1980), 19.

59 As a general rule, political acts are excluded from the domain of "piracy" as defined in the 1982 United Nations Convention on the Law of the Sea, Article 101. The exact meaning of this qualification is, however, debatable; see, *e.g.*, Malvina Halberstam, "Terrorism on the High Seas: The *Achille Lauro*, Piracy and the IMO Convention on Maritime Safety" 82 *American Journal of International Law* (1988) 269, 272–284.

60 See, e.g., "Draft Convention on Piracy, *supra* no28, 789, stating that "[p]iracy in territorial waters has as little to do with international law as other robberies within the territory of a State [...]. Piracy is, and has always been, a crime against the safety of traffic on the open sea, and therefore it cannot be committed anywhere else than on the open sea". There may, however, be exceptions to this rule, as discussed *infra*, 7.2.

Indiscriminate effect is not, of course, *per se* tantamount to "heinousness"; a mugger on a dark street will likely operate opportunistically and "indiscriminately", but this does not render him subject to universal jurisdiction. The key nuance here is that piracy has the potential to affect every *State* (and, by extension, every citizen). This helps to justify the response to a shared "heinous" threat through universal jurisdiction. The "indiscriminate" justification does not in itself satisfactorily explain, however, why universal jurisdiction might be exercisable over a broader range of crimes (such as genocide or crimes against humanity)[61] that usually occur within State borders and where a given State will possess more of a vested interest than others.[62] Accordingly, although we can treat the indiscriminate effect of piracy as a factor contributing to its perceived "heinousness", we must look further for a thorough explanation of this proposition.

6.1.3 *"Beyond all Borders"*

There is something significant, certainly, in the fact that pirates operate beyond all borders.[63] At the 1717 trial of "Black" Sam Bellamy's surviving crew in Boston,[64] the colonial Admiralty Court claimed that "as piracy is in itself a complication of treason, oppression, murder, assassination, robbery and theft, so it denotes the crime to be perpetrated on the high sea [...], whereby it becomes more atrocious".[65]

The very fact that piracy occurs beyond State territory arguably renders it a "heinous" act. According to the prosecution in *Bellamy*, "those crimes ought to be punished with the utmost severity, which cannot without the greatest difficulty be prevented".[66] Piracy gains strength from "the fundamental fact of

61 Chapter 1 (introduction).

62 Though see International Court of Justice, *Arrest Warrant of 11 April 2000* (Democratic Republic of the Congo v. Belgium) (2002), joint separate opinion of Judges Higgins, Kooijmans and Buergenthal, para., 61 (p81), noting that "[w]ar crimes and crimes against humanity are no less harmful to the interests of all because they do not usually occur on the high seas". Discussed at 8.1, *infra*.

63 See, *e.g.*, Anthony Sammons, "The Under-Theorisation of Universal Jurisdiction: Implications for Legitimacy on Trials of War Criminals by National Courts" 21 *Berkeley Journal of International Law* (2003) 111, 126, and Goodwin, *supra* no58, 1002.

64 Bellamy himself had died in a shipwreck six months prior, along with all but nine of his crew.

65 *The Trial of Eight Persons Indicted for Piracy* (concerning the crew of "Black" Sam Bellamy), Boston, 1717 (cited in Joel H. Baer, "'The Complicated Plot of Piracy': Aspects of English Criminal Law and the Image of the Pirate in Defoe", 23 *The Eighteenth Century* (1982) 3, 8).

66 *Ibid.*

the lack of governmental control" so that, in the lack of an effective judicial system, pirates "hop[e] thereby to commit their crimes with impunity" from State-made law.[67]

Universal jurisdiction can provide legal redress for such offences and, more importantly, provide a deterrent by placing pirates in fear of justice, regardless of the location of their crime or the identity of their victim. According to this idea, all States "have an interest in eliminating piracy even if pirates have not attacked their own vessels either because the State may be a direct victim in the future, or they may suffer the economic consequences of such attacks".[68] Our interest in seeing piracy prevented and punished extends beyond the immediate human interest in discouraging violence and theft, given that we also hold a universal interest in the *libertas commerciorum* and seeing the threat of famine, for instance, averted.[69]

By operating "beyond the State", on the dynamic and uncertain legal space of the high seas, pirates become something more than everyday criminals. Whereas purely domestic criminals such as murderers or highwaymen elect not to follow "the rules" of the legal system in place, rendering their actions criminal and punishable according to the law in effect in a given territory, pirates go one step further by deliberately acting *outside* the rules, seeking to apply their own "laws" from their extraterritorial *locus*. Manifesting in a *locus delicti* that leaves victims of piracy more vulnerable (given enforcement difficulties) than victims of crimes on *terra firma*, piracy becomes "more atrocious" because it occurs *without* the State and its associated laws and enforcement mechanisms.[70] In so doing it subverts State-made "civil" laws and leaves State subjects vulnerable to the legal vacuum of the oceans. From this standpoint pirates "take advantage of the absence of legitimate criminal justice systems that can or will prosecute

---

67 Willard B. Cowles, "Universality of Jurisdiction over War Crimes" 33 *California Law Review* (1945) 177, 193, making this claim by reference to brigandage. By contrast, pirates would have considered the State and its laws "antithetical to freedom of any kind": Bruce Buchan, "Anarchism and Liberalism" in Nathan J Jun (ed.), *Brill's Companion to Anarchism and Philosophy* (Leiden: Brill, 2017) 51, 57.

68 Miriam Cohen, "The Analogy between Piracy and Human Trafficking: A Theoretical Framework for the Application of Universal Jurisdiction" 16 *Buffalo Human Rights Law Review* (2010) 201, 217. See also Dino Kritsiotis, *supra* no58, 322, noting that "[o]f decisive importance is that this jurisdiction was regarded as lawful because the international community regarded piracy as damaging to the interests of all".

69 In 2009 piracy was estimated to cost between $13 and $16 billion every year, in addition to hindering sustained development in Africa: James Kraska and Brian Wilson, "Piracy Repression, Partnering and the Law" 40 *Journal of Maritime Law & Commerce* (2009) 44, 45.

70 Geoffrey Robertson, *Crimes Against Humanity: The Struggle for Global Justice* (3rd ed.) (London: Penguin, 2006), 240.

and punish their actions".[71] They threaten and subvert the otherwise ubiquitous global order and jurisdiction of the "civilised" Westphalian State.

Universal jurisdiction responds to this threat by reaffirming the reach of "civilised" law over the high seas, in a "communal quasi-territorial" manner.[72] In the context of piracy the victim's "sense of dignity and security that [...] criminal [law] affords them is sufficiently important to warrant conferring upon *every* State the power to punish perpetrators [...] extraterritorially".[73] In other words, universal jurisdiction fills the vacuum and restores a sense of order to the high seas, this being necessary for the protection of potential victims or for retribution on behalf of actual victims.

The manner in which pirates have been treated, historically, seems to confirm the idea that their harsh treatment (in tandem with universal jurisdiction) was designed, at least in part, as a deterrent, intended to restore order beyond the State itself. Pirates were, historically, given the harshest of penalties; executions were commonplace[74] and the bodies of the deceased were regularly displayed at prominent coastal settings where they could serve as a visual warning to passing crews.[75] Pirates who were convicted, but not executed, were reportedly sometimes branded with a hot iron in the shape of a "P" to serve as a warning to others.[76] The elaborate "savage beast" rhetoric with which pirates were denounced also seemed designed to warn off prospective pirates from an immoral way of life (but then, pirates *were* concerned with fostering a fearsome image).[77] A deterrence justification for universal jurisdiction is not specific to universal jurisdiction,[78] of course, but the point is that a deterrent effect for pirates can *only* effectively exist if universal jurisdiction is in place, given its intrinsically international character.[79] In any case realising

71 Sammons, *supra* no63, 126.

72 6.1, *supra*.

73 Chehtman, *supra* no6, 119. Chehtman is discussing crimes against humanity, yet the same point applies by extension to piracy.

74 Goodwin, *supra* no58, 997–999.

75 David Cordingly, *Life Among the Pirates: The Romance and the Reality* (London: Abacus, 1995), 261–263. See also Cordingly, *Spanish Gold: Captain Woodes Rogers and the Pirates of the Caribbean* (London: Bloomsbury, 2011), 176–177, noting how Blackbeard's severed head was prominently displayed as a deterrent aboard the *Adventure*.

76 David Cordingly and John Falconer, *Pirates: Fact & Fiction* (London: Collins & Brown Ltd, 1992), 85.

77 3.2.1, *supra*.

78 Chehtman, *supra* no6, 91 and 125.

79 See, e.g., Cedric Ryngaert, in the first edition of *Jurisdiction in International Law* (Oxford: OUP, 2008), 107, noting that "[b]y sending this signal – 'no impunity' – a State prevents future violations in other States and serves the common interests of all States".

any deterrent effect would require concentrated, systematic prosecutions, not merely a handful for "expressive or symbolic value".[80]

Taking this line of argument further, universal jurisdiction becomes necessary, in respect of piracy, for the continued survival of the State itself. The territorial jurisdiction of States is justified based on the need to uphold the "collective interest" of the human community present there,[81] so that, by extension, universal jurisdiction might be seen as the application of the same Hobbesian political philosophy to the international sphere in that it gives sovereign States a power to enforce laws that threaten an international community.[82] This approach to jurisdiction perhaps resembles a return to the essence of Grotian natural law[83] reconceptualised as broadly applicable municipal law in a manner envisaged by Blackstone.[84] In this way piracy transcends murder (for example), *even if* that murder occurs on the high seas. While murder (at sea or otherwise) must, of course, be considered a serious crime, loss of human life is not the only indicator by which we can measure "seriousness".[85] Piracy, like genocide (for example), "is grave for its effect, and potential effect, on a *shared community value*".[86] The threat posed by piracy is of a different order, against the State, and against what that represents. Consequently, pirates became the original *hostes humani generis*.

---

80 Eugene Kontorovich and Steven Art, "An Empirical Examination of Universal Jurisdiction for Piracy", 104 *American Journal of International Law* (2010) 436, 436.

81 Chehtman, *supra* no6, 56–59; Policante, *supra* no45, 89; Hans Kelsen, *General Theory of Law and State* (trans. Anders Wedberg) (Cambridge, MA: Harvard University Press, 1949), 233.

82 In reference to Thomas Hobbes' idea of the State in his 1651 work *Leviathan: or, the Matter, Forme, & Power of a Commonwealth Ecclesiasticall and Civill* discussed *supra*, 4.1.3, note 134. The State (or "commonwealth") is depicted as providing protection from the lawless "state of nature" that would otherwise exist. Pirates, as dishonourable robbers, form part of said state of nature; see discussion in Policante, *ibid.*, 89.

83 4.2.2, *supra*.

84 5.4, *supra*.

85 As exemplified by the decision of the International Criminal Court in *Prosecutor v Bahar Idriss Abu Garda*, "Decision on the Confirmation of Charges" (Pre-Trial Chamber I, 8 February, 2010), 30, holding that "the gravity of crimes should be assessed according to both quantitative and qualitative factors" with the latter referring to "issues of the nature, manner and impact" of the crimes. A similar decision was rendered by Pre-Trial Chamber II in "Decision Pursuant to Article 15 of the Rome Statute on the Authorization of an Investigation into the Situation in the Republic of Kenya" (31 March 2010), 56.

86 Roger L Phillips, "Pirate Accessory Liability: Developing a Modern Legal Regime governing Incitement and Intentional Facilitation of Maritime Piracy" 25 *Florida Journal of International Law* (2013) 271, 287 (emphasis added). Also instructive is Hannah Arendt's statement that the difference between murder and genocide is that "an altogether different order is broken and an altogether different community is violated": *Eichmann in Jerusalem: A Report on the Banality of Evil* (1963) (New York: Penguin, 2006), 272.

The threat posed by piracy, then, is recognised as being twofold: they pose a threat to merchants plying their vital trade outwith the protection of the State *and* they pose an inherent and indiscriminate threat to the international community of States itself (by reference to the *libertas commerciorum*). Universal jurisdiction is arguably *required* to maintain realistic prospects for prosecution and to reinforce deterrent effect. Thus, piracy's occurrence on the high seas (by definition) does explain, to an extent, why it ought to be subject to non-traditional bases of jurisdiction. Here we begin to uncover the real meaning of "heinous" in the specific context of piracy.

6.1.4 *Consensus*

Stemming from the idea that piracy affects States indiscriminately is the related notion that universal jurisdiction attaches to piracy because all States *agree* that it should.[87] For instance the United States *Restatement (Third) of Foreign Relations* suggests that universal jurisdiction is "based on the assumption that some crimes are *so universally condemned* that the perpetrators are the enemies of all people".[88] Universal condemnation must surely be a prerequisite to the existence of universal jurisdiction,[89] the acceptance and effectiveness of which can in turn only be realised by collective acquiescence in its practice.[90] Yet universal condemnation cannot, of itself, justify the exercise of universal jurisdiction, as this logic is defeated, again, by the "ordinary crime" obstacle: the fact that a murderer, for example, will not be subjected to universal jurisdiction, despite being punishable by the penal codes of all States.[91] More accurately, then, the emergence of universal jurisdiction reflects State acquiescence in the universal *enforcement* of criminal law in respect of specific offences, regardless of where or by whom such offences have been committed.[92] Piracy

87 Douglas Guilfoyle, *International Criminal Law* (Oxford: OUP, 2016), 38.

88 Section 404, emphasis added. Examples mentioned include "piracy, slave trade, attacks on or hijacking of aircraft, genocide, war crimes, and perhaps certain acts of terrorism". See also Alfred P. Rubin, *The Law of Piracy* (Honolulu: University Press of the Pacific, 2006), 203.

89 Kontorovich, "Positive Theory", *supra* no46, 35. See also *US v Hasan,* 747 F.Supp.2d 599, 2010 A.M.C. 2705, 608, noting that "universal jurisdiction over a crime is established by international consensus". By contrast, bilateral treaties "do not have general but only particular character" since their "norms are not valid for all states, but only for two or a larger or smaller group of states": Hans Kelsen, *Principles of International Law* (New York: Rinehart & Co, 1952), 324.

90 Noura Erakat, "*The U.S. v. The Red Cross*: Customary International Humanitarian Law and Universal Jurisdiction" 41 *Denver Journal of International Law and Policy* (2013) 225, 253–254.

91 Unless his acts form part of a pattern amounting to a "core" international crime. See *supra*, no21.

92 Aisling O'Sullivan, *Universal Jurisdiction in International Criminal Law: The Debate and the Battle for Hegemony* (Oxon: Routledge, 2017), 116. In respect of the "core" international

provides the paradigm example of this, as an offence over which the application of universal jurisdiction is not disputed.[93]

The underlying importance of universal condemnation can be explored through a consideration of nineteenth century attempts to extend the principle to slavery,[94] a development that suggested a deeper moral element to the use of universal jurisdiction, given that "the slave trade did not threaten commerce or other interaction among nations in the same way as piracy".[95] The rationale for this leap of logic appeared to be that "the severity of [slavery's] infringement on individual liberty was considered uniquely atrocious",[96] marking the moment at which universal jurisdiction was reconceived as a tool for promoting a universal concept of morality.[97] The invocation of universal jurisdiction initially failed, however, given that slavery was not universally condemned at the time.[98] Comparisons drawn between piracy and slavery were rebutted in the 1816 British Admiralty case *Le Louis,*[99] in which Sir William Scott held that

crimes, such enforcement can, of necessity, *only take* place in the asserting State's territory (with piracy forming the exception due to its exceptional *locus delicti*).

93 The consensus is helped by the fact that piracy is, by definition, apolitical. The application of "new" universal jurisdiction to "core" international crimes has often been frustrated by political obstacles; see Kontorovich, "Positive Theory", *supra* no46, 18, and discussion *infra*, 8.2.2.

94 For instance the US declared the slave trade to be "piracy" in 1820 (Act of May 15, 1820, ch. 113, 3 Stat. 600). The 1826 *Convention Between Great Britain and Brazil, for the Abolition of the African Slave Trade,* at Article 1, also stated that carrying on the slave trade "shall be deemed and treated as piracy". Similarly, Article 1 of the 1841 London *Treaty between Great Britain, Austria, France, Prussia, and Russia for the Suppression of the African Slave Trade* denounced traffic in slaves as "piracy" with consequence that a slaving vessel lost "all right to the protection of their flag". See Jean Allain, *The Law and Slavery: Prohibiting Human Exploitation* (Leiden: Brill, 2015), 8–9.

95 Fausto Pocar and Magali Maystre, "The Principle of Complementarity: A Means Towards a More Pragmatic Enforcement of the Goal Pursued by Universal Jurisdiction?" in Morten Bergsmo (ed.), *Complementarity and the Exercise of Universal Jurisdiction for Core International Crimes* (FICHL Publication Series, 2010), 247, 265.

96 *Ibid.*

97 See, e.g., "First Report from the Select Committee on Slave Trade", *House Of Commons* 102 (1848) reprinted in 4 *British Parliamentary Papers* (1847–48), 19, in which Lord Palmerston described suppression of the slave trade as being in "the interest of humanity" and a "moral duty". See also Jenny S. Martinez, "Antislavery Courts and the Dawn of International Human Rights Law" 117 *Yale Law Journal* (2008) 550, 632, describing the antislavery movement as a "precursor to the modern international human rights movement".

98 Lauren Benton, "Toward a New Legal History of Piracy: Maritime Legalities and the Myth of Universal Jurisdiction" 23 *International Journal of Maritime History* (2011) 225, 234.

99 (1817) 165 Eng. Rep. 1464 (Adm. Ct.). The case involved a French vessel seized by Britain during peacetime under the authority of the 1807 *Act for the Abolition of the Slave Trade,* which permitted the Navy to board ships it suspected of carrying slaves. The Act

> There are still nations which adhere to the practice of enslavement under all the encouragement which their own laws can give it. [...] [T]heir practice is to be respected [...]. A nation is not justified in assuming rights that do not belong to her, merely because she means to apply them to a laudable purpose [...]. Nor is it to be argued, that because other nations approve the ultimate purpose, they must therefore submit to every measure which any one State or its subjects may inconsiderably adopt for its attainment.[100]

Given the lack of universal agreement over the abolition of slavery, then, one State's prosecution of another's slaver may have violated the latter's sovereignty.[101] Universal condemnation was required as a precursor to universal jurisdiction. In the context of piracy, this was driven by the various points discussed above, making piracy a threat against a *vital* and *universal* interest.

6.2 Against "Heinousness"

> [T]he rationale for piracy's unique jurisdictional status had nothing to do with the heinousness or severity of the offence.[102]
>
> EUGENE KONTOROVICH

Part 6.1 outlined the various reasons why piracy might be considered to be, in fact, a "heinous" offence, leading to the emergence of universal jurisdiction as a means of denouncing and containing it. Several themes weave together here, supporting an argument that, regardless of whether piracy could properly be deemed "heinous", it was the threat against a vital and universal interest of the community of States that warranted their admonishing and the corresponding development of innovative jurisdictional tools.

---

was applied in any region not under the dominion of a European State based on the logic that "the laws of nature would proscribe slavery there by default"; see Tara Helfman, "The Court of Vice Admiralty at Sierra Leone and the Abolition of the West African Slave Trade" 115 *Yale Law Journal* (2006) 1122, 1141 and 1150–1152.

100 *Le Louis, ibid.* Similar reasoning was espoused in the earlier case of *The Amedie*, (1810) 12 Eng. Rep. 92 (P.C.).

101 Rubin, *Ethics and Authority in International Law* (Cambridge: CUP, 2007), 107. See also Guilfoyle, *supra* no87, 39, noting that universal jurisdiction does not apply to slavery because "all the nineteenth and twentieth century treaties covering the slave trade by sea appeared to leave prosecution in the hands of the ship's flag State".

102 *Supra* no6, 186.

Opponents of the "piracy analogy" refute that piracy could plausibly have been considered "heinous", however, amounting to mere robbery at sea. Part 6.1 (read against the historical context of Chapter 5) has largely dispelled this theory, yet some counter-arguments need addressing. The analogy to privateering (the argument that piracy could not have been particularly serious, as States were responsible for identical conduct) has already been dealt with.[103] Two remaining issues stand to be dealt with now. These are, firstly, the idea of "reverse heinousness" and, secondly, the claim that universal jurisdiction became attached to piracy for practical reasons (*i.e.* due to the difficulty of containing it) rather than out of any sense of "heinousness".

6.2.1 *"Reverse Heinousness"*

An alternative approach to the "heinousness" debate might be sought in Judge Trott's suggestion in *Bonnet* that, in contrast to piracy, "I need not expatiate to you upon the heinousness of the sin of murder, a crime which carries its own natural horror and guilt along with it, so that it is altogether needless for me to aggravate it".[104] This might suggest that universal jurisdiction was attached to piracy as a way of highlighting the seriousness of it, whereas murder did not require this measure to be taken. In other words, piracy was never actually perceived to be "heinous" – rather, this was an invention designed to discourage it, with universal jurisdiction an artifice designed to substantiate this claim. The paucity of actual universal jurisdiction cases (despite frequent *obiter* claims to its legitimacy) throughout the eighteenth and nineteenth centuries suggests that there may be some weight to this point of view, with such rhetorical claims perhaps made to improve prospects that legislatures and courts elsewhere should pursue pirates more vociferously. This is, however, a largely spurious line of reasoning, and does not detract from the weight of authority that *does* support a "heinousness" argument concerning piracy and universal jurisdiction.[105]

Of relevance here is the 1820 US Supreme Court case, *United States v Furlong*.[106] Attempting to untangle the definition of piracy espoused by Congress,[107] the Court iterated that it could not claim jurisdiction over an act simply by labelling it "piracy", when the act in question did not constitute an offence under the "law of nations". "Murder" was cited as an example of an offence that, unlike piracy, was not "universally cognisable":

---

103 3.1, *supra*.

104 *Supra* n011.

105 6.1, *supra*.

106 18 U.S. (5 Wheat.) 184 (1820).

107 See discussion *supra*, 5.4.

> Robbery on the seas is considered an offense within the criminal jurisdiction of all nations [...]. Not so with the crime of murder. It is an offence too abhorrent to the feelings of man, to have made it necessary that it also should have been brought within this universal jurisdiction. And hence, punishing it when committed within the jurisdiction [...] of another nation, has not been acknowledged as a right [of States].[108]

Furlong's logic appears to be that society understands, already, that murder is a serious crime, whereas piracy required the application of universal jurisdiction in order to "enforce" such an understanding.[109] The Court does not, at any point, suggest that piracy is any less serious than murder. Commenting on the case, Kontorovich suggests that:

> Murder inflicts a uniquely grave injury, depriving the victim of his life, while piracy [...] deprives him only of property. [...] Because robbery shocks the conscience less than murder, it is less likely that a directly injured nation would be determined to prosecute pirates, and thus less likely that it would be offended if another nation stepped in to do so. [...] *Furlong* [...] contradicts the theory that the recognition of universal offenses in the law of nations turns on the heinousness of the offense or the universal repugnance it generates.[110]

Kontorovich concludes that *Furlong* "shows that the heinousness theory would not be consistent with universal jurisdiction over piracy because piracy was not considered one of the most heinous offenses".[111] This analysis seems erroneous given that this is not the court's actual suggestion: its point was that piracy was simply not as well entrenched as murder in terms of being popularly understood as a "heinous" crime. While this could not be doubted with murder, piracy was, until the eighteenth century at least, regarded more ambiguously (as history shows).[112] Furthermore, Kontorovich is mistaken in equating piracy simply with "robbery at sea" – a characterisation that we have shown to be overly simplistic (notwithstanding that "piracy" can embrace manifold

108 *Supra* no106, 196–197.

109 Parallels may here be drawn with *Bonnet, supra* no11, in which Judge Trott noted that murder was an established "sin", whereas the act of piracy required him to elaborate on what, exactly, rendered it a heinous offence, the perpetrators of which were *hostes humani generis*.

110 *Supra* no6, 229.

111 *Ibid.*, 228.

112 3.2.1, *supra*.

constituent offences, such as torture or murder,[113] which might be tried under the header of piracy or, as in the case of *Kidd*, tried separately).[114] Moreover, *Furlong* should be read against the context of a plethora of cases suggesting that piracy is indeed "heinous".[115] The compound "heinousness" explanation for universal jurisdiction over piracy cannot easily be easily dismissed, and has the potential for nuanced expansion to other offences.[116]

6.2.2 *Forum Conveniens*

> Piracy occurs in a place, the high seas, which *requires* universal jurisdiction, as the alternative to there being no jurisdiction at all.[117]

A commonly encountered reason for the emergence of universal jurisdiction in relation to piracy, distinct from any notion that piracy is "heinous", is that of *forum conveniens*: from a sea-policing point of view, it simply makes sense for the State capturing a pirate to prosecute him.[118] The nature of piracy requires, by definition, that a jurisdictional response (at an enforcement level) must be extraterritorial. In other words, "piracy occurs in a place, the high seas, which *requires* universal jurisdiction, as the alternative to there being no jurisdiction at all".[119] This "pragmatic" justification for universal jurisdiction

113 See *In re Piracy Jure Gentium*, [1934] A.C., 594, in which the Privy Council denounced as nonsense the proposition that "armed men, sailing the seas [...] could attack and kill everybody on board another vessel [...] without committing the crime of piracy unless, they stole, say an article worth sixpence". See also Peter MacDonald Eggers QC, "What is a pirate? A common law answer to an age-old question" in Douglas Guilfoyle (ed.), *Modern Piracy: Legal Challenges and Responses* (Cheltenham: Edward Elgar, 2013), 250, 256–257.

114 5.2, *supra*.

115 *Ibid.*

116 Harvard "Draft Convention on Jurisdiction", *supra* no28, 571–572.

117 Robertson, *supra* no70, 274.

118 See, *e.g.*: Henry Wheaton, *Elements of International Law* (8th ed.), ed. Richard Henry Dana (Boston: Little, Brown & Co., 1866), s.124 (p193); Michael Davey, "A Pirate Looks at the Twenty-First Century: The Legal Status of Somali Pirates in an Age of Sovereign Seas and Human Rights" 85 Notre Dame Law Review (2010) 1197, 1203; Harvard "Draft Convention on Jurisdiction", supra no28, 566 and 739; *Arrest Warrant*, supra no62, Declaration of Judge Ranjeva, 55–56; Sammons, supra no63, 126; Martin Murphy, "Piracy and UNCLOS: Does International Law Help Regional States Combat Piracy?" in Peter Lehr (ed.), *Violence at Sea: Piracy in the Age of Global Terrorism* (New York: Routledge, 2007) 155, 161; Paige, "Piracy and Universal Jurisdiction", *supra* no6, 148–151; Anna Petrig, "Piracy" in Donald R. Rothwell, Alex G. Oude Elferink, Karen N. Scott, and Tim Stephens (eds), The Oxford Handbook of the Law of the Sea 843, 861; Martin N Murphy, Contemporary Piracy and Maritime Terrorism: The Threat to International Security (London: Routledge 2007), 12.

119 Robertson, *supra* no70, 274.

over piracy is sometimes merged with a "heinousness" explanation,[120] though it is also cited by several scholars as being the *only* reasonable explanation for universal jurisdiction,[121] so that practical considerations *per se* would justify the capturing State's right to prosecute any pirate. According to this theory, then, universal jurisdiction simply serves to "plug the gaps" which arise because of piracy's unique *locus delicti*.[122] This theory is damaging for the "piracy analogy" justification for the exercise of universal jurisdiction over "core" international crimes. Tamsin Paige, for instance, argues that piracy "attracts the concurrent municipal jurisdiction of all States to enforce and prosecute, distinguishing it from other *jus cogens* crimes which attract a universal jurisdiction".[123] According to this argument, the genealogy of universal jurisdiction is distinct as between piracy and the "core" international crimes, so that *Eichmann's* invocation of piracy as a precursor to genocide becomes a somewhat dubious precedent.[124]

This argument seems difficult to sustain, however, given that this state of affairs is only permitted by the pre-existing universal proscription of piracy and consensus in the use of universal jurisdiction.[125] That consensus has been fuelled by a rich history of resentment and disenfranchisement explored throughout the book so far. If the "pragmatic" argument is, today, the sole basis on which universal jurisdiction over piracy can be justified, it did not originate that way, nor is there an obvious "transition period" when the theoretical basis might have shifted.

Consider the fact that "ordinary" crimes are not subject to universal jurisdiction even when committed at sea. A cruise ship in the mid-Atlantic on which, say, a serial killer is operating cannot, without prior arrangement, be boarded by the crew of an unassociated passing naval vessel, the flag-State of which may wish to bring the perpetrator to justice. States do not possess universal

---

120 See, *e.g.*, Mohamed M. El Zeidy, "Universal Jurisdiction *In Absentia:* Is it a Legal Valid Option for Repressing Heinous Crimes?" 37 *The International Lawyer* (2003) 835, 838, suggesting that "[w]hile the gravity of the piracy crime and the need to protect the interest of the international community was an element for triggering universal jurisdiction, the fact that it was committed outside the territorial jurisdiction of any State was the rationale for its application".

121 *Supra*, no118.

122 Jan Klabbers, "Piracy in Global Law and Global Governance" in Panos Koutrakos and Achilles Skordas (eds), *The Law and Practice of Piracy at Sea: European and International Perspectives* (Oxford: Hart, 2014) 329, 330.

123 Tamsin Paige, "Piracy and Universal Jurisdiction" *supra* no6, 154.

124 Kontorovich, "Piracy Analogy", *supra* no6.

125 See, e.g., Robin Geiss and Anna Petrig, *Piracy and Armed Robbery at Sea: The Legal Framework for Counter-Piracy Operations in Somalia and the Gulf of Aden* (Oxford: OUP, 2011), 147.

jurisdiction over such events.[126] This exception can be explained by the fact that in this scenario there are clear jurisdictional links to interested States; for instance, the cruise ship's State of registration, the last port of call, the territorial sea State (if applicable) or the home States of either the offender or the victim,[127] so that "[i]t is not true that all nations have jurisdiction over all offences committed at sea. On the contrary, no nation has any jurisdiction at sea, but over its own citizens or vessels, or offences against itself".[128] Exceptions to this rule only arise in instances of piracy.[129] This tells us something about the unique nature of piracy, itself a "warlike activity"[130] requiring the invasion of one vessel from another, which by its indiscriminate nature and effects on global trade, can cause deeper consequences than might affect a few private civilians.[131] The "pragmatic" approach "seems to cast [pirates] less as enemies of all than as simple criminals that any party might try given the geography of their criminal activity".[132]

Moreover, it does not make sense that universal jurisdiction should exist as *merely* a gap-filling tool, considering that piracy *could* be dealt with under "traditional" concepts of jurisdiction.[133] The counter-argument might be that this would create considerable difficulty in arresting pirates *in locus delicti* or in acting as a deterrent, which of course it would, but there are two plausible responses to this. Firstly, the very fact that piracy is so difficult to contain is part

126 Chehtman, *supra* no6, 91.

127 Kate Lewins and Nick Gaskell, "Jurisdiction over criminal acts on cruise ships: perhaps, perhaps, perhaps?" 37 *Criminal Law Journal* (2014) 221.

128 Speech of the honourable John Marshall, delivered in the US House of Representatives, 1800; reproduced in Frank Moore, *American Eloquence: A Collection of speeches and addresses, by the most eminent orators of America*, 21 (New York: D. Appleton, 1851).

129 Strictly speaking, of course, "core" international crimes such as genocide, crimes against humanity may also, of course, be committed at sea and, in so doing, may attract universal jurisdiction. One might also include the "transnational" crimes outlawed by the "suppression conventions" (examples include the 1936 *Convention for the Suppression of the Illicit Traffic in Dangerous Drugs*, the 1963 *Convention on Offenses and Certain Other Acts Committed on Board Aircraft*, the 1979 *International Convention Against the Taking of Hostages*, the 1997 *International Convention for the Suppression of Terrorist Bombing*, the 2000 *Convention against Transnational Organized Crime* and the 2005 *International Convention for the Suppression of Acts of Nuclear Terrorism*); see Boister, "Transnational Criminal Law?" 14 *European Journal of International Law* (2003) 953. Piracy is nevertheless the only crime defined by a high seas *locus delicti* which may be subject to universal jurisdiction.

130 Abi-Saab, "Proper Role", *supra* no28, 600.

131 *Rex v Dawson*, *supra* no17.

132 Gould, *supra* no6, 34.

133 Kontorovich, "Positive Theory", *supra* no46, 19.

of what makes it "heinous", as considered above.[134] Secondly, the "considerable difficulty" counter-argument can only explain why States might be granted the right to capture and arrest pirates. Consequently, if we follow this approach, there would be no reason why the suspect should not be handed to a more "interested" State for prosecution (as indeed often happens).[135] However, the fact that the apprehending State is, under international law, granted a right to conduct its own trial of the suspect suggests that there are more complex issues at play.[136]

The "pragmatic" or "*forum conveniens*" approach to universal jurisdiction over piracy nevertheless serves as a useful and necessary side-effect, a "mutual convenience" which has conserved its vitality.[137] In this way, universal jurisdiction might be seen as a natural and necessary complement to the "agreed vital interest"[138] of the *libertas commerciorum*, by which every State accepts policing duties, in turn sustaining the international community of States. "Pragmatism" and "heinousness" need not be mutually exclusive explanations for universal jurisdiction. Rather, they complement each other.[139]

6.3 Conclusion

> The threat the pirates present has never been greater. Their intent is to cause terror and destruction until civilization simply ceases to function.[140]
>
> WOODES ROGERS, *Black Sails*

This account demonstrates that there is no *single* reason for the emergence of universal jurisdiction, as claims and counter-claims blur against other and fail to clearly materialise. To be sure, this exercise never was going to be scientific in nature, such are the ambiguities and variables of (legal) history, and it may

---

134 6.1.3, *supra*.

135 See, e.g., United Nations Office on Drugs and Crime, online page on "Maritime Crime Programme – Indian Ocean", reporting on cases of Somali pirates transferred to Kenya, Tanzania, Mauritius and The Seychelles, a UN-supported trend that has "seen States in the Indian Ocean region take ownership of a regional security issue that affects them directly".

136 UNCLOS, *supra* no59, Article 105.

137 Kontorovich, "Positive Theory", *supra* no46, 21.

138 *Eichmann*, *supra* no2, para. 12.

139 Phillips, *supra* no86, 290.

140 Episode "XXXVI" (dir. Uta Briesewitz). Rogers is a real-life character, of course, though rendered here in fictional form.

be that universal jurisdiction gains its strength from a combination of arguments (for "the strength of the thread does not reside in the fact that some one fibre runs through its whole length, but in the overlapping of many fibres").[141]

Some things are clear, however, and Rogers' claim, here, suggests an essential truth. To regard piracy as "heinous" is to re-evaluate the meaning of the term to take account of the perceived overarching threats to society at the time. The central issue appears to have been the effect of piracy on maritime commerce, itself an "agreed vital interest of [an] international community"[142] increasingly committed to industry and diplomacy. Its vitiation threatened to undermine the State itself as the principal mode of human organisation. This central claim can then be built upon and complemented by related factors, so that piracy becomes a greater concern due to its indiscriminate nature and extraterritorial *locus delicti*. These are factors that, in turn, helped States to reach a consensus regarding the proscription of piracy and the right to exercise universal jurisdiction over it. The simple pragmatism of universal jurisdiction is also likely to have been a factor behind its emergence, yet should be seen as complementing the "heinousness" rationale rather than replacing it. These factors all flow from that initial violation of an internationally pervasive norm, that of the *libertas commerciorum*, without which the State and its peoples could not *be*. It is a *vital* and a *universal* interest, warranting the application of an innovative form of jurisdiction applied by the world at large. This appears to be how universal jurisdiction was conceived.

Analogies to "new" universal jurisdiction, over "core" international crimes, become increasingly apparent, the later trend having developed in in *ad hoc* manner in response to certain egregious offences, designed to proscribe and contain an enemy who "offen[ds] against the conscience of the civilized world".[143] An argument emerges for the existence of a "golden thread" that spans the ages and unites the exercise of universal jurisdiction in response to difference offences, in each case perpetrated by those who most threaten the evolving "agreed vital interests" of the international community.[144] To quote Hannah Arendt, the difference between murder and genocide is that "an

141 Ludwig Wittgenstein, *Philosophical Investigations* (trans. GEM Anscombe) (Oxford: Blackwell, 1958), 32.

142 *Eichmann, supra* n02, para. 12.

143 Menno T. Kamminga, "Lessons Learned from the Exercise of Universal Jurisdiction in Respect of Gross Human Rights Offenses" 23 *Human Rights Quarterly* 940, 943.

144 Policante, *supra* n045, 171–172. "International community" is defined, in this context, at the opening of Chapter 8, *infra*.

altogether different order is broken and an altogether different community is violated".[145] The same applies to piracy.

This is not the end of the story of universal jurisdiction over piracy, of course, which would be seized upon and rewritten in UNCLOS,[146] invoked at Nuremberg[147] and analogised to genocide during the *Eichmann* trial in the 1960s.[148] As such the application of universal jurisdiction appears to evolve to respond to new threats to society. It is to these final chapters in the story that we now turn.

---

145 *Supra* no86. In this context see also the discussion on the Grotian definition of, and response to, the pirate, in 4.1.3 and 4.2.2, *supra*.

146 *Supra* no59.

147 Secretary-General of the United Nations, *The Charter and Judgment of the Nuremberg Tribunal: History and Analysis*, U.N. Doc. A/CN.4/5 (1949), 80. See also 1.2.1, *supra*.

148 *Supra* no2.

CHAPTER 7

Uncertain Waters: Combating Piracy in the 21st Century

In September 2008 the Danish naval vessel *Absalon* captured ten pirates operating in seas near Somalia.[1] Rather than denouncing the pirates as *hostes humani generis* and transporting them to Denmark for trial, via the exercise of universal jurisdiction, the captain opted instead to dump the pirates, weaponless, on a Somali beach. The failure to act against the pirates may have been due to reservations over whether the pirates could be deported back to Somalia after any sentences had been served,[2] or perhaps down to flaws in the applicable Danish legislation.[3] The *Absalon* episode was not a unique occurrence; rather, it represented a common trend among States to release captured pirates without trial. A United Nations report from 2010 suggested that nine out of ten captured pirates were being released without charge at this time.[4] Allowed to continue, this trend would empower pirates to proceed unchecked and permit a culture of impunity to take root in the region.

This situation is difficult to reconcile with the image of piracy that was propagated almost three hundred years earlier, when Boston minister Cotton Mather told a group of condemned pirates that "[a]ll nations agree to treat your tribe as the common enemies of mankind, and [to] extirpate them out of the world".[5] The forceful manner of Mather's rhetoric seems to have been overlooked by a disparate community of States that lack either the requisite motivation, resources or legal expertise to carry out the prophesied extirpation. The practice of "catching and releasing" pirates suggests that States have regressed in their approach to piracy in the three centuries since Captain Kidd's

1 Oliver Hawkins, "What to do with a captured pirate", BBC News, 10 March 2009.

2 Lloyds List, "Danes free pirates from Navy ship", 26 December 2008.

3 Joseph M. Isanga, "Countering Persistent Contemporary Sea Piracy: Expanding Jurisdictional Regimes", 59 *American University Law Review* (2010) 1267, 1277.

4 Jack Lang, *Report of the Special Adviser* [*on legal issues related to piracy*] *to the Secretary-General on Legal Issues Related to Piracy off the Coast of Somalia*, 25 January 2011, 3. See also Eugene Kontorovich and Steven Art, "An Empirical Examination of Universal Jurisdiction for Piracy", 104 *American Journal of International Law* (2010) 436, 445, noting that less than 1.5 *per cent* of reported pirate attacks between 1998 and 2009 resulted in a universal jurisdiction prosecution.

5 Cotton Mather, *Instructions to the Living, From the Conditions of the Dead* (Boston, 1717), 17; reproduced in Marcus Rediker, *Villains of All Nations* (London: Verso, 2004), 127.

 | DOI:10.1163/9789004390461_008

brethren were denounced as *hostes humani generis*, perpetrators of "the most mischievous and prejudicial [depredations upon] trade that can happen".[6] Although the situation in Somalia has since vastly improved,[7] the failure to react in a timely manner suggests that there may be flaws in the contemporary notion of pirates as *hostes humani generis*, particularly as regards pirates' subjection to universal jurisdiction. There are clearly issues to work through, and serious questions to be asked concerning the role of universal jurisdiction in piracy prevention. The reasons behind recent improvements in the "Somalia situation" also warrant attention, particularly in terms of examining why and how attitudes have shifted, the role that universal jurisdiction has played, and lessons that may be learned for arresting piracy in other regions. This chapter addresses the contemporary issues surrounding universal jurisdiction over piracy specifically. It examines the reasons why States have struggled to respond to piracy since the early 2000s, by reference to the applicable international law and the way States have interpreted their rights and duties under it.

Particular focus is paid to the outbreak of "Somali" piracy, analysing how the phenomenon has tested the resolve and capacity of States and considering why it has since been largely overcome. Low-level piracy has been occurring in the region since the collapse of Somalia's Siad Barre government in 1991,[8] ostensibly in response to overfishing by outsiders and illegal toxic dumping in Somali territorial seas.[9] Activity in the region increased from 2004 onwards, influenced by the collapse of the secessionist Puntland government (but leaving just enough stability and infrastructure for organised piracy to be viable),[10] new clan allegiances within Somalia and the emergence of more efficient business models, including the use of "motherships" that allowed pirates to operate at a much greater range.[11] Geography was also an important factor, as Somalia's proximity

6 *Kidd's Trial*, 14 Howell's State Trials 123 (1701).

7 International Chamber of Commerce / International Maritime Bureau, *Piracy and Armed Robbery against Ships*, "Report for the Period 1 January to 31 December 2017", documenting nine attacks (including both piracy *stricto sensu* and "armed robbery" in territorial waters) "off Somalia" in 2017. See also *International Chamber of Commerce*, "Piracy attacks in East and West Africa dominate world report", 19 January 2012, and "Maritime piracy and armed robbery reaches 22-year low, says IMB report", 10 January 2018.

8 Douglas Guilfoyle, "Piracy in Somalia and Counter-Piracy Efforts" in Guilfoyle (ed.), *Modern Piracy: Legal Challenges and Responses* (Cheltenham: Edward Elgar, 2013), 35, 36–38.

9 *Ibid.*, 36–38, suggesting, however, that there is no solid evidence for these claims.

10 Guilfoyle, *ibid.*, 43.

11 Jay Bahadur, *Deadly Waters: Inside the hidden world of Somalia's pirates* (London: Profile, 2011), 32–34.

to major shipping lanes allowed the pirates to thrive.[12] The unique combination of factors facilitated the most significant outbreak since the "golden age".[13] In 2004, there were nine reported attacks in the region, a figure that rose to 219 attacks in 2010 and peaked at 275 attacks in 2011 (from a total of 439 pirate attacks reported worldwide).[14] This level of attacks created serious challenges to "the international community at large because of the repercussions they have on world trade and international security [,] estimated to cost between $13 and $16 billion every year".[15] This is in addition to the human impacts of violence and kidnapping, with 1,090 hostages taken by Somali pirates in 2010.[16] From 2011, however, these figures began to fall. 2012 saw only 75 reports of attacks in the region, and 2013 saw only fifteen,[17] while 2014 saw eleven.[18] There were no reported piracy attacks in 2015 and, although 2016 and 2017 have seen a small resurgence (with nine reported attacks in 2017),[19] the figures remain far short of their 2011 peak. The figures suggest that a comprehensive strategy has been put in place to contend with the problem and that history is repeating as States learn, anew, how to best apprehend and suppress the threat. Nevertheless, piracy continues to thrive in other parts of the globe, predominantly off the coasts of West Africa (notably the Gulf of Guinea) and Southeast Asia (especially around Indonesia and The Philippines).[20] The threat of piracy thus persists.

The following analysis is separated into two distinct but related areas. Part 7.1 examines the international law regime applicable to piracy, States' obligations under it, and shortcomings that may have enabled piracy to thrive (with

12 Guilfoyle, *supra* no8, 38.

13 Helmut Tuerk, "The Resurgence of Piracy: A Phenomenon of Modern Times" 17 *University of Miami International and Comparative Law Review* (2009) 1, 5.

14 Figures from International Chamber of Commerce, "Piracy attacks in East and West Africa", *supra* no7. The actual figures may well be much higher, as instances of piracy are believed to be vastly under-reported; see Douglas Guilfoyle, *Shipping Interdiction and the Law of the Sea* (Cambridge: CUP, 2009), 46 and 51.

15 Tuerk, *supra* no13, 5. See also Robert S. Jeffrey, "An Efficient Solution in a Time of Economic Hardship: The Right to Keep and Bear Arms in Self-Defence against Pirates" 41 *Journal of Maritime Law and Commerce* (2010) 507, 509–513, listing several indirect costs of piracy such as higher insurance premiums and the need to take longer alternative shipping routes.

16 Kaija Hurlburt, "The Human Cost of Somali Piracy, 2011", report for *Oceans Beyond Piracy*.

17 International Chamber of Commerce, "Somali pirate clampdown caused drop in global piracy, IMB reveals", 15 January 2014.

18 International Chamber of Commerce, "SE Asia tanker hijacks rose in 2014 despite global drop in sea piracy, IMB report reveals", 12 January 2015.

19 See sources cited *supra*, no7.

20 International Maritime Bureau 2017 Report, *ibid.* The "piracy" in this area occurs predominantly within territorial waters, however.

particular reference to the outbreak of "Somali" piracy). Part 7.2 looks at the strategies that have been formulated in response to the crisis, revealing how universal jurisdiction can be applied effectively and collaboratively in order to re-establish control over the outlaw sea. In so doing, it examines the differences between tackling piracy now and in the eighteenth century, suggesting ways in which universal jurisdiction must evolve to account for unique contemporary issues. Part 7.3 forms a conclusion, reflecting on progress made and on the proper role of universal jurisdiction in combating piracy today.

7.1 The Modern Legal Framework

The rights and obligations of States regarding piracy are today set out in the 1982 *UN Convention on the Law of the Sea* (UNCLOS),[21] though the legal framework set out in the treaty is actually much older than this. Formal international standards began to take shape in the late 1800s, when several draft treaties sought to formally proscribe piracy among States and affirm the existence of universal jurisdiction in relation to it.[22] These failed to gain widespread support, however, due to the perception that piracy was no longer a pressing issue. In 1924 the League of Nations attempted to draft a multilateral Piracy Convention,[23] though this was ultimately scrapped due to perceptions that the subject was "not one of vital interest for every State, or one the treatment of which can be regarded as in any way urgent",[24] a statement that reflected the low level of piracy at this time.[25]

21 UNCLOS has been widely ratified, with 167 parties at the time of writing. The United States of America is a notable absentee.

22 Examples include the 1878 *Treaty to Establish Uniform Rules for Private International Law*, Article 34(3) of which provides for piracy to be subject to universal jurisdiction (the treaty was only ever ratified by Peru); the 1889 *Treaty on International Penal Law*, Article 13 of which states "Crimes considered as piracy by public international law fall within the jurisdiction of the State under whose power the criminals come" (ratified by several South American States); and the 1928 *Bustamente Code*, annexed to the *Convention on Private International Law*, Article 308 of which provides that "Piracy, […] shall be punished by the captor in accordance with the penal laws of the latter".

23 League of Nations Committee of Experts for the Progressive Codification of International Law, *Questionnaire No. 6*, adopted January 1926; (reproduced in 20 *American Journal of International Law* (1926)) 222.

24 Statement of Polish representative to the League Council, 13 June 1927, reproduced in 22 *American Journal of International Law* (1928), supplement, 222.

25 Edwin D. Dickinson, "Is the Crime of Piracy Obsolete?", 38 *Harvard Law Review* (1925) 334; Harvard "Draft Convention on Piracy with Comments", 26 *American Journal of International Law* (1932) supplement, 764.

The relevant UNCLOS provisions in force today are largely drawn from the 1932 "Draft Convention on Piracy" and accompanying commentary, researched and drafted at Harvard University.[26] The drafters attempted to reconcile several centuries of case law and scholarship,[27] though they were ultimately hampered by the "startling lack of international case authority and modern state practice, as large scale piracy disappeared long before".[28] It would have been difficult for the drafters to apply centuries-old case law and legal logic to the existing situation. Nevertheless the Harvard Drafters acknowledged the "gravity of the former dangers of piratical enterprises to the sea-borne commerce of the world",[29] a comment that recognised the serious threat that piracy posed to the "free sea" principle. Regardless of the difficulties faced, the drafters produced a definition of piracy and delineated the scope of permitted universal jurisdiction in terms that were adopted (with small amendments)[30] into the 1958 *Convention on the High Seas*[31] and, subsequently, into UNCLOS. As such the present legal framework for dealing with piracy is built around a 1932 definition, drafted at a time when piracy was not perceived to be an issue. The Harvard research group would be surprised at this turn of (non-)events, as they did not envisage that theirs was the last word on the matter.[32] Importantly, the present legal setup does not allow for the subsequent proliferation of sovereign States (particularly in Africa) or the political mechanics of the UN system. These problems will become apparent as we inspect the details and shortcomings of the existing regime.

7.1.1 *Defining Piracy*

Piracy is defined in Article 101 of UNCLOS as

> Any illegal acts of violence or detention, or any act of depredation, committed for private ends by the crew or the passengers of a private ship [...], and directed [...] on the high seas, against another ship [...].

26 "Draft Convention", *ibid.*, 749.

27 "Draft Convention", *ibid.*, 769.

28 Martin Murphy, "Piracy and UNCLOS: Does International Law Help Regional States Combat Piracy?" in Peter Lehr (ed.), *Violence at Sea: Piracy in the Age of Global Terrorism* (New York: Routledge, 2007) 155, 157.

29 "Draft Convention", *supra* no25, 757.

30 A close examination of the various permutations can be found in Alfred P. Rubin, *The Law of Piracy* (Honolulu: University Press of the Pacific, 2006), 305–337, and in Barry H. Dubner, *The Law of International Sea Piracy* (The Hague: Martinus Nijhoff, 1980), 37–89 and 103–123.

31 Geneva, 29 April 1958; in force 30 September 1962.

32 Dubner, *supra* no30, 54.

Acts that meet this internationally approved and recognised definition of piracy may, in conjunction with Article 105, be the subject of universal jurisdiction, as exercised by States. As such, it is in States' interest to adopt this definition into domestic legislation,[33] given that usage of a *different* definition may create disputes between States as to whether a particular claim to jurisdiction is indeed permitted.[34] The system provided for under UNCLOS is thus one whereby piracy is *defined* in international law but *enforced* at a municipal level via "implementing" domestic legislation.[35] The two should be aligned for this to succeed. It can be debated whether piracy is directly criminalised under international criminal law or whether the criminalisation occurs purely at a domestic level (based on the UNCLOS definition) and universal jurisdiction over it is simply "allowed".[36] In *either* case, universal jurisdiction acts as an enabling mechanism for putting international law (as explicated in UNCLOS) into practice.

The reference to "illegal acts" in Article 101 seems somewhat tautological, though it is designed to rule out actions taken in self-defence or that may be in some other way justifiable.[37] This formulation may be necessitated by the

33 Robin Geiss and Anna Petrig, *Piracy and Armed Robbery at Sea: The Legal Framework for Counter-Piracy Operations in Somalia and the Gulf of Aden* (Oxford: OUP, 2011), 144. See also UN Security Council Resolution 1918, 27 April 2010, "*Reaffirming* that international law, as reflected in the United Nations Convention on the Law of the Sea of 10 December 1982 [...], sets out the legal framework applicable to combating piracy and armed robbery at sea, as well as other ocean activities" (preamble, para. 3).

34 See, *e.g.*, Permanent Court of International Justice, *The Case of the S.S. "Lotus" (France v Turkey)*, 7 September 1927, dissenting opinion of Judge Moore, 70, noting that "the municipal laws of many States denominate and punish as 'piracy' numerous acts which do not constitute piracy by law of nations, and which therefore are not of universal cognizance, so as to be punishable by all nations". See also *US v Dire et al*, US Court of Appeals, 4th Circuit, 23 May 2012, establishing that universal jurisdiction can only be exercised in relation to the internationally recognised definition of piracy, which the Court ruled was contained in UNCLOS.

35 Rubin, *supra* no30, 328.

36 Arguing the former position see, *e.g.*, Hans Kelsen, *General Theory of Law and State* (trans. Anders Wedberg) (Cambridge, MA: Harvard University Press, 1949), 344–345, and P.K. Menon, "The International Personality of Individuals in International Law: A Broadening of the Traditional Doctrine" 1 (1992) 151, 175. The latter claim is more common, however; see, *e.g.*, H.E. José Luis Jesus, "Protection of Foreign Ships against Piracy and Terrorism at Sea: Legal Aspects" 18 *International Journal of Marine and Coastal Law* (2003) 363, 374, Rubin, *ibid.*, 311, and Geiss & Petrig, *supra* no33, 141. Relevant UN Security Council Resolutions further support the latter theory by suggesting the need for States to "implement fully their relevant obligations" under UNCLOS (Resolution 2383, 7 November 2017, para. 27), thereby suggesting the criminalisation must take place at the domestic level.

37 John E. Noyes, "Introduction to the International Law of Piracy", 21 *California Western International Law Journal* (1990) 105, 106–107. See also Tuerk, *supra* no13, 12.

otherwise very broad scope of the phrase "any [...] acts of violence", which is intentionally vague.[38]

These technical points aside, the definition presents three key "contingencies" of piracy, inherent aspects of the offence that serve to demarcate jurisdictional limitations.[39] The first is the limitation of the definition to "private ends", a qualification that, based on the historical study preceding this chapter, seems uncontroversial. The distinction would, historically, have been applied to distinguish the acts of pirates from those of State-sponsored privateers,[40] and it formed a key part of Grotius' analysis of piracy.[41] The private motivation of the pirate remains applicable insofar as it distinguishes the pirate from a politically motivated actor (such as a State, a rebel group or a terrorist), who is not acting with an indiscriminate "animus against the whole world"[42] but instead directing his violence against a given State (or group thereof), towards a tangible political end.[43] On the contrary, theft or violence *for its own sake* is a defining feature of an act of piracy.[44] This is not to say that the actions of a politically motivated actor should not be treated equally seriously (depending

38 Michael Davey, "A Pirate Looks at the Twenty-First Century: The Legal Status of Somali Pirates in an Age of Sovereign Seas and Human Rights" 85 *Notre Dame Law Review* (2010) 1197, 1217.

39 Dino Kritsiotis, "The Contingencies of Piracy", 41 *California Western International Law Journal* (2011) 305.

40 3.1, *supra*. But see *Institute of Cetacean Research v Sea Shepherd Conservation Society*, United States District Court, W.D. Washington, 13 June 2016, holding that "[i]n the context of a piracy claim, an act taken for a 'private end' is one 'not taken on behalf of a state'" and that "essential to piracy's definition is not the actor's intent, but whether any state can be held liable for the actor's actions". The holding, seemingly based on analysis of a single journal article (Michael Bahar, "Attaining Optimal Deterrence at Sea: A Legal and Strategic Theory for Naval Anti-Piracy Operations", 40 *Vanderbilt Journal of Transnational Law* (2007) 1) seems incorrect in drawing such a rigid distinction.

41 See, e.g., *De Jure Praedae* (c. 1604) (trans. Martine Julia van Ittersum) (Indianapolis: Liberty Fund, 2006), 449, and 4.1.2, *supra*.

42 Gerry Simpson, "Piracy and the Origins of Enmity", in Matthew Craven, Malgosia Fitzmaurice and Maria Vogiatzi (eds), *Time, History and International Law* (Leiden: Martinus Nijhoff, 2007), 219, 228.

43 The drafters of the 1932 "Draft Convention on Piracy" suggested that "there seems no good reason why jurisdiction over genuine cases of this type should not be confined to the injured State": *supra* no25, 786.

44 Note that the definition of piracy is widely accepted as extending beyond robbery *per se*, so that "[i]f [a pirate] wilfully sinks or destroys an innocent merchant ship, without any other object than to gratify his lawless appetite for mischief, it is just as much a piratical aggression [...] as if he did it solely and exclusively for the sake of plunder": *United States v Smith* (18 US 5 Wheat 153), 232. See also Peter MacDonald Eggers QC, "What is a pirate? A common law answer to an age-old question" in Guilfoyle (ed.), *supra* no8, 250, 255–258.

on the facts), but that separate procedures and mechanisms should apply.[45] Attacks carried out with clearly political purposes (as opposed to purposed of private gain *per se*) would clearly not qualify as "piracy". As such, for example, the 1961 *Santa Maria* episode (a luxury liner seized by Portuguese rebels),[46] the 1985 *Achille Lauro* incident (a cruise ship hijacked by Palestinian terrorists demanding the release of fifty political prisoners being held by Israel)[47] or the 2010 Gaza flotilla raid (the Israeli raid on six humanitarian aid vessels headed to Gaza)[48] do not meet the definition of piracy. Less obviously, acts of maritime sabotage carried out by environmentalist groups such as the "Sea Shepherds" serve a political, rather than purely private, purpose, and similarly ought not to be treated as instances of "piracy".[49] Other acts may blur this distinction so that "only the consideration of the relevant circumstances of the case will tell which way to go".[50] Somali pirates claim to act as "coastguards", protecting their waters from foreign over-fishing and illegal dumping,[51] yet the immediate aim of their attacks is pecuniary gain through the seizure of goods or the demand for ransoms. Their apprehension should not pose a problem under the definition of piracy espoused in UNCLOS.

The second contingency inherent in the UNCLOS definition is its exclusive application to piracy on the high seas. Again, history reveals why this ought to be the case – by usurping the common good of the high seas, pirates were viewed as an indiscriminate and universal enemy whereas, by contrast,

45 As noted in the "Draft Convention", *supra* no25, 802. The 1988 *Convention on the Suppression of Unlawful Acts against the Safety of Maritime Navigation* (10 March 1988) is intended to deal with such situations. It establishes a right of States to claim jurisdiction in a range of circumstances (Article 7, albeit requiring some connection to the State) over a broad set of offences defined by action rather than motive (Article 3). Since coming into effect, "it would appear to be a lost cause to continue insisting on considering [any] politically-motivated act as piracy" (Jesus, *supra* no36, 378).

46 Ferenc A. Váli, "The Santa Maria Case" 56 *Northwestern University Law Review* (1961) 168. On the distinction between piracy and terrorism more generally see Robert Haywood and Roberta Spivak, *Maritime Piracy* (Oxford: Routledge, 2012), 75–76.

47 Malvina Halberstam, "Terrorism on the High Seas: The *Achille Lauro*, Piracy and the IMO Convention on Maritime Safety" 82 *American Journal of International Law* (1988) 269.

48 Andrzej Makowski and Laurence Weinbaum, "The Mavi Marmara Incident and the Modern Law of Armed Conflict at Sea" 7 *Israel Journal of Foreign Affairs* (2013) 75.

49 Milena Sterio, "Are Sea Shepherds Pirates? The United States Supreme Court May Decide Soon", blog post at *Communis Hostis Omnium*, 9 June 2015; Jesus, *supra* no36, 79.

50 Jesus, *ibid.*, 379, suggesting as an example "the situation of a person or group of persons that rob or arrest a ship and crew for a ransom as a fundraiser scheme to fund their political activities, a practice followed by some rebel groups".

51 *Supra* no9. Although disputed, the "coastguard narrative" nevertheless serves as a useful ruse; see Christian Bueger, "Practice, Pirates and Coast Guards: the grand narrative of Somali piracy", 34 *Third World Quarterly* (2013), 1811.

"[p]iracy in territorial waters has as little to do with international law as other robberies within the territory of a State [...]. Piracy is, and has always been, a crime against the safety of traffic on the open sea, and therefore it cannot be committed anywhere else than on the open sea".[52] The delineation of applicable *locus delicti* might also be justified by reference to State sovereignty over territorial waters and the corresponding notion that "the coastal state could resolve this situation by enacting its own municipal legislation".[53] This justification comes with a presumption, however, that States possess functioning governments, effective navies and sufficient resources (as may have been the case in 1932, with large swathes of the world under colonial control). Yet this has not been the case in Somalia since the collapse of the Barre regime 1991. The situation has been exacerbated by the expansion of territorial seas to twelve nautical miles in UNCLOS,[54] a provision that vastly reduces the geographic range of States' permitted anti-piracy operations (excluding the territorial State, of course). The issues raised by this nuance, and solutions thereto, are discussed in more detail later.[55]

The third contingency is the "two boats" condition that requires an external attack on the victim vessel. This serves to exclude crimes committed by passengers already on board vessels and preserves the indiscriminate and "warlike" aspect of the definition of piracy.[56] This contingency is not controversial or overtly restrictive.

7.1.2 *Universal Jurisdiction*

Universal jurisdiction over piracy is permitted and defined in Article 105 of UNCLOS, which provides that

> On the high seas, or in any other place outside the jurisdiction of any State, every State may seize a pirate ship [...], and arrest the persons [...] on board. The courts of the State which carried out the seizure may decide upon the penalties to be imposed[.][57]

52 "Draft Convention on Piracy", *supra* n025, 789.

53 Dubner, *supra* n030, 17.

54 Article 3. There is general consensus that the definition of piracy applies with the "exclusive economic zones" of States, which expand for 200 nautical miles from the coastline; see Martin Murphy, *Contemporary Piracy and Maritime Terrorism: The Threat to International Security* (London: Routledge 2007), 15.

55 7.2, *infra*.

56 Rosemary Collins and Daud Hassan, "Applications and Shortcomings of the Law of the Sea in Combating Piracy: A South East Asian Perspective" 40 *Journal of Maritime Law and Commerce* (2009) 89, 100–101.

57 It seems to be common consensus that this provision does not *restrict* jurisdiction to the capturing State, thereby allowing for transfer agreements; see J. Ashley Roach, "General

This legal provision bears similarities to Britain's historic claim to authority over the high seas in common with all other States, as exemplified, for instance by the Admiralty Court's 1718 declaration in *Bonnet's Trial* that "the King of England hath [...] an undoubted jurisdiction and power, in concurrency with other princes and States, for the punishment of all piracies and robberies at sea, in the most remote parts of the world".[58] The drafters of the 1932 "Draft Convention on Piracy" considered this "extraordinary basis of jurisdiction"[59] to be justified by reference to the need to "ensure the safety and passage of vessels travelling over the high seas".[60] This was despite the fact that historical instances of universal jurisdiction were very rare,[61] so that the provision is effectively based on secondary opinion and naturalist reasoning rather than actual State practice.[62] Nevertheless, there were sound policy reasons for adopting this provision (based on the reasons established in Chapter 6), which subsequently became an uncontroversial basis for universal jurisdiction over piracy. The lack of actual practice at the time of its drafting, however, means that there was no opportunity to explore and address weaknesses in its application. As such, given that States historically "had little incentive to actually focus on and incorporate international norms governing piracy into their domestic realities [...], the international community appears to have only recently noticed that States have generally failed to implement universal jurisdiction anti-piracy legislation".[63]

Article 105 is relatively straightforward in allowing a universal enforcement jurisdiction to States and, by extension, universal legislative and adjudicatory jurisdiction. When read in conjunction with Article 101, Article 105 provides for a system of universalised enforcement tied to an internationally agreed definition. Article 105 does, however, leave a large amount of discretion to States; apprehension of pirates is *permitted* rather than obliged and States are

Problematic Issues on Exercise of Jurisdiction over Modern Instances of Piracy" in Clive R. Symmons (ed.), *Selected Contemporary Issues in the Law of the Sea* (Leiden: Martinus Nijhoff, 2011) 119, 129–131.

58 *Bonnet's Trial*, 15 State Trials (Howell) 1231 (Am. Vice Adm. 1718).

59 "Draft Convention" *supra* no25, 768.

60 Paraphrased in Dubner, *supra* no30, 120.

61 "Draft Convention", *supra* no25, 756.

62 Rubin, *supra* no30, 311.

63 Yvonne M. Dutton, "Maritime Piracy and the Impunity Gap: Domestic Implementation of International Treaty Provisions" in Michael J. Struett, Jon D. Carlson, and Mark T. Nance (eds), *Maritime Piracy and the Construction of Global Governance* (New York: Routledge, 2013) 71, 72.

under no explicit subsequent obligation to take any concrete action following capture, such as prosecuting or extraditing captured suspects.[64] As such, while international law permits action to be taken against pirates, it does not ensure that effective action will be taken.[65] Under this provision any decision to "catch and release", while undesirable, would be compatible with international law.

7.1.3 *Duty to Cooperate*

The above provisions are supplemented by a "duty to cooperate" as stated in Article 100 of UNCLOS:

> All States shall cooperate to the fullest possible extent in the repression of piracy on the high seas or in any other place outside the jurisdiction of any State.

Article 100 obliges States to suppress piracy by any means available to them, but is remarkably vague, being deliberately intended to allow "a certain latitude as to the measures it should take to this end in any individual instance".[66] The provision was drafted amidst disagreement between delegations over whether a failure to take action against pirates should be considered a violation of international law,[67] hence the forceful but vague formulation, intended as a "statement of intent" rather than imposing any definite duty.[68] The failure to establish a specific standard suggests that the same level of cooperation cannot be required of every State; rather, the standard will likely differ widely in terms of access to resources and expertise.[69] The vagueness of the provision, however, makes it difficult to pin definite obligations on States, rendering it of limited use in practice.[70]

---

64 Beatriz López Lorca, "Harmonisation of National Criminal Laws on Maritime Piracy: a Regulatory Proposal for the Crime of Piracy and its Penalties", 23 *European Journal on Criminal Policy and Research* (2017) 115, 118.

65 Tullio Treves, "Piracy and the International Law of the Sea" in Guilfoyle (ed.), *supra* no8, 117, 123.

66 International Law Commission, 2 *Yearbook of the International Law Commission* (1955) 25.

67 Dubner, *supra* no30, 109.

68 *Ibid.*, 110.

69 *Ibid.*

70 Collins and Hassan, *supra* no56, 104, suggesting that the provision is "flawed because it fails to define what level of cooperation is required".

7.1.4 *Issues Arising*

From the foregoing analysis it seems fair to conclude that "[t]he law of piracy, [...] is adequate on the international level, provided that more is done on the municipal level".[71] The UNCLOS regime provides the bare bones for States to build upon in taking the necessary action, but it does little more than that. There is no obligation on States to do *anything* specific, such as devote resources to policing the seas or even to formulate effective anti-piracy laws.

Although many States do have domestic laws criminalising piracy (in some form),[72] the content of these laws vary widely.[73] Some States specify the UNCLOS definition of piracy in their domestic laws[74] while others make reference broadly to "piracy according to the law of nations".[75] Many, however, fail to directly criminalise the offence, opting to penalise, instead, constituent acts such as "seizing or taking control over any ships by force".[76] Applicable penalties also vary massively.[77] There are also significant discrepancies in terms of the invocation of universal jurisdiction over piracy, with many States failing to incorporate

71 Thomas A. Clingan, Jr, "The Law of Piracy" in Eric Ellen (ed.), *Piracy at Sea* (Paris: ICC Publishing, 1986) 168, 171.

72 Lorca, *supra* no64 (writing in 2016) noting that, where data is available, "out of 80 countries, 64 jurisdictions have classified a crime of piracy and 16 jurisdictions have not yet specifically classified it".

73 Ilja Van Hespen, "Developing the Concept of Maritime Piracy: A Comparative Legal Analysis of International Law and Domestic Criminal Legislation" 31 *International Journal of Marine and Coastal Law* (2016) 279 (analysing relevant legal texts from 66 States), 298–299; Milena Sterio, "Incorporating International Law to Establish Jurisdiction over Piracy Offences: A Comparative Examination of the Laws of the Netherlands, South Korea, Tanzania, India and Kenya" in Michael P. Scharf, Michael A. Newton and Milena Sterio (eds), *Prosecuting Maritime Piracy: Domestic Solutions to International Crimes* (Cambridge: CUP, 2015) 75.

74 Seventeen States have done this (Lorca, *supra* no64, 122); examples include the UK, South African and Malta. Kenya, Tanzania, Cyprus, Liberia and Australia incorporate UNCLOS with subtle variation (Dutton, *supra* no63, 80).

75 Examples include the US, New Zealand, Canada, Singapore and Malaysia (Dutton, *ibid.*, 78–79). Such an approach allows flexibility for changes in international law, but might create issues in terms of determining what the "law of nations" is at a given moment in time; for instance, in *US v Said*, 757 F. Supp. 2d 555 (E.D. Va. 2010), the Eastern District of Virginia Court based this assessment on the 1820 case of *United States v Smith* (18 US 5 Wheat 153), rather than on UNCLOS, though this was later overturned on appeal (*US v Dire, supra* no34).

76 Examples include Thailand, Japan, Greece, Estonia, Ukraine and Germany (Dutton, *ibid.*, 80–81). The example cited is taken from Thailand's anti-piracy law.

77 Lorca, *supra* no64, 122.

it into domestic law.[78] Indeed, many States fail to define piracy (in conformity with UNCLOS or otherwise) *or* provide for universal jurisdiction over it.

Such diversity of approach creates issues in practice. Definitions of piracy that do not meet the UNCLOS definition may cause complications when States seek to claim jurisdiction[79] or might not accurately describe (and, therefore, proscribe) the conduct of pirates.[80] The failure to adopt universal jurisdiction, as permitted under international law, will create enforcement gaps (or may be used as an excuse for failing to prosecute). Discrepancies in domestic approach will inherently limit the effectiveness of UNCLOS. Conversely, "[i]f all States have jurisdiction over [piracy], then at least some perpetrators may be prosecuted some of the time, thereby providing more deterrence, retribution, and condemnation of the crimes, and more incapacitation and perhaps even rehabilitation of perpetrators, than would otherwise exist".[81] Otherwise, "universal" jurisdiction will exist in name and aspiration only, and pirates will have little to fear.[82]

Even with satisfactory laws, States may not possess sufficient willpower, resources or expertise to safely and legally capture pirates or to conduct a trial (which will inevitably be more complex than "ordinary" criminal cases). States can become reluctant to act due to the prohibitive costs associated with the apprehension, trial and incarceration of suspects, problems with obtaining evidence, transporting in witnesses, translation, and the possibility of suspects claiming asylum.[83] Moreover judges may be unable "to understand the context and intricacies of maritime crimes and thus hand out inappropriate verdicts".[84] States may also be dissuaded from detaining pirates due to the

---

78 Including Sri Lanka, Denmark and Turkey (Dutton, *supra* no63, 81). The latter's position is that "the responsibility for the prosecution of piracy-related events should remain within the countries of the region", a less than "universal" view.

79 See *supra* no34.

80 As with the *Alondra Rainbow* case, discussed *infra*.

81 Madeline H. Morris, "Universal Jurisdiction in a Divided World" 35 *New England Law Review* (2001) 337, 338.

82 See also Kontorovich and Art, *supra* no4, 436, noting that "deterrent effect depends on [the] incidence [of prosecutions] relative to the number of perpetrated crimes".

83 See, *e.g.*: Dutton, *supra* no63, 72–73; Sofia Galani, "Somali Pirates and the Human Rights of Seafarers", *Netherlands Quarterly of Human Rights* 34 (2016) 71; and Michael J. Stepek, "Challenges of Jurisdiction and Prosecution" in Charles H. Norchi and Gwenaële Proutière-Maulion (eds), *Piracy in Comparative Perspective: Problems, Strategies, Law* (Paris: Pédone, 2012) 331, 334–335.

84 "Piracy – is India Prepared to Handle the Challenge it Poses", blog post at *The United Service Institution of India*, 2 September 2014.

possibility of human rights claims against them. In the 2014 European Court of Human Rights cases *Ali Samatar and Others v France*[85] and *Hassan and Others v France*,[86] France was held to be in violation of Articles 5(1) and (3) of the European Convention on Human Rights for failing to bring captured Somali pirates promptly before a judge. Having transported the suspects from the Gulf of Aden to France over a period of up to six days, the suspects had been held on French soil for a further 48 hours before being charged, a period held to be excessive in the circumstances. Although the French authorities were clearly at fault by not charging the suspects as soon as they had arrived in France, the decision is likely to have had a chilling effect on other States seeking to return pirates to their territory for trial.

The case of the *Alondra Rainbow* provides a colourful example of the various issues that States have faced in capturing and prosecuting high seas piracy in the modern age. In November 1999 the Indian Navy apprehended the *Alondra Rainbow* near Cochin. The ship was registered in Panama, owned by Japan, crewed by Filipinos, and had been hijacked near Indonesia by pirates of Indonesian origin.[87] The suspected hijackers (the fifteen men found on board) were dropped off in Mumbai, where the Indian authorities reluctantly decided to put them on trial.[88] The trial was "the first in history to use international law and specifically the law of the sea to claim 'universal jurisdiction' for an act of piracy having nothing to do with the prosecuting country".[89] Although India claimed universal jurisdiction over the pirates, the crime of "piracy" did not exist in its domestic law, so that the men were charged *inter alia* with armed robbery, theft and attempted murder.[90] The legal process moved slowly, with one of the suspects dying in detention before the trial had even begun.[91] The trial finally commenced in early 2001 and lasted two years, over which the prosecution introduced 24 witnesses and a range of circumstantial evidence.[92] The defence produced no evidence and elected not to cross-examine important

85 Application nos. 17110/10 and 17301/10, 4 December 2014.

86 Application nos. 46695/10 and 54588/10, 4 December 2014.

87 Langewiesche, *The Outlaw Sea: A World of Freedom, Chaos and Crime* (New York, NY: North Point Press, 2004), 71.

88 *Ibid.*, 75, noting that it would be normal practice to "shoo" the pirates away.

89 *Ibid.*, 76.

90 *Ibid.*, 76. The charges would nevertheless have corresponded with the deliberately broad definition of piracy contained in Article 101 of UNCLOS.

91 *Ibid.*

92 *Ibid.*, 77–78.

witnesses (such as the hijacked Japanese captain) due to language difficulties.[93] The pirates were convicted in February 2003 and handed seven-year sentences,[94] but just over two years later, in April 2005, the judgement was overruled by the Mumbai High Court and the pirates acquitted, due to "systemic and organisation failures" at trial.[95] The *Alondra Rainbow* case provides a snapshot of the many difficulties inherent in trying piracy: general reluctance, inadequate laws, difficulties acquiring evidence, procedural rights that may be difficult to guarantee in the unique circumstances.[96] Yet with assistance from affected States (Indonesia or Japan, for instance), or with financial help and legal expertise, India might have stood a better chance of conducting a successful trial. It is a case study in the need for mutual assistance and cooperation.

The *Alondra Rainbow* episode is also a case study in the "regionalisation" of universal jurisdiction. When piracy occurs close to capable and well-resourced States, effective prosecutions will come more easily than in regions that lack the necessary expertise and resources. The "golden age" Caribbean pirates, for instance, operated in the vicinity of relatively wealthy colonies and, although they were experts in elusion, were ultimately sought out and hunted down by increasingly well-equipped navies. Trials were relatively easy, quick and efficient (generally lasting only a few days), albeit lacking in procedural guarantees for the accused.[97] Following the conclusion of the 1713 *Peace of Utrecht*,[98] former enemies began to work together, cooperating and pooling resources to suppress piracy. These conditions do not pertain, however, in the modern world.[99] Pirates avoid developed regions and, instead, thrive off the legal vacuum of governmental weakness or, even, outright collapse. "Universal jurisdiction" is, perhaps paradoxically, only of use in the hands of States that are both *willing* and *able* to use it.[100] Rather than create a toolkit for the effective suppression of pirates by all States, UNCLOS represents a blind restatement of ineffective, outdated ideas pioneered by powerful States *for* powerful States.

---

93 *Ibid.*, 78–80.

94 *Ibid.*, 80–81.

95 "Piracy – is India Prepared to Handle the Challenge it Poses", *supra* no84.

96 On which see, further, Tamsin Paige, "The Impact and Effectiveness of UNCLOS on Counter Piracy Operations" 22 *Journal of Conflict & Security Law* (2017) 97, 108–111.

97 5.2, *supra*.

98 Randall Lesaffer, "The Peace of Utrecht and the Balance of Power", available online through *Oxford Historical Treaties*; discussed at 5.3, *supra*.

99 See, e.g., Isanga, *supra* no3, 1299, noting that "[c]ontemporary piracy is a completely different threat than traditional piracy envisioned under the UNCLOS".

100 *Ibid.*, 1270.

Cooperation, then, becomes key, particularly in terms of States helping each other to apprehend pirates, communicating effectively, sharing expertise (*e.g.* drafting suitable laws, facilitating fair trials), and sharing resources. Without international cooperation, the provisions of UNCLOS will remain frustrated possibilities. However, the gradual but effective suppression of piracy around East Africa illustrates how well cooperative schemes between States can work. It is to this more successful chapter (for States, that is) in the history of piracy that we now turn.

7.2 "Universalising" Universal Jurisdiction over Piracy

> As long as pirates perceive that the international community is unwilling or lacking the capacity to prosecute, piracy will continue to thrive.[101]

The outbreak in Somali piracy in the early 2000s provided the first real test for universal jurisdiction in terms of its role in maintaining the Grotian ideal of the free sea.[102] In the absence of effective local enforcement mechanisms, more capable States might have been expected to take captures and prosecutions into their own hands, via universal jurisdiction, in order to maintain the safety and freedom of the global commons. As such it ought to be "inconceivable that piracy, a crime regarded as one that is committed against the human race, should not be suppressed and prosecuted at the international level as effectively as other internationally cognizable offenses".[103] In reality the response was sluggish (as the figures cited demonstrate),[104] with no systematic response mechanism in place, either locally (involving East African States, for instance) or at a global level.

The number of pirate attacks in the region has since declined, however. A study of the circumstances surrounding the ultimately successful response to Somali piracy reveals that universal jurisdiction is best realised as part of a collaborative effort among States. The initial trigger for more effective cooperation appears to have been UN Security Council (UNSC) Resolution 1816,[105]

---

101 *Ibid.*, 1273.

102 4.1.2, *supra*.

103 Isanga, *supra* n03, 1297.

104 Introduction to Chapter 7, *supra*.

105 Issued 2 June 2008. The trigger for the Resolution appears to have been the hijacking of a French yacht, *Le Ponant*.

itself in response to pressure from the International Maritime Organisation (IMO)[106] and a request from the Somali Transitional Government.[107] The Resolution was significant in finding a breach of "international peace and security"[108] based on "the threat that acts of piracy [...] pose to the prompt, safe and effective delivery of humanitarian aid to Somalia, the safety of commercial maritime routes and to international navigation"[109] and, consequently, the Resolution's issuance under Chapter VII of the UN Charter.[110] On the basis of such a finding, the Security Council authorised States to "[e]nter the territorial waters of Somalia for the purpose of repressing acts of piracy and armed robbery at sea"[111] and, more broadly, to suppress piracy by "all necessary means".[112] The positive response triggered by the string of Resolutions indicate that anti-piracy strategies work best when coordinated at a supra-national level. This is notwithstanding the fact that the operative provisions are restricted temporally and geographically, and, moreover, that "[t]he reference to the consent by the coastal state concerned greatly limits the 'revolutionary content' of

106 IMO Assembly, "Piracy and Armed Robbery against Ships in Waters off the Coast of Somali", Doc. A 25/Res 1002, 6 December 2007, para 6.

107 *Supra* no105, para. 9.

108 *Ibid.*, preamble, para. 12.

109 *Ibid.*, preamble, para. 2.

110 *Ibid.*, para. 12. The UNSC tied the "threat" to the ongoing instability in Somalia by suggesting that piracy "exacerbate[s] the situation". Nevertheless, the purpose of the Resolution is specifically aimed at and triggered by piracy in the region, this being described as a "grave concern". The Resolution's reference to the broader problem in Somalia was likely intended to provide a more acceptable basis for a finding of a "threat to the peace" and to assuage the concerns of other States, like Indonesia, who expressed concern at its potential precedential value (UN Press Release, "Security Council Condemns Acts of Piracy, Armed Robbery off Somalia's Coast, Authorizes for Six Months 'All Necessary Means' to Repress Such Acts", 2 June 2008, SC/9344).

111 *Ibid.*, para. 7(a). Pirate attacks carried out within the territorial waters do not, strictly speaking, qualify as piracy *jure gentium* within the terms of UNCLOS. Arguably, given Somalia's inability to police its own territorial waters, this rule loses its operative meaning, so that States may detain and prosecute pirates based on default claims to universal jurisdiction, permitted under Article 105 of UNCLOS "in a place outside the jurisdiction of any State". The Transitional Government's consent might be viewed as a cession of this right, which appears not to have posed an obstacle to trials in the region. The right to enter Somali waters was initially issued temporarily, but has since been renewed several times, most recently (at the time of writing) by Resolution 2383 (7 November 2017), para. 14, extending the authority to enter Somali waters for a further twelve months, while noting "the primary role of Somali authorities in the fight against piracy and armed robbery at sea off the coast of Somalia".

112 *Ibid.*, para. 7(b).

the resolutions".[113] The UNSC strategy was proportionate to the threat and, in time, achieved the desired objective.

The solution was unique to the situation, however; its success here does not guarantee that a similar approach can necessarily be utilised elsewhere.[114] By contrast UNSC Resolution 2018 (2011),[115] designed to offer a solution to the issue of piracy in the Gulf of Guinea, offers an alternative solution. Whilst again expressing "deep concern about the threat that piracy and armed robbery at sea in the Gulf of Guinea pose to international navigation, security and the economic development of states in the region",[116] it omits to take action under Chapter VII while maintaining the pelagic territorial integrity of the littoral States and calling for greater cooperation amongst them.[117] The key difference from the "Somalia" situation" is that the States in the region are, in theory, capable of policing their own territorial waters and adjoining high seas and, as such, have not requested UNSC intervention on a similar scale to that in Somalia. Nigeria and Benin, for instance, routinely conduct patrols in the region,[118] whereas in Somalia the inexistence of a State navy required novel measures to fill the enforcement gap. Piracy (and "armed robbery" taking place within territorial waters) continues to escalate in the region,[119] however, while legislative and judicial responses remain sluggish.[120]

UNSC intervention did not prove to be a panacea even on the eastern coast of Africa, as instances of piracy initially continued to grow in number and State

113 Tuerk, *supra* n013, 37.

114 Anna Petrig, "Piracy", in Donald R. Rothwell, Alex G. Oude Elferink, Karen N. Scott and Tim Stephens (eds), *The Oxford Handbook of the Law of the Sea* (Oxford: OUP, 2015) 843, 863.

115 31 October 2011.

116 *Ibid.*, preamble, para. 1.

117 *Ibid.*, paras 3–6.

118 As noted in preamble, para. 9, *ibid.*

119 The IMB reported 22 attacks (covering both piracy *stricto sensu* and "armed robbery" in territorial waters) in the seas off Nigeria in the first quarter of 2018 (International Chamber of Commerce / International Maritime Bureau, *Piracy and Armed Robbery against Ships*, "Report for the Period 1 January – 31 March 2018"), while 33 were reported in the entirety of 2017 (2017 report, *supra* n07), second only behind Indonesia, with 43.

120 Nigeria, for instance, does not specifically criminalise piracy and does not allow for universal jurisdiction; "Nigeria Piracy Law" in the *Piracy Law Database* maintained by *Oceans Beyond Piracy* (available online). There have (at the time of writing) been no convictions: Oceans Beyond Piracy, *State of Maritime 2016: Assessing the Economic and Human Cost: West Africa* (2 May 2017).

navies persisted with the practice of "catch and release".[121] Over time, relevant UNSC Resolutions called for greater and closer levels of cooperation along more specific lines. Resolution 1851 (December 2008), for instance, obliged States *inter alia* to "increase regional capacity [...] to effectively investigate and prosecute piracy",[122] while Resolution 1918 (27 April 2010) required States "to criminalise piracy under their domestic law and favourably consider the prosecution of suspected, and imprisonment of convicted, pirates apprehended off the coast of Somalia".[123] With assistance lent by the United Nations Office on Drugs and Crime (UNODC) and advice on coordination devised by the Contact Group on Piracy off the Coast of Somalia (comprising a transnational network of up to 100 legal experts),[124] these further Resolutions have catalysed concrete cooperation between States.[125] Prosecutions of piracy have become commonplace in the region (predominantly via cases transferred to Kenya, The Seychelles and Mauritius, *inter alia*), aided by effective laws and local capacity building.[126] The UNODC has worked to build capacity in the region by providing judicial and prosecutorial training, recruiting lawyers and translators, assisting with evidence collection, building and improving courtrooms and prisons, repatriating convicts post-sentence and facilitating legislative reform (including in Somalia itself).[127] The UNODC's work has been

121 Lang report, *supra* n04, 13.

122 16 December, 2008, para. 5.

123 27 April 2010, para. 2.

124 Christian Bueger, "Experts in an Adventure with Pirates: A Story of Somali Piracy Expertise" in Anna Leander and Ole Waever (eds), *Assembling Exclusive Expertise: Knowledge, Ignorance and Conflict Resolution in the Global South* (Oxford: Taylor & Francis, 2018), Chapter 2.

125 A summary of relevant initiatives is provided in the lengthy preamble to UNSC Resolution 2383 (2017); these include EU-led naval operation "Operation Atalanta", NATO-led "Operation Ocean Shield", US-led "Combined Task Force 151", a piracy database maintained by INTERPOL, and guidance and support from the IMO (among others). See also Michael J Struett, "Maritime Piracy and Global Security" in Philip Reichel and Ryan Randa (eds), *Transnational Crime and Global Security* (Santa Barbara, CA: ABC-CLIO, 2018) 23, 35, summarising the multilateral incentives being undertaken by States.

126 Treves, *supra* n065, 138; Efthymios Papastavridis, "Who Will Prosecute Piracy in Africa?" in Charles Chernor Jalloh and Ilias Bantekas (eds), *The International Criminal Court and Africa* (Oxford: OUP, 2017), 320, 328–329; Sterio, "Incorporating International Law" *supra* n073, 89–90 and 95–100; Aruna Narain, "Preparing for piracy trials in Mauritius", 39 *Commonwealth Law Bulletin* (2013) 53.

127 UNODC, Global Maritime Crime Programme, *Annual Report 2016* (Nairobi, 2016); Oceans Beyond Piracy, *supra* n0120; UN Secretary-General, "Report on Specialized Anti-piracy Courts in Somalia and other States in the region", U.N. Doc. S/2012/50 (Jan. 20, 2012); US

supplemented by the IMO-funded *Djibouti Code of Conduct concerning the Repression of Piracy and Armed Robbery against Ships in the Western Indian Ocean and the Gulf of Aden,* which requires signatory States to cooperate towards the repression of piracy, establishes an information-sharing network and has supported the reform of national piracy laws.[128] It has been signed by 20 regional States in the region and is generally regarded as a success.[129] *In lieu* of addressing the root causes of piracy (an ideal response would be one that builds peace and self-sufficiency in Somalia),[130] the cooperative regime overseen by the UNSC and facilitated (*inter alia*) by the UNODC has proved successful.

The work of the UNODC and cooperative regime of *Djibouti* make international law and universal jurisdiction *accessible* to States. Consider the position of The Seychelles which, as a State located close to pirate hotspots, was losing an estimated four *per cent* of its economy to pirates at the peak of the crisis (due to loss of boats, fishing and tourism, and investment in maritime security).[131] A country of roughly 94,000 people,[132] The Seychelles possesses only two courtrooms and capacity for 100 prisoners,[133] yet between 2010 and 2016 it oversaw the trial of 152 suspected pirates.[134]

The Seychellois government announced the formation of a piracy court in 2010, designed to receive and try suspects detained by European Union patrols.[135] Successful trials required legislative reform, however, given that the penal code defined piracy by reference to "the law of England for the time

---

Department of Justice, "Major Achievements in the Courtroom: Piracy Cases", available online.

128 9 January 2009; see Guilfoyle, *supra* no8, 52, and J. Ashley Roach, "Countering Piracy off Somalia: International Law and International Institutions" 104 *American Journal of International Law* (2011) 397, 410–411.

129 *Ibid.*

130 Paige, *supra* no96, 116; Christian Bueger, Jan Stockbruegger and Sascha Werthes, "Pirates, fishermen and peacebuilding: options for counter-piracy strategy in Somalia" 32 *Contemporary Security Policy* (2011) 356.

131 President James Michel, cited in Mark Lowe, "Pirate's Prison" *Maritime Security Review*, 8 March 2012.

132 Figure from CIA World Factbook, estimate from July 2017.

133 Michael Onyiego, "Seychelles to Establish Regional Court to Prosecute Pirates", *Voice of America*, 5 May 2010.

134 Oceans Beyond Piracy, *supra* no120. By contrast, 164 were tried in much larger Kenya over the same period.

135 Onyiego, *supra* no133; UNODC, *Annual Report 2016, supra* no127.

being in force",[136] requiring an investigation of "the common law prevailing in England as at the 29th June 1976 [...] when Seychelles attained independence from Britain".[137] Establishing the relevant law therefore would have required investigating of obsolete statutes, case law, and reliance on the 1958 *Convention on the High Seas*[138] (incidentally this interpretation would have allowed for the use of universal jurisdiction, with the 1934 Privy Council case *In re Piracy Jure Gentium* as authority).[139] In cognisance of this issue, the applicable law was revised in 2010 so as to define piracy in terms almost identical to the relevant provisions in UNCLOS,[140] obviating the need to arbitrarily establish the law pertaining in England in June 1976. The Seychelles Supreme Court subsequently confirmed in *Talenduic* that

> universal jurisdiction makes it possible for the arresting State, like the Republic of Seychelles in this case, to freely prosecute suspected pirates, from anywhere in the world, and punish them if found guilty under the municipal law[.][141]

This reads like a statement of intent from the Seychelles,[142] which has since processed 152 suspected pirates through its resource-limited system, assisted by UNODC which has financed detention centres, provided assistance at trial (particularly by providing trained lawyers and translators), and facilitated prisoner transfers to Somalia.[143] The UNODC claims that "no trial has failed due to lack of due process or availability of witnesses".[144] In 2015 the Seychelles

136 *Seychelles Penal Code*, Cap 158, s65.

137 See, e.g., *R v. Abdi Ali & Ten Others* (CR 14/2010) ("*Intertuna II*"), para. 2.

138 *Supra* n031.

139 "*Intertuna II*", *supra* n0137, para. 34, citing *In re Piracy Jure Gentium* [1934] A.C., 589.

140 Seychelles Penal Code, Cap 158, as amended by Act no. 2 of 2010, s65. The definition criminalises piracy that occurs within Seychellois territorial waters as well as on the high seas. See, further, Anthony Francis Tissa Fernando, "An Insight into piracy prosecutions in the Republic of Seychelles", 41 *Commonwealth Law Bulletin* (2015) 173.

141 *R v. Mohamed Ahmed Ise & Four Others* (CR 76/2010) ("*Talenduic*"), para. 22.

142 See, further, Mileno Sterio, "Pirates' Right to a Speedy Trial" in Michael P. Scharf, Michael A. Newton and Milena Sterio (eds) *supra*, 73, 200.

143 *Annual Report 2016*, *supra* n0127.

144 *Ibid.* As of 2015, 138 out of 142 suspects had been convicted, with those acquitted repatriated to Somalia (Rassin Vannier and Sharon Uranie, "First trial starts before the Seychelles dedicated court for piracy and maritime crime cases", *Seychelles News Agency*, 2 June 2015).

opened a dedicated piracy court, funded by UNODC, the United Kingdom, the Netherlands and the Trust Fund on Piracy off the Coast of Somalia (administered by the Contact Group on Piracy off the Coast of Somalia).[145] The Seychelles, Kenya[146] and Mauritius sit at the centre of a cooperative web that sees inter-State organisations cooperating to arrest, prosecute, detain and (if needed) repatriate pirates, with UNODC playing a supporting role throughout. The trials demonstrate a marked improvement from India's somewhat experimental *Alondra Rainbow* case and showcase the benefits of inter-State cooperation and resource sharing.[147] Although piracy in the East African region has now largely been brought under control,[148] it continues to thrive in other areas, most notably in the Gulf of Guinea, Southeast Asia[149] and around parts of South America.[150] Any learning from the Somalia situation must be applied to these and any future outbreaks. In any case, in order to keep piracy under control, close cooperation and creative use of universal jurisdiction remains necessary.

145 Vannier and Uranie, *ibid.*

146 A similar success story has ensued in Kenya, again despite initial legal difficulties. A 2010 court judgement refused to recognise that it possessed universal jurisdiction over high seas piracy, though this was reversed in 2012, with the Kenyan Court of Appeal noting that "the offence of piracy on the coast of Somalia, which we are dealing with in this appeal, is of great concern to the international community as it has affected the economic activities and thus the economic well-being of many countries including Kenya. All States, not necessarily those affected by it, have therefore a right to exercise universal jurisdiction to punish the offence": *In re Mohamud Mohammed Hashi, et al*, 18 October 2012. See commentary in Alexander M. Muteti, "Prosecution of piracy cases – the Kenya experience" 39 *Commonwealth Law Bulletin* (2013) 73. Kenya has however been severely pushed in terms of resources and has faced criticisms regarding the human rights of defendants; see Yvonne M. Dutton, "Bringing Pirates to Justice: A Case for Including Piracy within the Jurisdiction of the International Criminal Court", 11 *Chicago Journal of International Law* (2010) 197, 224–227.

147 Though see Tamsin Paige, "Emerging Voices: Pirates of the Indian Ocean – Enforcement in the Seychelles", blog post at *opiniojuris.org*, 19 August 2013, noting issues particularly as regards training, facilities, and payment of defence counsel.

148 UN Security Council, "Report of the Secretary-General on the Situation with Respect to Piracy and Armed Robbery at Sea off the Coast of Somalia", UN Doc S/2015/276 (12 October 2015), para 3, though see IMB report for 2017, *supra* n07, and Michael Scharf and Mistale Taylor, "A Contemporary Approach to the Oldest Crime" 33 *Utrecht Journal of International and European Law* (2017) 77, at 77, warning of the continued threat in the region.

149 IMB report, *ibid.*

150 *Ibid.;* "Pirates 'massacre' Guyana fishermen off Suriname coast", BBC News, 4 May 2018.

7.3 Conclusion

This overview of recent developments raises questions about the continued relevance of terms such as *"hostes humani generis"*, the usefulness of universal jurisdiction as a tool in the fight against piracy, and the pertinence of the "piracy analogy" as a means of establishing the heredity of extraterritorial prosecutions of "core" international crimes. The potential of universal jurisdiction appears to have fallen short when called upon to contend with piracy today; it does not appear to be "universal" in a true sense, given that only certain States possess the motivation and ability to use it. The outdated and equivocal terms of UNCLOS seem designed to appeal to an obsolete geopolitics whereby State navies *were* willing and able to apprehend any pirates they encountered on the high seas. The claimed "undoubted jurisdiction and power, in concurrency with other princes and States, for the punishment of all piracies and robberies at sea, in the most remote parts of the world"[151] might work for certain States, in certain parts of the world, but *de facto* it is a somewhat exclusive right, better realised by collaborative efforts such as those outlined above.

The paradigm of unilateral universal jurisdiction, which might have been successful three hundred years ago during the "golden age" of piracy, has no practical basis in the real world. Rather, we have "a nineteenth century regulatory framework, implemented by twentieth century institutions, trying to resolve a problem for an industry and world that has rapidly moved into the twenty-first century".[152] As pirates continue to terrorise the seas, a rethink of the applicable legal apparatus is required, otherwise Isanga's prediction ("as long as pirates perceive that the international community is unwilling or lacking the capacity to prosecute, piracy will continue to thrive") will prove correct.[153]

The exercise of universal jurisdiction has to evolve in order to best contain the problem of modern piracy. The radically different geographies and politics of contemporary piracy call for a revised response, one of collaborative effort and resource sharing. UN Security Council resolutions, improved international cooperation, and competence-building projects led by the UNODC have, so far, all helped in making universal jurisdiction prosecutions more effective (as the example of The Seychelles shows) and in securing the seas around the

151 *Bonnet's Trial,* 15 State Trials (Howell) 1231 (Am. Vice Adm. 1718).

152 Haywood and Spivak, *supra* no46, 70.

153 *Supra* no101.

Gulf of Aden. The work of the UNODC in States such as The Seychelles, Kenya and Mauritius serves as examples of how collaborative efforts towards eradicating piracy may be the key to clearing the seas of danger in other areas. With piracy on the rise again in the Gulf of Guinea and Southeast Asia, it is increasingly essential that lessons are learned and effective action taken.

CHAPTER 8

Ancient Promise or False Hope?: the Legacy of the Piracy Analogy

> In the modern age, humanitarian and practical considerations have combined to lead the nations of the world to recognize that respect for fundamental human rights is in their individual and collective interest. […] [T]he torturer has become – like the pirate […] before him – *hostis humani generis,* an enemy of all mankind.[1]

These words of the US Circuit Court in *Filártiga v Peña-Irala* echo the *Eichmann* case in suggesting a linear progression from the pirate to (in this example) the torturer. *Both* are *hostes humani generis,* the enemies of all mankind, the uniting theme being, in the words of the Court, their affront to the global "individual and collective interest" in human rights. The ideology espoused here represents the modern-day variant of the *jus gentium* (as described by Cicero)[2] and draws heavily on the Israeli Supreme Court's appeal to "agreed vital interests" in the *Eichmann* case.[3] Yet it speaks of new concerns, imperatives, and global interests.

A redefining moment appears to have taken place. International law has shifted from a State-centred model to a more complex system that (in theory at least) places importance on the human rights of individuals.[4] Documents such as the United Nations (UN) Charter and a plethora of human rights and

1 *Filártiga v Peña-Irala*, 630 F.2d 876 (2d Cir. 1980), 890. The case set a precedent in the United States for tortious suits on the basis of universal civil jurisdiction.

2 *De Officiis*, III, s.107 (1913 edition by Walter Miller, with an English Translation; Cambridge, MA: Harvard University Press, 1913); discussed *supra*, 2.2.

3 *Eichmann v. A-G Israel* (Supreme Court), 36 *International Law Reports* (1968) 227, para. 12.

4 P.K. Menon, "The International Personality of Individuals in International Law: A Broadening of the Traditional Doctrine" 1 *Journal of Transnational Law & Policy* (1992) 151, 153; Jure Vidmar, "Norm Conflicts and Hierarchy in International Law: Towards a Vertical International Legal System?" in Erika de Wet and Jure Vidmar (eds), *Hierarchy in International Law: The Place of Human Rights* (Oxford: OUP, 2012) 13, 16; Nigel White, "The United Nations System: Conference, Contract or Constitutional Order?" 4 *Singapore Journal of International and Comparative Law* (2000) 281, 290; and Wouter Werner and Geoff Gordon, "Kant, Cosmopolitanism, and International Law" in Anne Orford and Florian Hoffmann (eds), *The Oxford Handbook of the Theory of International Law* (Oxford: OUP, 2016) 505, 515.

 | DOI:10.1163/9789004390461_009

humanitarian law treaties bear witness to this trend.[5] Reinforcing this reconceived community interest is the emergence of international criminal law as a super-national discipline, providing a tool by which those in violation of human rights (on a massive scale) may be prosecuted in domestic or international courts. Though the system is imperfect (inadequate, even), it nevertheless hints at the existence of a universally valid and applicable value system,[6] with the "values" set internationally, though enforceable domestically.[7] Universal jurisdiction has developed in parallel, its permissive exercise by States generally recognised in response to instances of genocide, crimes against humanity, war crimes, torture and aggression,[8] offences that the preamble to the Rome Statute describes as "unimaginable atrocities that deeply shock the conscience of humanity [and] threaten the peace, security and well-being of the world".[9] These words define the present moral stance of the international community against a somewhat different threat to that posed by the Caribbean pirates.

Whereas universal jurisdiction originally developed to enable early Westphalian States to self-identify and to remove external threats, the twentieth century saw it transform into a tool designed to maintain acceptable standards of conduct *within* that community, effectively enabling States to "undercut"

5 The UN Charter (San Francisco, 1945) vows to "reaffirm faith in fundamental human rights, in the dignity and worth of the human person, [and] in the equal rights of men and women" (preambular paragraph 2). Subsequent developments include the ratification of the 1948 Universal Declaration of Human Rights, adopted by the General Assembly in 1948 without a dissenting vote (General Assembly Resolution 217A (III), 10 December 1948), the 1966 International Covenant on Economic, Social and Cultural Rights (Adopted by GA Res 2200A (XXI), 16 December 1966) and the 1966 International Covenant on Civil and Political Rights (also adopted by Adopted by GA Res 2200A (XXI)). Every State has ratified at least four major multilateral human rights treaties; figures taken from website of the UN Office of the High Commissioner for Human Rights (correct as of November 2018). Moreover every UN Member State has ratified all four of the 1949 Geneva Conventions; information from ICRC website (as of November 2018). See also references *ibid.*

6 Kai Ambos, *Treatise on International Criminal Law (vol 1)* (Oxford: OUP, 2013), 57–60; Robert Cryer, *Prosecuting International Crimes: Selectivity and the International Criminal Law Regime* (Cambridge: CUP, 2005), 12.

7 On the relationship between the two sources of law in this context, see Ann Marie Slaughter, "Defining the Limits: Universal Jurisdiction and National Courts" in Macedo (ed.), *Universal Jurisdiction: National Courts and the Prosecution of Serious Crimes under International Law* (Philadelphia: University of Pennsylvania Press, 2004), 168.

8 Chapter 1, *supra* (introductory section). On the issue of universal jurisdiction over aggression see Michael P. Scharf, "Universal Jurisdiction and the Crime of Aggression" 53 *Harvard International Law Journal* (2012) 358. The crime of torture does not appear as a crime *per se* in the Rome Statute, (though widespread and systematic use would constitute a crime against humanity) but it is nevertheless recognised as an offence subject to universal jurisdiction.

9 Rome Statute of the International Criminal Court, 1998, preamble, paras 1–3.

the sovereignty of others by judging the conduct of their civilians or, even, their officials.[10] As such, "[t]he enemy of all [...] is no longer someone willingly on the outside of the international community [...]; it is instead a member of the international community that must be forcefully cast out of it".[11] The stateless pirate had given way to the *pirate State*.

The phrase "international community" (a cause of consternation for some scholars)[12] describes, in this context, the unified stance of States in response to certain norms that are purportedly universally accepted, such as the right to inter-State commerce (as violated by piracy) or certain international human rights standards (as violated by the "core" crimes).[13] This is not a static concept but one that, instead, varies depending on what the pressing international concerns of the age may be.[14] As such the identity of *hostes humani generis* at a given point in time appears to hinge on the pressing concerns

10 Amedeo Policante, *The Pirate Myth: Genealogies of an Imperial Concept* (Abingdon: Routledge, 2015), 170–171; Devika Hovell, "The Authority of Universal Jurisdiction 29 European Journal of International Law (2018) 427, 443.

11 *Policante, ibid.*, 171.

12 See, especially, Dino Kritsiotis, "Imagining the International Community" 12 *European Journal of International Law* (2002) 961, and Georges Abi-Saab, "Whither the International Community" 9 *European Journal of International Law* (1998) 248.

13 John Rawls, *The Law of Peoples* (Cambridge, MA: Harvard University Press, 1999) 79, suggesting that "[t]here are a special class of urgent rights, such as freedom from slavery and serfdom, liberty [...] of conscience, and security of ethnic groups from mass murder and genocide. The violation of this class of rights is equally condemned both by reasonable liberal peoples and decent hierarchical peoples". The term is used in this way in, e.g.: Rosalyn Higgins, *Problems & Process: International Law and How We Use It* (Oxford: Clarendon, 1995), 58; Theodor Meron, "Reflections on the Prosecution of War Crimes by International Tribunals", 100 *American Journal of International Law* (2006) 551, 552; Hersch Lauterpacht, *The Function of Law in the International Community* (Oxford: Clarendon, 1933), 434–443; Kai Ambos: *Treatise on International Criminal Law (vol 1)* (Oxford: OUP, 2013), 57–60; and Bruno Simma & Andreas L. Paulus, "'The International Community': Facing the Challenge of Globalisation" 9 *European Journal of International Law* (1998) 266. It also forms the basis of decisions in, *inter alia*: *Eichmann* (Supreme Court), *supra* no3, para. 11; ICTY, *Prosecutor v. Tadić*, "Decision on the Defence Motion for Interlocutory Appeal on Jurisdiction" (Appeals Chamber) 2 October 1995, para. 59; ICTR, *Prosecutor v. Rutaganda*, Judgement and Sentence, 6 December 1999, para. 455; Special Court for Sierra Leone, *Prosecutor v. Charles Ghankay Taylor* (Appeals Chamber), "Decision on Immunity from Jurisdiction", 31 May 2004, para. 6; and International Court of Justice, *Legality of the Threat or Use of Nuclear Weapons*, 8 July 1996, Declaration of President Bedjaoui, para. 12.

14 See, *e.g.*, William Schabas, *Unimaginable Atrocities: Justice, Politics, and Rights at the War Crimes Tribunals* (Oxford: OUP, 2012), 31, noting that "Nuremberg was part of a dynamic process" and, citing prosecutor Robert Jackson, adding that "every custom has its origin in some single act".

of contemporary society – be it the anarchical economic or societal subversion of the pirate or (to borrow from the *Filartiga* example) the deprivation of human dignity by the State-sponsored torturer.[15] The "piracy analogy" remains relevant, then, in terms of the historically authenticated justification it lends to the use of universal jurisdiction, by reference to dynamic community interests.[16]

The history of States' interactions with pirates, via universal jurisdiction, has proved to be influential in informing the prosecution of "core" international crimes, *i.e.*, genocide, crimes against humanity, war crimes and (in theory) aggression. Chapter 1 has already charted the history of how the "piracy analogy" was subtly invoked at Nuremberg and in Israel's prosecution of Adolf Eichmann; the unique status of universal jurisdiction, as it applied to piracy, set a precedent for these pathbreaking events.[17] As such the "piracy analogy" has, arguably, already done its work by spawning and informing prosecutions of a broader set of "core" crimes. Doubtless, though, the "piracy analogy" has a continued role to play by informing discourses around the constantly contentious nature of "new" universal jurisdiction.[18]

This chapter examines the legacy that piracy has left for "core" international crimes, via an analysis of two areas. Part 8.1 expands on the argument advanced in Chapter 6 that universal jurisdiction over piracy developed in response to a perceived threat against an "agreed vital interest of the international community",[19] namely the sacrosanct principle of maritime trade (as influenced by several factors that exacerbated the perceived "heinousness" of piracy).[20] Here it is suggested that the same logic applies, by extension, to "core" international crimes which, in their own way, threaten the redefined international community of today. Part 8.2, by contrast, examines the limitations of this approach by reference to the present state of international law and suggests what action might be taken to ensure the future of universal jurisdiction. Part 8.3 forms a conclusion.

---

15 David Luban, "Human Dignity, Humiliation, and Torture" 19 *Kennedy Institute of Ethics Journal* (2009) 211; Office of the High Commissioner for Human Rights, *Report of the Special Rapporteur on torture and other cruel, inhuman or degrading treatment or punishment*, August 2015.

16 Policante, *supra* n010, 171–172.

17 1.2.1, *supra*.

18 1.2.3, *supra*.

19 *Eichmann, supra* n03, para. 12.

20 6.1, *supra*.

8.1 Ancient Promise? The Piracy Analogy and "New" Universal Jurisdiction

> No longer do [universal jurisdiction's] precise historical functions and applications, such as trials of pirates [...], remain salient. New purposes growing out of the turbulence of our times claim greater attention.[21]

With this quote Henry Steiner suggests that universal jurisdiction's original function, as a means of suppressing piracy, has today given way to broader and, arguably, more pressing concerns. Pirates might have been the original *hostes humani generis* based on their twofold subversion of State economies and perceived opposition to the State itself as a form of human organisation.[22] The emergence of universal jurisdiction was intended to facilitate pirates' eradication in a renewed global community founded on peaceful mercantilism.[23] The abhorrence towards them was informed and compounded by exacerbating factors such as piracy's indiscriminate effect, its extraterritorial *locus*, and State consensus regarding its proscription (and, as a corollary, regarding universal jurisdiction).[24] It was piracy's indiscriminate effect on a valuable and universal interest that rendered its perpetrators *hostes humani generis*,[25] an action "grave for its effect, and potential effect, on a *shared community value*".[26] Thought of in this way, universal jurisdiction might be said to create "an international community of interest",[27] uniting States (and the individuals who comprise them) towards common standards of practice and morality while penalising individuals whose actions fall outside the bounds of outside those standards. It is an extension of the Hobbesian social contract, on a global scale.[28]

---

21 Henry J. Steiner, "Three Cheers for Universal Jurisdiction – Or Is It Only Two?" 5 *Theoretical Inquiries in Law* (2004) 199, 201.

22 Hugo Grotius, *The Rights of War and Peace* (ed. Richard Tuck, from the edition by Jean Barbeyrac), (Indianapolis: Liberty Fund, 2005), Book 3, Chapter 3, s2; see 4.1.3, *supra*.

23 As suggested with the adoption of the 1713 Peace of Utrecht: Randall Lesaffer, "The Peace of Utrecht and the Balance of Power", available online through *Oxford Historical Treaties*. Discussed *supra*, 5.3.

24 6.1, *supra*.

25 *Ibid.*

26 Roger L Phillips, "Pirate Accessory Liability: Developing a Modern Legal Regime governing Incitement and Intentional Facilitation of Maritime Piracy" 25 *Florida Journal of International Law* (2013) 271, 287 (emphasis added).

27 Adeno Addis, "Imagining the International Community: The Constitutive Dimension of Universal Jurisdiction" 31 *Human Rights Quarterly* (2009) 129, 133.

28 6.1.3, *supra*.

There is some debate over whether the corpus of international criminal law directly criminalises individual actions at an international level or whether it imposes an *erga omnes* obligation (*i.e.* applicable to all) on States to criminalise such actions.[29] A similar debate can be observed in the context of piracy.[30] Scrutiny of this debate would go beyond the scope of this book; for our purposes, it is sufficient to conclude that, whatever the truth of this, "there is a necessary connection between universal jurisdiction and the idea of universal criminality. Universal jurisdiction is the primary international-law vehicle for affirming the idea that certain acts are universally criminal".[31] Universal jurisdiction attaches to the "core" international crimes to enable enforcement, wherever feasible, at a domestic level, alongside international courts and tribunals (which, perhaps counterintuitively, have generally *not* possessed universal jurisdiction).[32] A distinction should, however, be drawn between "international criminalisation", the dynamic process by which offences are recognised as being international causes for concern and thereby proscribed (directly or indirectly) in international legal instruments, and universal jurisdiction, the principle which allows for the domestic enforcement of such offences *in lieu* of other jurisdictional bases. Universal jurisdiction does not attach to international crimes *ipso facto*,[33] a process that occurs via treaty, custom, or a combination of the two. Universal jurisdiction over war crimes and torture, for instance, was originally established by treaty in the form of "extradite of prosecute" provisions, though has since arguably become customary international

29 The former is the more common view; see, *e.g.*, Robert Cryer, "The Doctrinal Foundations of International Criminalisation" in M. Cherif Bassiouni (ed.), *International Criminal Law: Sources, Subjects, and Content* (Vol I) (Leiden: Martinus Nijhoff, 2008, (3rd ed.)) 107, 108, noting that "[t]he fundamental point to understand about these crimes is that the *locus* of the criminal prohibition is not the domestic, but the international legal order". Kevin Jon Heller, "What Is an International Crime? (A Revisionist History)" 58 *Harvard International Law Journal* (2017) 353, provides a thoughtful defence of the latter view.

30 7.1.1, *supra*.

31 Heller, *supra* no29, 400; International Court of Justice, *Arrest Warrant of 11 April 2000 (Democratic Republic of the Congo v. Belgium)* (2002), Joint Separate Opinion of Judges Higgins, Kooijmans and Buergenthal, 81 (para 61).

32 See Olympia Bekou and Robert Cryer, "The International Criminal Court and Universal Jurisdiction: A Close Encounter?" 56 *International and Comparative Law Quarterly* (2007) 49, noting that the more limited jurisdiction that the International Criminal Court possesses (based on territoriality and nationality) has facilitated greater uptake among States.

33 Mitsue Inazumi, *Universal Jurisdiction in Modern International Law: Expansion of National Jurisdiction for Prosecuting Serious Crimes under International Law* (Antwerp: Intersentia, 2005; School of Human Rights Research Series), 152.

law.[34] In the context of genocide, crimes against humanity and aggression, the process has occurred through customary international law.[35] Substantial progress has occurred as States adopt the Rome Statute and, in many cases, implement the definitions of the various "core" crimes into domestic law, often alongside universal jurisdiction provisions.[36] That universal jurisdiction flows as a natural consequence of international criminalisation has, however, been the focus of some disagreement.[37]

In any case, invoking the "piracy analogy" to claim jurisdiction over other acts perceived as being "heinous" carries a huge amount of rhetorical power and has the potential to expand the scope of universal jurisdiction.[38] Defining Adolf Eichmann, for instance, as a "pirate-by-analogy" rendered him *hostis humani generis*, a cause of concern for *all* States, a ubiquitous transgressor who ought to be subject to universal jurisdiction. Applying this logic, the "piracy analogy" creates a continuity of reason, a logical theoretical connection between one *hostis humani generis* and the next (with the attendant State rights to exercise universal jurisdiction as a corollary).[39] As the international community reconceived itself around universal standards of human rights and humanitarian law in the middle of the twentieth century,[40] so the focus of universal jurisdiction expanded to embrace pressing renewed "agreed vital interests of the international community" (to borrow from the Israeli Supreme Court in *Eichmann*).[41] These "vital interests" are today embodied by the "core"

34 On the relevant treaty bases see notes 38 and 30 to Chapter 1, *supra*. In their study of customary international humanitarian law, Jean-Marie Henckaerts and Louise Doswald-Beck note a right under customary international law for States "to vest universal jurisdiction in their national courts over war crimes": ICRC *Customary International Humanitarian Law, Volume I: Rules* (Cambridge: CUP), 604 (Rule 157, "Jurisdiction over War Crimes"). But see, *contra*, Matthew Garrod, "Unraveling the Confused Relationship Between Treaty Obligations to Extradite or Prosecute and 'Universal Jurisdiction' in the Light of the *Habré* Case" 59 *Harvard International Law Journal* (2018) 125, 165, arguing that "it is false to read treaty obligations to extradite or prosecute as either permitting or mandating universal jurisdiction".

35 See Inazumi, *supra* no33, 62, plus Introduction to Chapter 1, *supra*, and discussion at 8.2.1, *infra*.

36 See, *e.g.*, Arturo J. Carrillo and Annalise K Nelson, "Comparative Law Study and Analysis of National Legislation relating to Crimes Against Humanity and Extraterritorial Jurisdiction" 46 *George Washington International Law Review* (2014) 481.

37 Discussed *infra*, 8.2.

38 Dino Kritsiotis, "The Contingencies of Piracy", 41 *California Western International Law Journal* (2011) 305, 319.

39 Policante, *supra* no10, 171–172.

40 *Supra*, nos 4 and 5.

41 *Eichmann*, *supra* no3, para. 12.

international crimes (genocide, crimes against humanity, war crimes, torture and aggression).[42] Although pirates continue to pose an indiscriminate threat to the global economy, the diversified application of universal jurisdiction to "core" international crimes indicates that Steiner is correct: the interests of the international community have developed to embrace a broader set of pressing concerns, derived from universally accepted human rights norms.[43] Nevertheless the development and of this broad set of offences, and the corollary of universal jurisdiction, owes a great deal to the "piracy analogy".

Different international crimes can be said to reflect various dynamic concerns of the "international community": the proscription of piracy (historically and in modern times) represents concerns about the survival of the Westphalian State (particularly via its economy), the safety of commerce and the assertion of law upon the *terra nullius* of the high seas;[44] the prohibition of genocide represents a desire to protect the diversity of the human race (particularly minority groups, and especially at the hands of States or State-like groups);[45] the proscription of crimes against humanity (and torture *per se* within the terms of the Convention Against Torture)[46] represents a basic expression of human rights, outlawing persecution by States (or similarly empowered organisation) against their citizens;[47] the prohibition of war crimes expresses a yearning for law, order and justice in conflict situations;[48] and the crime of aggression

42 See introduction to Chapter 1, *supra*. On the concept of "core" crimes see introduction to Chapter 1, *supra*, and Cryer, *supra* no6, 108. The concept of "agreed vital interests" is broadly synonymous with that of "obligations *erga omnes*"; see *infra*, no66, and accompanying text.

43 See *supra*, no5.

44 6.1, *supra*.

45 International Court of Justice, *Reservations to The Convention on The Prevention and Punishment of the Crime of Genocide*, Advisory Opinion of 28 May 1951, 23, suggesting that the object of the Convention is "to safeguard the very existence of certain human groups and [...] to confirm and endorse the most elementary principles of morality"; Schabas, *supra* no14, 113, suggesting that "[u]nderpinning the concept of genocide is the idea that the survival of national, ethnic, racial and religious groups is not only a right of the victims themselves but also a value of profound importance to humanity as a whole. [...] There is something enriching about this diversity, of benefit to us all". See also *Prosecutor v Jean-Paul Akayesu*, Judgement, 2 September 1998, para 469,

46 Mads Andenas and Thomas Weatherall, "International Court of Justice: Questions Relating to the Obligation to Extradite or Prosecute (Belgium v Senegal) Judgment of 20 July 2012" 62 *International & Comparative Law Quarterly* (2013) 753, 768; *Akayesu, ibid.*

47 David Luban, "A Theory of Crimes Against Humanity" 29 *Yale Journal of International Law* (2004) 85, 116–200; *Akayesu, ibid.*

48 Willard Cowles, "Universality of Jurisdiction Over War Crimes" 33 *California Law Review* (1945) 177, 193–194; International Committee of the Red Cross, *Repression of Infringements of the Humanitarian Conventions* (1948), 2; Richard van Elst, "Implementing Universal

represents intolerance of the destruction and loss of life inevitably caused by aggressive war.[49] These offences, each one "heinous" in their own right, comprise the "core" international crimes subject to the jurisdiction of the Rome Statute (with the exception of piracy), each having been recognised as subject to universal jurisdiction.[50]

The "piracy analogy" informs the creation of new categories of international crimes, each in response to a specific threat to the core interests of the international community, as it is conceived at any given point in time. These various "core" international crimes are each informed by a *threat* against a given "agreed vital interest of the international community",[51] be it (for example) the survival of the Westphalian State as the recognised mode of human governance (incorporating mercantilist rights within it), basic standards of human rights, or the objective of peace as the desired state of human existence. As such universal jurisdiction may be said to be a constitutive "process through which the international community imagines its identity".[52] Whereas Matthew Garrod (*inter alia*) suggests that "the heinous nature of piracy has nothing to do with universal jurisdiction and is therefore incapable of providing a rationale for it; and by extension, it does not provide a valid precedent for universal",[53] this study has shown that the inverse, in fact, appears to be true.[54]

This cataloguing of atrocities, however, tells us little about how or why these crimes are deemed to be those that "most serious crimes of concern to the international community"[55] at the exclusion of other potentially heinous offences. The straightforward answer to this problem is that "we might say that a crime is an international crime because international lawmakers so decide",[56]

Jurisdiction Over Grave Breaches of the Geneva Conventions" 13 *Leiden Journal of International Law* (2000) 815, 823–824; *Akayesu, ibid.*

49 Trial of the Major War Criminals, Judgment and Sentences (Nuremberg IMT, 1 October 1946), reprinted in 41 *American Journal of International Law* (1947) 172, 186, suggesting that "[t]o initiate a war of aggression, therefore, is not only an international crime; it is the supreme international crime differing only from other war crimes in that it contains within itself the accumulated evil of the whole".

50 See the introduction to Chapter 1, *supra*, and also Amnesty International, "Universal Jurisdiction: A Preliminary Survey of Legislation Around the World – 2012 Update", 9 October 2012.

51 *Eichmann, supra* n03, para. 12.

52 Addis, *supra* n027, 132.

53 Garrod, *supra* n034, 167, drawing on Eugene Kontorovich, "The Piracy Analogy: Modern Universal Jurisdiction's Hollow Foundations", 45 *Harvard International Law Journal* (2004) 183 and Tamsin Paige, "Piracy and Universal Jurisdiction", 12 *Macquarie Law Journal* (2013) 131.

54 See *supra*, Chapter 6.

55 Rome Statute, *supra* n09, preamble, para 4.

56 Schabas, *supra* n014, 35

with each being developed over time in response to specific historical events;[57] the proscription of piracy, for instance, as a response to Captain Kidd's seizure of the *Quedagh Merchant*,[58] the development of war crimes derived, over time, from Henry Dunant's advocacy following his adverse reaction to the aftermath of the Battle of Solferino,[59] the outlawing of genocide as a direct response to The Holocaust (and due largely to the efforts of Raphael Lemkin),[60] the devising of "crimes against humanity", similarly, as a response to the horrors of The Holocaust,[61] the outlawing of aggressive war as a retort to the warmongering of jingoistic Nazi Germany,[62] and the international criminalisation of torture as a response to its use during twentieth century wars of independence and by autocratic regimes in 1970s Latin America.[63] International crimes develop over time, then, in response to genuine threats that humanity has experienced.

We could go further in seeking an answer to the question of why these crimes should be contained within the Rome Statute and not, for example, (mass) murder *per se*, or terrorism. This takes us into murky waters, as the explanation of *why* the "core" crimes qualify as such, at the exclusion of others, has been subject to much debate.[64] Perhaps the most common explanation for "international criminalisation" is the "normative universalist position" or "moralist" position, recognising "the existence of certain core values that are

57 See, *e.g.,* Nuremberg Prosecutor Robert Jackson's opening "Report to the President on Atrocities and War Crimes", June 7, 1945, noting that "every custom has its origin in some single act, and every agreement has to be initiated by the action of some State".

58 5.2, *supra.*

59 Henry Dunant, *A Memory of Solferino* (Geneva: International Committee of the Red Cross, 1939 (orig. 1862)); Burrus M. Carnahan, "Lincoln, Lieber and the Laws of War: The Origins and Limits of the Principle of Military Necessity" 92 *American Journal of International Law* (1998) 213.

60 Schabas, *supra* no14, 104–105; Raphael Lemkin, "Genocide", 15 *American Scholar* (1946) 227.

61 Though the term was originally coined to denounce the 1915 massacre of ethnic Armenians in the Ottoman Empire; see Jonas Nilsson, "Crimes Against Humanity" in Antonio Cassese (ed), *The Oxford Companion to International Criminal Justice* (Oxford: OUP, 2009) 284, 285.

62 Jens Ohlin, "Aggression", in Cassese, *ibid.*, 236, at 236.

63 J. Hermann Burgers and Hans Danelius, "*The United Nations Convention Against Torture: A Handbook on the Convention Against Torture and Other Cruel, Inhuman, or Degrading Treatment or Punishment"* (Dordrecht: Martinus Nijhoff, 1988), 14.

64 See, *e.g.*, M. Cherif Bassiouni, "International Crimes: The *Ratione Materiae* of International Criminal Law" in Bassiouni (ed.), *supra* no29, 129 at 132, noting that "[t]he writings of scholars are uncertain, if not tenuous, as to what they deem to be the criteria justifying the establishment of crimes under international law".

shared by the international community".[65] Such values are, "[b]y their very nature the concern of all states. In view of the importance of the rights involved, all states can be held to have a legal interest in their protection; they are obligations *erga omnes*".[66] As Immanuel Kant theorised, "[t]he peoples of the earth have [...] entered in varying degrees into a universal community, and it has developed to the point where a violation of rights in one part of the world is felt everywhere".[67] As a corollary, then, the existence of such interests and obligations give rise to the creation of international crimes which *any* State may prosecute, regardless of whether it has a connection to the crime.[68] A court prosecuting such crimes, whether a domestic court or internationally constituted, would in effect be acting on behalf of humanity itself.[69] As the International Criminal Tribunal for the former Yugoslavia acknowledged in *Tadić*,

> In such circumstances, the sovereign rights of States cannot and should not take precedence over the right of the international community to act appropriately as they affect the whole of mankind and shock the conscience of all nations of the world.[70]

This theory is not without its problems, however, notably the vagueness of the *erga omnes* standard suggested and the impracticality of discerning what the stated "core values" might be at any given point in time.[71]

The categorisation of certain offences as "core" crimes might alternatively be justified by reference to the involvement of a State or, at least, organisations with "the capability to perform acts which infringe on basic human values".[72]

---

65 M. Cherif Bassiouni, "The History of Universal Jurisdiction and Its Place in International Law" in Stephen Macedo (ed.), *supra* no7, 39, 42.

66 Kenneth C. Randall, "Universal Jurisdiction under International Law", 66 *Texas Law Review* (1987–1988) 785, 823, citing International Court of Justice, *Case Concerning the Barcelona Traction, Light and Power Company, Ltd* (Belgium v Spain), ICJ Reports 1964, 6.

67 This is the basis of Kant's "common interest rationale" as proposed in "Perpetual Peace: A Philosophical Sketch": Hans Reiss, ed., *Kant's Political Writings* (trans. H.B. Nisbet, Cambridge: CUP, 1970), 107–108.

68 Bassiouni, "International Crimes", *supra* no64.

69 *Einsatzgruppen*, Trials of War Criminals Before the Nuremberg Military Tribunals Under Control Council Law No. 10, IV, 411, 498; Aisling O'Sullivan, *Universal Jurisdiction in International Criminal Law: The Debate and the Battle for Hegemony* (Oxon: Routledge, 2017), 192.

70 *Tadić*, *supra* no13, para 42. Paraphrased, later, in the preamble to the 1998 Rome Statute (para 2).

71 Addis, *supra* no27, 139–140.

72 International Criminal Court, Situation in the Republic of Kenya, Pre-Trial Chamber II, "Decision Pursuant to Article 15 of the Rome Statute on the Authorization of an

Under this line of reasoning, "crime is internationalised primarily because of impunity before the national jurisdiction, that is, because national justice systems fail to prosecute [usually] because the government itself is complicit".[73] An offence becomes "internationalised" once the local State can no longer solve its own problems, due to its own complicity in a crime or due to the overwhelming activity of an evasive group resembling a State in terms of organisation and power. Outrage at The Holocaust, for example, might be said to be rooted in basic conceits of humanity, and therefore satisfy "the normative universalist position"[74] yet, more concretely, one might say that humanity's "shocked conscience"[75] was derived from the fact that this gross barbarism at the hands of the State could affect people in a similar situation anywhere.[76] In such cases the protective structures we have built actively pursue us, so that, as everyone is governed by such structures, "the ensuing crimes inherently concern humanity as a whole".[77] As a single "juristic community", humanity possesses an interest in seeing rules upheld by the States to which they have entrusted their safety, dignity and general day-to-day existence.[78] By contrast, "ordinary" crimes, even those of a significant scale, are usually adequately dealt with without any need to resort to procedural internationalisation.[79] This approach embraces the notion of universal jurisdiction as a "victim-driven" tool designed to administer justice to those who have suffered in a situation where it would otherwise be lacking.[80] Such a theorisation of international crime (if we were to adopt it) does not *obviously* embrace piracy, a crime that is defined, in part, by non-State perpetrators. However, the internationalised crime of piracy *does* fit this theory insofar as it involves an offence committed by a State-like entity that affects international society indiscriminately, violates values fundamental to organised human society, and cannot necessarily

Investigation into the Situation in the Republic of Kenya" (ICC-01/09-19), 31 March 2010, para. 90, citing M. Di Filippo, "Terrorist crimes and international co-operation: critical remarks on the definition and inclusion of terrorism in the category of international crimes", 19 *European Journal of International Law* (2008) 533, 567.

73 Schabas, *supra* no14, 44. See, however, the critique of this approach in Frédéric Mégret, "Is the ICC Focusing too much on Non-State Actors?" in Margaret M Deguzman and Diane Marie Amann (eds), *Arcs of Global Justice: Essays in Honour of William A. Schabas* (Oxford: OUP, 2018), 173.

74 *Supra* no65.

75 *Supra* no9.

76 Larry May, "Humanity, International Crime and the Rights of Defendants", 20 *Ethics & International Affairs* (2006) 373, 376.

77 Luban, "Crimes Against Humanity", *supra* no47, 116–120.

78 Quincy Wright, "War Criminals", 39 *American Journal of International Law* (1945) 257, 282.

79 Schabas, *supra* no14, 150.

80 Hovell, *supra* no10, 449–455.

be prosecuted by any given single State.[81] Nevertheless the prosecution of the "core" crimes undoubtedly raises problems that we do not see in the prosecution of piracy, given that States are often complicit in (and therefore obstructive of) the former.[82] That piracy has not (yet) undergone criminalisation in the statute of an international court or tribunal is indicative of its somewhat different nature and perception as compared with the "core" crimes.[83]

A full consideration and analysis of the various theories set out above falls outside the ambit of this book. What *is* important is that each "core" crime has arisen as a response to a historical event, something the international community has perceived as being unacceptable and has agreed should lead to the vitiation of traditional concepts of sovereignty via international criminalisation. There is something in the (admittedly vague) "normative universalist position", then, though we need not obsess over exactly how this principle works: we can link to historical events that chart the progress of this idea. As Cryer points out, "international society has not reached full consensus on *a priori* moral precepts, and the best evidence of fundamental principles of behaviour in the world is that which has been accepted as criminal by virtue of the normal processes of international law".[84]

Universal jurisdiction was never intended to be merely a "gap-filling" tool in cases where there is an "absence or uncertainty of a jurisdiction capable of being effectively exercised over the crime in question".[85] Although a useful premise, it does not account for the historical development of universal jurisdiction and cannot provide a full explanation of the concept. We ought to move away from that basic premise. The "piracy analogy", then, provides an anchoring point for the application of universal jurisdiction to each of these proscribed acts, a dynamic rationalisation by historicity that sustains contemporary practice. In time, new "internationalised" issues may through the same process: possible contenders include terrorism,[86] gender-based

81 5.2, *supra*.

82 Discussed *infra*, 8.2.2.

83 See, *e.g.*, discussion in Yvonne M Dutton, "Bringing pirates to justice: A Case for Including Piracy within the Jurisdiction of the International Criminal Court" 11 *Chicago Journal of International Law* (2010) 197.

84 Cryer, "Doctrinal Foundations" *supra* no29, 113, adding that there is no certain way to identify the contents of international criminal law at any given moment (124–127).

85 Christopher Staker, "Jurisdiction" in Malcolm D. Evans, (ed.) *International Law* (4th ed.) (Oxford: OUP, 2014), 309, 322.

86 See discussion in the Special Tribunal for the Lebanon, Appeals Chamber decision, "Interlocutory Decision on The Applicable Law: Terrorism, Conspiracy, Homicide, Perpetration, Cumulative Charging", STL-11-01/1, 16 February 2011, 49–74.

crimes,[87] environmental degradation,[88] "participating in a manifestly unlawful war",[89] and (more speculatively, perhaps) the abolition of nuclear weapons.[90]

There is a historical continuity and consistency in terms of the exercise of universal jurisdiction across the ages between, for example, the claim of the Scottish Admiralty Court, in the 1705 *Tryal of Captain Thomas Green and his crew*, to possess jurisdiction over "crime[s] against the law of nations, [...] which all mankind have an interest to pursue",[91] and the jurisdiction of the Extraordinary African Chambers (tasked with the 2016 trial of Hissène Habré) to "prosecute and try the [...] persons most responsible for crimes and serious violations of international law [and] customary international law" committed in Chad in the 1980s.[92] This demonstrated historicity ought to allow for greater confidence and certainty in claims to universal jurisdiction. While this reality will not, perhaps, denote a revolution in the way States approach international crime, the affirmation of the "piracy analogy" and long history of universal jurisdiction does reaffirm its continuity, its veracity, and its validity. It provides a starting point for reconsidering everything we thought we knew about the principle.

Rescuing the authenticity of the "piracy analogy", however, does not *per se* spell victory for universal jurisdiction. The principle itself remains hotly contested, as demonstrated by equivocal State practice and divided scholarly opinion. Although the existence of universal jurisdiction over piracy remains uncontested,[93] its application to "core crimes" raises fundamentally different stakes in that the State itself is often (allegedly) implicated in the commission

87 See, *e.g.*, Nicole Hallett, "The Evolution of Gender Crimes in International Law" in Samuel Totten (ed.), *Plight and Fate of Women During and Following Genocide* (New Brunswick: Transaction, 2009), 183.

88 Jessica Durney, "Crafting a Standard: Environmental Crimes as Crimes Against Humanity Under the International Criminal Court" 24 *Hastings Environmental Law Journal* (2018) 413.

89 Alejandro Chehtman, "Revisionist Just War Theory and the Concept of War Crimes" 21 *Leiden Journal of International Law* (2018) 171.

90 Richard Falk, "Nuclear Weapons, War, and the Discipline of International Law" in Richard Falk and David Krieger (eds), *At the Nuclear Precipice* (New York: Palgrave Macmillan, 2008), 225.

91 14 *Howell's State Trials* 1199 (1705).

92 *Statute of the Extraordinary African Chambers within the courts of Senegal created to prosecute international crimes committed in Chad between 7 June 1982 and 1 December 1990*, Article 3, unofficial translation by Human Rights Watch. The Statute does not mention "universal jurisdiction" explicitly, but uses the principle as the basis for its jurisdictional reach.

93 See introduction to Chapter 1, *supra*.

of such crimes.[94] The "suspect" State is, naturally, likely to object to what it perceives as interference in its own sovereign affairs – as the United States did when faced with the possibility of a former president facing prosecution in Belgium,[95] and as China did when dealing with the proposition of its own former officials being implicated in a Spanish universal jurisdiction case.[96] These are not isolated examples; indeed, many States have objected to the existence of universal jurisdiction, either in response to specific cases or as a general rule.[97] As such, the support for a customary rule in favour of universal jurisdiction is not clear cut.

There is a pervasive issue, then, in terms of whether universal jurisdiction is indeed "universal". Part 8.2 considers this point, and potential solutions, read within the context of the "piracy analogy".

8.2 False Hope? The Limitations of Universal Jurisdiction

> The exercise of universal jurisdiction is not as widespread nor as accepted and supported by State practice as some scholars and human rights organisations present it to be [...]. [As such] reaching an international understanding on the terms and the scope of universal jurisdiction seems difficult in theory and impossible in practice.[98]

Piracy forms something of a "golden thread" linking a historicised theory of universal jurisdiction with contemporary practice. Despite this, there remains (and will remain) disagreement, among States and among scholars, regarding the scope of the principle. In this quote Noora Arajärvi warns against proclaiming any kind of victory for universal jurisdiction just yet. Although it may be morally and pragmatically desirable for States to exercise universal jurisdiction in relation to the "core" international crimes, a

94 Maximo Langer, "The Diplomacy of Universal Jurisdiction: The Political Branches and the Transnational Prosecution of International Crimes", 105 American Journal of International Law (2011) 1, 5; M. Cherif Bassiouni, *Crimes Against Humanity: Historical Evolution and Contemporary Application* (Cambridge: CUP, 2011), 10.

95 Discussed at 1.2.2, *supra*.

96 *Ibid.*

97 *Infra*, 8.2.1.

98 Noora Arajärvi, "Looking Back from Nowhere: Is There a Future for Universal Jurisdiction over International Crimes?" 16 *Tilburg Law Review* (2011) 5, 22.

position lent historical and philosophical weight by reference to the "piracy analogy", it is not clear that this position is empirically supported as a matter of customary international law.[99] Looking to the sources of international law, we ought to see universal jurisdiction permitted as a matter of either treaty law or customary international law. In the case of treaty-based universal jurisdiction, for instance in relation to war crimes, this poses little problem.[100] In instances where customary international law purports to provide the legal basis for universal jurisdiction, however, the legal situation is more problematic.

In such cases, customary international law should be supported by State practice and accompanying *opinio juris*[101] (as opposed, for example, to being "deduced" from prevailing notions of morality).[102] The "piracy analogy" can rationalise the use of universal jurisdiction by situating it within a historical narrative whereby certain conduct on the part of individuals triggers the right of all States to respond. What it cannot do is create and govern the applicable legal regime. To be clear, the dispute over the scope of universal jurisdiction is not a dispute about the existence of these crimes.[103] Rather, the issue is that not every State and not every scholar agrees that the perpetration of "core" crimes should lead to a reordering of the normal jurisdictional order and, with it, the requisitioning of State sovereignty.

There are three main aspects to Part 8.2. examines the present legality of universal jurisdiction under customary international law, while 8.2.2 sets out reasons for the ambiguous legal position and proposes solutions, with a particular emphasis on subsidiarity.

99 See, *e.g.*, contrasting views in Langer, *supra* n094 and Garrod, *supra* n034.

100 In this case the treaty basis is further substantiated by relevant custom; Henckaerts and Doswald-Beck, *supra* n034.

101 Statute of the International Court of Justice, Article 38; see, further, James Crawford, *Brownlie's Principles of Public International Law* (8th ed.) (Oxford: OUP, 2012), 23–32. The level of uniformity and duration needed to substantiate a given rule may vary depending on the nature of the rule in question (Crawford, 24).

102 Mari Takeuchi, "Beyond Dichotomy between Deduction and Induction – Critical Appraisal on the Approaches to Universal Jurisdiction" 64 *Okayama Law Journal* (2014) 388, 360 (note the reverse page numbering of this journal); Cryer, "Doctrinal Foundations" *supra* n029, 112–113.

103 See, e.g., Cedric Ryngaert, *Jurisdiction in International Law* (2nd ed.) (Oxford: OUP, 2015), 128, noting that "[c]onceptually, all States may indeed consider perpetrators of core crimes as *hostes humani generis*, and have no qualms about them being prosecuted by any State" but that "[i]n practice, however, qualms may abound".

8.2.1 *The Shape of "New" Universal Jurisdiction: the Position in International Law*

Scholarly debate over the validity of universal jurisdiction can be roughly sorted into two levels, each of which is typified by polarised positions. The first level of debate is characterised by the friction between moralism (reminiscent of the "normative universalist position")[104] and the principles of sovereign inviolability and equality. Bartram Brown, for instance, suggests that international law "rises above the narrow interests of States in recognising the universal jurisdiction of all to prosecute those responsible for certain special crimes of concern to the entire international community".[105] The "piracy analogy" might be seen as an element of this line of reasoning by drawing on the notion of "community interest".[106] The counter-argument, as expressed by Luke Reydams (by way of example), stipulates that "universal jurisdiction does not refer to an absolute right for individual States to prosecute gross human rights violations committed abroad. It simply cannot because limitations on States' jurisdiction are the logical precondition for the existence of a multi-State system".[107] These counter arguments are often expressed in policy-based concerns, most notably Henry Kissinger's objection that universal jurisdiction "risk[s] substituting the tyranny of judges for that of governments".[108]

The second level of debate concerns the applicable international law at a positivist level, particularly as regards the content of relevant customary international law. Although there may be moralist (or naturalist) arguments in favour of universal jurisdiction, and "Statist" arguments against them, the key to either argument ought to lie in the extent to which States have adopted universal jurisdiction and expressed relevant *opinio juris* in relation to it. At this level of technical legal discourse, we find, again, proponents and opponents. The proponent argument is characterised by Máximo Langer's empirical claim that "universal jurisdiction has been expanding, not decreasing in recent years; there have been more universal jurisdiction statutes and trials".[109]

104 *Supra* n065.

105 Bartram S. Brown, "The Evolving Concept of Universal Jurisdiction" (2001) 35 New England Law Review 383, 391. A similar line of reasoning can be seen in *Tadić, supra* n013.

106 8.1, *supra*.

107 "The Rise and Fall of Universal Jurisdiction", Leuven Centre for Global Governance Working Paper No. 37, January 2010, 28.

108 "The Pitfalls of Universal Jurisdiction" 90 *Foreign Affairs* (2001) 86. See, further, Mark Chadwick, "Modern Developments in Universal Jurisdiction: Addressing Impunity in Tibet and Beyond", 9 *International Criminal Law Review* (2009) 359, 380–387.

109 Maximo Langer, "Universal Jurisdiction is Not Disappearing" 13 *Journal of International Criminal Justice* (2015) 245, 249.

The opposing argument is typified by Matthew Garrod's claim that "universal jurisdiction is, at present, a hollow concept without State practice".[110] Given the inherently elusive nature of customary international law, however, the debate has struggled to progress beyond these opposing arguments, each interpreting State practice and accompanying *opinio juris* in their own way.[111]

An initial point to consider, here, is the provenance of the *Lotus* principle, this being a point of law on which some adherents to universal jurisdiction build their argument.[112] In the 1927 *Lotus* case, the Permanent Court of International Justice held that

> International law [...] leaves [States] a wide measure of discretion which is only limited in certain cases by prohibitive rules; as regards other cases, every State remains free to adopt the principles it regards as best and most suitable.[113]

Accordingly, universal jurisdiction ought to be permissible under international law unless explicitly shown to be *im*permissible. Given the ambiguous nature of State practice on the matter, *Lotus* ought to allow us to reach a conclusion that universal jurisdiction is, indeed, permissible.

This is a problematic proposition, however, particularly considering the factual situation of the case itself, namely a jurisdictional dispute between Turkey over France in a case involving the collision of two ships, one of each nationality.[114] As such the issue in case was one of concurrent territoriality and the outcome was, simply, that Turkey could not be barred from exercising jurisdiction under the existing legal regime. Moreover, the principle has not found consistent application, as the International Court of Justice (ICJ) has since sought to ascertain a degree of uniformity of State practice in before confirming rules

110 *Supra* no34, 129. Garrod's claim is based on a dual argument suggesting that the "extradite or prosecute" provisions of the Geneva Conventions (*inter alia*) have been mischaracterised as universal jurisdiction and that there is little evidence to support the existence of universal jurisdiction as a matter of customary international law.

111 On which see Devika Hovell, 433–434, and Separate Opinion of Judges Higgins, Kooijmans and Buergenthal, *supra* no31, 79 (para 52).

112 See, e.g., Mohamed El Zeidy, "Universal Jurisdiction *In Absentia*: Is it a Legal Valid Option for Repressing Heinous Crimes?" (2003) 37 *International Lawyer* 835, 859, and Scharf, *supra* no8, 379–380.

113 Permanent Court of International Justice, *The Case of the S.S. "Lotus"*, September 7th, 1927, paras 18–19.

114 *Ibid.*

of customary international law.[115] The standard suggested by the ICJ in the *Nicaragua* case conceded that "for a rule to be established as customary, the corresponding practice [does not have to] be in absolutely rigorous conformity with the rule".[116] This is still a somewhat different standard from the *Lotus* principle, requiring a certain degree of positive State practice to establish the *existence* of a customary law (in this case relating to the use of force in self-defence).

In any case, the liberal methodology of *Lotus* is arguably outdated in the much-altered contemporary world, an important point noted by Judge Shahabuddeen in his dissenting opinion to the ICJ Advisory Opinion on the *Legality of the Threat or Use of Nuclear Weapons*:

> The notions of sovereignty and independence which the "*Lotus*" Court had in mind did not evolve in a context which visualized the possibility that a single State could possess the capability of wiping out the practical existence both of itself and of all other States.[117]

Shahabuddeen recognised the unsuitability of *Lotus* in contemporary circumstances where States possess the power to bring about the apocalypse, so that it would be dangerous, today, to allow unilateral action that is otherwise unsubstantiated by positive international norms. Shahabuddeen's cautious tone has been built upon, in the specific context of universal jurisdiction, in the Joint Separate Opinion of Judges Higgins, Buergenthal and Kooijmans to the ICJ *Arrest Warrant* case. The judges noted that the *Lotus* principle

> represents the high water mark of *laissez-faire* in international relations, and an era that has been significantly overtaken by other tendencies. [...] [T]hose States and academic writers who claim the right to act unilaterally to assert a universal criminal jurisdiction over persons committing such acts, invoke the concept of acting as "agents for the international community". This vertical notion of the authority of action is significantly

115 See the following International Court of Justice cases: *Colombia v Peru* ("*Asylum*"), ICJ Reports, 1950, 266, 276–277; *United Kingdom v Norway* ("*Anglo-Norwegian Fisheries*"), ICJ Reports, 1951, 116, at 131 and 138; and *Federal Republic of Germany v Netherlands* ("*North Sea Continental Shelf*"), ICJ Reports 1969, 3, 43.

116 *Nicaragua v. United States of America* ("*Case Concerning Military and Paramilitary Activities In and Against Nicaragua*"), ICJ Reports, 1986, 14, 98 (para 186).

117 *Legality of the Threat or Use of Nuclear Weapons* (Advisory Opinion), ICJ Reports 1996, 226, 395.

> different from the horizontal system of international law envisaged in the *Lotus* case.[118]

The judges suggest that an unambiguous conventional or customary international law ought to exist as a legal basis for action. Disagreements over the exercise of universal jurisdiction are not bilateral in nature but, instead, implicate the entire international order, so that stricter standards are justifiably required.[119] As such, a proper investigation into the extent of relevant State Practice and applicable *opinio juris* remains necessary.

Dismissing the *Lotus* principle, then, as a useful legal precedent, any analysis of relevant State practice (and accompanying *opinio juris*) runs into a problem of *visibility*. Although States *may* introduce and exercise universal jurisdiction laws under an impression of legal entitlement, its auxiliary nature means that it is nevertheless likely to be exercised only in exceptional circumstances.[120] As such any attempt to draw a connection between the lawfulness of universal jurisdiction and the existence of State practice arguably becomes self-defeating, for "until courts engage in the practice, it will not be lawful; yet, as long as the practice it is not lawful, courts will not engage in the practice".[121] Nevertheless individual instances of universal jurisdiction have been reasonably commonplace since the turn of the millennium,[122] giving States ample opportunity to voice their approval or disapproval of the principle (either as a general principle, or in relation to individual cases).

A substantial number of States have implemented universal jurisdiction laws in relation to the "core" crimes found in the Rome Statute. A 2012 study by Amnesty international found that out of 193 UN Member States, 136 States had universal jurisdiction in place in relation to war crimes, 80 States possessed it in relation to crimes against humanity, 94 possessed it in relation to genocide and 95 possessed it in relation to torture (no data on aggression).[123] If we

---

118 *Supra* no31, 78 (para 51). See also the Separate Opinion of Judge Guillame, 43 (paras 14 and 15).

119 *Ibid.*, 79 (para. 52), suggesting that a "general rule of positive international law" may be required.

120 Hovell, *supra* no10, 435. Moreover, many States recognise a principle of "subsidiarity", giving preferential status to a State possessing a closer link to the suspected offence.

121 *Ibid.*

122 TRIAL International, *Make Way for Justice (#4): Momentum towards accountability: Universal Jurisdiction Annual Review 2017*, 6; Maximo Langer, "Not Disappearing" *supra* no109; Wolfgang Kaleck, "From Pinochet to Rumsfeld: Universal Jurisdiction in Europe 1998–2008" 30 *Michigan Journal of International Law* (2009) 927.

123 Amnesty International, *Universal Jurisdiction: A Preliminary Survey of Legislation around the World – 2012 Update.*

exclude war crimes (universal jurisdiction over which may be better linked to States' duties under the Geneva Conventions),[124] less than half of States possess universal jurisdiction for the other "core" international crimes documented in the study. It is difficult to draw much of a conclusion from these figures. As indicated by Judges Higgins, Kooijmans and Buergenthal (in 2000), "national legislation may be illuminating as to the issue of universal jurisdiction, but not conclusive as to its legality. [...] In short, national legislation and case law – that is, State practice – is neutral as to exercise of universal jurisdiction".[125] Examining the figures provides only half of the picture for, as further indicated by the judges Higgins *et al*, such a study sheds little insight on the *opinio juris* expressed by States.[126] It is pertinent to enquire, for instance, is whether non-implementing States object to the principle or otherwise do not believe there is a basis for it in international law,[127] something that cannot be ascertained from a cursory study.

The debate at the General Assembly Sixth (Legal) Committee that opened in 2009 and has been ongoing since (at the time of writing) has shed further light on the views and attitudes of States.[128] Throughout the discussions States have expressed a spectrum of opinions on the matter and have been unable to reach agreement.[129] Yet tellingly, as indicated by the Chair of the Sixth Committee Working Group, "[n]o delegation had rejected the concept of universal jurisdiction", although "the approaches to its meaning, scope and application had been many and varied".[130]

124 See, further, Garrod, *supra* no34, 168, suggesting that the study presents "examples of treaty-based jurisdiction as universal jurisdiction [thereby] creating an inaccurate empirical picture because the degree of state practice in support of universal jurisdiction (and its importance as a tool for preventing impunity) are overstated". Notwithstanding the merits of this argument, it is not clear how this can be the case when universal jurisdiction is in many cases clearly based on perceived customary law rights or obligations, for instance in relation to genocide or crimes against humanity.

125 *Supra* no31, 77 (para 45).

126 *Ibid.*

127 See Ryan Rabinovitch, "Universal Jurisdiction In Absentia" 28 *Fordham International Law Journal* (2005) 500, 510.

128 UN General Assembly Sixth (Legal) Committee, 64th Session (2009), "The scope and application of the principle of universal jurisdiction (agenda item 84)". On the background to the debate, see Martin Mennecke, "The African Union and Universal Jurisdiction" in Charles Chernor Jalloh and Ilias Bantekas (eds), *The International Criminal Court and Africa* (Oxford: OUP, 2017), 10, 25–32.

129 UN Document GA/L/3549, 11 October 2017, "Tackling Scope, Application of Universal Jurisdiction, Sixth Committee Speakers Debate Best Venue for Further Discussions on Principle's Definition".

130 UN General Assembly Official Records, 66th Session, 17th meeting (U.N. Doc. A/C.6/66/SR.17), October 21, 2011, para 18.

Australia, for instance, has noted that it "recognises universal jurisdiction as a well-established principle of international law" which "vests in every State the competence to exercise criminal jurisdiction over those individuals responsible for the most serious crimes of international concern regardless of where the conduct occurs" and recognised its application (under customary international law) to genocide, war crimes, crimes against humanity, slavery and torture.[131] Belgium has similarly suggested that there are "customary obligations which require States to incorporate rules of universal jurisdiction in their domestic law in order to try persons suspected of crimes of such seriousness that they threaten the international community as a whole, such as grave crimes under international humanitarian law", subject to the suspect's presence on Belgian territory (as required by the post-2003 universal jurisdiction law).[132] Germany, Norway, Sweden, the Netherlands, New Zealand and South Africa have also accepted a broad interpretation of the principle, along similar lines.[133] The United States, an aggressive adversary of several universal jurisdiction cases initiated in Europe against its own nationals, has recognised that universal jurisdiction exists over offences governed by international treaties, as well as "a small subset of offences – crimes like piracy, genocide and torture – for which the authority to exercise such broad jurisdiction derives, at least in part, from recognition of the offence as a universal crime under customary international law".[134] A general point of agreement among these States is that the presence of the accused is required within State territory in order to initiate proceedings (though a case may, presumably, be constructed in advance). This is in contrast to piracy, whereby States, of necessity, claim enforcement jurisdiction over suspects not within State territory.

Other States appear to oppose the principle in practice, except in limited circumstances. China, for instance, claimed that "[o]ther than with regard to acts of piracy, there is clear disagreement and dispute among States over the question of whether or not universal jurisdiction exists in other situations, as well as over the scope and conditions of its application".[135] A similar stance has

131 "Australian Views on the Scope and Application of the Principle of Universal Jurisdiction", presented to the 65th Session of the UN General Assembly, Sixth (Legal) Committee, 2010.

132 "Observations by Belgium on the scope and application of the principle of universal jurisdiction", submitted to 65th Session of the UN General Assembly Sixth (Legal) Committee, para. 11.

133 See presentations of these States to the 65th Session of the UN General Assembly, Sixth (Legal) Committee, 2010.

134 "Information and Observations on the Scope and Application of the Principle of Universal Jurisdiction", presented at the 66th Session of the UN General Assembly, Sixth (Legal) Committee, 2011.

135 China's statement to the 65th session of the UN General Assembly Sixth (Legal) Committee, 15 September 2010, on "The scope and application of the principle of universal jurisdiction", 6.

been adopted by several African States, for instance Malawi, Cameroon, Ethiopia, Tunisia and Mauritius, each opining that universal jurisdiction should only be utilised in instances where it is explicitly provided for in treaties, due to the lack of clarity in relevant customary international law.[136] Iraq has also put forward a similar position.[137] The objections appear to be linked to the *form that* universal jurisdiction takes, rather than to the principle itself.

A further set of States fall somewhere between these two positions, notably the United Kingdom which has suggested, in a noncommittal statement, that

> under international law, universal jurisdiction in its true sense is only clearly established for a small number of crimes: piracy and war crimes [...]. [T]here is a further limited group of crimes which some States consider to attract universal jurisdiction, including genocide and crimes against humanity, but there is a lack of international consensus on the issue. [A] careful study of State practice and *opinio juris* would be required to determine whether they are established under customary international law as crimes of universal jurisdiction.[138]

Although frustratingly evasive, the UK statement provides a fairly accurate summary of the state of the law. Yet, despite setbacks to the principle in the early 2000s,[139] States continue to adopt the principle into national law and universal jurisdiction cases continue to arise.[140] In their dissenting opinion to the ICJ *Arrest Warrants* case, judges Higgins, Kooijmans and Buerguenthal, adopted a statement from *Oppenheim's International Law* claiming that

> While no general rule of positive international law can as yet be asserted which gives to States the right to punish foreign nationals for crimes against humanity in the same way as they are, for instance, entitled to punish acts of piracy, there are clear indications pointing to the gradual evolution of a significant principle of international law to that effect.[141]

136 See presentations of these States to the 65th Session of the UN General Assembly, Sixth (Legal) Committee, 2010. On Africa's relationship with universal jurisdiction more generally, see Mennecke, *supra* no128.

137 *Ibid.*

138 UK Mission to the UN, "Scope and Application of the Principle of Universal Jurisdiction", 15 April 2011, presented at 66th session of Legal Committee of the UN General Assembly. France expressed similar views; see its submission, "The scope and application of the principle of universal jurisdiction", presented to the 65th Session of the UN General Assembly, Sixth (Legal) Committee, 2010.

139 Discussed *supra*, 1.2.2, and *infra*, 8.2.2.

140 See TRIAL *International*, *supra* no122.

141 *Supra* no31, 80 (para. 52), citing *Oppenheim's International Law* (9th ed.), 998.

This appears to be as accurate today as it was in 2000, the picture being one of "gradual evolution". The "piracy analogy", as we previously noted, presents an anchoring point for the use of universal jurisdiction in new contexts, so that we see its gradual acceptance as a necessary mechanism enabling States to address contemporary "agreed vital interests of the international community".[142] The emergence of "new" universal jurisdiction has been anything but smooth, however. The next section considers some of the reasons behind the stuttered acceptance of the principle, as compared with universal jurisdiction over piracy, and suggests tentative solutions.

8.2.2 *W(h)ither Universal Jurisdiction? Recognising and Overcoming Issues*

The previous section suggests an evolutionary yet indeterminate legal basis for the emergence of "new" universal jurisdiction. The reasons for this may be manifold; Chapter 1 outlined several "formalist" objections to the principle of universal jurisdiction, for instance the risk of "politically motivated" trials,[143] the perceived interference with principles of sovereign equality and non-intervention,[144] or the potential for "judicial chaos".[145] As previously noted, such criticisms are often conflated with politicised objections to specific instances of universal jurisdiction.[146] It is outside the scope of this book to address these points in detail,[147] though some comments are in order.

With acceptance of the piracy analogy comes recognition that States have collaborated and cooperated for over 300 years when faced with hideous threats to foundational, globally accepted, principles. Prosecution of the "core" crimes raises unique issues, however, that domestic courts have not experienced in the investigation and prosecution of piracy. For instance, such investigations often implicate the apparatus of the State of which the suspect is a national or, even, an official.[148] In such circumstances, the defendant's State may "have its diplomats lobby and threaten reprisals against the prosecuting State",[149] as has

142 *Eichmann* (Supreme Court), *supra* no03, para. 12.

143 O'Sullivan, *supra* no069, 115.

144 Luc Reydams, Universal Jurisdiction: International and Municipal Legal Perspectives (Oxford: OUP, 2003), 224–225.

145 Separate Opinion of Judge Guillame to *Arrest Warrant, supra* no031, 44; Kissinger, *supra* no108.

146 1.2.2, *supra*.

147 See Chadwick, *supra* no108, for a further discussion of these points.

148 *Supra* no072 and associated text.

149 Langer, "Diplomacy", *supra* no094, 5, adding, at 6, that "the diplomatic pressures and potential reprisals by foreign states would [...] rise or fall as a consequence of the nationality of the defendant".

happened on numerous occasions.[150] Although such objections may, in reality, be rooted in politics, there is nevertheless a legal basis underpinning them, namely that any universal jurisdiction case will take away a slice of jurisdictional sovereignty that the territorial State (or State of nationality, *etc*) would otherwise be able to claim.[151]

As previously noted, however, no State appears to have explicitly objected to the *idea* of universal jurisdiction, so that objections based on sovereign interference may be something of a red herring. Rather, States appear to be more perturbed by specific individual exercises of the principle, as opposed to the principle itself.[152] The 2009 *AU-EU Expert Report on the Principle of Universal Jurisdiction* provides a compelling example of this phenomenon.[153] The report was assembled at the request of the African Union (AU) in response to a string of universal jurisdiction cases targeting African States,[154] and was negotiated by legal experts appointed by both the AU and the European Union. The Report states that as a general matter "African states welcome the principle of universal jurisdiction, and are committed to addressing impunity"[155] but goes on to claim that

> African states take the view that they have been singularly targeted in the indictment and arrest of their officials and that the exercise of universal jurisdiction by European states is politically selective against them.[156]

The view of the AU, as expressed via the report, is that States will tend to support the idea of universal jurisdiction[157] but may take exception to *when* and *how* the principle is enforced, particularly when it implicates that State's own nationals.

150 1.2.2, *supra*; discussed further in this section, *infra*.

151 Hovell, *supra* n010, 439.

152 Roger O'Keefe, "Universal Jurisdiction: Clarifying the Basic Concept", 2 *Journal of International Criminal Justice* (2004) 735, 754.

153 Council of the European Union, *The AU-EU Expert Report on the Principle of Universal Jurisdiction*, 16 April 2009.

154 *Ibid.*, para. 34 (p35). See also "The Government of Rwanda's report on information and observations on the scope and application of the principle of universal jurisdiction" (undated), presented at 65th session of the Legal Committee of the UN General Assembly, 2, lamenting that universal jurisdiction "has been used to settle political scores. Particularly, Rwanda has been a victim of the abuse of this principle".

155 *Ibid.*, para 33.

156 *Ibid.*, para 34.

157 As indicated by the adoption of an *African Union Model National Law on Universal Jurisdiction over International Crimes* (Doc. EX.CL/731(XXI)c) in 2012.

The short but eventful history of "new" universal jurisdiction appears to consolidate and confirm this point. The *Eichmann* case set a benchmark for the extension of universal jurisdiction beyond piracy, and its promise was initially sustained throughout the 1970s and 80s by further prosecutions of erstwhile Nazis seeking refuge around the world.[158] These cases proceeded without objections given the universal abhorrence generated by the acts of the Nazi regime. These were outcasts who, like pirates, were rejected by every State and whose acts fell, by consensus, beyond the limits of acceptable conduct. Nazi *génocidaires* had become the new *hostes humani generis*, finding no favour with an international community guided by fundamental moral standards.[159] As Langer points out, "States have incentives to concentrate on defendants about whom there is broad agreement in the international community and whom their own state of nationality is not willing to defend".[160]

The 1990s brought the next wave of universally condemned *hostes humani generis*. The racially motivated conflicts in the former Yugoslavia and Rwanda spawned atrocities similar in nature (if not in scope) to the genocidal massacres of the Nazis.[161] The perpetrators of these atrocities became, like the Nazis before them, the subjects of uncontested universal jurisdiction prosecutions,[162] representatives of discredited regimes whose actions had

158 See, e.g.: *Demjanjuk v. Petrovsky*, 776 F.2d 571, (US, 6th Circuit, 1985; extradition hearing), 580–583; *Polyukhovich v Australia*, (1991) 172 CLR 501, F.C. 91/026; *R v Finta* [1994] S.C.R. 701 (Canada); *Fédération Nationale des Déportés et Internés Résistants et Patriotes and Others v Barbie* 78 I.L.R. 125 (Fr. Cass. Crim. 1983); and *R v Sawoniuk* (UK, Central Criminal Court 1999) (unpublished).

159 Gerry Simpson, "Didactic and Dissident Histories in War Crimes Trials" 60 *Albany Law Review* (1997) 801, 811, describing Nazism as "an exemplification of evil in the world and also as an exception to universal humanism".

160 Langer, "Diplomacy", *supra* no94, 3.

161 See, e.g., ICTY case *Prosecutor v Radislav Krstić*, Appeals Chamber judgement (19 April 2004) at para. 37, affirming that "Bosnian Serb forces committed genocide" at the July 1995 Srebrenica massacre; see also ICJ *Case Concerning Application of the Convention on the Prevention and Punishment of the Crime of Genocide* (*Bosnia and Herzegovina v. Serbia and Montenegro*) (26 February 2007), para. 297. It is generally accepted that genocide occurred in Rwanda in 1994, as acknowledged in several ICTR cases; see, e.g., *Prosecutor v Jean Kambanda*, 4 September 1998, para. 16.

162 See, e.g., *Tadić*, Federal Supreme Court, 13 February 1994 (Germany); *Djajić*, Judgment, (Higher Regional Court of Bavaria, 23 May 1997); *Jorgić*, Judgment, Higher Regional Court at Düsseldorf, 6 September 1997; *Sokolović*, Judgment, Federal Supreme Court (Germany), 21 February 2001; *Cvjetković*, Landesgericht, Salzburg (Austria), 31 May 1995; *Knesević*, Supreme Court of the Netherlands, 11 November 1997, translated in 1 *Yearbook of International Humanitarian Law* (1998) 600; *Higaniro et al* ("The Butare Four") (Belgium), Unreported, Cour d'Assises de l'Arrondissement Administratif de Bruxelles-Capital, 8 June 2001. See also 1.2.1, *supra*.

been universally condemned by the international community as a whole. The institution of the UN-sponsored *ad hoc* International Criminal Tribunals for the former Yugoslavia and for Rwanda seemingly affirmed their "universal offender" status.[163] Universal jurisdiction could be assured of its uncontested "universal" character in these circumstances, given the unanimity of negative opinion over the atrocities committed during these conflicts and the lack of any influential regime to protest on the perpetrators' behalf.[164]

Many universal jurisdiction cases from the late 1990s onwards chose to venture beyond such politically "safe" targets. For instance, Augusto Pinochet's 1999 London arrest (requested by Spain based on an investigation authorised under universal jurisdiction laws)[165] drew ire from a Chilean government which considered him immune from prosecution under domestic amnesty laws.[166] Successful cases against former Argentine military officers Adolfo Scilingo[167] and Ricardo Miguel Cavallo[168] followed, alongside an investigation into the conduct of former Guatemalan President Ríos Montt, accused of overseeing a genocide against indigenous Mayans.[169] Despite initial objections, these investigations helped to drive political revolution in the countries targeted – in Chile and Argentina, for instance, domestic amnesty laws were overturned and a wave of criminal cases opened into atrocities carried out by the erstwhile military dictatorships in those countries.[170] As with their predecessor cases, these investigations were able to succeed thanks largely to acquiescence by the "home" State, notwithstanding initial reluctance.

Later Spanish cases did not produce such positive outcomes, however. For instance, a 2005 case against several high-ranking Chinese officials (including

163 Chadwick, *supra* no108, 365–366.

164 Langer, "Diplomacy", *supra* no94, 2 and 49.

165 Reed Brody and Michael Ratner, *The Pinochet Papers: The Case of Augusto Pinochet in Spain and Britain* (The Hague: Kluwer Law International, 2000).

166 Naomi Roht-Arriaza, *The Pinochet Effect: Transnational Justice in the Age of Human Rights* (Philadelphia: University of Pennsylvania Press, 2005), 37 and 70–71.

167 See Giulia Pinzauti, "An Instance of Reasonable Universality: The *Scilingo* Case" 3 *Journal of International Criminal Justice* (2005) 1092. Scilingo was tried and imprisoned in Spain.

168 Roht-Arriaza, *supra* no166, 140–149. Cavallo was extradited back to Argentina in 2008 to stand trial there; see Wolfgang Kaleck, "From Pinochet to Rumsfeld: Universal Jurisdiction in Europe 1998–2008" 30 *Michigan Journal of International Law* (2009) 927, 955–956.

169 Hervé Ascensio, "The Spanish Constitutional Tribunal's Decision in Guatemalan Generals: Unconditional Universality is Back" 4 *Journal of International Criminal Justice* (2006) 586; Amy Ross, "The Ríos Montt case and universal jurisdiction" 18 *Journal of Genocide Research* (2016) 361.

170 Roht-Arriaza, *supra* no166, chapters 3 and 4.

former president Jian Zemin) for the alleged genocide of ethnic Tibetans[171] was met with angry protest from China, which decried the investigation as "a complete fabrication and a complete slander", adding that "we strongly oppose any country using the so-called Tibetan issue to interfere in China's internal affairs".[172] As such the Spanish executive was forced to take account of "international relations costs that the defendant's state of nationality would impose if a prosecution and trial take place".[173] The law in question was subsequently curtailed in 2009, limiting legal proceedings to instances where a connection to Spain could be ascertained.[174]

A similar situation unfolded in Belgium throughout the 2000s. increasingly ambitious investigations into high-profile US war crimes suspects George H.W. Bush (for alleged war crimes during the 1991 Gulf War) and General Tommy Franks (for suspected offences committed during the 2003 Iraq conflict) caused the US to threaten the withdrawal of funding from NATO's Brussels headquarters and to boycott future meetings.[175] Belgium's expansive *Act Concerning Punishment for Grave Breaches of International Humanitarian Law* (passed in 1993, amended 1999)[176] was subsequently modified in August 2003, limiting future prosecutions under universal jurisdiction to instances where it is required under a treaty *and* the suspect is present in Belgian territory, thereby curtailing the breadth of the Belgian law.[177] Although Spain and Belgium still possess universal jurisdiction laws, the trend appeared to be one of "retreat", fuelled by a backlash against certain cases targeting suspects from certain

171 Order of 10 January 2006, Audiencia Nacional (Plenary); see Christine Bakker, "Universal Jurisdiction of Spanish Courts over Genocide in Tibet: Can it Work?" 4 *Journal of International Criminal Justice* (2006) 595.

172 "China Warns Spain over Tibet Lawsuit", at *International Herald Tribune,* 6 June 2006. Similar language appears in China's statement to the 65th session of the UN General Assembly Sixth (Legal) Committee, 15 September 2010, in the context of the debate on "The scope and application of the principle of universal jurisdiction".

173 Langer, "Diplomacy", *supra* no94, 2.

174 See Arajärvi, *supra* no98, 18, and Ignacio de la Rasilla del Moral, "The Swan Song of Universal Jurisdiction in Spain", 9 *International Criminal Law Review* (2009) 777. A further 2014 amendment to the law limited proceedings to instances where the suspect is present in Spain: Amnesty International, *Spain: Current Human Rights Concerns and a Setback in the Struggle Against Impunity,* Submission to the UN Universal Periodic Review, January 2015.

175 Diane F. Orentlicher, "Whose Justice? Reconciling Universal Jurisdiction with Democratic Principles", 92 *Georgetown Law Journal* (2004) 1057, 1062.

176 As described in "Observations by Belgium on the scope and application of the principle of universal jurisdiction", submitted to 65th Session of the UN General Assembly Sixth (Legal) Committee.

177 Steven R. Ratner, "Belgium's War Crimes Statute: A Postmortem" 97 *American Journal of International Law* (2003) 888, 890–891.

States.[178] The curtailment of the laws in both countries might, however, be better viewed as a symptom of the backlash against "absolute" universal jurisdiction (a procedural variation on the principle where the suspect's presence is not required) than against the principle itself.[179]

Later cases bucked the "retreat", with a year-on-year rise in universal jurisdiction cases in the 2010s.[180] Where investigations target regimes that have been discredited or lack international support, a smooth trial is more likely. For instance, the UK prosecution of Afghan warlord Faryadi Zardad (2005),[181] the US prosecution of "Chuckie" Taylor (son of former President and convicted war criminal Charles Taylor) (2008),[182] the Senegalese trial of erstwhile Chadian President Hissene Habré (2015),[183] and the present wave of European trials against suspected "Islamic State" militants[184] have all proceeded (or are proceeding) with little or no dissent. In these cases, the home State of the accused has been willing to cooperate with the trial, the prosecutions being "just and reasonable both from the defendants' perspective and from the perspective of the States concerned. The proceedings unfolded in a sphere of mutual assistance in criminal matters and international law was used to *solve* problems, as it should".[185] Obvious discrepancies remain, with the effectiveness of universal jurisdiction apparently dependent on the identity of the perpetrator. As Langer suggests,

> universal jurisdiction will never establish a minimum international rule of law – that is, it will never substantially close the impunity gap regarding international crimes or be applied equally across defendants – since

178 O'Sullivan, *supra* no69, 164.

179 *Ibid.*, 199; Antonio Cassese, "Is the Bell Tolling for Universality? A Plea for a Sensible Notion of Universal Jurisdiction" 1 *Journal of International Criminal Justice* (2003) 589.

180 See citations *supra*, no122.

181 *R v. Zardad* (Cent. Crim. Ct. July 18, 2005) (Eng.); *R v. Zardad*, [2007] EWCA (Crim) 279 (Eng.).

182 US Court of Appeal, 11th Circuit, *US v. Roy M. Belfast, Jr., a.k.a. Chuckie Taylor*, case no. 09-10461, 15 July 2010.

183 Celeste Hicks, *The Trial of Hissène Habré: How the People of Chad Brought a Tyrant to Justice* (London: Zed Books, 2018).

184 See examples in: Alison Smale, "Iraqis' Arrest in Finland Highlights Difficulties in Prosecuting Distant Crimes", New York Times, 24 December 2015; Human Rights Watch, "'These are the Crimes we are Fleeing': Justice for Syria in Swedish and German Courts", 3 October 2017; and Patrick Kroker and Alexandra Lily Kather, "Justice for Syria? Opportunities and Limitations of Universal Jurisdiction Trials in Germany", blog post at EJIL:*Talk!*, 12 August 2016.

185 Luc Reydams, "The Rise and Fall of Universal Jurisdiction", Leuven Centre for Global Governance Working Paper No. 37, January 2010, 24.

> high-cost, most mid-cost, and many low-cost defendants are beyond the reach of the universal jurisdiction enforcement regime.[186]

By referring to the "cost" of potential defendants, Langer acknowledges that certain suspects are more vigorously protected by their home States, based on the political influence they possess and the force with which they will contest a claim to universal jurisdiction from another State. Although international law is, by its very nature, shaped and defined by politics and by "the free will of States",[187] this variegated and heavily politicised approach should not be tolerated. This is an undue prioritisation of the "concrete" over the "normative",[188] for genocide is genocide, wherever or by whomever it is committed (and the same applies to the other "core" international crimes).[189] *Génocidaires*, like pirates, should be *hostes humani generis* regardless of identity. The prospects for prosecution in a given case should not, from a normative standpoint, depend on the relative political influence of the territorial or national State. *This* is where the sovereign equality principle is potentially breaking down, with certain States able to protect suspects, while others cannot. The treatment of pirates, by contrast, is utterly removed from this problem. As stateless and "apolitical" beings by definition, pirates do not benefit from political barriers to prosecution.[190] They operate on behalf of none and threaten to undermine all.[191] Historically, as we know, this was not the case: States *could*, prior to the 1856 Declaration of Paris, offer protection to "pirates" by engaging them as privateers. Today, though, State-sponsored piracy would be unacceptable, potentially an act of aggression or the war crime of pillage. Similarly, State-sponsored genocide remains genocide and, subject to the availability of evidence, should be prosecuted and punished as such.

There seems to be a disparity, in any case, between the acceptance of the principle itself and the acceptance of its actual application on a case by case basis. The problems raised are issues of form rather than substance, objections

---

186 Langer, "Diplomacy", *supra* n094, 2–3. Langer suggests States should "concentrate on broadly agreed-upon defendants" (49).

187 Werner and Gordon, *supra* n04, 507–509.

188 Martti Koskenniemi, *From Apology to Utopia: The Structure of International Legal Argument* (2005 Reissue) (Cambridge: CUP, 1989), 513.

189 Notwithstanding the evidential difficulties of proving this to the appropriate legal standard.

190 Eugene Kontorovich, "A Positive Theory of Universal Jurisdiction", Bepress Legal Series, Working Paper 211 (2004), 14.

191 See Chapter 6, *supra*, in general, charting the relevant legal reasoning that rendered pirates *hostes humani generis* and subject to universal jurisdiction.

to specific of proceedings brought by specific States, rather than being objections to the principle of universal jurisdiction itself.[192] This might be overcome, to a large extent, by the introduction of a principled regime designed to take account of objections. This may be in the form of "subsidiarity", a principle whereby "a State may only exercise its jurisdiction if another State with a purportedly stronger nexus to the case fails to do so in ways that are reasonably acceptable to the [...] international community at large".[193] The principle is not new; Hugo Grotius suggested that States possess "much more right in regard to offences by which they are injured in particular" so that "the State [...] where the delinquent is, ought to bring no obstacle to the right which belongs to the other power".[194]

The notion of subsidiarity as a procedural prerequisite to the exercise of universal jurisdiction is supported in the laws of several States[195] and the works of several scholars,[196] with one commentator speculating that "the principle of subsidiary universal jurisdiction [...] is in the process of developing into a rule of customary international law".[197] It also forms a core part of the reasoning of judges Higgins, Kooimans and Buerguenthal in their separate opinion to the ICJ *Arrest Warrants* case.[198] "Subsidiarity" provisions have been built into the universal jurisdiction laws of several States; Spanish law, for instance, requires that "[c]riminal proceedings initiated in a Spanish court shall be temporarily

192 O'Sullivan, *supra* n069, 155, noting that "a sense that greater attention to the parameters of the principle [is] needed, given the general acceptance of the validity of universal jurisdiction".

193 Ryngaert, *supra* n0103, 214.

194 *The Rights of War and Peace* (ed. Richard Tuck), (Indianapolis: Liberty Fund, 2005), Book II, Chapter 21, s3.

195 Discussed *infra,* though see also the responses of US, Rwanda, Ethiopia, and Israel (*inter alia*) to the 65th session of the UN General Assembly (Legal Committee).

196 Jo Stigen, "The Relationship between the Principle of Complementarity and the Exercise of Universal Jurisdiction for Core International Crimes" in Morten Bergsmo (ed.), *Complementarity and the Exercise of Universal Jurisdiction for Core International Crimes* (FICHL Publication Series, 2010), 133; Fannie Lafontaine, "Universal Jurisdiction – the Realistic Utopia?" 10 *Journal of International Criminal Justice* (2012) 1277, 1286–1302; Mennecke, *supra* n0128, 19–20; *Institut de droit international*, "Resolution on Universal criminal jurisdiction with regard to the crime of genocide, crimes against humanity and war crimes", 15 May 2006.

197 Laura Burens, "Universal Jurisdiction Meets Complementarity: An Approach towards a Desirable Future Codification of Horizontal Complementarity between the Member States of the International Criminal Court" 27 *Criminal Law Forum* (2016) 75, 77.

198 *Supra* n031, 81 (para 59), suggesting that a State seeking to exercise universal jurisdiction "must ensure that certain safeguards are in place [that] are absolutely essential to prevent abuse and to ensure that the rejection of impunity does not jeopardize stable relations between States".

stayed where it has been established that proceedings based on the alleged acts have been initiated in [another] country".[199] In Belgium, the Federal Prosecutor has discretion to refuse prosecution where a case is already "before a court in the place where the facts occurred, or before the courts of the State of which the perpetrator is a national or those of the place where he is present".[200] Similarly, in Germany, the Federal Prosecutor has the discretion to give priority to proceedings in an interested State given the "special interest of the State of the perpetrator and victim" so that universal jurisdiction should constitute "a subsidiary competence, which should prevent impunity, yet not appropriately push aside the primary competent jurisdictions".[201] This approach should eliminate inter-jurisdictional conflict by engaging in a balancing act that gives priority to countries able to demonstrate a traditional jurisdictional connection to the suspect and who are willing to act,[202] a process that is "convenient both for States genuinely seeking to combat international crimes and for states reluctant to interfere in other States' affairs".[203] Under this model, universal jurisdiction operates as a default form of jurisdiction, and will likely become more broadly accepted (in terms of practice and application) as a result.[204] An internationally entrenched subsidiary regime can in turn complement the work of the International Criminal Court (ICC) in a three-tier international justice system[205] comprising (i) domestic prosecutions under traditional bases of jurisdiction, (ii) universal jurisdiction applied selectively based on subsidiarity, and (iii) international prosecutions at the ICC based on complementarity (should the first two options fail).[206]

Such a solution will not be a panacea of itself, by any means. There will likely be a complex series of questions that will have to be worked through, such as: how to measure the "adequacy" of proceedings in the more interested State (*i.e.* whether any proceedings against a given suspect are genuine, or designed to shelter them from prosecution elsewhere);[207] what the appropriate stage of

199 Organic Act No. 6/1985, amended 2009, Article 23(4).

200 Preliminary Title of the Belgian Code of Criminal Procedure 1878, as amended, Art 10, 1*bis* and 12*bis*.

201 *Centre for Constitutional Rights et al v Donald Rumsfeld et al* (11 February 2005), reproduced in 45 *International Legal Materials* (2006) 119, 120.

202 Antonio Cassese, "When May Senior State Officials Be Tried for International Crimes? Some Comments on the Congo v. Belgium Case", 13 *European Journal of International Law* (2002) 853, 857.

203 Stigen, *supra* n0196, 141.

204 Cassese, "Bell Tolling", *supra* n0179, 2003.

205 Naomi Roht-Arriaza, *supra* n0166, 201.

206 Chadwick, *supra* n0108, 389–390.

207 LaFontaine, *supra* n0196, 1298; Burens, *supra* n0197, 90–91.

intervention will be;[208] the availability of evidence (or, otherwise, the prospects for a successful trial); whether the defendants' rights can be protected in line with international standards;[209] whether there are compelling reasons *not* to intervene (to preserve a fragile peace, for instance);[210] and the inevitable procedural question of *how* these issues might be resolved (or, of course, whether States would cooperate).[211] These areas are worthy of further investigation and discussion.

This analysis leaves an ambiguous legacy for the "piracy analogy". The historical response to piracy, as charted in earlier chapters, arguably does provide a sound rationale for the extended application of universal jurisdiction today, characterised as a response mechanism to those who, at any given point in human history, are *hostes humani generis* and a threat to the international community as a whole (as represented in either cooperative mercantilist terms or in a universally moralistic sense). The correlation between old and new is not always an easy one to draw, however. Pirates and perpetrators of "core" international crimes are fundamentally different in terms of their motivations, their political affiliations, and their place in the international community. Although States generally agree on the severity of the "core" crimes and appear not to object to the existence of universal jurisdiction in principle, they are likely to disagree over whether individual cases should proceed, particularly if their own interests are at stake. Those who advocate universal jurisdiction should proceed with care, along the lines suggested.

---

208 This may take account of traditional justice systems; see Mark Drumbl, *Atrocity, Punishment, and International Law* (Cambridge: CUP, 2007), 188–193, calling for "qualified deference" to such processes.

209 Danielle Ireland-Piper, *Accountability in Extraterritoriality: A Comparative and International Law Perspective* (Cheltenham: Edward Elgar, 2017), 178.

210 See, *e.g.*, Eugene Kontorovich, "The Inefficiency of Universal Jurisdiction" 1 *University of Illinois Law Review* (2008) 389, arguing that "[n]on-prosecution is sometimes socially optimal, that is, increasing the net welfare of perpetrators, victims and even third-parties" (392) and suggesting that "[i]n between prosecution and waiver lie a number of settlement options" (396).

211 Ryngaert, *supra* no103, 184–187.

8.3 Conclusion

> What's to be done with the unwanted ones? The men who do not fit, whom civilisation must prune from the vine to protect its sense of itself. Every culture since earliest antiquity has survived this way, defining itself by the things it excludes.[212]
>
> PRISON KEEPER, *Black Sails*

The argument put forward in the first half of this chapter is that the twin concepts of *hostes humani generis* and universal jurisdiction have continuously evolved to identify, proscribe and deter those who endanger what the Israeli Supreme Court called the "agreed vital interests of the international community".[213] As the Prison Keeper in the final episode of *Black Sails* suggests, these enemies from "beyond the pale" have existed since earliest antiquity. The identity of these dynamic "enemies of all" reflect the diverse and changeable existential concerns of the international community,[214] so that universal jurisdiction might be characterised as "a marker of the international community at a given historical time",[215] a Ciceronian response to an evolving series of enemies. Contrary to the claim that the "piracy analogy" cannot sustain "new" universal jurisdiction because piracy was never considered to be particularly heinous,[216] the opposite appears to be true. Universal jurisdiction provides the link between the relevant international law identifying the *hostes humani generis* in question and the ability of States to take action to punish or repress such enemies. This process has been occurring for hundreds of years. The "piracy analogy" provides a starting point, justification and rationale for the expansion and further use of universal jurisdiction, based in historical circumstances that remain valid today.

It may be fine to reference the validity and historicity of the "piracy analogy", but this cannot be enough, *ipso facto*, to sustain the principle. When read together, Chapters 7 and 8 chart a history of mixed fortune for universal jurisdiction in the twentieth and twenty-first centuries. If universal jurisdiction over modern piracy has proved to be difficult to apply,[217] the transposition from piracy to "core" international crimes has proved even more vexing. The ancient

212 Episode "*XXXVIII*", dir. Jonathan E. Steinberg.

213 *Eichmann, supra* n03, para. 12.

214 Policante, *supra* n010, 171–172.

215 Addis, *supra* n027, 149.

216 Eugene Kontorovich, "The Piracy Analogy: Modern Universal Jurisdiction's Hollow Foundation" 45 *Harvard International Law Journal* (2004) 183, 186.

217 Chapter 7, *supra*.

promise of the "piracy analogy" cannot be applied and endorsed unthinkingly in relation to the use of "new" universal jurisdiction, given that perpetrators of genocide, crimes against humanity, war crimes or aggression can be closely linked with to the inner workings of powerful States. As agents of the State itself they obtain protection and become difficult to prosecute. In the same way that England protected the pirate-cum-privateer Sir Francis Drake, so today's superpowers are similarly likely to protect suspects who operate (or are perceived to operate) on their behalf. If the piracy analogy serves as a promise of the historical *potential* of universal jurisdiction, it is also a warning about its limits. Universal jurisdiction must, for now, tread a careful path between Kantian cosmopolitanism and the *realpolitik* of international relations.[218] This is nothing new, of course. The adoption of a principled system of subsidiarity, as requested and supported by States and scholars, would go a long way to assisting in this endeavour.

218 Werner and Gordon, *supra* n04, 507–509.

CHAPTER 9

On Stranger Tides: Conclusion

> The seas and the weathers are what is; your vessels adapt to them or sink.
>
> JACK SHANDY, *On Stranger Tides*[1]

Throughout his adventures in the Caribbean, John Chandagnac, the protagonist of *On Stranger Tides*, is forced to constantly adapt to change. He is forced to adapt to the ways of piracy after the hijacking of the ship he is a passenger on, taking the pirate name "Jack Shandy". After gaining the trust of his fellow pirates and himself becoming a sea-robber of some repute, he is forced to contend with the demise of piracy in the Caribbean and, ultimately, to summon up the courage to perform a daring rescue in the face of almost certain death.

Much as Chandagnac is forced to adapt to a changing situation, so the international community has been forced to contend with shifting imperatives. States initially united in their response to piracy, the perpetrators of which constituted a threat to Cicero's *jus gentium*, to Gentili's conception of the "just" State, and to Grotius' sacrosanct model of international commerce. The response to piracy provides an analogy for the modern day "moral imperative", whereby perpetrators of "core" international crimes – *génocidaires*, perpetrators of crimes against humanity, war criminals, and (by some accounts) torturers and wagers of aggressive war – threaten the universally applicable moral standards that bind international society. In this context, universal jurisdiction is best interpreted as a response to such pervasive threats. The "piracy analogy" allows us to draw a direct connection between old and new threats to the reconstructed global *civitas*, serving as both a historical *and* modern justification for the exercise of universal jurisdiction. It intimates at the ability of States, as a collective, to adapt and respond to truly "heinous" conduct, to draw the moral boundaries of today's society and to react to those who fall outside those boundaries.

The usefulness of this analogy is restricted, however, by limits both political and mechanical. Universal jurisdiction over piracy today is dependent on

1 Tim Powers, *On Stranger Tides* (New York: Ace Books, 1987), 71.

 | DOI:10.1163/9789004390461_010

motivation and resources, and is best realised through inter-State collaboration, so that it becomes difficult, in fact, to analogise the control of modern piracy to that of its ancestral form. Similarly, it is difficult to apply the analogy straightforwardly to "new" universal jurisdiction over "core" international crimes. Although the reasons for exercising universal jurisdiction may be essentially the same, there are additional factors to consider that limit the use of "new" universal jurisdiction in practice; foremost among these is that fact that States do not appreciate being judged by their peers.

The book opened with the 1961 *Eichmann* case, wherein the Israeli Supreme Court invoked the historical exercise of universal jurisdiction over piracy in order to justify its own novel claim to universal jurisdiction over Adolf Eichmann, Nazi logistician and facilitator of The Holocaust.[2] *Eichmann* expressed the basic concept of the "piracy analogy", whereby the history and tradition of universal jurisdiction over piracy (the perpetrators of which were historically branded *hostes humani generis*) is used to justify the extension of the concept to other supposedly "heinous" international offences such as (*inter alia*) genocide, crimes against humanity, war crimes, torture and aggression (the "core" international crimes).[3] The "piracy analogy" appears to lend the controversial principle added legitimacy, particularly via its intimation that universal jurisdiction possesses an ancient pedigree.[4] This is of particular importance given the ambiguous status of universal jurisdiction in customary international law.[5]

The "piracy analogy" has been questioned, however, particularly on the ground that piracy was never particularly "heinous", or at least certainly not considered serious enough to justify analogising it to "core" international crimes today (an argument sustained in part based on piracy's similarity to State-sponsored privateering).[6] With this debate regarding the pertinence of the "piracy analogy" in mind, the book set out to investigate two key questions, namely: (i) the rationale for the application of universal jurisdiction to piracy; and (ii) whether the "piracy analogy" can sustain the extension of universal jurisdiction to the "core" international crimes.

Chapter 2 sought to address the manner in which "piracy" was addressed in ancient Rome, with particular emphasis on Pompey's campaign against the Mediterranean "pirates" and Cicero's influential discourse on the matter.

2 Supreme Court of Israel, *Eichmann v. A-G Israel*, 36 *International Law Reports* (1968) 227; see introduction to Chapter 1, *supra*.

3 Eugene Kontorovich, "The Piracy Analogy: Modern Universal Jurisdiction's Hollow Foundation" 45 *Harvard International Law Journal* (2004) 183.

4 *Ibid.*, 208.

5 8.2.1, *supra*.

6 Kontorovich, *supra* no3, 208.

Consideration of the relevant Roman history is necessary given the influential history of the era on later scholars such as Gentili and Grotius. Cicero's divisive ideology (the "Ciceronian paradigm" of piracy) has since proved to be particularly influential, continuing to permeate modern thought and policy regarding piracy today.[7] as such, the chapter provided the ideological bedrock for the ideas pursued throughout the rest of the book. It established that piracy was accepted as largely legitimate prior to the rise of Rome, after which the constant antagonism of the Cilician sea-peoples (or *peiratēs*) prompted their forcible eradication from the Mediterranean.[8] This process was influenced by the Roman adoption of territorial governance (a geopolitical construct to which the *peiratēs* could not conform) as well as increased dependency on overseas trade (particularly for grain and slaves).[9] There is some debate over the precise identity of the *peiratēs,* along the lines of whether they were simply seaborne criminals or, rather, political enemies comparable to combatants.[10] The important point, however, for our purposes, is that Cicero regarded these peoples as enemies of Rome, "*communes hostes omnium*" who, by their maritime predation and contempt for commerce, opposed his conception of the universal *jus gentium.*[11] The relevant issue in this period was not the claim of universal jurisdiction *per se*, but rather with drawing that basic division between the civilised and "primordial" worlds, the latter occupied by the *peiratēs*. This schism would allow for the conditions in which universal jurisdiction could later arise.[12] This division, inherent in the "Ciceronian paradigm" of piracy, forms a cornerstone of international law.

Building on the ancient histories, Chapter 3 showed how the polities of medieval Europe were forced to deal with piratical plunderers who represented no recognised State. The act of plundering was not, *per se*, problematic, as it was common practice among States. At issue, rather, was the question of identity and the perception that "unauthorised" pirates, who could not claim the backing of any State, threatened the rough system of mutually recognising European "peer polity" States.[13] Having established the crucial distinction between pirates and privateers, the chapter showed that a considerable degree of difficulty existed in terms of defining and dealing with piracy, an act that somehow defied political or legal categorisation. While disputes concerning

7 Harry D, Gould, "Cicero's Ghost: Rethinking the Social Construction of Piracy", in Michael J. Struett, Jon D. Carlson, and Mark T. Nance (eds), *Maritime Piracy and the Construction of Global Governance* (New York: Routledge, 2013) 23, 24–25.

8 2.1.5, *supra*.

9 2.1.2, 2.1.3, *supra*.

10 2.1.5, *supra*.

11 2.2, *supra*.

12 2.3.1, *supra*.

13 3.1, *supra*.

privateering could be dealt with as inter-State disputes, stateless pirates presented jurisdictional issues. The English judge and jurist Lord Coke sought to contend with the problem of piracy via several legal cases and in his deeply influential *Institutes of the Laws of England*.[14] Whilst affirming that pirates were subject to nationality jurisdiction or a territoriality link based on the registration of the ship(s) involved, Coke stopped sort of ascribing "universal jurisdiction" to piracy, a conclusion that appears to support contemporary practice across the rest of Europe.[15] His conclusion was complicated, however, by his characterisation of pirates as *hostes humani generis*, a rhetorical catachresis designed not so much to legitimise a broad claim to jurisdiction as to, simply, affirm the serious nature of piracy – very much as an extension of Ciceronian reasoning.[16] The term remains in use in this way today.

Chapter 4 introduced to the debate the late sixteenth and early seventeenth century works of influential scholars Alberico Gentili and Hugo Grotius. For Gentili, the danger of the pirate lay in his subversive threat to the emergent European territorial State. The pirate was a plunderous entity that represented only peculation rather than righteous "public cause".[17] In this way, Gentili represents a continuation of Cicero, which is perhaps unsurprising given his absorption with Roman law and jurisprudence. Grotius, in turn, characterised the pirate in a more nuanced manner as an enemy not just of the civilised State, but also of the divinely bestowed right of free commerce between States (this being the key aspect of Grotius' doctrine of "*mare liberum*", the free sea).[18] Grotius' politically motivated characterisation drew on the actions and identity of pirates and, in so doing, effectively promulgated the modern definition of pirates as stateless (in terms of being unauthorised) sea-robbers.[19] These legal-historical developments that would, in turn, inform State policies of the 1700s, when universal jurisdiction over piracy began to emerge.

Chapter 5 demonstrated how a rapidly changing political situation across Europe and the American colonies catalysed novel responses to piracy. Beginning in 1699 with an abrupt clampdown on piracy (epitomised by the trial and execution of Captain Kidd), States began to claim a broad and unlimited universal jurisdiction over pirates.[20] This novel concept allowed States a broad remit to prosecute any pirate captured anywhere, bypassing the rigid

14 *The Third Part of the Institutes of the Laws of England; Concerning High Treason, and Other Pleas of the Crown and Criminal Causes* (c. 1628).

15 3.2.3, *supra*.

16 *Ibid*.

17 Alberico Gentili, *De Jure Belli Libri Tres* (trans. John C. Rolfe) (Oxford: Clarendon Press, 1933), 25; discussed at 4.1.1, *supra*.

18 4.1.2, *supra*.

19 4.1.3, *supra*.

20 5.2, *supra*.

jurisdictional constructions put forward by Lord Coke, whilst simultaneously affirming the moral superiority represented by Statehood.[21] Although claims to universal jurisdiction at this time were primarily being invoked in English (or British, depending on the era) courts, and predominantly against English-born or colony-born pirates, there were instances of other States trying and executing foreign pirates without protest.[22] More importantly, the *idea* of universal jurisdiction appeared to gain broad acceptance, even if genuine instances of its use were rare. Hyperbolic language denouncing pirates as monstrous "*hostes humani generis*" accompanied the trials, being designed to legitimise the ruthless process of judicial extermination and intentionally bolstered the notion that pirates were universally condemned.[23] Doubtless, the language of these cases led to later conceptions that piracy is somehow a "heinous" practice, "need[ing] no aggravation, it being evident to the reason of all men".[24]

This is something of a simplification, however – Chapter 6 established that the actual reason why piracy might be considered to be "heinous" lies in a number of factors, such as the threat to commerce (this being, certainly, the principal factor behind abhorrence of piracy), the fact that piracy theoretically harms all States indiscriminately, the consensus among States regarding its proscription and subject to universal jurisdiction (as opposed to slavery, for instance, in the early nineteenth century), the notion that piracy thrives on the power vacuum of the high seas, and that it may simply be technically difficult to prosecute under traditional bases of jurisdiction.[25] As such the proposed "heinousness" of piracy should be understood as a combination of several factors. These are factors that might, by analogy, also apply to the "core" international crimes. That piracy represented a universal threat to a vital interest of the reconceptualised (as of the late 1600s) international community is the key conclusion of Chapter 6.

---

21 5.1, *supra*. See also Douglas R. Burgess, "Piracy in the Public Sphere: The Henry Every Trials and the Battle for Meaning in Seventeenth-Century Print Culture", 48 *Journal of British Studies* (2009) 887.

22 *E.g. Tryal of Captain Thomas Green and his crew* (Scotland), 14 Howell's State Trials 1199 (1705); *Flying King* trial (Portuguese Brazil), reported in Captain Charles Johnson, *A General History of the Robberies and Murders of the most notorious Pirates* (1724) (with an introduction by David Cordingly; London: Conway Maritime Press, 1998), 83.

23 See, e.g., *Kidd's Trial*, 14 Howell's State Trials 123 (1701), *Quelch's Trial*, 14 Howell's State Trials 1067 (1704), *Bonnet's Trial*, 15 State Trials (Howell) 1231 (Am. Vice Adm. 1718), 1235, and *The Trial of Eight Persons Indicted for Piracy* (concerning the crew of "Black" Sam Bellamy), Boston, 1717 (cited in Joel H. Baer, "'The Complicated Plot of Piracy': Aspects of English Criminal Law and the Image of the Pirate in Defoe", 23 *The Eighteenth Century* (1982) 3, 8).

24 *Bonnet, ibid.*

25 Chapter 6, *supra*.

It seems apt to reject as over-simplistic, then, the view that "the foundation of piracy is the stateless nature of the crime and not the heinousness of the crime".[26] On the contrary, *both* of these assertions are true, the former feeding into the latter. That universal jurisdiction was apparently only exercised by a handful of States at this time does not defeat these conclusions given that this insubstantial practice informed modern international piracy law.[27] As codified through the UN Convention on the Law of the Sea, the practice of the "golden age" today finds universal acceptance and recognition.[28]

Chapters 2 to 6 build up a chain of legal and political events that lend precedent to universal jurisdiction today. Together, they form a coherent sequence of events that helps to explain the genesis of and rationale for the phenomenon.

Chapter 7 built on this rich history to demonstrate how modern piracy continues to pose a serious threat to trade, causing consternation for the international community (as demonstrated by the impact of twenty-first century Somali piracy and the response of the UN Security Council).[29] However, eighteenth century counter-piracy practice has not transferred well to the modern age given the lengthy absence of any real pirate menace, resource inequality among States, and the lack of any firmly established cooperative response mechanism. Inter-State cooperation is required to reignite the ancient promise of universal jurisdiction, with the virtual eradication of piracy the Gulf of Aden region providing a modern success story and a model for innovation elsewhere.[30] We ought not to blindly apply notions such as *hostes humani generis* to pirates and simply insist on the universal right of States to prosecute them. Concrete strategies are, instead, required.

Chapter 8 investigated the crossover between historic universal jurisdiction over piracy, as established throughout Chapters 2 to 6, and the application of universal jurisdiction to contemporary "core" international crimes. These are offences that grossly infringe internationally recognised human rights or humanitarian law standards rather than the economic or subversive concerns reflected by the proscription of piracy, yet these crimes can nevertheless be assimilated together with piracy under the heading of universally recognised

26 Tamsin Paige, "Piracy and Universal Jurisdiction", 12 *Macquarie Law Journal* (2013) 131, 147.

27 7.1, *supra*.

28 See, e.g., UN Security Council Resolution 1918, 27 April 2010, "*Reaffirming* that international law, as reflected in the United Nations Convention on the Law of the Sea of 10 December 1982, in particular its articles 100, 101 and 105, sets out the legal framework applicable to combating piracy and armed robbery at sea, as well as other ocean activities" (preamble, para. 3).

29 7.2, *supra*.

30 *Ibid.*

"agreed vital interests of the international community" (to cite *Eichmann*).[31] As the only pre-existing example of an "international" crime in relation to which universal jurisdiction could be claimed, it made sense that piracy was invoked as a precedent for extending this principle to other crimes of widespread concern, particularly where claiming jurisdiction might otherwise be difficult. As such the "piracy analogy" can provide an anchoring point for the application of universal jurisdiction to "core" international crimes, as rationalised and supported by historic practice.[32]

There is a coherent relationship, then, between universal jurisdiction over piracy and over "core" international crimes, yet this anchoring point cannot *per se* spell success for the principle, particularly as existing State practice indicates a somewhat ambiguous approach towards "new" universal jurisdiction.[33] The "piracy analogy" can sustain the *idea* of universal jurisdiction, but novel mechanisms tailored to the realities of modern law and politics (for instance the introduction of subsidiarity as a precursor to exercises of universal jurisdiction) are required to sustain it in *practice*.[34]

Let us return to the aims of this book, then, as set out in the introduction. It becomes possible to make an informed consideration of (i) the rationale for the link between piracy and universal jurisdiction; and (ii) the relevance of the "piracy analogy" for claims of universal jurisdiction over modern day "core" international crimes.[35] It will be useful to recall, here, the rejection of the "piracy analogy" by Eugene Kontorovich, who suggests that

> piracy's unique jurisdictional status had nothing to do with the heinousness or severity of the offense. Indeed, piracy was not regarded in earlier centuries as being an egregiously heinous crime, at least not in the way that most human rights offenses are heinous.[36]

This proposition is supported largely by reference to the State-sponsored practice of privateering, based on the argument that "[s]ea robbery was historically not seen as an inherent wrong of this kind, as is clear from the issuance by every maritime nation of licenses to engage in sea robbery".[37] Kontorovich also

31 *Eichmann, supra* no2, para. 12.
32 8.1, *supra*.
33 8.2.1, *supra*.
34 8.2.2, *supra*.
35 1.3, *supra*.
36 *Supra* no3, 186.
37 *Ibid.*, 223.

cites various sources (notably *United States v Furlong*)[38] to support a theory that piracy was "no more heinous than robbery".[39] We are now in a position to answer the question(s) posed above and to make an informed response to Kontorovich.

The link between piracy and universal jurisdiction is derived, initially, from the ancient Ciceronian castigation of "piracy". It is the perpetuation of this divide, throughout the centuries, that effectively forms the basis for universal jurisdiction.[40] It drives the rhetorical yet powerful notion of "*hostes humani generis*" and lent force to the oft-cited remarks of Alberico Gentili and Hugo Grotius, who together reintroduced the "Ciceronian paradigm" for a new audience by juxtaposing the threat of piracy against the instabilities of the Westphalian State. With the Ciceronian paradigm firmly established, the next step was to further demonise the pirate for his negative effect on seaborne commerce and his appropriation of the problematic maritime space. Against this background of division and disenfranchisement, the next step was proscription and punishment, which had to be done in a manner that allowed States to curtail an extraterritorial, "extra-jurisdictional" offender. Universal jurisdiction was a natural fit for the problem, a solution based on a unanimous abhorrence of piracy in an age of diplomacy and commerce. Universal jurisdiction could be justified by reference to: (i) piracy's threat to the universally endorsed *libertas commerciorum* as engendered by a subversive non-State actor;[41] (ii) the idea that piracy affected all States indiscriminately (without which "piracy" would be the concern of a single State, or small group thereof);[42] (iii) the nature of piracy's "extra-jurisdictional" occurrence on the high seas (so that the lack immediate State response rendered it a more serious threat);[43] (iv) consensus over the operation of universal jurisdiction (a criterion that is reliant on piracy being abhorred under points i-iii);[44] and (v) the useful practical implications of allowing the State capturing a pirate to proceed with a prosecution.[45] The first of these factors is the most crucial, namely the notion that piratical outsiders frustrated friendly inter-State trade. As trade became an important factor in the development of colonial economies, so piracy became the "enemy of all",

38 18 U.S. (5 Wheat.) 184 (1820). See discussion of this case in Chapter 5, *supra*, pp133–134.
39 *Supra* n03, 223.
40 See, e.g., Gould, *supra* n07, 35–36.
41 6.1, *supra*.
42 6.2, *supra*.
43 *Ibid.*
44 *Ibid.*
45 *Ibid.*

an opponent of the commercial State, and deserved a proportionate and representative response.

The idea that "heinousness" alone is the rationale for universal jurisdiction is over-simplistic and misleading. Rather, what is needed – based on this comprehensive study – is an assessment of the "agreed vital interests" of the international community.[46] The relevance of piracy as a precedent for wider exercises of universal jurisdiction is suitable, if characterised in this manner. It sustains "new" universal jurisdiction over "core" international crimes, which it is up to the international community to conceive of and define depending on the pressing concerns of the age. The atrocities of World War II led to several decades of international law-making whereby human rights and humanitarian law became enshrined as key principles of the UN-led international system, with international criminal law designed to punish the most serious violations of these norms, as enforced via universal jurisdiction or, where appropriate, by international tribunals.

In summary, the "piracy analogy" lends credence to universal jurisdiction by affirming its historic role as a constitutive element of the international community and as a response mechanism to those who threaten its core values. Understood in this way, universal jurisdiction (and indeed, the corpus of international criminal law more generally) retains a powerful link to piracy. This explanation revolutionises how we view the history of piracy and helps, in turn, to rationalise the existence, validity and purpose of universal jurisdiction.

There are important limitations to this approach, however. The analogy may well validate Bassiouni's claim that universal jurisdiction is justified by "the normative universalist position, which recognises the existence of certain core values that are shared by the international community",[47] but this argument can only work if States are willing to investigate, or allow investigations into, genuine suspects of the "core" international crimes. Having established the ancient pedigree of the principle of universal jurisdiction, the next stage should be to realise it in practice, redefined for a new world and for new purposes.

46 *Eichmann, supra* no2, para. 12.

47 M. Cherif Bassiouni, "The History of Universal Jurisdiction and Its Place in International Law" in Stephen Macedo (ed.), *Universal Jurisdiction: National Courts and the Prosecution of Serious Crimes under International Law* (Philadelphia: University of Pennsylvania Press, 2004) 39, 42.

Bibliography

Case Law

Domestic

Australia

Polyukhovich v Australia, (1991) 172 CLR 501, F.C. 91/026.

Austria

Republic of Austria v Cvjetković, Landesgericht, Salzburg, 31 May 1995.

Belgium

Higaniro et al ("The Butare Four") (Belgium), Unreported, Cour d'Assises de l'Arrondissement Administratif de Bruxelles-Capital, 8 June 2001.

Canada

R v Finta [1994] S.C.R. 701.

England/Scotland/UK

Scadding's Case, 1 January 1608, 80 E.R. 91.

Re Admiralty, (1610) 12 Coke Reports 79, 77 E.R. 1357.

R v Marsh, (1615) 3 Bulstrode 27, 81 E.R. 23.

Hildebrand, Brimston, & Baker's Case, 1 Rolle 285 (1615), King's Bench, Hilary Term.

Southern v Howe, 2 Rolle 5 (1617).

Rex v Dawson, 13 *Howell's State Trials* 451 (1696).

Kidd's Trial, 14 Howell's State Trials 123 (1701).

Quelch's Trial, 14 Howell's State Trials 1067 (1704).

Tryal of Captain Thomas Green and his crew, 14 Howell's State Trials 1199 (1705).

Trial of Eight Persons Indicted for Piracy, Boston, 1717.

Bonnet's Trial, 15 State Trials (Howell) 1231 (Am. Vice Adm. 1718).

The Amedie, (1810) 12 Eng. Rep. 92 (P.C.).

Le Louis (1817) 165 Eng. Rep. 1464 (Adm. Ct.).

Re Tivnan 122 E.R. 971 (1864).

A-G of Hong Kong v Kwok-A-Sing [1873] LR 5 PC 179.

R v Keyn (1876) 2 Ex D 63.

In re Piracy Jure Gentium, [1934] A.C., 589.

R v Sawoniuk (UK, Central Criminal Court 1999) (unpublished).

R v Bow Street Metropolitan Stipendiary Magistrate Ex p. Pinochet Ugarte (No. 3) House of Lords, 24 March 1999; [2000] 1 A.C. 147.

R v. Zardad (Cent. Crim. Ct. July 18, 2005).

France

Fédération Nationale des Déportés et Internés Résistants et Patriotes and Others v Barbie 78 I.L.R. 125 (1987).

Germany

Tadić, Federal Supreme Court, 13 February 1994.

Public Prosecutor v. Djajić, Judgment, Higher Regional Court of Bavaria, 23 May 1997.

Jorgić, Judgment, Higher Regional Court at Düsseldorf, 6 September 1997.

Sokolović, Judgment, Federal Supreme Court, 21 February 2001.

Centre for Constitutional Rights et al v Donald Rumsfeld et al (11 February 2005), reproduced in 45 *International Legal Materials* (2006) 119.

Israel

A-G Israel v. Eichmann (1961), 36 *International Law Reports* (1968) 5.

Eichmann v. A-G Israel, 36 *International Law Reports* (1968) 227.

Kenya

In re Mohamud Mohammed Hashi, et al, Court of Appeal, 18 October 2012.

Netherlands

Prosecutor v Knesević, Supreme Court of the Netherlands, 11 November 1997.

Senegal

Chambre Africaine Extraordinaire d'Assises, Ministère Public v Hissein Habré, Judgement, 30 May 2016.

Seychelles

R v. Abdi Ali & Ten Others (CR 14/2010) ("Intertuna II").

R v. Mohamed Ahmed Ise & Four Others (CR 76/2010) ("Talenduic").

Seychelles v Houssein Mohammed Osman & Ten Others (October 12, 2011).

Spain

Scilingo, Case No. 10049/2006-P, July 3 2007.

United States

United States v Palmer 16 U.S. (3 Wheat) 610 (1818).

United States v Klintock 18 U.S. (5 Wheat) 144 (1820).

United States v Smith, 18 U.S. (5 Wheat) 153 (1820).

United States v Furlong 18 U.S. (5 Wheat) 184 (1820).

Brig Malek Adhel, 43 U.S. (2 How.) 210 (1844).

United States v Ambrose Light, 25 F. 408, 412 (S.D.N.Y. 1885).
People v Lol-Lo and Saraw, 43 Philippine Islands 19 (1922).
Filártiga v Peña-Irala, 630 F.2d 876 (2d Cir. 1980).
Demjanjuk v Petrovsky, 776 F.2d 571 (6th Circuit, 1985).
United States v Yunis 681 F. Supp. 896 (D.D.C. 1988).
United States v Yousef, 327 F.3d 56 (3d Cir. 2002).
United States v Hasan, 747 F.Supp.2d 599, 2010 A.M.C. 2705.
United States v Said, 757 F. Supp.2d 555 (E.D. Va. 2010).
United States v Roy M. Belfast, Jr., a.k.a. Chuckie Taylor, case no. 09-10461, US Court of Appeal, 11th Circuit, 15 July 2010.
Institute Of Cetacean Research v Sea Shepherd Conservation Society Court of Appeals, 9th Circuit, 9 October 2010.
United States v Dire, Court of Appeals, 4th Circuit, 23 May 2012.

International

European Court of Human Rights

Jorgic v. Germany, 12 July 2007.
Ely Ould Dah v France, 17 March 2009.
Ali Samatar and Others v France, 4 December 2014.
Hassan and Others v France, 4 December 2014.

International Court of Justice

"Asylum" (Colombia v Peru), ICJ Reports, 1950, 266.
Reservations to the Convention on The Prevention and Punishment of the Crime of Genocide, Advisory Opinion, ICJ Reports 1951, 15.
"Anglo-Norwegian Fisheries" (United Kingdom v Norway), ICJ Reports, 1951, 116.
"North Sea Continental Shelf" (Federal Republic of Germany v Netherlands), ICJ Reports 1969, 3.
Case Concerning the Barcelona Traction, Light and Power Company, Ltd (Belgium v Spain), ICJ Reports 1964, 6.
Case Concerning Military and Paramilitary Activities In and Against Nicaragua (Nicaragua v. United States of America), ICJ Reports, 1986, 14.
Legality of the Threat or Use of Nuclear Weapons (Advisory Opinion), ICJ Reports 1996, 226.
Case Concerning the Arrest Warrant of 11 April 2000 (Democratic Republic of the Congo v. Belgium), ICJ Reports 2002, 3.
Case Concerning Application of the Convention on the Prevention and Punishment of the Crime of Genocide (Bosnia and Herzegovina v. Serbia and Montenegro), ICJ Reports 2007, 43.
Questions Relating to the Obligation to Prosecute or Extradite (Belgium v. Senegal), ICJ Reports 2012, 422.

International Criminal Court

Prosecutor v Bahar Idriss Abu Garda, "Decision on the Confirmation of Charges", 8 February, 2010.

Kenya (situation), "Decision Pursuant to Article 15 of the Rome Statute on the Authorization of an Investigation into the Situation in the Republic of Kenya", 31 March 2010.

International Criminal Tribunal for the Former Yugoslavia

Prosecutor v. Tadić, "Decision on the Defence Motion for Interlocutory Appeal on Jurisdiction" (Appeals Chamber) 2 October 1995; Appeal Judgement, 10 August 1995.

Prosecutor v Anto Furundžija, Judgement, 10 December 1998.

Prosecutor v Radislav Krstić , Appeals Chamber, 19 April 2004.

International Criminal Tribunal for Rwanda

Prosecutor v Jean-Paul Akayesu, Judgement, 2 September 1998.

Prosecutor v Jean Kambanda, Judgement, 4 September 1998.

Prosecutor v. Rutaganda, Judgement and Sentence, 6 December 1999.

Nuremberg International Military Tribunal

Prosecutor Robert Jackson, "Report to the President on Atrocities and War Crimes", June 7, 1945.

Trial of the Major War Criminals, Judgment and Sentences (Nuremberg IMT, 1 October 1946), reprinted in 41 *American Journal of International Law* (1947) 172.

Control Council Law No 10

Einsatzgruppen, IV, 411.

Permanent Court of International Justice

The Case of the S.S. "Lotus" (France v Turkey) 7 September 1927.

Special Court for Sierra Leone

Prosecutor v. Charles Ghankay Taylor (Appeals Chamber), "Decision on Immunity from Jurisdiction," 31 May 2004.

Special Tribunal for the Lebanon

"Interlocutory Decision on The Applicable Law: Terrorism, Conspiracy, Homicide, Perpetration, Cumulative Charging", Appeals Chamber, STL-11-O1/1, 16 February 2011.

Legal Instruments

Domestic

England/UK

Offences at Sea Act 1536.
An Act for the more effectual Suppressions of Piracy 1698.
Prize Act 1708.
Act for the Abolition of the Slave Trade 1807.

Belgium

Belgian Code of Criminal Procedure 1878, as amended.

Seychelles

Seychelles Penal Code.

Spain

Organic Act No. 6/1985, as amended.

United States

US Constitution, 1787.
Act of March 3, 1819.
Lieber Code (Instructions for the Government of Armies of the United States in the Field, United States War Sept., General Orders 100, April 24, 1863).
Restatement (Third) of the Foreign Relations Law of the United States (1988) s404.

International

Treaty of Madrid, 1670.
Peace of Utrecht, 1715.
Treaty of Amity, Commerce, and Navigation (between Britain and the US), 19 November 1794.
Convention Between Great Britain and Brazil, for the Abolition of the African Slave Trade, 1826.
Treaty between Great Britain, Austria, France, Prussia, and Russia for the Suppression of the African Slave Trade, 1841.
Declaration of Paris, April 16, 1856.
Treaty to Establish Uniform Rules for Private International Law, 7 November 1878.
Treaty on International Penal Law, 23 January 1889.
Hague Convention (IV) Respecting the Laws and Customs of War on Land, 18 October 1907.

Washington Treaty Relating to the Use of Submarines and Noxious Gases in Warfare, 6 February 1922.

Convention on Private International Law 20 February 1928.

Convention for the Suppression of the Illicit Traffic in Dangerous Drugs 1936.

Charter of the United Nations, 26 June 1945.

Convention on the Prevention and Punishment of the Crime of Genocide, 9 December 1948.

Universal Declaration of Human Rights, 10 December 1948.

Geneva Convention I for the Amelioration of the Condition of the Wounded and Sick in Armed Forces in the Field, 12 August 1949.

Geneva Convention II for the Amelioration of the Condition of Wounded, Sick and Shipwrecked Members of Armed Forces at Sea, 12 August 1949.

Geneva Convention III Relative to the Treatment of Prisoners of War, 12 August 1949.

Geneva Convention IV Relative to the Protection of Civilian Persons in Times of War, 12 August 1949.

Geneva Convention on the High Seas 29 April 1958.

Convention on Offenses and Certain Other Acts Committed on Board Aircraft 1963 *International Covenant on Civil and Political Rights*, 16 December 1966.

International Covenant on Civil and Political Rights, 16 December 1966.

International Covenant on Economic, Social and Cultural Rights, 16 December 1966.

Protocol (I) Additional to the Geneva Conventions of 1949, Relating to the Protection of Victims of International Armed Conflicts, 8 June 1977.

International Convention Against the Taking of Hostages, 1979.

UN Convention on the Law of the Sea, 10 December 1982.

Convention Against Torture and Other Cruel, Inhuman or Degrading Treatment or Punishment, 10 December 1984.

Convention on the Suppression of Unlawful Acts against the Safety of Maritime Navigation, 10 March 1988.

San Remo Manual on International Law Applicable to Armed Conflicts at Sea, June 1994.

Hague Convention on Parental Responsibility and Protection of Children, 19 October 1996.

International Convention for the Suppression of Terrorist Bombing, 1997.

Rome Statute of the International Criminal Court, 17 July 1998.

Convention against Transnational Organized Crime, 2000.

Regional Cooperation Agreement on Combating Piracy and Armed Robbery against Ships in Asia, 2004.

International Convention for the Suppression of Acts of Nuclear Terrorism, 2005.

African Union Model National Law on Universal Jurisdiction over International Crimes (Doc. EX.CL/731(XXI)c).

Documents and Resolutions of International Organisations

European Union

Council of the European Union, "The AU-EU Expert Report on the Principle of Universal Jurisdiction", 16 April 2009.

International Law Commission

Draft Code of Crimes Against the Peace and Security of Mankind, adopted at Forty-Eighth Session, U.N. Doc. A/51/10 (1996).
Report of the Work of Its Sixty-Sixth Session, U.N. Doc. A/69/10 (2014).

League of Nations

League of Nations Committee of Experts for the Progressive Codification of International Law, *Questionnaire No. 6*, January 1926, reproduced in 20 *American Journal of International Law* (1926) 222.

United Nations

Secretary-General of the United Nations, *The Charter and Judgment of the Nuremberg Tribunal: History and Analysis*, U.N. Doc. A/CN.4/5 (1949).
"Security Council Condemns Acts of Piracy, Armed Robbery off Somalia's Coast, Authorizes for Six Months 'All Necessary Means' to Repress Such Acts", 2 June 2008, SC/9344.
UN General Assembly Sixth (Legal) Committee, 64th Session (2009), "The scope and application of the principle of universal jurisdiction (agenda item 84)".
"Australian Views on the Scope and Application of the Principle of Universal Jurisdiction", presented to the 65th Session of the UN General Assembly, Sixth (Legal) Committee, 2010.
"Observations by Belgium on the scope and application of the principle of universal jurisdiction", submitted to 65th Session.
"Information from and observations by China on the scope and application of the principle of universal jurisdiction", presented at 65th Session.
Permanent Mission of France to the United Nations, "The scope and application of the principle of universal jurisdiction", presented to the 65th Session.
"The scope and application of the principle of universal jurisdiction: information provided by Spain", presented at the 65th Session.
"The Government of Rwanda's report on information and observations on the scope and application of the principle of universal jurisdiction" (undated), presented at 65th Session.
UK Mission to the UN, "Scope and Application of the Principle of Universal Jurisdiction", 15 April 2011, presented at 66th session of the Sixth (Legal) Committee of the UN General Assembly.

United States submission, "Information and Observations on the Scope and Application of the Principle of Universal Jurisdiction", presented at the 66th session.

Lang, *Report of the Special Adviser [on legal issues related to piracy] to the Secretary-General on Legal Issues Related to Piracy off the Coast of Somalia*, 25 January 2011.

UN General Assembly Official Records, 66th Session, 17th meeting (U.N. Doc. A/C.6/66/SR.17), October 21, 2011.

UN Secretary-General, "Report on Specialized Anti-piracy Courts in Somalia and other States in the region", (U.N. Doc. S/2012/50), Jan. 20, 2012.

Office of the High Commissioner for Human Rights, *Report of the Special Rapporteur on torture and other cruel, inhuman or degrading treatment or punishment*, August 2015.

United Nations Office on Drugs and Crime, Global Maritime Crime Programme, *Annual Report 2016* (Nairobi, 2016).

UN Document GA/L/3549, 11 October 2017, "Tackling Scope, Application of Universal Jurisdiction, Sixth Committee Speakers Debate Best Venue for Further Discussions on Principle's Definition".

Security Council Resolutions

827, 25 May 1993.

955, 8 November 1994.

1816, 2 June 2008.

1851, 16 December, 2008.

1877, 7 July 2009.

1918, 27 April 2010.

2018, 31 October 2011.

2184, 12 November 2014.

General Assembly Resolutions

2625 (XXV), 24 October 1970.

71/149 (adopted by the Sixth Committee), 13 December 2016.

International Maritime Bureau

Piracy and Armed Robbery against Ships, "Report for the Period 1 January to 31 December 2017" and "Report for the Period 1 January to 31 March 2018".

International Maritime Organisation

"Piracy and Armed Robbery against Ships in Waters off the Coast of Somali", Doc. A 25/Res 1002, 6 December 2007.

Institut de Droit International

"Resolution on Universal criminal jurisdiction with regard to the crime of genocide, crimes against humanity and war crimes", 15 May 2006.

NGOs

Amnesty International

"International Law Commission: The Obligation to Extradite or Prosecute", 2009.

"Universal Jurisdiction: A Preliminary Survey of Legislation Around the World – 2012 Update", 9 October 2012.

"Spain: Current Human Rights Concerns and a Setback in the Struggle Against Impunity", Submission to the UN Universal Periodic Review, January 2015.

FIDH

"Position Paper to the United Nations General Assembly at its 64th Session", October 2009.

"Pascal Simbikangwa convicted of genocide and complicity in crimes against humanity", 14 March 2014.

Human Rights Watch

"The Long Arm of Justice: Lessons from Specialised War Crimes Units in France, Germany and the Netherlands", September 16, 2014.

Statute of the Extraordinary African Chambers within the courts of Senegal created to prosecute international crimes committed in Chad between 7 June 1982 and 1 December 1990, unofficial translation by Human Rights Watch.

"Q&A: The Case of Hissène Habré before the Extraordinary African Chambers in Senegal", 31 August 2015.

"'These are the Crimes we are Fleeing': Justice for Syria in Swedish and German Courts", 3 October 2017.

International Committee of the Red Cross

Repression of Infringements of the Humanitarian Conventions (1948).

Oceans Beyond Piracy

State of Maritime Piracy 2016: Assessing the Economic and Human Cost (2 May 2017).

Hurlburt, Kaija, "The Human Cost of Somali Piracy, 2011" (report for *Oceans Beyond Piracy*).

Redress

"Onesphore Rwabukombe convicted of accessory to genocide", February 2014.

TRIAL International

Make Way for Justice (#3): Universal Jurisdiction Annual Review 2017, 3.

Journal Articles

Anonymous, "The Nyon Arrangements: Piracy by Treaty?" 19 *British Yearbook of International Law* (1938) 198.

Abi-Saab, "Whither the International Community" 9 *European Journal of International Law* (1998) 248.

Abi-Saab, "The Proper Role of Universal Jurisdiction" 1 *Journal of International Criminal Justice*, (2003) 596.

Addis, "Imagining the International Community: The Constitutive Dimension of Universal Jurisdiction" 31 *Human Rights Quarterly* (2009) 129.

Akehurst, "Jurisdiction in International Law" 46 *British Yearbook of International Law*, (1972–1973) 145.

Andenas and Weatherall, "International Court of Justice: Questions Relating to the Obligation to Extradite or Prosecute (Belgium v Senegal) Judgment of 20 July 2012" 62 *International & Comparative Law Quarterly* (2013) 753.

Arajärvi, "Looking Back from Nowhere: Is There a Future for Universal Jurisdiction over International Crimes?" 16 *Tilburg Law Review* (2011) 5.

Ascensio, "The Spanish Constitutional Tribunal's Decision in Guatemalan Generals: Unconditional Universality is Back" 4 *Journal of International Criminal Justice* (2006) 586.

Avidov, "Were the Cilicians a Nation of Pirates?" 12 *Mediterranean Historical Review* (1997) 5.

Azubuike, "International Law Regime against Piracy" 15 *Annual Survey of International and Comparative Law* (2009) 43.

Baer, "'The Complicated Plot of Piracy': Aspects of English Criminal Law and the Image of the Pirate in Defoe" 23 *The Eighteenth Century* (1982) 3.

Bakker, "Universal Jurisdiction of Spanish Courts over Genocide in Tibet: Can it Work?" 4 *Journal of International Criminal Justice* (2006) 595.

Bassiouni, "International Crimes: *Jus Cogens And Obligatio Erga Omnes*" 59 *Law and Contemporary Problems* (1996) 63.

Bekou and Cryer, "The International Criminal Court and Universal Jurisdiction: A Close Encounter?" 56 *International and Comparative Law Quarterly* (2007) 49.

Bekou, "Doing Justice for the Liberian Victims of Mass Atrocity NGOs in Aid of Universal Jurisdiction" 13 *Journal of International Criminal Justice* (2015) 219.

Ben-Ari, "Universal Jurisdiction: Chronicle of a Death Foretold?" 43 *Denver Journal of International Law and Policy* (2015) 165.

Benton, "Legal Spaces of Empire: Piracy and the Origins of Ocean Regionalism" 47 *Comparative Studies in Society and History*" (2005) 700.

Benton, "Toward a New Legal History of Piracy: Maritime Legalities and the Myth of Universal Jurisdiction" 23 *International Journal of Maritime History* (2011) 225.

Berg, "'You're Gonna Need a Bigger Boat': Somali Piracy and the Erosion of Customary Piracy Suppression" 44 *New England Law Review* (2010) 343.

Bergsmo, "The Jurisdictional Regime of the International Criminal Court" 6 *European Journal of Crime, Criminal Law and Criminal Justice* (1998) 345.

Birnie, "Piracy: Past, Present and Future" 11 *Marine Policy* (1987).

Boister, "Transnational Criminal Law?" 14 *European Journal of International Law* (2003) 953.

Bueger, Stockbruegger and Werthes, "Pirates, fishermen and peacebuilding: options for counter-piracy strategy in Somalia" 32 *Contemporary Security Policy* (2011) 356.

Bueger, "Practice, Pirates and Coast Guards: the grand narrative of Somali piracy" 34 *Third World Quarterly* (2013), 1811.

Burens, "Universal Jurisdiction Meets Complementarity: An Approach towards a Desirable Future Codification of Horizontal Complementarity between the Member States of the International Criminal Court" 27 *Criminal Law Forum* (2016) 75.

Burgess, "Hostis Humani Generi: Piracy, Terrorism and a New International Law" 13 *University of Miami International & Comparative Law Review* (2006) 293.

Burgess, "Piracy in the Public Sphere: The Henry Every Trials and the Battle for Meaning in Seventeenth-Century Print Culture" 48 *Journal of British Studies* (2009) 887.

Burleigh, "Coercion, Conviction, Conversion: Sovereign Selves and Interior States in Colonial Piracy Trials and Narratives" 24 *Law & Literature* (2012) 151.

Burns, "Piracy as an Islamic-Christian Interface in the Thirteenth Century" 11 *Viator* (1980) 165.

Buxbaum, "Territory, Territoriality, and the Resolution of Jurisdictional Conflict" 57 *American Journal of Comparative Law* (2009) 631.

Bykhovsky, "An Argument against Assertion of Universal Jurisdiction by Individual States" 21 *Wisconsin International Law Journal* (2003) 161.

Carnahan, "Lincoln, Lieber and the Laws of War: The Origins and Limits of the Principle of Military Necessity" 92 *American Journal of International Law* (1998) 213.

Carpenter, "Eustace the Monk" in *Oxford Dictionary of National Biography* (OUP) (available online).

Carrillo and Nelson, "Comparative Law Study and Analysis of National Legislation relating to Crimes Against Humanity and Extraterritorial Jurisdiction" 46 *George Washington International Law Review* (2014) 481.

Cassese, "When May Senior State Officials be tried for International Crimes? Some Comments on the *Congo v Belgium* Case" 13 *European Journal of International Law* (2002) 853.

Cassese, "Is the Bell Tolling for Universality? A Plea for a Sensible Notion of Universal Jurisdiction" 1 *Journal of International Criminal Justice* (2003) 589.

Chadwick, "Modern Developments in Universal Jurisdiction: Addressing Impunity in Tibet and Beyond" 9 *International Criminal Law Review* (2009) 359.

Chehtman, "Revisionist Just War Theory and the Concept of War Crimes" 21 *Leiden Journal of International Law* (2018) 171.

Cohen, "The Analogy between Piracy and Human Trafficking: A Theoretical Framework for the Application of Universal Jurisdiction" 16 *Buffalo Human Rights Law Review* (2010) 201.

Colangelo, "The New Universal Jurisdiction: *In Absentia* Signaling Over Clearly Defined Crimes" 36 *Georgetown Journal of International Law* (2005) 537.

Collins and Hassan, "Applications and Shortcomings of the Law of the Sea in Combating Piracy: A South East Asian Perspective" 40 *Journal of Maritime Law and Commerce* (2009) 89.

Conklin, "The Myth of Primordialism in Cicero's Theory of *Jus Gentium*" 23 *Leiden Journal of International Law* (2010) 479.

Cooperstein, "Letters of Marque and Reprisal: The Constitutional Law and Practice of Privateering" 40 *Journal of Maritime Law and Commerce* (2009) 221.

Cowles, "Universality of Jurisdiction over War Crimes" 33 *California Law Review* (1945).

Craze, "Prosecuting privateers for piracy: How piracy law transitioned from treason to a crime against property" 28 *International Journal of Maritime History* (2016) 654.

Crockett, "Toward a Revision of the International Law of Piracy" 26 *DePaul Law Review* (1976) 78.

Davey, "A Pirate Looks at the Twenty-First Century: The Legal Status of Somali Pirates in an Age of Sovereign Seas and Human Rights" 85 *Notre Dame Law Review* (2010) 1197.

Dicker, "A Few Reflections on the Current Status and Future Direction Of Universal Jurisdiction Practice" 107 *American Society of International Law Proceedings* (2013) 233.

Dickinson, "The Analogy between Natural Persons and International Persons in the Law of Nations" 26 *Yale Law Journal* (1917) 564.

Dickinson, "Is the Crime of Piracy Obsolete?" 38 *Harvard Law Re*view (1925) 334.

Dilts, "To Kill a Thief: Punishment, Proportionality and Criminal Subjectivity in Locke's Second Treatise" 40 *Political Theory* (2012) 58.

Doeg, "PMCs on the High Seas: the Solution to Somali Piracy or a Failure to Learn from History?" 1 *University of Miami National Security & Armed Conflict Law Review* (2011) 139.

Durney, "Crafting a Standard: Environmental Crimes as Crimes Against Humanity Under the International Criminal Court" 24 *Hastings Environmental Law Journal* (2018) 413.

Dutton, "Bringing pirates to justice: A Case for Including Piracy within the Jurisdiction of the International Criminal Court" 11 *Chicago Journal of International Law* (2010) 197.

El Zeidy, "Universal Jurisdiction *In Absentia:* Is it a Legal Valid Option for Repressing Heinous Crimes?" 37 *The International Lawyer* (2003) 835.

Erakat, "*The U.S. v. The Red Cross*: Customary International Humanitarian Law and Universal Jurisdiction" 41 *Denver Journal of International Law and Policy* (2013) 225.

Ferencz, "A Nuremberg Prosecutor's Response to Henry Kissinger" 8 *Brown Journal of World Affairs* (2001) 177.

Fernando, "An Insight into piracy prosecutions in the Republic of Seychelles" 41 *Commonwealth Law Bulletin* (2015) 173.

Filippo, "Terrorist crimes and international co-operation: critical remarks on the definition and inclusion of terrorism in the category of international crimes" 19 *European Journal of International Law* (2008) 533.

Frohock, "The Word and the Grand Pirate, Captain George Cusack" 42 *Early American Literature* (2007) 263.

Galani, "Somali Pirates and the Human Rights of Seafarers" *Netherlands Quarterly of Human Rights* 34 (2016) 71.

Gardner, "Piracy Prosecutions in National Courts" 10 *Journal of International Criminal Justice* (2012) 797.

Garrod, "Piracy, the Protection of Vital State Interests and the False Foundations of Universal Jurisdiction in International Law" 25 *Diplomacy and Statecraft* (2014) 195.

Garrod, "Unraveling the Confused Relationship Between Treaty Obligations to Extradite or Prosecute and "Universal Jurisdiction" in the Light of the *Habré* Case" 59 *Harvard International Law Journal* (2018) 125.

Gertwagen, Ruthy "Venice, Genoa and the Fights over the Island of Tenedos (Late Fourteenth and Early Fifteenth Century) 67 *Studi Veneziani* (2013) 35.

Gibbon, Edward, *History of the Decline and Fall of the Roman Empire*, Volume I (1776) (London: Penguin, 1985).

Golden, "Patent Privateers: Private Enforcement's Historical Survivors" 26 *Harvard Journal of Law and Technology* 545.

Goodwin, "Universal Jurisdiction and the Pirate: Time for an Old Couple to Part", 39 *Vanderbilt Journal of Transnational Law* (2006) 973.

Greene, "*Hostis Humani Generis*" 34 *Critical Enquiry* (2008).

Guilfoyle, "The Laws of War and the Fight Against Somali Piracy: Combatants or Criminals?" 11 *Melbourne Journal of International Law* (2010) 1.

Halberstam, "Terrorism on the High Seas: The *Achille Lauro*, Piracy and the IMO Convention on Maritime Safety" 82 *American Journal of International Law* (1988) 269.

Hans, "Providing for Uniformity in the Exercise of Universal Jurisdiction" 15 *Transnational Law* (2002) 357.

Harpham, "The case of Captain William Kidd – a 300 year old miscarriage of justice?" 3 *New Histories* (July 2012).

Harvard Research Group, "Draft Convention on Piracy with Comments" 26 *American Journal of International Law* (1932) supplement, 749.

Harvard Research Group, "Draft Convention on Jurisdiction with Respect to Crime" 29 *American Journal of International Law* (1935) supplement, 435.

Hayes, "Pirates, Privateers and the Contract Theories of Hobbes and Locke" 39 *History of Political Thought* (2008) 461.

Helfman, "The Court of Vice Admiralty at Sierra Leone and the Abolition of the West African Slave Trade" 115 *Yale Law Journal* (2006) 1122.

Heller, "What is an International Crime? (A Revisionist History)" 58 *Harvard International Law Journal* (2017) 353.

Hovell, "The Authority of Universal Jurisdiction" 29 European Journal of International Law (2018) 427.

Isanga, "Countering Persistent Contemporary Sea Piracy: Expanding Jurisdictional Regimes" 59 *American University Law Review* (2010) 1267.

Jeffrey, "An Efficient Solution in a Time of Economic Hardship: The Right to Keep and Bear Arms in Self-Defence against Pirates" 41 *Journal of Maritime Law and Commerce* (2010) 507.

Jesus, "Protection of Foreign Ships against Piracy and Terrorism at Sea: Legal Aspects" 18 *International Journal of Marine and Coastal Law* (2003) 363.

Jones, "A Roman Law Concerning Piracy", 16 *Journal of Roman Studies* (1926) 155.

Joyner, "Arresting Impunity: The Case for Universal Jurisdiction in Bringing War Criminals to Accountability" 59 *Law & Contemporary Problems* (1996) 153.

Kahn, "Speaking Law to Power: Popular Sovereignty, Human Rights, and the New International Order" 1 *Chicago Journal of International Law* (2000) 1, 4.

Kaleck, "From Pinochet to Rumsfeld: Universal Jurisdiction in Europe 1998–2008" 30 *Michigan Journal of International Law* (2009) 927.

Kamminga, "Lessons Learned from the Exercise of Universal Jurisdiction in Respect of Gross Human Rights Offenses" 23 *Human Rights Quarterly* 940.

Kavanagh, "The Law of Contemporary Sea Piracy" 5 *Australian International Law Journal* (1999) 127.

Kazemi, "Justifications for Universal Jurisdiction: Shocking the Conscience is Not Enough" 49 *Tulsa Law Review* (2013) 1.

Kempe, "'Even in the Remotest Corners of the World': Globalised Piracy and International Law, 1500–1900" 5 *Journal of Global History* (2010) 353.

Kissinger, "The Pitfalls of Universal Jurisdiction" 80 *Foreign Affairs* (2001) 86.

Kontorovich, "The Piracy Analogy: Modern Universal Jurisdiction's Hollow Foundation" 45 *Harvard International Law Journal* (2004a) 183.

Kontorovich, "A Positive Theory of Universal Jurisdiction" Bepress Legal Series, Working Paper 211 (2004b).

Kontorovich and Art, "An Empirical Examination of Universal Jurisdiction for Piracy" 104 *American Journal of International Law* (2010) 436.

Kontorovich, "A Guantánamo on the Sea: The Difficulty of Prosecuting Pirates and Terrorists" 98 *California Law Review* (2010) 243.

St. Korowicz, "The Problem of the International Personality of Individuals" 50 *American Journal of International Law* (1965) 533.

Kraska, "Prize Law" in *Max Planck Encyclopaedia of Public International Law* (available online).

Kraska and Wilson, "Piracy Repression, Partnering and the Law" 40 *Journal of Maritime Law & Commerce* (2009) 44.

Kritsiotis, "Imagining the International Community" 12 *European Journal of International Law* (2002) 961.

Kritsiotis, "Public International Law and its Territorial Imperative" 30 *Michigan Journal of International Law* (2009) 547.

Kritsiotis, "The Contingencies of Piracy" 41 *California Western International Law Journal* (2011) 305.

Lafontaine, "Universal Jurisdiction – the Realistic Utopia?" 10 *Journal of International Criminal Justice* (2012) 1277.

Land, "Flying the Black Flag: Revolt, Revolution and the Social Organisation of Piracy in the 'Golden Age'" 2 Management and Organisational History (2007) 169.

Langer, "The Diplomacy of Universal Jurisdiction: The Political Branches and the Transnational Prosecution of International Crimes" 105 American Journal of International Law (2011) 1.

Langer, "Universal Jurisdiction is Not Disappearing" 13 *Journal of International Criminal Justice* (2015) 245.

Lapidoth, "Freedom of Navigation – its Legal History and its Normative Basis" 6 *Journal of Maritime Law & Commerce* (1975) 259.

Leeson, "An-*aargh*-chy: The Law and Economics of Pirate Organisation" 115 *Journal of Political Economy* (2007).

Leeson, "Rationality, Pirates and the Law: A Retrospective" 59 *American University Law Review* (2010) 1219.

Lemkin, "Genocide" 15 *The American Scholar* (1947) 227.

Lesaffer, "The Peace of Utrecht and the Balance of Power" available online through *Oxford Historical Treaties*.

Lewins and Gaskell, "Jurisdiction over criminal acts on cruise ships: perhaps, perhaps, perhaps?" 37 *Criminal Law Journal* (2014) 221.

Lewis, "Responsibility for Piracy in the Middle Ages" 19 *Journal of Comparative Legislation and International Law* (1937) 77.

Lim, "From *Haijin* to *Kaihai*: The Jiajing Court's Search for a *Modus Operandi* along the South-eastern Coast (1522–1567)" 2 *Journal of the British Association for Chinese Studies* (2013) 1.

Lorca, "Harmonisation of National Criminal Laws on Maritime Piracy: a Regulatory Proposal for the Crime of Piracy and its Penalties: a Regulatory Proposal for the Crime of Piracy and its Penalties" 23 *European Journal on Criminal Policy and Research* (2017) 115.

Luban, "A Theory of Crimes Against Humanity" 29 *Yale Journal of International Law* (2004) 85.

Luban, "Human Dignity, Humiliation, and Torture" 19 *Kennedy Institute of Ethics Journal* (2009) 211.

Malkin, "The Inner History of the Declaration of Paris" 8 *British Yearbook of International Law* (1927).

Mann, "The doctrine of jurisdiction in International Law" 111 *Recueil des Cours* (1964) 1.

Martinez, "Antislavery Courts and the Dawn of International Human Rights Law" 117 *Yale Law Journal* (2008) 550.

May, "Humanity, International Crime and the Rights of Defendants" 20 *Ethics & International Affairs* (2006) 373.

Menon, "The International Personality of Individuals in International Law: A Broadening of the Traditional Doctrine" 1 *Journal of Transnational Law & Policy* (1992) 151.

Meron, "Common Rights of Mankind in Gentili, Grotius and Suarez" 85 *American Journal of International Law* (1991) 110.

Meron, "Reflections on the Prosecution of War Crimes by International Tribunals" 100 *American Journal of International Law* (2006) 551.

Mikhail, "Is the Prohibition of Homicide Universal? Evidence from Comparative Criminal Law" 75 *Brooklyn Law Review* (2009) 497.

Milanović, "From Compromise to Principle: Clarifying the Concept of State Jurisdiction in Human Rights Treaties" 8 *Human Rights Law Review* (2008) 411.

Morris, "Universal Jurisdiction in a Divided World" 35 *New England Law Review* (2001) 337.

Muteti, "Prosecution of piracy cases – the Kenya experience" 39 *Commonwealth Law Bulletin* (2013) 73.

Narain, "Preparing for piracy trials in Mauritius" 39 *Commonwealth Law Bulletin* (2013) 53.

North, "Sources of Productivity Change in Ocean Shipping, 1600–1850" 76 *Journal of Political Economy* (1968) 953.

Noyes, "Introduction to the International Law of Piracy" 21 *California Western International Law Journal* (1990) 105.

O'Keefe, "Universal Jurisdiction: Clarifying the Basic Concept" 2 *Journal of International Criminal Justice* (2004) 735.

O'Keefe, "The Grave Breaches Regime and Universal Jurisdiction" 7 *Journal of International Criminal Justice* (2009) 811.

Orentlicher, "Whose Justice? Reconciling Universal Jurisdiction with Democratic Principles" 92 *Georgetown Law Journal* (2004) 1057.

Orford, "Jurisdiction Without Territory: From the Holy Roman Empire to the Responsibility To Protect" 30 *Michigan Journal of International Law* (2009) 981.

Paige, "Piracy and Universal Jurisdiction" 12 *Macquarie Law Journal* (2013a) 131.

Paige, "The Impact and Effectiveness of UNCLOS on Counter Piracy Operations" 22 *Journal of Conflict & Security Law* (2017), 117.

Paradisi, "International Law and Social Structure in the Middle Ages" 2 *Indian Year Book of International Affairs* (1964) 154.

Passman, "Protections Afforded to Captured Pirates Under the Law of War and International Law" 33 *Tulane Maritime Law Journal* (2008).

Phillips, "Pirate Accessory Liability: Developing a Modern Legal Regime governing Incitement and Intentional Facilitation of Maritime Piracy" 25 *Florida Journal of International Law* (2013).

Pinzauti, "An Instance of Reasonable Universality: The *Scilingo* Case" 3 *Journal of International Criminal Justice* (2005) 1092.

Plescia, "Conflict of Laws in the Roman Empire" 38 *Labeo Rassegna di Diritto Romano* (1992) 30.

Policante, "The New Pirate Wars" 3 *Global Discourse* (2013) 52.

Porras, "Constructing International Law in the East Indian Seas: Property, Sovereignty, Commerce and War in Hugo Grotius' *De Iure Praedae,* or 'On how to Distinguish Merchants from Pirates'" 31 *Brooklyn Journal of International Law* (2005–06) 741.

Power, "Maritime Terrorism: A New Challenge for National and International Security" 10 *Barry Law Review* (2008) 111.

Rabinovitch, "Universal Jurisdiction *In Absentia*" 28 *Fordham International Law Journal* (2005) 500.

Radin, "The Roman Law of Delphi and the *Lex Gabinia*" 23 *The Classical Journal* (1928) 678.

Randall, "Universal Jurisdiction under International Law" 66 *Texas Law Review* (1987–1988) 785.

Rasilla del Moral, "The Swan Song of Universal Jurisdiction in Spain" 9 *International Criminal Law Review* (2009) 777.

Ratner, "Belgium's War Crimes Statute: A Postmortem" 97 *American Journal of International Law* (2003) 888.

Rech, "Rightless Enemies: Schmitt and Lauterpacht on Political Piracy" 32 *Oxford Journal of Legal Studies* (2012) 235.

Reydams, "*Niyonteze v. Public Prosecutor*" 96 *American Journal of International Law* (2002) 231.

Reydams, "Belgium's First Application of Universal Jurisdiction: the Butare Four Case" 1 *Journal of International Criminal Justice* (2003a) 428.

Reydams, "The Rise and Fall of Universal Jurisdiction" Leuven Centre for Global Governance Working Paper No. 37, January 2010.

Roht-Arriaza, "Universal Jurisdiction: Steps Forward, Steps Back" 17 *Leiden Journal of International Law* (2004) 375.

Ross, "The Ríos Montt case and universal jurisdiction" 18 *Journal of Genocide Research* (2016) 361.

Ryngaert, "Universal Jurisdiction in an ICC Era" 14 *European Journal of Crime and Criminal Justice* (2006) 46.

Sammons, "The Under-Theorisation of Universal Jurisdiction: Implications for Legitimacy on Trials of War Criminals by National Courts" 21 *Berkeley Journal of International Law* (2003) 111.

Schabas, "State Policy as an Element of International Crimes" 98 *Journal of Criminal Law and Criminology* (2008) 953.

Schabas, "The Contribution of the *Eichmann* Trial to International Law" 26 *Leiden Journal of International Law* (2013) 667.

Scharf, "Universal Jurisdiction and the Crime of Aggression" 53 *Harvard International Law Journal* (2012) 357.

Schmitt, "The Concept of Piracy (1937)" 2 *Humanity: An International Journal of Human Rights, Humanitarianism and Development* (2011) 27.

Schwarzenberger, "The Problem of an International Criminal Law" 3 *Current Legal Problems* (1950) 263.

Shaw, "Fear and Loathing: The Nomad Menace and Roman Africa" 52 *Revue de l'Université d'Ottawa* (1982) 25.

Shaw, "Bandits in the Roman Empire" 105 *Past and Present* (1984) 3.

Simma and Paulus, "'The International Community': Facing the Challenge of Globalisation" 9 *European Journal of International Law* (1998) 266.

Simpson, "Didactic and Dissident Histories in War Crimes Trials" 60 *Albany Law Review* (1997) 801.

Sponsler, "The Universality Principle of Jurisdiction and the Threatened Trials of American Airmen" 15 *Loyola Law Review* (1968–69).

Steiner, "Three Cheers for Universal Jurisdiction – Or Is It Only Two?" 5 *Theoretical Inquiries in Law* (2004) 199.

Swart, "The Legal Foundation for Criminalizing International Crimes: A Response to Kevin Jon Heller" (available at the Harvard International Law Journal website, 20 March 2018).

Tai, "Marking Water: Piracy and Property in the Pre-Modern West" presentation at *Seascapes, Littoral Cultures, and Trans-Oceanic Exchanges,* Washington, DC, 12–15 February 2003.

Tai, "Restitution and the Definition of a Pirate: The Case of Sologrus de Nigro" 19 *Mediterranean Historical Review* (2004) 34.

Tai, "The Legal Status of Piracy in Medieval Europe" 10 *History Compass* (2012) 838.

Takeuchi, "Beyond Dichotomy between Deduction and Induction – Critical Appraisal on the Approaches to Universal Jurisdiction" 64 *Okayama Law Journal* (2014) 388.

Thorup, "The horror of the 'enemy of humanity' – on pirates, terrorists and states" presentation at "Fear, Horror & Terror", 1st Global Conference, Mansfield College, Oxford, September 10–12, 2007.

Tomuschat, "The Legacy of Nuremberg" 4 *Journal of International Criminal Justice* (2006) 830.

Treves, "Piracy, Law of the Sea, and Use of Force: Developments off the Coast of Somalia" 20 *European Journal of International Law* (2009) 399.

Tuerk, "The Resurgence of Piracy: A Phenomenon of Modern Times" 17 *University of Miami International and Comparative Law Review* (2009).

Váli, "The Santa Maria Case" 56 *Northwestern University Law Review* (1961) 168.

van Elst, "Implementing Universal Jurisdiction Over Grave Breaches of the Geneva Conventions" 13 *Leiden Journal of International Law* (2000) 815.

Van der Vyver, "Prosecution and Punishment of the Crime of Genocide" 23 *Fordham International Law Journal* 286 (1999), 321.

Van der Wilt, "Universal Jurisdiction under Attack: An Assessment of African Misgivings towards International Criminal Justice as Administered by Western States" 9 *Journal of International Criminal Justice* (2011) 1043.

Von Mehren, "Adjudicatory Jurisdiction: General Theories Compared and Evaluated" 63 *Boston University Law Review* (1983) 279.

Wagner, "Lessons of Imperialism and of the Law of Nations: Alberico Gentili's Early Modern Appeal to Roman Law" 23 *European Journal of International Law* (2012) 873.

Waldron, "Foreign Law and the Modern *Ius Gentium*", 119 *Harvard Law Review* (2005–06) 129.

Wedgwood, "The Revolutionary Martyrdom of Jonathan Robbins" 100 *Yale Law Journal* (1990) 229.

Whatley, "Historical Sketch of the Law of Piracy" 3 *Law Magazine and Review* (1874) 618.

White, "The United Nations System: Conference, Contract or Constitutional Order?" 4 *Singapore Journal of International and Comparative Law* (2000) 281.

Wright, "War Criminals" 39 *American Journal of International Law* (1945) 257.

Zaid, "Will or Should the United States Ever Prosecute War Criminals?: A Need for Greater Expansion in the Areas of both Criminal and Civil Liability" 35 *New England Law Review* (2001) 447.

Books

Anon, *The Grand Pyrate: Or, the Life and Death of Capt. George Cusack the Great Sea-Robber* (London: Jonathan Edwin, 1676).

Abulafia, *The Great Sea* (Oxford: OUP, 2011).

Allain, *The Law and Slavery: Prohibiting Human Exploitation* (Leiden: Brill, 2015).

Ambos, *Treatise on International Criminal Law (vol 1)* (Oxford: OUP, 2013).

Anand, *Origin and Development of the Law of the Sea* (The Hague: Martinus Nijhoff, 1983).

Anand, *New States and International Law* (2nd ed) (Gurgaon: Hope India Publications, 2008).

Anghie, *Imperialism, Sovereignty and the Making of International Law* (Cambridge: CUP, 2005).

Appian, *Roman History: The Mithridatic Wars* (c. 150) (trans. Horace White) (New York: Macmillan, 1899).

Arendt, *Eichmann in Jerusalem: A Report on the Banality of Evil* (1963) (New York: Penguin, 2006).

Augustine, *The City of God* (5th Century AD) (ed. RW Dyson) (Cambridge: CUP, 1998).

Ayala, *Three Books on the Law of War and on the Duties Connected with War and on Military Discipline* (1582) (ed. John Westlake) (Washington DC: Carnegie, 1912).

Azzo of Bologna, *Summa Codicis* (c. 1210).

Bahadur, *Deadly Waters: Inside the hidden world of Somalia's pirates* (London: Profile, 2011).

Baker, *An Introduction to English Legal History* (Butterworths, 2002).

Baldwin, "The Territorial State" in Hyman Gross and Ross Harrison (eds), *Jurisprudence: Cambridge Essays* (Gloucs: Clarendon Press, 1992).

Banner, *Who Owns the Sky?* (Cambridge, MA: Harvard University Press, 2008).

Barrie, *Peter and Wendy* (Hodder & Stoughton, 1911).

Bartolus of Saxoferrato, *De Captivis et Postliminio Reversis Rubrica* in *Apostilla domini Bartoli de Saxoferato super secunda parte Digesti novi* (Milan: Johanes Antoni de Donato, 1486).

Bassiouni, *Crimes Against Humanity: Historical Evolution and Contemporary Application* (Cambridge: CUP, 2011).

Bauman, *Crime and Punishment in Ancient Rome* (London: Routledge, 1996).

Bellamy, *Just Wars: From Cicero to Iraq* (Cambridge: Wiley, 2006).

Belli, *De Re Militari et Bello Tractatus* (1563) (trans. Herbert C. Nutting) (Oxford: Clarendon, 1936).

Benton, *A Search for Sovereignty: Law and Geography in European Empires, 1400–1900* (Cambridge: CUP, 2010).

Berger, *Encyclopaedic Dictionary of Roman Law* (Philadelphia: American Philosophical Society, 1968).

Black, *The Atlantic Slave Trade in World History* (NY: Routledge, 2015).

Borrow, (ed.), *Celebrated Trials and Remarkable Cases of Criminal Jurisprudence,* Volume IV (London: Knight and Lacey, 1825).

Boyer, *Sir Edward Coke and the Elizabethan Age* (Palo Alto, CA: Stanford University Press, 2003).

Bradford, *Flying the Black Flag: A Brief History of Piracy* (Westport, CT: Greenwood Publishing Group, 2007).

Brody and Ratner, *The Pinochet Papers: The Case of Augusto Pinochet in Spain and Britain* (The Hague: Kluwer Law International, 2000).

Brody, *Victims bring a Dictator to Justice: The Case of Hissène Habré* (2nd ed.) (Berlin: Bread for the World, 2017).

Burgers and Danelius, "*The United Nations Convention Against Torture: A Handbook on the Convention Against Torture and Other Cruel, Inhuman, or Degrading Treatment or Punishment*" (Dordrecht: Martinus Nijhoff, 1988).

Byron, *The Corsair* (London: John Murray, 1814).

Caesar, *The Civil Wars* (trans. W.A. McDevitte and W.S. Bohn) (Loeb Classical Library, 1917).

Cassese, Gaeta, *Cassese's International Criminal Law* (Oxford: OUP, 2013).

Chehtman, *The Philosophical Foundations of Extraterritorial Punishment* (Oxford: OUP, 2010).

Champlin and Lintott, *The Cambridge Ancient History* (*Vol X: The Augustan Empire, 43 BC – AD 69*) (Cambridge: CUP, 1996).

Childs, *Pirate Nation: Elizabeth I and her Royal Sea Rovers* (Barnsley: Seaforth, 2014).

Cicero, *De Officiis* (ed. Walter Miller, with an English Translation) (Cambridge, MA: Harvard University Press, 1913).

Cicero, *De Republica,* (54–51 BC) (trans. Clinton Walker Keyes) (London: Heinemann, 1928).

Cicero, *Verrine Orations,* (trans. C.D. Yonge) (London: George Bell & Sons, 1903).

Cicero, *De Imperio Gnaei Pompei* ("On Pompey's Command") (66 BC) (trans. C.D. Yonge) (London: Henry G. Bohn, 1856).

Coke, *The Third Part of the Institutes of the Laws of England; Concerning High Treason, and Other Pleas of the Crown and Criminal Causes.* (c. 1628).

Conklin, *Hegel's Laws: The Legitimacy of a Modern Legal Order* (Stanford, CA: Stanford University Press, 2008).

Cordingly, *Life among the Pirates: The Romance and the Reality* (London: Abacus, 1995).

Cordingly, *Spanish Gold: Captain Woodes Rogers and the Pirates of the Caribbean* (London: Bloomsbury, 2011).

Cordingly and Falconer, *Pirates: Fact & Fiction* (London: Collins & Brown Ltd, 1992).

Crawford, *The Creation of States in International Law* (2nd ed) (Oxford: OUP, 2006).

Crawford, *Brownlie's Principles of Public International Law* (8th ed.) (Oxford: OUP, 2012).

Cryer, *Prosecuting International Crimes: Selectivity and the International Criminal Law Regime* (Cambridge: CUP, 2005).

Cryer, Friman, Robinson, and Wilmshurst, *An Introduction to International Criminal Law and Procedure* (3rd ed.) (Cambridge: CUP, 2014).

Dawidowicz, *The War Against the Jews* (New York: Bantam, 1986).

De Souza, *Piracy in the Graeco-Roman World* (Cambridge: CUP, 2002).

Dio, *History of Rome* (c. 229 AD) (trans. E. Cary) (Cambridge, MA: Loeb Classical Library, 1924).

Domingo, *The New Global Law* (Cambridge, CUP, 2011).

Drews, *The End of the Bronze Age: Changes in Warfare and the Catastrophe ca. 1200 BC* (Princeton, NJ: 1993).

Drumbl, *Atrocity, Punishment, and International Law* (Cambridge: CUP, 2007).

Dunant, *A Memory of Solferino* (Geneva: International Committee of the Red Cross, 1939 (orig. 1862)).

Dubner, *The Law of International Sea Piracy* (The Hague: Martinus Nijhoff, 1980).

Earle, *The Pirate Wars* (New York: Thomas Dunne Books, 2003).

Edmonds and Oppenheim, *Land Warfare: An Exposition of the Laws and Usages of War on Land, for the Guidance of Officers of His Majesty's Arms* (London, 1914).

Elden, *Terror and Territory: The Spatial Extent of Sovereignty* (University of Minnesota Press, 2009).

Florus, *Epitome of Roman History*, Book 1, XLI, III, 6 (trans. E.S. Forster) (Loeb Classical Library, 1929).

Foucault, *The Birth of Biopolitics: Lectures at Collège du France , 1978–79* (New York: Palgrave Macmillan).

Fraser, *The Pyrates* (1983) (London: HarperCollins, 1996).

Fuller and Leslie-Melville, *Pirate Harbours and Their Secrets* (London: Stanley Paul & Co., 1935).

Fulton, *The Sovereignty of the Sea* (Clark, NJ: The Lawbook Exchange Ltd, 1911).

Garnsey, *The Roman Empire: Economy, Society and Culture* (Berkeley, CA: University of California Press, 1987).

Gavouneli, *Functional Jurisdiction in the Law of the Sea* (Leiden: Martinus Nijhoff, 2007).

Geiss and Petrig, *Piracy and Armed Robbery at Sea: The Legal Framework for Counter-Piracy Operations in Somalia and the Gulf of Aden* (Oxford: OUP, 2011).

Gentili, *De Jure Belli Libri Tres* (1589) (trans. John C. Rolfe) (Oxford: Clarendon Press, 1933).

Gibbs, *On the Account in the 'Golden Age': Piracy and the Americas, 1670–1726* (Brighton: Sussex Academic Press, 2014).

Glueck, *War Criminals: Their Prosecution and Punishment* (New York: A.A. Knopf, 1944).

Goldsmith and Wu, *Who Owns the Internet?* (Oxford: OUP, 2006).

Gosse, *The History of Piracy* (1932) (Mineola, NY: Dover Publications, 2007).

Gottmann, *The Significance of Territory* (Charlottesville: University Press of Virginia, 1973).

Gottschalk, and Flanagan, *Jolly Roger With an Uzi: The Rise and Threat of Modern Piracy* (Naval Institute Press, 2008).

Grotius, *Commentary on the Law of Prize and Booty* (ed. Ittersum) (Indianapolis: Liberty Fund Inc, 2006).

Grotius, *The Free Sea* (trans. Richard Hakluyt, ed. David Armitage) (Indianapolis: Liberty Fund, 2004).

Grotius, *Mare Liberum 1609–2009* (ed. Robert Feenstra) (Leiden: Brill, 2009).

Grotius, *The Rights of War and Peace* (ed. Richard Tuck, from the edition by Jean Barbeyrac) (Indianapolis: Liberty Fund, 2005).

Grünewald, *Bandits in the Roman Empire: Myth and Reality* (1999) (trans. by John Drinkwater) (London: Routledge, 2004).

Guilfoyle, *Shipping Interdiction and the Law of the Sea* (Cambridge: CUP, 2009).

Guilfoyle, *International Criminal Law* (Oxford: OUP, 2016).

Hall, *International Law*, 8th ed. (1924).

Hamilton, Madison and Jay (eds), *The Federalist Papers* (1788) (New York: New American Library, 1961).

Haywood and Spivak, *Maritime Piracy* (London: Routledge, 2012).

Heebøll-Holm, *Ports, Piracy and Maritime War: Piracy in the English Channel and the Atlantic, c. 1280 - c. 1330* (Leiden: Brill, 2013).

Hegel, *Elements of the Philosophy of Right* (1820) (ed. Allen W. Wood) (Cambridge: CUP, 1991).

Heller-Roazen, *The Enemy of All: Piracy and the Law of Nations* (Brooklyn: Zone Books, 2009).

Henckaerts and Doswald-Beck, ICRC *Customary International Humanitarian Law, Volume I: Rules* (Cambridge: CUP).

Henkin, *How Nations Behave: Law and Foreign Policy* (2nd ed.) (New York: Columbia University Press, 1979).

Higgins, *Problems & Process: International Law and How We Use It* (Oxford: Clarendon, 1995).

Hostettler, *Sir Edward Coke: A Force for Freedom* (Chichester: Barry Rose Law Publishers, 1997).

Inazumi, *Universal Jurisdiction in Modern International Law: Expansion of National Jurisdiction for Prosecuting Serious Crimes under International Law* (Antwerp: Intersentia, 2005; School of Human Rights Research Series).

Ireland-Piper, *Accountability in Extraterritoriality: A Comparative and International Law Perspective* (Cheltenham: Edward Elgar, 2017).

Israel, *The Dutch Republic: Its Rise, Greatness, and Fall 1477–1806,* (Oxford: Clarendon, 1995).

James, *Europe's Barbarians AD 200–600* (Abingdon: Routledge, 2014).

Johnson, *A General History of the Robberies and Murders of the Most Notorious Pirates* (1724) (with an introduction and commentary by David Cordingly) (London: Conway Maritime Press, 1998).

Jowitt, *The Culture of Piracy, 1580–1630: English Literature and Seaborne Crime* (Farnham: Ashgate Publishing, 2010).

Justinian, *Digest* (ed. Alan Watson) (Philadelphia: University of Pennsylvania Press, 2011).

Kelsen, *General Theory of Law and State* (trans. Anders Wedberg) (Cambridge, MA: Harvard University Press, 1949).

Kelsen, *Principles of International Law* (New York: Rinehart & Co, 1952).

Konstam, *Piracy: The Complete History* (Oxford: Osprey, 2008), 10; Benerson Little, *Pirate Hunting* (Washington DC: Potomac Books, 2010).

Kraska, *Contemporary Maritime Piracy: International Law, Strategy, and Diplomacy at Sea: International Law, Strategy, and Diplomacy at Sea* (Santa Barbara, CA: ABC-CLIO, 2011).

Kuhn, *Life Under the Jolly Roger: Reflections on Golden Age Piracy* (Oakland, CA: PM Press, 2009).

Langewiesche, *The Outlaw Sea: A World of Freedom, Chaos and Crime* (New York, NY: North Point Press, 2004).

Latimer, *Buccaneers of the Caribbean: How Piracy Forged An Empire 1607–1697* (Cambridge, MA: Harvard University Press, 2009).

Lauterpacht, Hersch, *The Function of Law in the International Community* (Oxford: Clarendon, 1933).

Lavan, *Slaves to Rome: Paradigms of Empire in Roman Culture* (Cambridge: CUP, 2013).

Lemnitzer, *Power, Law and the End of Privateering* (London: Palgrave Macmillan).

Lepage, *Medieval Armies and Weapons in Western Europe: An Illustrated History* (Jefferson, NC: McFarland, 2014).

Lewis and Short, *A Latin Dictionary* (Oxford: Clarendon Press, 1879).

Liddell and Scott, *An Intermediate Greek-English Lexicon* (Oxford: Clarendon Press, 1889).

Lipstadt, *The Eichmann Trial* (New York: Schocken, 2011).

Little, *The Sea Rover's Practice: Pirate Tactics and Techniques, 1630–1730* (Lincoln, NE: Potomac Books, 2005).

Livy, *History of Rome* (c. 27–25 BC) (trans. A.C. Schlesinger) (Cambridge, MA: Loeb Classical Library, 1959).

Locke, *Two Treatises of Government* (1690) (ed. P Laslett) (Cambridge: CUP, 1998).

Lunsford, *Piracy and Privateering in the Golden Age Netherlands* (Gordonsville, VA: Palgrave Macmillan, 2005).

Maitland and Montague, *A Sketch of English Legal History* (New Jersey: The Lawbook Exchange, 2010).

Marley, *Pirates: Adventurers of the High Seas* (London: Arms and Armour Press, 1997).

Marley, *Wars of the Americas: a chronology of armed conflict in the New World, 1492 to the Present* (Santa Barbara: ABC-CLIO, 1998).

Mather, *The Wonders of the Invisible World (Being an account of the Tryals of Several Witches lately executed in New England)* (Boston & London: John Dunton, 1693).

Meijer, *A History of Seafaring in the Classical World* (Beckenham: Croom Helm, 1986).

Molloy, *De Maritimo et Navali: or, a Treatise of Affairs Maritime and of Commerce* (1707), vol. i.

Moore, *American Eloquence: A Collection of speeches and addresses, by the most eminent orators of America* (New York: D. Appleton, 1851).

Morris (ed.), *American Heritage Dictionary of the English Language* (Boston, MA: American Heritage Publishing and Houghton Mifflin, 1969).

Murphy, *Contemporary Piracy and Maritime Terrorism: The Threat to International Security* (London: Routledge, 2007).

O'Connell, *The Influence of Law on Sea Power* (Manchester: University of Manchester Press, 1975).

Octavian, *Res gestae Divi Augusti* (Loeb Classical Library, 1924).

Oppenheim, *International Law: A Treatise* (London: Longmans, Green & Co, 1905).

Ormerod, *Piracy in the Ancient World* (Baltimore: JHU, 1997).

O'Sullivan, *Universal Jurisdiction in International Criminal Law: The Debate and the Battle for Hegemony* (Oxon: Routledge, 2017).

Papadatos, *The Eichmann Trial* (London: F.A. Praeger, 1964).

Parchami, *Hegemonic Peace and Empire: The Pax Romana, Britannica and Americana* (London: Taylor & Francis, 2009).

Phillipson, *The International Law and Custom of Ancient Greece & Rome* (London: Macmillan, 1911).

Piggott, *The Declaration of Paris, 1856: A Study, Documented* (London, 1919).

Pliny the Elder, *The History of the World* (c. 77–79 AD) (trans. Philemon Holland, 1601).

Plucknett, *A Concise History of the Common Law* (1956) (Indianapolis: Liberty Fund, 2010).

Plutarch, *Parallel Lives of Greeks and Romans* (c. 100 AD) (trans. Bernadotte Perrin) (Cambridge, MA: Loeb Classical Library, 1917).

Policante, *The Pirate Myth: Genealogies of an Imperial Concept* (Abingdon: Routledge, 2015).

Polybius, *The Histories* (c. 150 BC) (trans. William R. Paton) (Cambridge, MA: Loeb Classical Library, 1954).

Powers, *On Stranger Tides* (New York: Ace Books, 1987).

Pufendorf, *De jure naturae at gentium* (1672), trans. Oldfather and Oldfather, 1934) (Oxford : Clarendon, 1934).

Rawls, *The Law of Peoples* (Cambridge, MA: Harvard University Press, 1999).

Rech, *Enemies of Mankind: Vattel's Theory of Collective Security* (Leiden, Martinus Nijhoff, 2013).

Rediker, *Villains of All Nations* (London: Verso, 2004).

Rennie, *Treasure Neverland: Real and Imaginary Pirates* (Oxford: OUP, 2013).

Reydams, *Universal Jurisdiction* (Oxford: OUP, 2003b).

Ritchie, *Captain Kidd and the War Against the Pirates* (Cambridge, MA: Harvard University Press, 1986).

Roberts and Guelff, *Documents on the Laws of War* (3rd ed.) (Oxford: OUP, 2000).

Robertson, *Crimes Against Humanity: The Struggle for Global Justice* (3rd ed.) (London: Penguin, 2006).

Roht-Arriaza, *The Pinochet Effect: Transnational Justice in the Age of Human Rights* (Philadelphia: University of Pennsylvania Press, 2005).

Rossi, *Sovereignty and Territorial Temptation* (Cambridge: CUP, 2017).

Rothwell and Stephens, *The International Law of the Sea* (Oxford: Hart, 2010).

Rubin, *The Law of Piracy* (Honolulu: University Press of the Pacific, 2006).

Rubin, *Ethics and Authority in International Law* (Cambridge: CUP, 2007).

Ruddy, *International law in the Enlightenment: the background of Emmerich de Vattel's Le Droit Des Gens* (New York: Oceana Publications, 1975).

Ryngaert, *Jurisdiction in International Law* (1st ed) (Oxford: OUP, 2008).

Ryngaert, *Jurisdiction in International Law* (2nd ed) (Oxford: OUP, 2015).

Sassen, *Territory, authority, rights: from medieval to global assemblages* (Princeton, NJ: Princeton University Press, 2006).

Schabas, *Genocide in International Law* (2nd ed.) (Cambridge: CUP, 2009).

Schabas, *Unimaginable Atrocities: Justice, Politics, and Rights at the War Crimes Tribunals* (Oxford: OUP, 2012).

Scharf, *Customary International Law in Times of Fundamental Change: Recognizing Grotian Moments* (Cambridge: CUP, 2013).

Schmitt, *The Nomos of the Earth* (1950) (trans. G.L. Ulmen) (New York: Telos Press, 2003).

Scott, *The Pirate* (Edinburgh: Archibald Constable, 1822).

Selden, *Mare Clausum*, 1635.

Senior, *A Nation of Pirates: English Piracy in its Heyday* (Newton Abbot: David & Charles, 1976).

Shakespeare, *Hamlet* (1603) (ed. Neil Taylor & Ann Thompson) (London: Puffin, 2006).

Sicking, *Neptune and the Netherlands: State, Economy and War at Sea in the Renaissance* (Brill, 2004).

Simpson and Weiner, *The Oxford English Dictionary* (2nd ed.) (Oxford: Clarendon, 1989).

Smith, *A General History of the Lives and Adventures of the Most Famous Highwaymen*, London, 1719.

Southey, *History of Brazil, Part III* (London: Longman, Hurst, Reed and Orme, 1819).

Spruyt, *The Sovereign State and its Competitors: An Analysis of Systems Change* (Princeton NJ: Princeton University Press, 1996).

Stein, Roman *Law in European History* (Cambridge: CUP, 1999).

Stern, *The Company State: Corporate Sovereignty & the Early Modern Foundations of the British Empire in India* (Oxford: OUP, 2011).

Stevenson, *Treasure Island* (Boston: Roberts Brothers, 1884).

Strayer, *On the Medieval Origins of the Modern State* (Princeton, NJ: Princeton University Press, 1970).

Svantesson, *Solving the Internet Jurisdiction Puzzle* (Oxford: OUP, 2017).

Tacitus, *Annals* (trans. J. Jackson) (Loeb Classical Library, 125–1937).

Tarwacka, *Romans and Pirates: Legal Perspective* (Warsaw: Wydawnictwo Uniwersytetu Kardynała Stefana Wyszyńskiego, 2009).

Taylor, *The Anatomy of the Nuremberg Trials: A Personal Memoir* (New York: Knopf, 1992).

Tellegen-Couperus, *A Short History of Roman Law* (NY: Routledge, 1993).

Tenenti, *Piracy and the Decline of Venice 1580–1615* (London: Longmans, 1961).

Tindall, *An Essay Concerning the Laws of Nations and the Rights of Soveraigns* (1694).

Tinniswood, *Pirates of Barbary* (London: Vintage, 2011).

Thesaurus Linguae Latinae, vol. VII, (Leipzig, 1934).

Thomson, *Mercenaries, Pirates and Sovereigns* (Princeton, New Jersey: Princeton University Press, 1994).

Thucydides, *History of the Peloponnesian War*, (trans. Charles Foster Smith) (Cambridge, MA: Loeb Classical Library, 1928).

Van Bynkershoek, *Two Books of Questions of Public Law*, (trans. Tenney Frank) (Washington, DC: Carnegie Endowment for International Peace, 1930).

Vattel, *The Law of Nations* (1758) (trans. Charles G. Fenwick) (Washington, DC: Carnegie Institution of Washington, 1916).

Velleius, *Historiae Romanae* (ed. Frederick W. Shipley) (Cambridge, MA: Loeb Classical Library, 1924).

Vreeland, *Hugo Grotius: The Father of the Modern Science of International Law* (Oxford: OUP, 1917).

Welwood, *An Abridgement of All Sea Laws*, 1615.

Wheaton, *Elements of International Law* (1836) (ed. Richard Henry Dana and George Grafton Wilson) (Oxford: Clarendon, 1936).

Wheaton, *Elements of International Law,* 8 th edition, ed. RH Dana (Boston: Little, Brown & Co., 1866).

Williams, *Captains Outrageous: Seven Centuries of Piracy* (London: Barrie and Rockliff, 1961).

Wittgenstein, *Philosophical Investigations* (trans. GEM Anscombe) (Oxford: Blackwell, 1958).

Wolff, *The Law of Nations Treated According to a Scientific Model* (1747) (trans. Joseph H. Drake) (Washington DC: Carnegie Endowment for International Peace, 1934).

Woodard, *The Republic of Pirates: Being the True and Surprising Story of the Caribbean Pirates and the Man who Brought Them Down* (London: Pan Macmillan, 2016).

Woolrych, *The Life of the Right Honourable Sir Edward Coke* (London: J & WT Clarke, 1826).

Wynne, *The Life of Sir Leoline Jenkins* (1724).

Zacks, *The Pirate Hunter: The True Story of Captain Kidd* (London: Headline, 2002).

Zouche, *An Exposition of Fecial Law and Procedure* (1650) (trans. James L. Brierly) (Washington, DC: Carnegie Endowment for International Peace, 1911).

Edited Collections (and Contents, Where Cited Specifically)

Amirell, and Müller (eds), *Persistent Piracy: Maritime Violence and State-Formation in Global Historical Perspective* (Basingstoke: Palgrave Macmillan, 2014).

- Amirell and Müller, "Introduction: Persistent Piracy in World History", 1.
- De Souza, "Piracy in Classical Antiquity: The Origins and Evolution of the Concept", 24.
- Price, "Ship-Men and Slaughter-Wolves: Pirate Polities in the Viking Age", 51.

Bassiouni (ed.), *International Criminal Law, Volume I: Sources, Subjects and Contents* (Leiden: Brill, 2008).

- Cryer, "The Doctrinal Foundations of International Criminalisation", 107.
- Bassiouni, "International Crimes: The *Ratione Materiae* of International Criminal Law", 129.

Bergsmo (ed.), *Complementarity and the Exercise of Universal Jurisdiction for Core International Crimes* (FICHL Publication Series, 2010).

- Stigen, "The Relationship between the Principle of Complementarity and the Exercise of Universal Jurisdiction for Core International Crimes", 133.
- Pocar and Maystre, "The Principle of Complementarity: A Means Towards a More Pragmatic Enforcement of the Goal Pursued by Universal Jurisdiction?" 247.

Blom (ed.), *Property, Piracy and Punishment: Hugo Grotius on War and Booty in De Iure Praedae: Concepts and Contexts* (Boston, MA: Brill, 2009).

- Winkel, "Problems of Legal Systematisation from *De Iure Praedae* to *De Iure Belli ac Pacis*", 61.
- Van, Ittersum, "Preparing *Mare Liberum* for the Press: Hugo Grotius' Rewriting of Chapter 12 of *De iure praedae* in November-December 1608", 246.
- Kempe, "Beyond the Law: The Image of Piracy in the Legal Writings of Hugo Grotius", 379.

Borradori, Giovanna, (ed.), *Philosophy in a time of terror: dialogues with Jürgen Habermas and Jacques Derrida* (University of Chicago Press, 2003).

Bull, Kingsbury and Roberts (eds), *Hugo Grotius and International Relations*, (Oxford: OUP, 2002).
- Kingsbury, and Roberts, "Grotian Thought in International Relations", 1.
- Bull, "The Importance of Grotius in the Study of International Relations", 65.
- Draper, "Grotius' Place in the Development of Legal Ideas about War", 177.
- Butler, "Grotius and the Law of the Sea", 209.

Cassese (ed.), *The Oxford Companion to International Criminal Justice* (Oxford: OUP, 2009).
- Ohlin, "Aggression", 236.
- Nilsson, "Crimes Against Humanity", 284.
- Henckaerts, "Lieber Code", 409.
- Stewart, "Pillage", 454.

Craven, Fitzmaurice and Vogiatzi, (eds), *Time, History and International Law* (Leiden: Martinus Nijhoff, 2007).
- Simpson, "Piracy and the Origins of Enmity", 219.

DeGuzman and Amann (eds), *Arcs of Global Justice: Essays in Honour of William A. Schabas* (Oxford: OUP, 2018).
- DeGuzman, "Criminal Law Philosophy in William Schabas's scholarship", 155.
- Mégret, "Is the ICC Focusing too much on Non-State Actors?", 173.

De Wet and Jure Vidmar (eds), *Hierarchy in International Law: The Place of Human Rights* (Oxford: OUP, 2012).
- Vidmar, "Norm Conflicts and Hierarchy in International Law: Towards a Vertical International Legal System?", 13.

Dupuy and Chetail (eds), *The Roots of International Law* (Leiden: Martinus Nijhoff, 2013).
- Chetail, "Vattel and the American Dream: An Inquiry into the Reception of the *Law of Nations* in the United States", 251.

Ellen (ed.), *Piracy at Sea* (Paris: ICC Publishing, 1986).
- Clingan, "The Law of Piracy", 168.

Evans (ed.), *International Law* (4th ed.) (Oxford: OUP, 2014).
- Staker "Jurisdiction", 309.

Falk and Krieger (eds), *At the Nuclear Precipice* (New York: Palgrave Macmillan, 2008).

– Falk, "Nuclear Weapons, War, and the Discipline of International Law", 225.

Fassbender and Peters (eds), *The Oxford Handbook of the History of International Law* (Oxford: OUP, 2012).

– Fernández, "*Hostes humani generis*: Pirates, Slavers and Other Criminals", 120.

Gerth (ed.) *From Max Weber: Essays in Sociology* (1948), 1991 reprint (Abingdon, Ox: Routledge, 1991).

– Weber, "Politics as a Vocation", 78.

Guilfoyle (ed.), *Modern Piracy: Legal Challenges and Responses* (Cheltenham: Edward Elgar, 2013).

– Guilfoyle, "Piracy in Somalia and Counter-Piracy Efforts", 35.
– Murphy, "Petro Piracy: Predation and Counter-Predation in Nigerian Waters", 61.
– Treves, "Piracy and the International Law of the Sea", 117.
– Eggers, "What is a pirate? A common law answer to an age-old question", 250.

Jalloh and Bantekas (eds), *The International Criminal Court and Africa* (Oxford: OUP, 2017).

– Martin Mennecke, "The African Union and Universal Jurisdiction", 10.
– Efthymios Papastavridis, "Who Will Prosecute Piracy in Africa?", 320.

Jowitt (ed.), *Pirates? The Politics of Plunder, 1550–1650* (Basingstoke: Palgrave Macmillan, 2007).

– Harding, "*Hostis Humani Generis* – The Pirate as Outlaw in the Early Modern Law of the Sea", 20.

Jun (ed.), *Brill's Companion to Anarchism and Philosophy* (Leiden: Brill, 2017).

– Bruce Buchan, "Anarchism and Liberalism", 51.

Kingsbury and Straumann (eds), *The Roman Foundations of the Law of Nations* (Oxford: OUP, 2010).

– Kingsbury and Straumann, "Introduction", 5.
– Panizza, "Alberico Gentili's *De Armis Romanis:* The Roman Model of the Just Empire", 53.
– Schröder, "Vitoria, Gentili, Bodin: Sovereignty and the Law of Nations", 163.
– Lesaffer, "Alberico Gentili's *ius post bellum* and Early Modern Peace Treaties", 210.
– Blaine, Alexis and Benedict Kingsbury, "Punishment and the *ius post bellum*", 241.

Koutrakos and Skordas (eds), *The Law and Practice of Piracy at Sea: European and International Perspectives* (Oxford: Hart, 2014).

– Proelss, "Piracy and the Use of Force", 53.
– Marauhn, "Counter-piracy Operations and the Limits of International Humanitarian Law", 67.
– Klabbers, "Piracy in Global Law and Global Governance", 329.
– Evans and Galani, "Piracy and the Development of International Law", 343.

Leander and Waever (eds), *Assembling Exclusive Expertise: Knowledge, Ignorance and Conflict Resolution in the Global South* (Oxford: Taylor & Francis, 2018).

– Bueger, "Experts in an Adventure with Pirates: A Story of Somali Piracy Expertise", Chapter 2.

Lehr (ed.), *Violence at Sea: Piracy in the Age of Global Terrorism* (New York: Routledge, 2007).

– Murphy, "Piracy and UNCLOS: Does International Law Help Regional States Combat Piracy?", 155.

Macedo (ed.), *Universal Jurisdiction: National Courts and the Prosecution of Serious Crimes under International Law* (Philadelphia: University of Pennsylvania Press, 2004).

– Bassiouni, "The History of Universal Jurisdiction and Its Place in International Law", 39.

– Slaughter, "Defining the Limits: Universal Jurisdiction and National Courts", 168.

Maquerlot and Willems (eds), *Travel and Drama in Shakespeare's Time* (Cambridge: CUP, 1996).

– Potter, "Pirates and 'turning Turk' in Renaissance Drama", 124.

McVeigh (ed.), *Jurisprudence of Jurisdiction* (Abingdon: Routledge, 2007).

– Dorsett, and McVeigh, "Questions of Jurisdiction", 3.

– Grantham, "The Man Who Shot Liberty Valance", 225.

Norchi and Proutière-Maulion (eds), *Piracy in Comparative Perspective: Problems, Strategies, Law* (Paris: Pédone, 2012).

– Stepek, "Challenges of Jurisdiction and Prosecution", 331.

Orford (ed.), *International Law and its Others* (Cambridge: CUP, 2006).

– Mégret, "From 'savages' to 'unlawful combatants': a postcolonial look at international humanitarian law's 'other'", 265.

Orford and Hoffmann (eds), *The Oxford Handbook of the Theory of International Law* (Oxford: OUP, 2016).

– Werner and Gordon, "Kant, Cosmopolitanism, and International Law", 505.

– Gregor Noll, "Theorising Jurisdiction", 600.

Parritt (ed.) *Violence at Sea: A Review of Terrorism, Acts of War and Piracy, and Countermeasures to Prevent Terrorism* (Paris, 1986).

– Ignarski, "Terrorism in a Maritime Context: Law, Insurance, and the Legal Implications of Armed Merchant Ships," 183.

Paschalis and Panayotakis (eds), *The Construction of the Real and the Ideal in the Ancient Novel* (Groningen: Barkhuis, 2013).

– Dowden, "'But there is a difference in the ends…': Brigands and Teleology in the Ancient Novel", 41.

Pennell (ed.), *Bandits at Sea: A Pirates Reader* (NYU Press, 2001).

– Pennell, "Introduction – Brought to Book: Reading about Pirates", 9.

– Pérotin-Dumon, "The Pirate and the Emperor: Power and the Law on the Seas, 1450–1850", 25.

– Rediker, The Seaman as Pirate: Plunder and Social Banditry at Sea", 139.
Powell (ed.), *The Greek World* (London: Routledge, 1997).
– De Souza "Greek Piracy", 179.
Reichel and Randa (eds), *Transnational Crime and Global Security* (Santa Barbara, CA: ABC-CLIO, 2018).
– Michael J Struett, "Maritime Piracy and Global Security", 23.
Reiss (ed.) *Kant's Political Writings* (trans. H.B. Nisbet, Cambridge: CUP, 1970).
Ronzitti (ed.), *Maritime Terrorism and International Law* (Dordrecht: Martinus Nijhoff, 1990).
– Menefee, "Piracy, Terrorism, and the Insurgent Passenger: A Historical and Legal Perspective", 43.
Rosow, Inayatullah and Rupert (eds), *The Global Economy as Political Space* (London: Lynne Rienner, 1994).
– Agnew, "Timeless Space and State-Centrism: The Geographical Assumptions of International Relations Theory", 87.
Rothwell, Elferink, Scott and Stephens (eds), *The Oxford Handbook of the Law of the Sea* (Oxford: OUP, 2015).
– Anna Petrig, "Piracy", 843.
Sabin, van Wees and Whitby (eds), *The Cambridge History of Greek and Roman Warfare* (Cambridge, 2007).
– Gabrielsen, "Warfare and the State", 248.
Scharf, Newton and Sterio (eds), *Prosecuting Maritime Piracy: Domestic Solutions to International Crimes* (Cambridge: CUP, 2015).
– Nanda, "Exercising Universal Jurisdiction over Piracy", 54.
– Sterio, "Pirates' Right to a Speedy Trial", 172.
Simmons (ed.), *Selected Contemporary Issues in the Law of the Sea* (Leiden: Martinus Nijhoff, 2011).
– Roach, "General Problematic Issues on Exercise of Jurisdiction over Modern Instances of Piracy", 119.
Spedding, Ellis, and Heath (eds), *The Works of Francis Bacon* v. XIII. (Boston: Houghton Mifflin, and Co., 1900).
Starkey, de Moor and Van Eyck van Heslinga, (eds), *Pirates and Privateers: New Perspectives on the War on Trade in the Eighteenth and Nineteenth Centuries* (Exeter: University of Exeter Press, 1997).
– Ritchie, "Government Measures against Piracy and Privateering in the Atlantic Area, 1750–1850", 10.
– Nadal, "Mediterranean Privateering between the Treaties of Utrecht and Paris, 1715–1856: First Reflections", 106.
– Starkey, "A Restless Spirit: British Privateering Enterprise, 1739–1815", 126.

- Kert, "Cruising in Colonial Waters: The Organisation of North American Privateering in the War of 1812", 141.

Struett, Carlson, and Nance (eds), *Maritime Piracy and the Construction of Global Governance* (New York: Routledge, 2013).

- Gould, "Cicero's Ghost: Rethinking the Social Construction of Piracy", 23.
- Heinze, "A Global War on Piracy? International Law and the Use of Force against Sea Pirates", 47.
- Dutton, "Maritime Piracy and the Impunity Gap: Domestic Implementation of International Treaty Provisions", 71.

Totten, *Plight and Fate of Women During and Following Genocide* (New Brunswick: Transaction, 2009).

- Nicole Hallett, "The Evolution of Gender Crimes in International Law", 183.

Watkins and Burton (eds), *Research Methods in Law* (Abingdon, Ox: Routledge, 2013).

- Handler, "Legal History", 85.

Miscellaneous

Historical Documents

Document AHU_ACL_CU_005, Cx 15, D1248, archived in the *Arquivo Hisrtórico Ultramarino*, Lisbon.

Calendar of State Papers Relating to English Affairs in the Archives of Venice, Volume 9 (1592–1603), 15 Feb 1603; Volume 10 (1603–1607), 18 May 1603 and 28 May 1603.

Mather, Cotton, *Instructions to the Living, from the Condition of the Dead*, Boston, 1717.

Boston Newsletter, April 16, 1722; December 2 and 16, 1717; January 16–24, 1724.

"First Report from the Select Committee on Slave Trade", *House Of Commons* 102 (1848) reprinted in 4 *British Parliamentary Papers* (1847–48).

British and Foreign State Papers, 1855–1856 (London, 1856), vol. 46, 831–2.

Policy Papers

The Princeton Principles on Universal Jurisdiction (Princeton University, 2001).

Magazines, Websites and Blogs

Edwards, "Lord of the Mongols", *National Geographic*, December 1996.

International Herald Tribune, "China Warns Spain over Tibet Lawsuit", 6 June 2006.

Kaslowsky and Webb, "Somali Pirates Seize Saudi Tanker Carrying $100 Million in Oil", *Washington Post*, 17 November 2008.

Lloyds List, "Danes free pirates from Navy ship", 26 December 2008.

BBC News, "Taylor's son jailed for 97 years", 9 January 2009.

Hawkins, "What to do with a captured pirate", *BBC News*, 10 March 2009.

Onyiego, "Seychelles to Establish Regional Court to Prosecute Pirates", *Voice of America*, 5 May 2010.

Dolmetsch and Van Voris, "Somali Pirate Muse Gets 34-Year Prison Sentence for Indian Ocean Hijacking", *Bloomberg*, 16 February 2011.

Schabas, William, "Crimes Against Humanity in Norway?", blog post at *PhD Studies in Human Rights*, 26 July 2011.

International Chamber of Commerce, Commercial Crime Services, "Piracy attacks in East and West Africa dominate world report", 19 January 2012.

Lowe, "Pirate's Prison" *Maritime Security Review*, 8 March 2012.

Heller, "A Response to Kontorovich and Gallagher About Piracy", blog post at *opiniojuris.org*, 27 February 2013.

Paige, "Emerging Voices: Pirates of the Indian Ocean – Enforcement in the Seychelles", blog post at *opiniojuris.org*, 19 August 2013b.

The World Bank, "The Pirates of Somalia: Ending the Threat, Rebuilding a Nation" (2013).

International Chamber of Commerce, "Somali pirate clampdown caused drop in global piracy, IMB reveals", 15 January 2014.

"Piracy – is India Prepared to Handle the Challenge it Poses", blog post at *The United Service Institution of India*, 2 September 2014.

Berenson, "Happy Talk Like A Pirate Day!" *Time Magazine*, 19 September 2014.

International Chamber of Commerce, "One coastal tanker hijacked every two weeks in SE Asia", 21 April 2015.

Vannier and Uranie, "First trial starts before the Seychelles dedicated court for piracy and maritime crime cases", *Seychelles News Agency*, 2 June 2015.

Sterio, "Are Sea Shepherds Pirates? The United States Supreme Court May Decide Soon", blog post at *Communis Hostis Omnium*, 9 June 2015.

"Tunisia attack: Cameron says IS fight 'struggle of our generation'", *BBC News*, 29 June 2015.

Harding, "Somalia warns of return to piracy", *BBC News*, 31 August 2015.

Smale, "Iraqis' Arrest in Finland Highlights Difficulties in Prosecuting Distant Crimes", *New York Times*, 24 December 2015.

Kroker and Kather, "Justice for Syria? Opportunities and Limitations of Universal Jurisdiction Trials in Germany", blog post at *EJIL:Talk!*, 12 August 2016.

International Chamber of Commerce / International Maritime Bureau, *Piracy and Armed Robbery against Ships*, "Report for the Period 1 January to 31 December 2017".

International Chamber of Commerce, "Maritime piracy and armed robbery reaches 22-year low, says IMB report", 10 January 2018.

BBC News, "Pirates 'massacre' Guyana fishermen off Suriname coast", 4 May 2018.

Film and Television

Treasure Island (dir. Byron Haskin, Disney), 1950.

Robin Hood: Prince of Thieves (dir. Kevin Reynolds), 1991.

Pirates of the Caribbean: The Curse of the Black Pearl (dir. Gore Verbinksi, Disney, 2003).

Captain Phillips (dir. Paul Greengrass, Sony, 2013).

Black Sails, Episode "I" (dir. Neil Marshall, 2014); Episode "XVIII" (dir. Steve Boyum, 2015); Episode "XXXVI" (dir. Uta Briesewitz); Episode "XXXVIII" (dir. Jonathan E. Steinberg, 2017).

Index